NSE4 Study Guide Series
Book One of Four

Introduction to Fortigate Part-I Infrastructure
Fortinet Network Security Introduction

By Daniel Howard
NSE8 #003255

For any comments or recommendations, please email me directly at
howardsinc@gmail.com

Introduction to FortiGate Part-I Infrastructure

Introduction to Fortigate Part-I Infrastructure

Copyright © 2020 iFirewall LLC

All rights reserved

Printed in the United States of America

No part of this book may be used or reproduced in any way without first obtaining written permission except in the case of quotation embodied in critical articles and review.

Black and White Edition

ISBN: 9798656785860

Imprint: Independently published

Dedication

To my wonderful wife Samantha for all her love
and support throughout this project.

To my wonderful kid's Araya, Darwin, and Ryker for being awesome
and allowing daddy time to write this book!

To the rest of my family, friends, and colleagues,
thanks for providing your support!

About the Author

Daniel Howard is an independent author and subject matter expert in many Fortinet technologies. He is only a few hundred to obtain the prestigious Fortinet Network Security Expert 8 certification, a grueling 2-day on-site lab examination. For the past decade, Daniel has worked in the carrier space, highly focused on consulting, managing, and maintaining Fortinet networks for Manage Security Service Providers (MSSPs). He has managed several carrier migration projects, deployments, provided technical training to customers, and served as a technical escalation point throughout his career. Daniel works at Fortinet as a Technical Account Manager to this day, consulting within the carrier space, and continues to assist various security engineering and operation teams.

To stay updated on my latest content, consider following my Facebook page, Amazon author page, or the Fortinet Press website.

https://www.facebook.com/fortinetpress/

https://www.amazon.com/Daniel-Howard/e/B08BS3B4NY

https://fortinetpress.com/

Enjoy!

Acknowledgments

This book took many, many hours of my life to write. I'm grateful that I've had awesome leadership and mentors throughout my career to help me get to this point to give back. I am certainly standing on the shoulders of giants. I appreciate all the feedback that has been provided. I want to stress that all the typos and errors that may have slipped into this book series are 100% my fault and have no reflection on Fortinet as a company and anyone who has helped me with this book's content. I am an independent author and publisher that writes during my free time when I'm not working as a Fortinet TAM or fulfilling my duties as a father and husband.

After I decided to publish this NSE4 study guide series, I honestly had doubts if I would keep writing and complete the series because I did think many folks would be interested in the book; however, I was very wrong. A few months after I published Part-I, this book started selling around the world literally. I had folks from Germany, Denmark, France, Japan, and the UK purchasing Part-I. I also had many folks that contacted me asking when Part-II would be released. I could not believe it. As a whole, I appreciate the support and feedback of the entire community, and I want to thank you for the motivation to keep writing! And here we are, Part-II is complete.

Introduction to FortiGate Part-I Infrastructure

Network Security Expert 4 (NSE4) Exam

The NSE4 certification recognizes your ability to install and manage the day-to-day configuration, monitoring, and operation of a FortiGate device to support specific corporate network security policies.

Who Should Attempt the NSE4 Certification?

The NSE4 exam is designed for security professionals involved in the day-to-day management, implementation, and administration of a security infrastructure using FortiGate devices. The current cost to attempt the exam is $400.

NSE4 Exam details

As of December 2020, there are two NSE4 exams available through Pearson Vue testing, which are:

1) **NSE4_FGT-6.2**
    a. 70 Questions
    b. Two hours to complete
    c. Available in English and Japanese
    d. Registration end 4/30/2021
2) **NSE4_FGT-6.4**
    a. 60 Questions
    b. 105 minutes
    c. Available in English and Japanese
    d. No posted end date

The high-level domains of knowledge covered by the NSE4 exam are:

1) System and Hardware
2) Firewall and NAT
3) Authentication
4) Content Inspection
5) Routing and L2 Switching
6) VPN
7) Logging and Diagnostics

Part-I & Part-II of this NSE4 study guide focuses on infrastructure technologies related to FortiGate. For example, layer-2, layer-3, layer-4, VPNs, HA, logging, SD-WAN, and troubleshooting.

Introduction to FortiGate Part-I Infrastructure

Table of Contents

About the Author 4

Acknowledgments 5

Network Security Expert 4 (NSE4) Exam 6

Introduction 10

    Chapter 1: Introduction to Fortinet 14

    Chapter 2: Layer 2 Switching 15

    Chapter 3: IPv4/IPv6 Routing 15

    Chapter 4: Firewall Policy and NAT 15

    RMA Processing 19

Chapter 1 | Introduction to FortiGate 28

    Getting Started with FortiGate 29

        Unboxing your FortiGate 30

        Intro to Modern Network Security and Challenges 34

        Security Profiles and FortiGuard Overview 37

        FortiGuard Technical Overview 39

    Security Processing Unit (SPU) Overview 40

    FortiOS Modes of Operations overview 42

    Basic FortiGate Administration 43

        Intro to the basic GUI navigation 43

        Intro to administrator access and permissions 54

        Intro to the network interface 61

    Intro to CLI and navigation 72

        Connecting to the Command Line Interface (CLI) 72

        FortiGate CLI Terminology 74

        Sub-commands examples 75

    General Administrative Task 85

        Product Life Cycle 93

        Basic Services 103

Chapter One Summary 106

Chapter One Review Questions 107

Chapter 2 | Layer Two Technologies 112

FortiGate Layer-2 Technologies.. 113

NAT Mode at Layer-2 114

MAC Learning and Forwarding... 115

Software Switch & Hardware Switch 120

    NAT Mode L2-Protocols 128

Spanning Tree Protocol (STP) 129

Link Aggregation Control Protocol (LACP) 132

VLAN Layer-3 Interface 142

Virtual Wire Pairing... 150

Virtual Extensible LAN (VXLAN) 153

Transparent Mode at Layer-2.. 154

    Transparent Mode Overview 154

    Transparent Mode Networking 156

    Layer-2 MAC learning Overview 156

    VLANs in Transparent Mode 163

    Summary... 170

    End of Chapter Two Questions 171

Chapter 3 | Layer Three Technologies 175

FortiOS Layer Three Technologies.. 176

    IP Routing Overview 177

    IPv4 Review 177

    IPv6 Review 181

FortiGate IP Routing 185

    Routing Table Overview 185

    Route Attributes and Selection.. 191

Session Table 197

FortiOS Routing... 208

Introduction to FortiGate Part-I Infrastructure

- Dynamic Routing Overview 216
- FortiOS Routing Features 222
- FortiOS IP Diagnostic 231
  - Summary 239
- Chapter Three Review Questions 240

Chapter 4 | Firewall Policy and NAT 244
- Firewall Policy and NAT Introduction 245
- Firewall Policy 246
  - Profile Based Policy Components 249
- Policy-Based Next-Generation Firewall 262
- Profile Based Policy Entry Features 265
- Firewall Policy Table Management 279
- Firewall Policy Section Summary 284
  - Network Address Translation (NAT) 285
- FortiOS Configuration Methods for NAT 285
  - Policy NAT Virtual IP (VIP) 287
  - IP Pool and SNAT 306
  - Central NAT 315
  - IPv4 and IPv6 NAT 318
  - Summary 326
  - Chapter Four Review Questions 328
- Book Summary - Intro to FortiGate Part-1 332
  - Appendix A: End of Chapter Answers 333

Introduction

Greetings! I want to be the first to welcome you on this journey into Fortinet Cyber Security technology, and I'm looking forward to helping you become Fortinet NSE4 certified! I love Fortinet products, but even better, I believe in them. I believe in them to protect a network better than any other product on the market. Aside from being the fastest firewall on the market, they are very effective and intuitive to use. I guess if I didn't think this, I wouldn't be writing this book, and if you didn't believe in them already somewhat, you would not have purchased this book. But If you need proof why FortiGate is a better firewall, then check out the 3rd party company NSS Labs who consistently ranks Fortinet as a Cyber Security leader.

But let's get down to business, if Fortinet knowledge is what you seek, then this is the right book for you whether you be a technology enthusiast with no Fortinet experience and are just intrigued by the FortiGate and its capabilities and want to learn more or you are or will be managing a Fortinet network and are required to be certified. Like you, I have searched the Internet looking for a comprehensive book that maps to the Network Security Expert 4 (NSE4) Fortinet certification exam, and like you, I did not find a lot of resources out there, and here we are.

I had to break down the subjects covered into four books, Part-I, Part-II, which covers infrastructure. Next, Part-III and Part-IV will cover FortiOS security features. The first two books will focus on FortiGate infrastructure, meaning network functionality, and

Introduction to FortiGate Part-I Infrastructure

reachability. The next two books will go over all the major security features that are offered on FortiOS. This is where we get into things like authentication, certificates, Web-Filtering, IPS, and AV! The books are designed to be read in sequence to build your FortiGate knowledge from the ground up, layer by layer, using the OSI model approach.

The goal of writing these books is to help you become an outstanding network security engineer who can effectively implement, engineer, support, and maintain a FortiGate

> DID YOU KNOW THAT THE AVERAGE FORTINET PRODUCTION ENGINEER SALARY IS 102K PER YEAR??

network. My career has been an enriching journey so far, and I have met many talented people, and becoming a Fortinet expert has changed my life forever, and I want the same for you. After reading this book and knowing it true, I promise you'll be on your journey to being a Fortinet Rockstar! But nothing is free, and it requires your effort and dedication. Are you ready?

Fortinet NSE Certifications

The first item I want to cover with you is the Fortinet certification structure. Five years ago, around 2015, Fortinet completely reworked its certification structure and created an 8-tier certification process. And so, the Network Security Expert certification path was born. Before the structure, Fortinet had ad hoc certifications for each product with little study material, and there was no way to identify an overall Fortinet expert that could deploy and integrate multiple cybersecurity products. Well, those days are long past now, and we have an evident certificate structure and path for self-development regarding Fortinet products.

Introduction to FortiGate Part-I Infrastructure

NSE certifications 1 through 3 are non-technical certifications and are meant for a high-level introduction into Fortinet products and solutions. You can think of the first three certifications being sales-related and for management teams that are trying to make strategic decisions for their environments. It's not until we get to the NSE-4 where we get the unveil the true potential of the FortiGate firewall and where the rubber meets the road. Compared to another vendor certification like Cisco, the NSE4 certification is pretty much equivalent to the CCNA. If you work in a Fortinet environment managing FortiGate(s), then at a minimum, you will be

required to hold NSE4 certification. And Fortinet partners are required to have so many on staff to maintain their partnership level. NSE 1 and 2 are free to the public and are accessible via https://training.fortinet.com

The NSE4 Network Security Professional certification focuses on the FortiGate firewall. The NSE 4 is not an entry-level certification; Fortinet expects you to have basic computer networking knowledge. If you have no prior experience or certifications, then I recommend you pursue the CompTIA Network+ and CompTIA Security+ certification first before attempting this one. The NSE4 certification focuses on vendor-specific features with a limited theory background. In total, there are 21 domains of material to master to be able to pass the NSE4 examination. The exam is taken at the Pearson VUE testing center. There are no prerequisites to take the exam.

Introduction to FortiGate Part-I Infrastructure

Next is the NSE5 Network Security Analyst certification, which lets you choose between four exams that cover the following Fortinet products: FortiAnalyzer, FortiManager, FortiSIEM, and FortiClient. You must successfully pass a minimum of any two of these exams to become NSE5 certified. These exams must also be taken at the Pearson VUE testing center. There are no prerequisites to take these exams.

The NSE6 Network Security Specialist certification lets you choose between nine exams mapping to the following products: FortiADC, FortiDDoS, FortiNAC, FortiWeb,

> *As of 2020 there are over 25,000 NSE4 certificate holders*

FortiVoice, FortiAuthenticator, FortiMail, FortiWifi, and FortiWLC. You must pass any four of these exams to become NSE6 certified. There are no prior prerequisites to take these exams. These exams must also be taken at the Pearson VUE testing center. The NSE6 certification is valid for two years from the date of completion. There are no prerequisites to take these exams.

The NSE7 Network, Security Architect certification, lets you choose between four exams: Advanced Threat Protection, Enterprise Firewall, Secure Access, and Cloud Security. You must pass any one of these exams to become NSE7 certified. There are no prerequisites to take these exams. The NSE7 is the next step beyond taking the NSE4 regarding FortiGate firewalls but requires knowledge of product integration. When comparing to other vendors like Cisco, the NSE7 is equivalent to their CCNP level certification. The NSE7 certification is valid for two years from the date of completion. The exam must be taken at the Pearson VUE testing center.

Lastly, the highest Fortinet certificate is the NSE8. Obtaining this certificate demonstrates the ability to design, configure, install, and troubleshoot a comprehensive network security solution in a live environment. You must pass a written exam at Person VUE first, and next must pass an extensive two-day hands-on lab exam in which you must successfully configure and validate a complete network topology involving multiple Fortinet products. Here you can find more details on NSE8 certification:
https://www.fortinet.com/content/dam/fortinet/assets/training/NSE8_Certification_ExamFAQ.pdf

In summary, all certifications are valid for two years. You can recertify by retaking the same exam or passing a higher-level exam, but there are some caveats, so for more information on Fortinet NSE certificates, please review:

https://training.fortinet.com/local/staticpage/view.php?page=nse

Introduction to FortiGate Part-I Infrastructure

Why Become Fortinet NSE4 Certified?

There are currently over 25,000 NSE4 certificate holders as of 2020. Fortinet is one of the fastest-growing cybersecurity companies in the world, and there is a shortage of talent in the market. More and more companies are converting their cybersecurity solutions to Fortinet technologies, and at this very moment, there are 1,000's of open positions for employers hiring people with a Fortinet background within the united states alone and even more open positions in Network Security around the world since Fortinet is a global company.

Obtaining the NSE4 Network Security Professional certificate will lay your Network Security skill set foundation and make you marketable to employers trying to secure their network infrastructure and services with FortiGate. The NSE4 certification would also qualify you to work in a Manage Security Service Provider (MSSP) environment supporting other enterprise security needs. Learning Fortinet has changed my life and has given me a specialized skill set that only a few people have within information technology specifically. If you're ready to separate yourself from the rest of the herd and double your pay, then the NSE4 will set you off on your path.

How do you become an NSE4?

As of 2020, you can earn an NSE4 certification when you pass the NSE4_FGT-6.2 or NSE4_FGT-6.0 exam at a Pearson Vue testing center; you are allowed 120 minutes, and there are 70 questions. For more information on Pearson Vue Fortinet testing, please see the below link:

https://home.pearsonvue.com/fortinet

Chapter 1: Introduction to Fortinet

Chapter 1, Ready to unbox your FortiGate? Here I provide a step-by-step introduction into the world of FortiOS and FortiGate hardware. I go over FortiCare and FortiGuard. I will walk you through a basic lab setup and give recommendations on how to be successful using this book, provide an overview of FortiOS features, initial setup, basic administration, built-in servers, and fundamental maintenance.

Introduction to FortiGate Part-I Infrastructure

Chapter 2: Layer 2 Switching

In chapter 2, we build a strong foundation on how FortiOS interacts with various layer two protocols and go over VLANs. You will learn about FortiOS transparent mode and how to broadcast domains are configured and handled. Configure soft-switch settings and understand spanning tree protocol

Chapter 3: IPv4/IPv6 Routing

In chapter 3, we get into the nitty-gritty routing engine FortiOS and explore the layer three routing features and attributes. How to implement policy-routes, layer-3 VLAN interfaces. What ECMP is and what it is used for. Learn about Reverse Path Forward (RPF) and different methods. Best practices regarding network design and routing. Learn how to use FortiOS packet capture tools.

Chapter 4: Firewall Policy and NAT

Chapter 4, We made it to the heart of the firewall.. the policy (known as ACL or rule in other vendors)! Here you'll learn the different components within firewall policies and how the matching algorithm works regarding these policies. How to configure firewall policies and logging. Understand policy IDs and sequence numbers. We also go over how to find firewall policy objects and perform Firewall policy management. We also discuss how FortiOS performs different types of NAT functions and how to configure these functions.

How to Use This Book

Each chapter is structured in the following manner:
1. Industry general overview of technology being discussed
2. Why we need it
3. Fortinet Vendor-specific details
4. How we Implement the technology on FortiGate
5. How to troubleshoot specific technology
6. Industry insight, this is where I add my personal experiences and advice
7. End of chapter questions similar to what is seen on the NSE4 exam

In short, if you are new to FortiGate technology, then make sure to read each chapter a couple of times and navigate to the provide URLs as needed for more information on any topics, do the quiz at the end of the chapter, and lastly, I

Introduction to FortiGate Part-I Infrastructure

recommend a hands-on approach as you navigate through these NSE4 books. Practice.. practice.. practice.. (google and flashcards are your friends) Lastly, read the questions at the end of each chapter first, so you know what to look for during each chapter.

If you are fairly confident with FortiGate Firewalls and want to further your knowledge, be sure to look into the troubleshooting sections and review the questions at the end of each chapter and go through any labs for technologies you're not familiar with.

By the end of this journey, you will be ready to pass your NSE4 exam with no issues. But even better, you will have the skill you need to be good at your job! And you will find a lot of people wanting to be your friend.

Where Do You Take the Exam?

NSE 1-3 are available at https://training.fortinet.com; signup and follow the instruction. NSE 4 – 8 written are available at Person Vue testing center https://home.pearsonvue.com/fortinet. NSE8 Lab, you must email training@fortinet.com to schedule one written exam is passed.

Next, I want to touch on a few Fortinet specific items like Licensing, support, and RMA. If you are new to working with Fortinet as a company, then you should take the time to read through the next sections.

Licensing

Licensing for cybersecurity products, in general, can get... complicated. Still, it is very important to understand that if you fail to renew contracts or licenses on a production device and it expires, this could cause a network outage, which does not make anyone look good. Some cybersecurity vendors require a license for the product itself and require a separate license per security features. These licenses might not co-term, meaning services beginning and ending on the same dates, which makes renewing easier.

Fortinet makes FortiGate firewall licensing much easier than other vendors being that one license can cover the entire product and all its security features, lucky for us. We do, however, need to choose what type of licenses we need for our FortiGate. Here is a quick overview.

> *"..if you fail to renew some contracts or licenses on a production device and it expires then this could cause a network outage.."*

FortiCare Entitlement

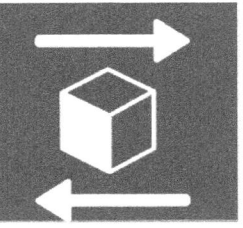

FortiCare entitlement for FortiGate is device-based vendor support. Having FortiCare entitlement on your FortiGate, once registered, allows you to open a support case against your devices' serial number through the Support Portal. FortiCare essentially allows you access to firmware images within the Support Portal, the option to engage Fortinet for Technical Assistance (TA) cases, and hardware replacement options. Hardware replacement is called Return Material Authorization (RMA). Before we get into the different types of tickets we can open and the different FortiCare options we have, let's first go over the RMA options and terminology.

Dead On Arrival DOA

DOA is when you receive a device, and it does not boot, it is dead. Fortinet will let you process this device as an RMA and will cover the shipping cost back to them and mark it as DOA, which is a plus. Note you only have up to 120 days to take advantage of this starting from the shipping date.

RMA Return and Replace

With this RMA method, you, the customer, are responsible for paying the shipping cost of returning the defective device to Fortinet. Once Fortinet receives the device, then A repaired or replacement unit will be shipped to you via ground carrier at Fortinet's expense within three business days after receipt of the failed unit.

RMA Advance Replacement

This method allows you to request a new device before sending the old one back, making the process a little quicker. Fortinet covers the shipping cost of sending you the new unit, and the customer must cover the shipping cost of returning the defective unit. The replacement unit will be ship the same business day if the request is before 2:00 PM of where the regional parts depot is. The shipping method will use next day delivery.

Portal Ticket Types

Next, let's look at all the different types of support cases we can choose from; these are found on the Fortinet support portal found under Assistance > Create A Ticket:

Introduction to FortiGate Part-I Infrastructure

- Technical Support Ticket (TA)
    - If you run into a technical issue, Fortinet TAC will assist you in solving it.
    - Ticket tracker is found in the support portal at Assistance > Manage Tickets
    - Must open a case with a Serial number with active FortiCare entitlement.
- Customer Service Ticket (CS)
    - CS can help you with any matter ranging from account issues, entitlement issues, extending support, or current contracts.
- Dead-On-Arrival (DOA) / Return Merchandise Authorization (RMA)
    - If your Fortinet product has a hardware issue (won't boot, etc.) and the device has FortiCare coverage, then Fortinet will replace your device.
- Anti-Virus Ticket / FortiGuard Service
    - If you have questions on IPS/AV signatures or need to report false positives
- Fortinet Converter ticket
    - This additional service can be purchased where Fortinet support will convert a 3rd party vendor configuration to a FortiGate configuration.

Next, let's go over the different types of FortiCare support service packages you can purchase for your device. Here is a high-level overview:

8x5 Support Standard Package

With 8x5 support, you can only engage Fortinet support agents Mon-Fri from 9 am-5 pm of where the device is registered. This is relative to what time zone of where the unit was initially registered to. This package has RMA Return & Replace Hardware entitlement meaning you must return defected device before Fortinet will send you a new one. Lastly, this package offers Telephone Support, Online Chat Support, Access to Support Portal, and firmware releases

24x7 Support Package

In addition to receiving all the deliverables in the 8x5 Support package, in the 24x7 package, you can engage Fortinet agents anytime. You also receive Premium RMA -

---

FortiCare 24x7 -- In addition to 24x7 phone and email support, this SKU covers automatic updates following databases: Application Control DB, Internet Service DB, Client ID DB, IP Geography DB, Malicious URL DB, and URL Whitelist DB.

Introduction to FortiGate Part-I Infrastructure

Advanced Hardware Replacement handling with Next-day Delivery. You can bundle FortiGuard updates with the FortiCare license.

360 Support Package

In addition to 24x7 and 8x5 Support deliverables, you also gain access to additional services like enhanced SLA, Health Monitoring, Monthly Reports, Access to Advanced Engineers (ASE) Support Services, Proactive Notification, and Malware Events. Fortinet also provides an add-on FortiCare Premium RMA Service as well. This includes the following options:

- Next-day Delivery: Parts are delivered the day following RMA approval by Fortinet support.
- 4-Hour Courier: Parts are delivered on-site 24 hours a day, seven days a week, within 4 hours of RMA approval by Fortinet support.
- 4-Hour On-site Engineer: Parts are delivered on-site with an engineer, 24 hours a day, seven days a week within 4 hours of RMA approval by Fortinet support.
- Secure RMA
    - Fortinet Secure RMA service supports customers that cannot return replaced hardware due to physical data protection requirements.

RMA Processing

Alright, I think we have a fairly good understanding of FortiCare and why we need it. Something that most engineers fret over is working through an RMA case because it's not something that has to be done often.

So, your device has died, and you want to process an RMA, now what? Well, the first thing you need to do is obtain the device's serial number. Also, gather all debug information that you have collected during troubleshooting the issue. This information could be console output, screenshot, or detailed troubleshooting steps. This step is a very important part because Fortinet TAC will not process an RMA without first troubleshooting; it is against the policy unless it's a no boot and no console access case.

Next, take all your information and navigate to your support portal, goto Assistance > Create A Ticket, and proceed to create a case with your device serial number and provide all details to the case.

The next step is what frustrates most people because your case will most likely be staged with TAC and not the RMA team. Once the case is assigned to a TAC engineer, they will most likely request that you format the FortiGate and upload fresh firmware via TFTP, which is a good troubleshooting step because if there is a

Introduction to FortiGate Part-I Infrastructure

corrupt file system, then a format will mark all the bad sectors. Another request could be to run an HQIP test; this stands for Hardware Quick Inspection Package. The HQIP image is a diagnostic image Fortinet uses for its hardware. There are two methods to perform this test.

- HQIP image is obtained from the Support Portal via Download > HQIP Image, and then enter your device serial number. Once entered, you will be presented with an HQIP.OUT image for your platform. You would need to upload this image to FortiGate from the BIOS via TFTP. To learn how to do this review, Section 'Formatting and loading firm TFTP' later in this chapter.
- Use built-in HQIP command for newer models
    - #diagnose hardware test

Lastly, in this test, you must use ethernet cables to wire each interface to one another. Since different platform models have different physical interface layouts, the wiring may differ from unit to unit. But once you load your HQIP image onto your FortiGate, you are present an ASCII wiring diagram to follow. Next, if the HQIP test indeed returns with a hardware failure result, then you will be allowed to proceed with the RMA request.

Image 1.3 - Wiring Diagram Example

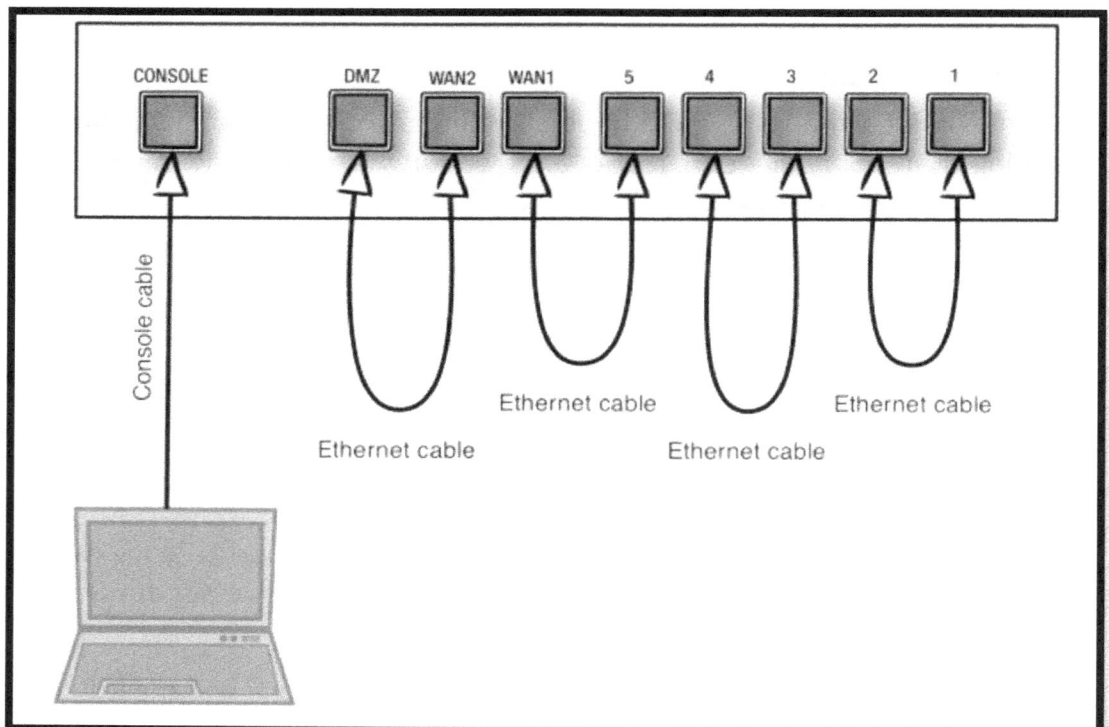

Lastly, in RMA processing are the steps to return the defective device, which are:

Introduction to FortiGate Part-I Infrastructure

- Obtain an RMA Number from Fortinet. RMA number is the same as the ticket number after RMA approval.
- Follow the RMA procedure indicated inside the online ticket after RMA approval.
- Ensure that all equipment and components you are returning are safely packed for transportation.
- Do not send back any accessories, mounting kit, mounting brackets, or user manuals. Please return only the failed device or any other component approved by Fortinet. Except in DOA cases, when you must return the defective unit along with all its original accessories, Fortinet RMA center is not responsible for returning accessories, which would have been shipped with the defective unit without Fortinet's pre-approval.
- Include a hard copy of the RMA form with your shipment and update the support ticket with a return tracking number.
- Clearly mark the RMA number on the outside of the return shipping container.
- Warehouse Opening Hours: Monday – Friday (Excluding Bank Holidays)
- 9:00AM to 12:00PM and from 2:00PM to 5:00PM
- Send returns to the following address:
    - (This will depend on where you are located; the information will be in RMA case)
- You are responsible for all costs associated with the return (e.g., shipping carrier, customs, etc.) except for DOA replacement, where Fortinet will bear the cost of shipment for both the return of the defective unit and the supply of the replacement unit. For 8*5 or 24*7 RMA replacement, shipments must be door to door.

After you receive your new unit, you must complete the following steps to move the license entitled from the defective unit to the new one. Hence, you must transfer the support contract to the replacement unit as follows:

- Login to https://support.fortinet.com
- Select Manage Products.
- Select the Serial Number of the defective unit.
- Under Registration > RMA Transfer, enter the new serial number of the replacement unit and click on Replace.

You can check FortiGate file system for issues with below command:
 # execute disk list
 # execute disk scan <value>

Introduction to FortiGate Part-I Infrastructure

Done! Too easy. Fortunately, you will most likely not need to perform a lot of these, but if you do, just come back to this section for a quick refresher!

FortiGuard Subscription Entitlement

FortiGuard is the keystone of the Fortinet security solution and is one of the main reasons Fortinet is regarded so highly within the industry. FortiGuard Labs are the threat intelligence and research organization within Fortinet, which consists of more than 200 cybersecurity professionals researching new security threats and developing security signatures as these threats are discovered. These signatures are available for download for Fortinet security devices that have active FortiGuard licenses. This allows FortiOS to maintain the most up to date security information on our FortiGate firewall.

Note, it is very important to remember to renew your FortiGuard Security Services before they expire. Firstly, of course, you will have more exposure to your internal network, but even worse could cause an outage for your network if certain security features are in use.

Let's proceed and touch on all the subscription services FortiGuard offers and then go over the subscription bundles they allow you to purchase. Here is the complete list of subscription services that FortiGuard offers:

- Antivirus (AV)
  - FortiGuard delivers the most up-to-date AV information to your FortiGate that protects against viruses, spyware, and other content level threats.
- Intrusion Prevention (IPS)
  - FortiGuard provides the most up to date IPS information that protects against network intrusions by matching and blocking threats before they reach their destination. Fortinet has over 6,800+ IPS signatures and counting!
- Application Control (App Control)
  - FortiGuard provides dynamic updates for application signatures. You can quickly create policies to control and monitor what applications are on your network.
- Security Rating Service
  - This is a fairly new feature where FortiGate will run a Security Rating check so to be able to identify critical vulnerability or configuration weakness within the Security Fabric. Also, it will provide you actual best practices for your network.
- Indicators of Compromise (IOC)

Introduction to FortiGate Part-I Infrastructure

- This feature is also only a few years old. The IOC uses log correlation to see if an endpoint on the network is compromised, and FortiGate has the feature to automatically quinine this host that triggered the IOC.
- Vulnerability Scan
  - FortiGuard vulnerability scan services
- Web Application Firewall (WAF)
  - FortiGuard provides dynamic WAF signature updates to protect against specialized attacks like SQL injections, Cross-site scripting, and many others.
  - Supports PCI DSS compliance by protecting against OWASP top-10 vulnerabilities and using WAF technology to block attacks.
- Web Filtering
  - This feature is a big one on FortiGate, and we have an entire chapter dedicated to this feature. This security feature provides granular blocking of various websites using white/blacklist also web categories.
- Antispam
  - Fortiguard offers dynamic updates Antispam security services that provide a multi-layer approach to detect and filter spam.
- Cloud Sandbox
  - This feature is an Advanced Threat Detection solution where FortiGate can dynamically upload a file to identify previously unknown malware. We go over this feature in our AV chapter.

Alright, next here, let's take a look at the FortiGuard Subscription bundles or what you can buy for your FortiGate; let's go shopping! :

- Advanced Threat Protection (ATP) Subscription
  - FortiCare
  - Application Control
  - Advanced Malware Protection (AV)
  - Intrusion Prevention (IPS)
- Unified Protection (UTM) Subscription
  - ATP Subscription items
  - Anti-Spam
  - Web Filtering
- Enterprise Protection (ENT) Subscription
  - ATP Subscription items
  - UTM Subscription items
  - Cloud Access Security Broker CASB
  - Security Rating Service
  - Industrial Security Service
- 360 Protection Subscription

Introduction to FortiGate Part-I Infrastructure

- ATP Subscription items
- UTM Subscription items
- ENT Subscription items
- FortiConverter Services
- SD-WAN One Click VPN Overlay
- SD-WAN Cloud Assist Monitoring
- FortiAnalyzer Cloud
- FortiManager Cloud

The most common FortiGuard security bundle I have worked with is the UTM, which are all the essential security features. Enterprise Protection and 360 Protection are great tools to help you evaluate your security posture and keep your network within compliance standards. The 360 Protection is fairly new as well, and if angle for enterprises wanting to take advantage of FortiGates SDWAN feature set.

Warranty

An important thing to know about is your Fortinet device warranty. Fortinet provides a one-year limited product hardware warranty. If any hardware issues arise with the FortiGate, you may return it via RMA. The one-year timer begins once you register your device. You should note that the warranty clock will begin 60 days after the device is shipped, even if you do not register the device. Fortinet also has a sunset requirement that requires all products must be registered within twelve months of the initial product sale, and if this point does not register the product in time, then the product will forfeit any warranty rights. So be sure and register your Fortigate!

Any warranty claims will be processed under FortiCare 24x7 support contact, which allows you to request a replacement to ship before return the defective unit. You must send the failed unit within 30 days after Fortinet begins the process of your RMA claim to avoid being billed. Also, DOA is handled as Advanced Replacements and will receive overnight shipping. Note that DOA must be reported no more than one hundred and twenty days from the shipment date.

Table 1.1 – Introduction to FortiGate

Objective	Chapter(s)
1.1 Identify platform features of FortiGate	1
1.2 Understand FortiGate Security Processor Unit SPU	1

Introduction to FortiGate Part-I Infrastructure

1.3 Identify the factory defaults	1
1.4 Understand different operational modes	1
1.5 Understand FortiGate relationship with FortiGuard and distinguish between live queries and package updates	1
1.6 Manage administrator profiles	1
1.7 Manage administrative users	1
1.8 Define the configuration method for administrative users	1
1.9 Manage network interface	1
1.10 Enable DHCP service	1
1.11 Backup and restore system configuration files	1
1.12 Understand the difference between restore requirements for plaintext and encrypted backup file	1
1.13 Identify the current firmware version	1
1.14 Upgrade firmware	1
1.15 Downgrade firmware	1

Table 1.2 - Layer 2 Switching

Objective	Chapter(s)
2.1 Configure VLANs	2
2.2 Describe VLANs and VLAN tagging	2
2.3 Understand Transparent mode vs. NAT mode	2
2.4 Configure basic FortiGate transparent mode settings	2
2.5 Understand transparent mode MAC address table	2
2.6 Understand Virtual Wire Pairing	2
2.7 Segment Layer 2 network into multiple broadcast domains	2

Introduction to FortiGate Part-I Infrastructure

2.8 Configure Soft Switch settings	2
2.9 Competence in Spanning Tree Protocol	2

Table 1.3 - IPv4/IPv6 Routing

Objective	Chapter(s)
3.1 Describe and Implement general routing capabilities	3
3.2 Describe the different dynamic routing protocol on FortiOS	3
3.3 Describe and Implement Policy routes	3
3.4 Route well-known Internet Services	3
3.5 Interpret route table	3
3.6 Identify active routes	3
3.7 Describe route attributes and how the best route is chosen	3
3.8 Describe and Implement Equal Cost Multiple Path ECMP	3
3.9 Describe and Implement route redundancy and load balancing	3
3.10 Describe Reverse Path Forwarding	3
3.11 Describe RPF check methods	3
3.12 Describe and Implement link health monitor	3
3.13 Apply network design best practices	3
3.14 Apply static route best practices	3
3.15 Use packet capture tools	3

Table 1.4 Firewall Policy and NAT

Objective	Chapter(s)
4.1 Identify components within firewall policies	4

Introduction to FortiGate Part-I Infrastructure

4.2 Describe how traffic is matched within firewall policies	4
4.3 Configure the firewall policies to secure network	4
4.4 Configure firewall policy logging	4
4.5 Describe policy list views	4
4.6 Explain policy IDs and policy sequence numbers	4
4.7 Describe where objects are referenced	4
4.8 Explain naming restrictions for firewall policies and objects	4
4.9 Perform firewall policies reordering	4
4.10 Describe matching policies for the traffic type	4
4.11 Describe and configure NAT and PAT	4
4.12 Describe and configure Session-Helpers	4
4.13 Describe and configure central NAT	4

Chapter 1 | Introduction to FortiGate

NSE4 Blueprint Topics Covered

- Identify platform features of FortiGate
- Describe Security Processor Unit SPU
- Identify factory defaults
- Understand the different operational modes
- Understand FortiGate and FortiGuard Relationship
- Manage administrator profiles
- Manage administrative profiles
- Manage network interfaces
- Manage basic services
- backup and restore config file
- upgrade and downgrade firmware
- Understand CLI structure
- Understand GUI navigation
- Initial Configuration

Chapter 1 | Introduction to FortiGate

Getting Started with FortiGate

Welcome to the world of Fortinet! I'm very excited to guide you on this amazing journey of introducing you to the FortiGate firewall. This book covers various Fortinet FortiGate firewall technologies and will help you prepare for your first technical certification within the Fortinet NSE certification track. Aside from helping you obtain your NSE4 certification, my main goal is for you to become an overall outstanding Fortinet engineer because I feel like that is what matters most. I'm writing this book from the perspective of onboarding a new Network Security Professional onto a team that manages FortiGate firewalls, and this is the book to get you up to speed!

We have a lot to cover in this first chapter to build your foundation and begin your emersion into all the FortiGate features and functions. FortiOS is a big subject, but do not fret because I walk you through everything step by step. We review everything from FortiGate licensing, to the FortiOS architecture, to basic FortiGate configuration in this chapter, and afterward, you will feel confident about what services Fortinet offers and how they relate to the FortiGate.

A little more information on FortiGate if you are brand new to the technology. FortiGate is a Next Generation, a stateful firewall that essentially provides Unified Threat Management (UTM) for enterprise networks. UTM just means bundling certain security features into one security device; we go over this further in this chapter. The FortiGate is an outstanding firewall and has been considered a market leader in

Chapter 1 | Introduction to FortiGate

edge security technologies year after year. Our powerful network security ally with many features that we can use to protect our network assets. However, it is yet still simple and intuitive to implement and manage.

So, Mr. or Ms. Network Security Analyst I, welcome to the team, and let's get started with your onboarding!

Unboxing your FortiGate

The day has finally come to unpack your brand new 60E FortiGate Firewall! This is an exciting moment with all its fresh, crisp white packaging and brand new UTM license so we can get fresh FortiGuard updates for stuff like AV and IPS! You are currently holding one of the most sophisticated network security products in the world. The package comes with some very important items:

- 60E FortiGate firewall
- Power Adapter
- Console cable (no USB adapter included)
- Ethernet Cable
- Wall Mount Hardware
- Information Supplement handbook

A couple of things to take notes of, on the bottom of the FortiGate (FGT), you will find the product serial number (SN). On top, you will find your FortiCloud key. I'll touch on FortiCloud here soon. The first thing you need to do is register your FortiGate SN! This can be done at https://support.fortinet.com. Yes, this is a very important step. This allows for:

- FortiGuard updates
    - FortiGate receives dynamic UTM updates (AV, IPS, etc..)
- Firmware upgrades
    - Ability to download FortiOS images via https://support.fortinet.com
- Technical support
    - Provides the ability to submit Technical Assist Cases to the Technical Assistance Center.
- Warranty Coverage
    - You can exchange your FortiGate if hardware defect via "Return Material Authorization" (RMA); more information found via RMA Knowledge Base

Chapter 1 | Introduction to FortiGate

Download FortiGate Virtual Machine

I want to encourage you to take time to set up a lab; this is a critical step in learning any new technology. I promise it is worth the effort!

If you do not have a FortiGate firewall to lab with. You can download a trial FortiGate-VM via support.fortinet.com. This is found via download> VM Images and select FortiGate Product, then the hypervisor platform, select Download. The trial

Figure 1.1 - Download FortiGate VM

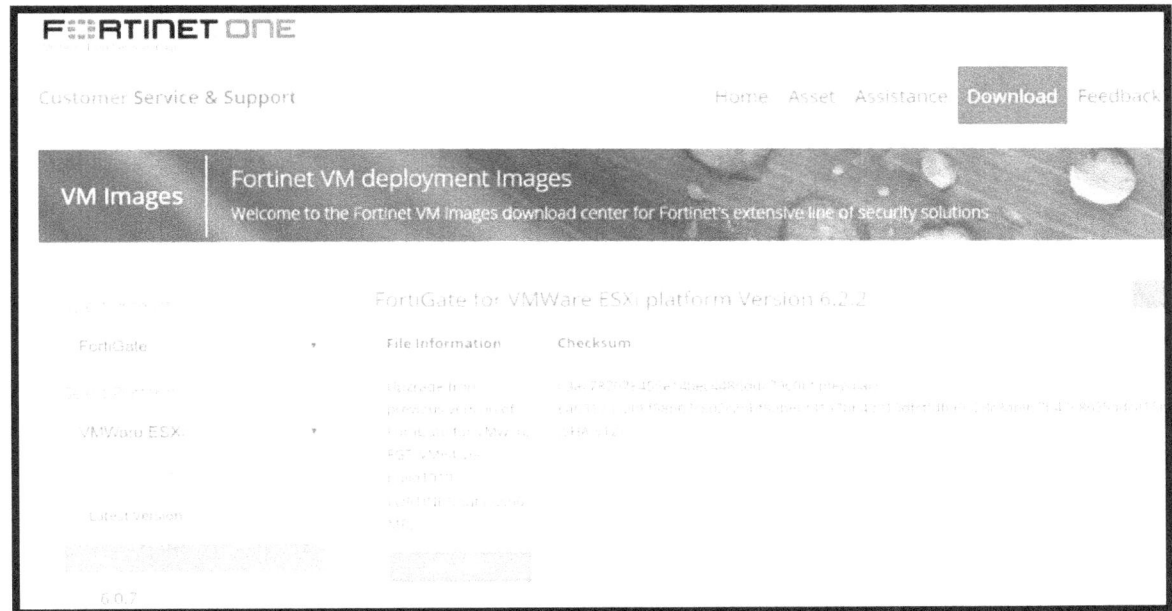

will last 14 days; once it expires, you need to download another FortiGate-VM image details are found in Figure 1.1. Also, 30E FortiGate can be found on many online retailers and would make for a great lab firewall!

For assistance creating a support.fortinet.com account visit the below URL and find "Create A Support Account.pdf"
https://kb.fortinet.com/kb/documentLink.do?externalID=FD32312

Chapter 1 | Introduction to FortiGate

Accessing FortiGate

Once you have registered your FortiGate on the Support Portal, it is now time to access your device! This can be done in a few different ways. You can access your new FortiGate via console port to provide the initial configuration if you would like, or you can use your HTTP(S) or SSH client to access the LAN side of the FortiGate. If you're new to working with FortiGate, then yes, you can access your device using management network protocols without any configuration by default, out of the box.

So, by default, FortiGate has HTTP(S) and SSH services running on the internal LAN interface you can interact with, along with a fully functional DHCP server! So, all you need to do is use the provided ethernet cable and attach your laptop or desktop computer's ethernet interface to your port1 interface on FortiGate.

> *Do not cable your new FortiGate internal interface(s) into your local SOC/NOC network, this will introduce a rogue DHCP server and black hole new DHCP clients!! (there is a reason I know this...)*

If your PC is set up as a DHCP client, then it receives an IP address in the 192.168.1.0/24 subnet ranges with your default gateway being 192.168.1.99, which is the default IP on your LAN internal interface(s) (please note this is only for entry-level models, higher-end models you will need to use console port for initial configuration). You can also set yourself a static IP within this range with the respective gateway above. Your initial login is:

- username: admin
- password: (blank) // just hit return key here

That's it! You now have access to your FortiGate device, and you are now one step closer to your journey of obtaining your Fortinet NSE4 certification! So, congratulations. In the coming up selections, we are shifting gears to go over Fortinet licensing, FortiOS features, and platform features. Also, I will be touching on Fortinet's services. GUI and CLI overview and then finish up with some basic FortiOS configuration. Let us get started!

FortiCloud

The first item on the docket, FortiCloud. What is it, and how is it useful to us? FortiCloud is an add-on service that comes with your FortiGate firewall without any additional cost! It operates as a single pane of glass cloud-based Software as a

Chapter 1 | Introduction to FortiGate

Service (SaaS) focused on device management, logging, and reporting solutions. Services include with FortiCloud are:

- FortiGate and FortiWiFi log retention, analysis, and reporting
- Cloud configuration Management for FortiGate, FortiWiFI, and FortiAP
- Cloud-based FortiSandbox for AV submission for heuristic evaluation
- FortiDeploy for one-touch provisioning.
- IOC Indicators of compromise service

> *A modern firewall does not only inspect traffic at the point of ingress into a network but also serves as a multi-functional device that inspects network traffic at perimeter as well as traffic internally within networks.*

One of the most useful features I found with ForitCloud is reporting. If you send your logs to FortiCloud, then it is very easy to set up daily, and weekly summary reports for your network traffic. Some of the report templates available are Cyber Threat Assessment, High Bandwidth applications, DNS, and Top Visited Websites. This is like having a free FortiAnalyzer! But if you decide to use this for your enterprise, note that the free version of the service only allows for 1Gb of logs; the paid version allows 200Gbs worth of logs. The service also allows for Cloud Sandboxing, meaning suspicious files evaluated by the local AV are sent to FortiCloud Sandbox for further analysis where heuristic malware detection is performed.

Every FortiGate comes with a FortiCloud key, located on the top of your device, that can be used to create an account on FortiCloud. You can register your firewall manually through the FortiCloud website, https://www.forticloud.com, or you can easily register and activate your account directly from your FortiGate GUI Dashboard Windowpane. Before you can activate a FortiGate Cloud account, you must first register your device! For more information, please see Forticloud Admin Guide 3.3.2.   In summary, FortiCloud works well for small to medium size FortiGate/FortiAP deployments. But for large deployment, I recommend investing in your own dedicated FortiManager and/or FortiAnalyzer deployment, and this allows for more scalable and granular solutions

Chapter 1 | Introduction to FortiGate

Image 1.2 - Top of FGT

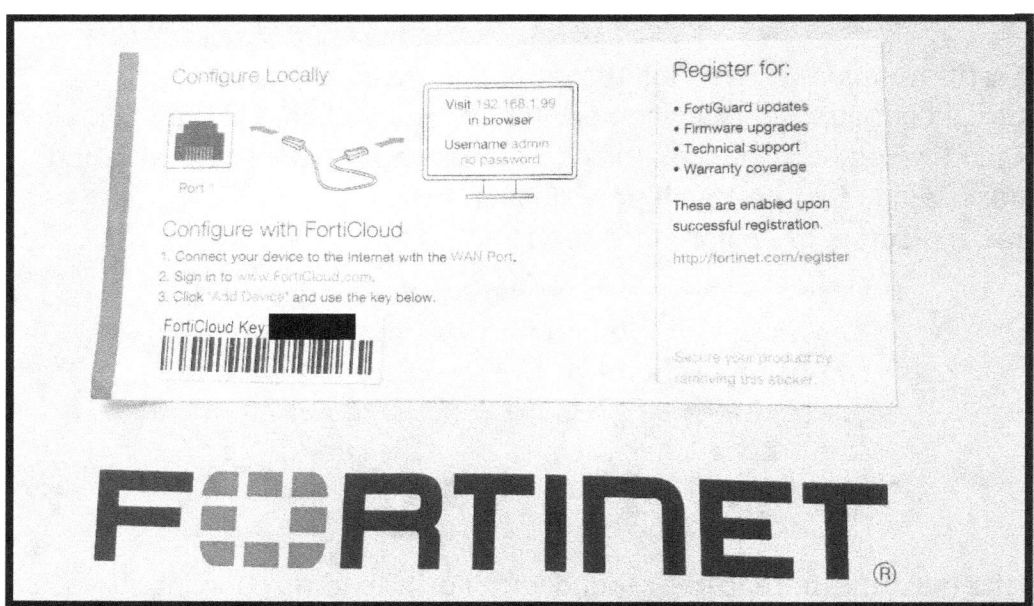

Intro to Modern Network Security and Challenges

Alright, let's get into some of the cooler stuff now. As the world of borderless Cyber Security networks unfolds, we have continued to come up with new methods to help secure networks. As technology changes and new methods of accessing networks are created, so then the requirements to protect these networks and applications also change, and so the more protection we add, the more unmanageable cybersecurity becomes.

Each security product has its own unique challenges and caveats, and it takes a lot of time and effort for cybersecurity professionals to learn and manage these products and even more challenges to make each security product work together for one united effort. So, if you have security products from 8 different vendors to manage on an enterprise network, protecting countless users and services, it eventually becomes unfeasible and too expensive to manage. So your expensive complex security solution is rendered ineffective; this is bad.

This is where the phrase Unified Threat Management comes in or UTM. UTM was created to address the chaos in cybers defense products, and vendors started to develop better methods to secure enterprise networks properly. Before UTM, there were security products for each unique networking problem, for example:

- Layer-3 and Layer-4 access control device
- VPN remote access device
- Load-balancer and decryption/encryption server device

Chapter 1 | Introduction to FortiGate

- Email SMTP(S) Application Service inspection device
- Email Spam filter device
- Web HTTP(S)Application Service inspection device
- Web Filtering device
- File Anti-Virus Scanning device
- Intrusion Prevention System (IPS) device
- Application Identification service and control device
- Data Leak Prevention device
- GEO-IP device
- Web-Proxy device

Could you imagine trying to manage all these different devices from different vendors specializing in a single problem? And then have all these products work together? Not fun. So that is why UTM is amazing; it takes all these solutions and places them inside one device... drum roll please... ... ... our FortiGate firewall.

The major problem UTM creates the amount of CPU processing power that is required from a single device, and for most devices, this creates a bottleneck in your network. Fortinet's solution to this problem is the specialized Application-specific Integrated Circuit (ASIC) chips, which are called the Security Processing Units (SPU). SPUs are a general label given to the ASIC chip suite, which are the NPx, CPx, and SoCx chips that offload network traffic and cryptography functions with FortiGate platforms, and this is especially critical for data centers and carriers where throughput is business-critical. We go over each of these chips in more detail in later chapters.

The FortiGate confronts the modern world of cybersecurity needs with UTM, the Security Fabric, and the processing power to handle the load. We go over all the major UTM features and hardware optimization in the next section, and I promise you will feel confident working with any one of these features by the end of this book.

In summary, FortiOS is the operating system that interfaces with FortiGate platforms or hypervisors. The platform hardware contains several specialized hardware ASIC chips that offload certain types of network traffic and cryptography services. FortiOS Utilizes UTM to provide robust modern protection for various types of networks like data centers, corporation enterprises, and MSSP's, each UTM module communicates with FortiGuard for security rating lookups or for dynamic database updates.

Chapter 1 | Introduction to FortiGate

Image 1.4 – FortiOS and Security Fabric Architecture

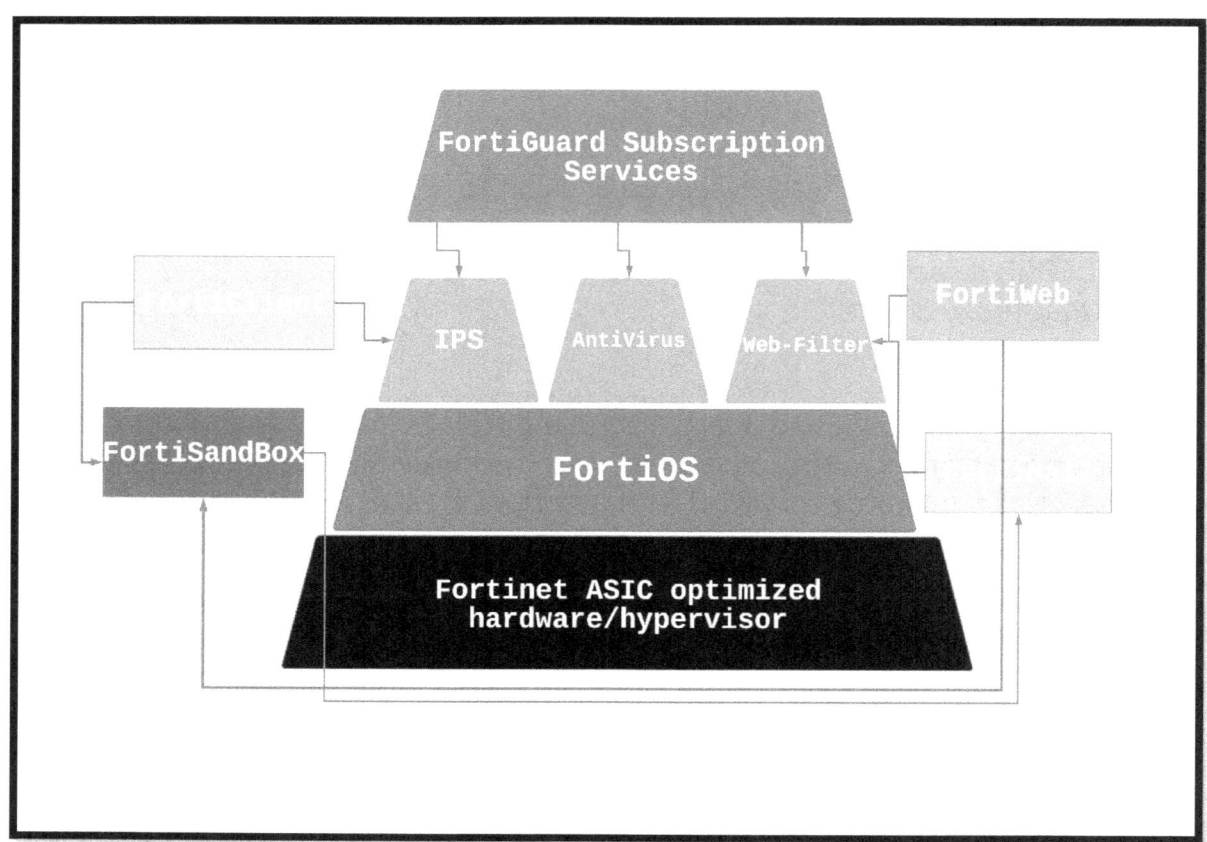

Image 1.4 provides a nice breakdown of some of the different Fortinet technologies and how they work together. At the bottom of image 1.4 is the foundation of all security-related functionally, the hardware. FortiGate has specialized ASIC's (application-specific integrated circuit) that helps FortiOS offload certain security-related or network-related tasks to a dedicated processor. Built on top of these dedicated specialized processors is the operating system, which is FortiOS. When you put your FortiOS with this specialized hardware, you get a FortiGate. As you can see in image 1.4, FortiGate has specific databases that provide security functionality to the network traffic; for example, IPS, AV, and Web Filtering. These security functions are then supported and updated by FortiGuard Distribution Network, and to obtain access to these FortiGuard services, a subscription is required. This guarantees that FortiOS is always using the latest security information to inspect traffic.

Also, in *Image 1.4*, you can see the inner communication between Fortinet products. For example, FortiClient can tell FortiGate about its local information and give great detail on the endpoint health. For example, it can report if a host has been

Chapter 1 | Introduction to FortiGate

compromised, and FortiGate can take action automatically and quarantine the host. Also, FortiClient and FortiGate have options to push suspicious files to FortiSandBox for further analysis through heuristic evaluation methods. Fortinet has many products you can add to the security fabric to create a multilayered security defense. For example, Fortinet offers specialized firewalls like FortiWeb and FortiMail that look only at certain applications and can easily be integrated with FortiGate.

Lastly, here I want to talk about the Security Fabric a little more. FortiOS communicates with other Fortinet products by sharing network information between security devices to obtain an in-depth view of the network security posture. For example, FortiGate can directly communicate with FortiClient endpoint software, FortiSandbox, FortiWeb, and FortiMail. The Security Fabric gives enterprise networks a holistic cybersecurity posture that is feasible to manage since every product is designed in-house to talk to one another via telemetry or API. This is an awesome security defense model, and by truly obtaining it completely, it carries with it the ultimate goal that every enterprise network security team is trying to reach, an effective security solution that is feasible to manage!

Security Profiles and FortiGuard Overview

Let's get started by digging into some of the juicy security features we have to work with on FortiGate firewalls. The FortiGate delivers the ability to perform full granular UTM on any type of traffic that can be isolated within a firewall policy. If you are wondering what all the security features FortiGate provides, below is the complete list of security profiles available on 6.2 FortioS:

- SSL/SSH Inspection Profile
    - This gives the ability to perform a Man-in-the-middle (MITM) attack on protocols secured with SSL/TLS encryption services. This is a very important feature because you cannot catch what you cannot see. By breaking the encryption, we now could see malicious traffic and control traffic as we see fit.
        - Supported protocols for MITM are:
            - HTTPS
            - SMTPS
            - POP3S
            - IMAPS
            - FTPS
- Web Filter Profile and DNS Filter Profile
    - This gives the ability to control where users can web browse on the internet. We can configure individual domains or use predefined

Chapter 1 | Introduction to FortiGate

categories to control user web traffic. Many features here, chapter 13 goes over this UTM feature.
- AntiVirus Profile
  - This feature gives the ability to scan network traffic for malicious files using a local signature database managed by our scanunitd daemon.
    - Support protocols for inspection are:
      - HTTP
      - SMTP
      - POP3
      - IMAP
      - MAPI
      - FTP
      - CIFS
- Intrusion Prevention (IPS)
  - This feature gives the ability to scan network traffic for known exploits or malicious traffic. Our IPS database currently has over 6,000+ signatures. This feature is managed by our IPSengine daemon.
- Application Control (App Control)
  - This feature gives the ability to identify the application running on the network and control this traffic. This feature is also used in SD-WAN for traffic steering and application reporting from logs sent to FortiAnalyzer or SIEM. Chapter 14 goes over this feature.
- Email Filter Profile (Anti-Spam)
  - This feature gives the ability to block malicious emails by domain and IP. You will learn about each email filter method in chapter 13.
- VoIP Profile
  - This feature gives us the ability to stop SIP spam from hitting your phone system. You will learn more about the VoIP profile in chapter 14.
- DoS Profile
  - This will prevent various Denial of service attacks from entering your network. We will learn more about this feature in chapter 16.
- ICAP Profile
  - we do not go over ICAP in this book for more information; please visit ICAP Cookbook
- Cloud Access Security Broker (CASB) Profile
  - CASB is designed to provide visibility, compliance, data security, and threat protection for cloud-based services employed by an organization.
- Data Leak Prevention Profile
  - Data Leak Preventions can be used to prevent things like Social Security number or Credit card numbers from leaving the network

Chapter 1 | Introduction to FortiGate

I have entire chapters dedicated to some of these features. We are going to have a lot of fun covering them fully later on!

FortiGuard Technical Overview

FortiGuard Subscription Services, what is it? The FortiGuard Distributed Network (FDN) is Fortinet's cloud support structure that provides the most up-to-date threat intelligence to many Fortinet product lines, including FortiGate. FortiGate is required to have a valid contract and Internet connection to receive threat updates and to perform live security rating queries. In short, having a valid license on your FortiGate guarantees, it always has the most up-to-date databases for your security features to use and allows real-time query access to FDN.

The IPS and AV UTM features download full signature databases from FDN (or can be pushed). The FortiGate obtains these databases from update.fortinet.net, which uses TCP (SSL/TLS) on ports 443/8890. The FortiOS UTM Security features that have local databases that receive dynamic updates from FortiGuard Servers are:

- Intrusion protection (IPS)
- Antivirus (AV)

Notice not all UTM features store their own database locally, and this is because these security databases are too large and change too often, and so this requires

> *AV and IPS are not the only features that have a local database on FortiOS that receive dynamic updates. A complete list can be found on cli with #diagnose autoupdate versions*

live queries to FDN for the most up-to-date security information. The FortiOS UTM Features that require live queries are:

- Web filtering
- DNS Filtering
- Antispam

You can also have the live queries use different ports and protocols, but by default, it is HTTPS on port 8888. The Port, Protocol, and FQDN for FDN live security rating queries are:

- securewf.fortiguard.net (FortiOS 6.2+)
    - Protocol HTTPS ports 53 or 8888
- service.fortiguard.net (6.0 and below)
    - Proprietary protocol UDP on port 53 or 8888.

Chapter 1 | Introduction to FortiGate

Here is the list of supported protocols for live FDN queries security ratings:

- Proprietary UDP/8888
- Proprietary UDP/53
- HTTPS/8888
- HTTPS/53

The protocol used can be changed via CLI:

```
#config system fortiguard
#    set protocol https
#    set port 8888
#end
```

As of 6.4 MR, to set custom FortiGuard Port, you must first configure: #fortiguard-anycast disable

By default, FortiGate can use any FortiGuard server location in the world, but this can be locked down to the region. FortiGate prefers a FortiGuard server in the nearest time-zone but adjusts its server-based on remote FortiGuard server load. By default, FortiGate checks for AV/IPS updates daily. This frequency can be changed via the GUI 'System > FortiGuard > Scheduled updates' and CLI is:

```
#config system autoupdate schedule
#    set frequency daily
#    set time 15:60
#end
```

That about wraps it up for FortiGuard Technical Overview. It is important to know what ports are required to communicate with FortiGuard and the FQDN for FDN services.

Security Processing Unit (SPU) Overview

All Fortinet hardware acceleration has been renamed to Security Processing Units SPUs, and this includes NPx, CPx, SPx, NPlite, and SoCx processor. These chips offload resource-intensive processing from the main CPU. I go over the SPU features and functionalities throughout the book and show you how to optimize these chips to work best with your security solution. Also, I show how to verify traffic is offloaded to the SPU chip, which is very important. Below are high-level capabilities for each chip

Chapter 1 | Introduction to FortiGate

Content Processor 9(CP9) Acceleration capabilities Overview

The CP help FortiOS accelerate traffic and optimize the entire system for a wide range of security function. CP chips are not bound to any interface but work more towards the application level. CP processors accelerate intensive cryptography tasks like SSL encryption/decryption and AV scanning. This chipset is responsible for various IPS functions, HMAC, Random number generator, various RSA functions, various SSL/TLS, and IPsec VPN functions.

Network Processors (NP7, NP6, NP6lite, and NP4) Capabilities Overview

Network Processor ASIC helps FortiOS with many networking tasking. A single NP6 ASIC can handle between 10 and 16 million sessions. This number depends on how much memory the platform has, and once the NP hits its session limit, all other sessions are sent to the CPU. The main CPU is only responsible for the initial session setup of the first couple of packet exchanges in a session, and once the CPU sees an outbound packet and a response packet for a new session, the session is then handed to the NP to manage (if qualifies). This frees up CPU cycles used in the packet forwarding process and lets the CPU focus more on more critical security tasks for the network. For a session to be offloaded or accelerated by an NP, that session must not require proxy-based security features, for example like Anti-virus scanning. The CPU must handle these sessions. Sessions that require flow-based security scanning can be offloaded to NP if FortiGate supports the NTurbo feature.

The NP7 is the newest NP and can handle up to 12 million sessions and 195 Gbps Firewall throughput. Also, NP7 handles offload of VXLAN termination, NAT, hardware logging, and policy enforcement. More information on NP7 can be found here: https://www.fortinet.com/products/fortigate/fortiasic.html#np7

System-on-a-Chip Processor SoC3

SoC chips are found in the entry-level FortiGate platform models and have a simpler system design but can still deliver high-speed performance. The SoC3 chip integrates the Network, Content, and RISC-based CPU(s) processors onto a single chip. These processors can obtain 1 Gbps to 1 Tbps of firewall throughput! And can still offload certain security and networking functions.

System-on-a-Chip Processor SoC4

The SoC4 chip is the newest SoC chip and is available on F series FortiGate. The SoC4 chip specializes in handling SDWAN traffic that delivers 10x higher performance than SoC3. SoC4 performs layer-7 offload security handling features. It can also handle up to 5 Gbps of firewall traffic offloading. More information found here: https://www.fortinet.com/products/fortigate/fortiasic.html#soc4

FortiOS Modes of Operations overview

So next, we are going to talk a little about FortiOS Operational modes. There are two modes FortiOS can operate in, NAT or Transparent, and this allows FortiOS to either operate as a Layer three device or a layer two device, respectfully. Enterprises need to evaluate their network requirements and see how FortiGate fits into the pictures. If only a bump in the wire is required and there is no need to change the layer-3 architecture, then maybe a Transparent mode is the right choice. But if FortiGate is used as a VPN concentrator or performs a routing function as well, then NAT mode would be required.

I have worked on NAT mode FortiGate's for most of my career, but the feature set for both modes are very similar. To decide which mode to deploy depends on your network requirements. You should consider your comfortability regarding managing a Layer-2 firewall versus a Layer-3 firewall.

NAT Mode Details

In this mode, FortiGate routes packets to their destination interface based on layer-3 header information and can have an IP address assigned to each interface. This mode requires a network redesign since FortiGate is acting as a layer-3 device. Essentially, this mode lets you have a router but also a full UTM firewall that betters the security posture of the network. The NSE4 is focused on NAT operational mode, and so is this book.

Transparent Mode Details

In this mode, FortiGate does not route packets but switches them to their destination interface by using layer-2 MAC address header information, and as a switch, there are no IP addresses assigned to interfaces. When a Transparent mode FortiGate is added to a network, it does not make any changes to the local IP address scheme; no layer-3 network changes are required. There can indeed be a layer-3 IP address configured for management access in Transparent Mode. In summary, this mode lets you have a switch and a firewall essentially and is used where security needs to be increased, but changing the network itself is impractical. For full feature comparison, please visit:

NAT/Route Mode vs. Transparent Mode :
https://help.fortinet.com/fos50hlp/54/Content/FortiOS/fortigate-transparent-54/1-Intro&Features/3-NAT-vs-Transparent.htm

Chapter 1 | Introduction to FortiGate

Basic FortiGate Administration

Shifting gears away from some of FortiGate's background information and back into the management and configuration of FortiOS. The Administration topics are an especially important section if you are new to managing FortiGate firewalls because here I show you how to navigate the FortiOS Graphical User Interface (GUI) and its Command Line Interface (CLI). The CLI for the FortiGate might be very different than the CLI of other devices you have managed in the past or if you come from a Cisco background.

I want you to think of this section as a tour of the FortiGate user interface. It is always a little scary learning a new vendor technology because every vendor is so different in how they implement their technology solutions, but you will find out quickly just how intuitive the GUI and CLI are to navigate and work with. This is one reason I made my career focus working with Fortinet products because they are just easy and fun to work with!

Intro to the basic GUI navigation

FortiOS has a powerful graphical user interface (GUI). Most configurations can be performed in the GUI, which in turn simplifies things a lot and saves you from memorizing endless lines of CLI commands. By default, we can access the GUI on

Image 1.5 – FortiGate Dashboard Widgets

If you do not have a FortiGate to follow along with then I encourage you to take a screen snippet or picture of this menu so when I reference locations in the GUI it makes sense to you.

Chapter 1 | Introduction to FortiGate

HTTP and HTTPS. The default username/password is admin, and the password is blank. Once you are on the GUI Dashboard page, the first thing you notice is the widgets at the top of the Dashboard windowpane as seen in *Image 1.5* and by default are:

Image 1.6 – FortiGate Dashboard Health Widgets

- System Information
  - This provides local system information:

Chapter 1 | Introduction to FortiGate

- Hostname
- Serial Number
- Firmware
- Virtual Domains Status
- System Time
- Uptime
- WAN IP
- Licenses
    - This provides registration status, support license, and UTM license status
- FortiGate Cloud
    - This provides information on your FortiCloud account status
- Security Fabric
    - The ICON's here give a quick high level of what is apart of the Security Fabric, for example, other FortiGates, FortiManager, FortiAnalyzer, FortiAP, and FortiSandbox.
- Administrators
    - This widget box gives a snapshot of what administrative protocols are being allowed on this FortiGate and what admin accounts are logged in, and how
        - In this example, 'admin' is logged in both HTTPS and SSH.

The next thing you see is the system health widgets. By default, they are CPU, Sessions, and memory. I have taken the liberty to add all of the widgets available on 60E 6.2.2, which can be found in *Image 1.6* below; take a second to check these out. There are many cool features here.

Right away, you can get a quick snapshot of the system's health and know if there are any high-level concerns regarding your system. Right now, I can see my CPU and memory are at good levels. My total session count is 176, and I even know what percentage of sessions are being offloaded to this SoC3 chip, 42% total, and 2.8% nTurbo. I can see that the average outbound bandwidth usage is 92.49. We see this is a standalone FortiGate, not an HA pair. The Advanced Threat Protection Statics would be for FortiSandbox, but I do not currently have one running on my network. In summary, the widgets on the FortiOS dashboard are an awesome tool for troubleshooting and makes it very easy to discover problems with your device and network. Take a few moments to look at *Image 1.6*.

Next, notice on the left side menu navigation windowpane, which allows us easily navigate different areas within the FortiOS GUI. I have VDOMs enabled on my FortiGate here, and I have root selected, which is management VDOM (we talk more about this in the VDOM chapter). Under root, we see all the different configuration domains neatly organized in an expandable tree. Next, I provide an overview of this navigation menu. Let the tour begin!

Chapter 1 | Introduction to FortiGate

Left GUI Navigation Configuration Menu Overview

Welcome to the navigation menu, where we can easily browse leisurely to many features FortiOS offers. Let's go over this real quick so you can understand the lay of the land.

Image 1.6.0 - Left Windowpane dropdown Navigation Pan

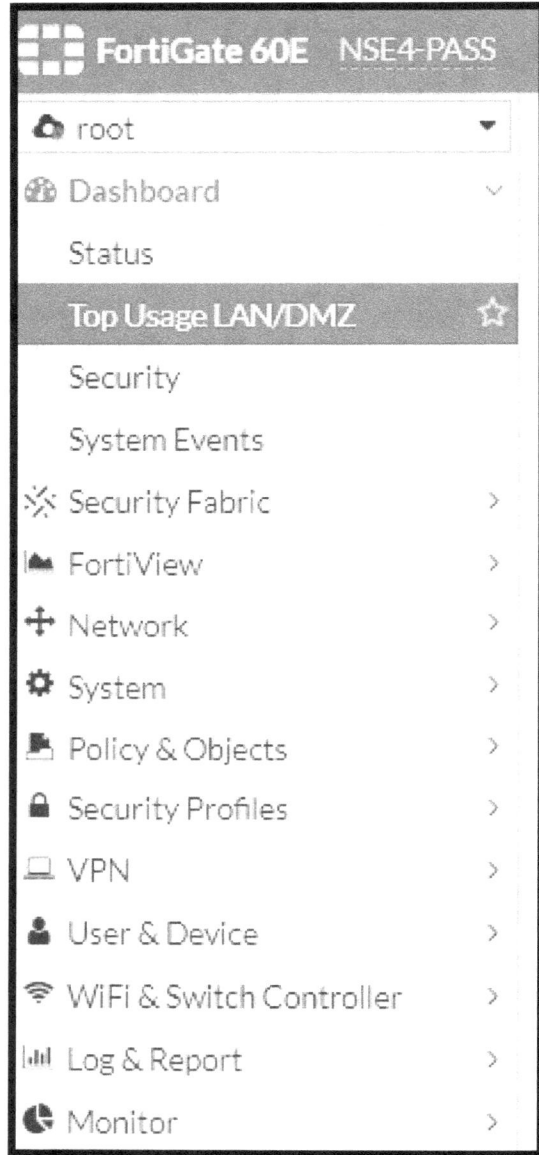

I will be referencing GUI configuration sections using the structure **'Top Menu > Sub Menu'**. For example, to reference the highlighted locate in *Image 1.7*, I would say 'Dashboard > Top Usage LAN/DMZ', which would take me to this Windowpane configuration section in the GUI.

Be sure to enable 'Features' in the GUI because some are hidden by default. I cannot tell you how many times this has bit me. Go to 'System > Feature Visibility' to change this.

Every related GUI configuration section is consolidated into a Top menu when selected, it will present sub-menus to choose from. This is how FortiOS tightly organizes all its features to be user-friendly. If you look at *Image 1.6.0*, and I say configure a *security profile* for a policy, where would you go first? Even if you never configured this before by looking at this menu, I'm pretty sure you would find the right place to begin to look.

Let us go ahead and move through all the top-level navigation drop-down menus here. I will give a brief overview of each one so you will have a general idea of where things are and how FortiGate is structured. Let us begin!

Chapter 1 | Introduction to FortiGate

Security Fabric Menu

This section provides a physical and logical visual of the Security Fabric this firewall is participating in. I love this feature because the more you add to the Security Fabric, the more this section will tell you about your network! You can see an

Image 1.6.1 – Security Fabric Topology

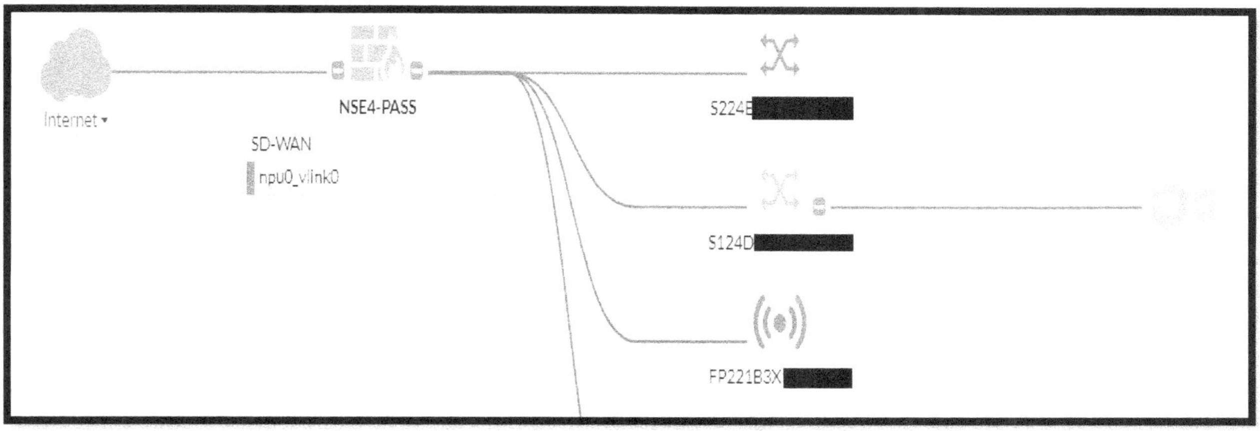

example view for the Physical Topology in *Image 1.6.1*. We can easily see our FortiGate is connected to an active FortiSwitch S124D and recognizes one inactive FortiAP and one inactive FortiSwitch. Hanging off the Active FortiSwitch S124D, we could drill down into our endpoint devices, note by the circle containing Windows icons, using this switch that FortiGate has detected or is apart of the Security Fabric. Talk about in-depth visibility!

FortiView Menu

Next is our FortiView section, which provides real-time network or security information in a friendly readable format. Yes, that is correct; the FortiGate GUI

Image 1.6.2 – FortiView Example

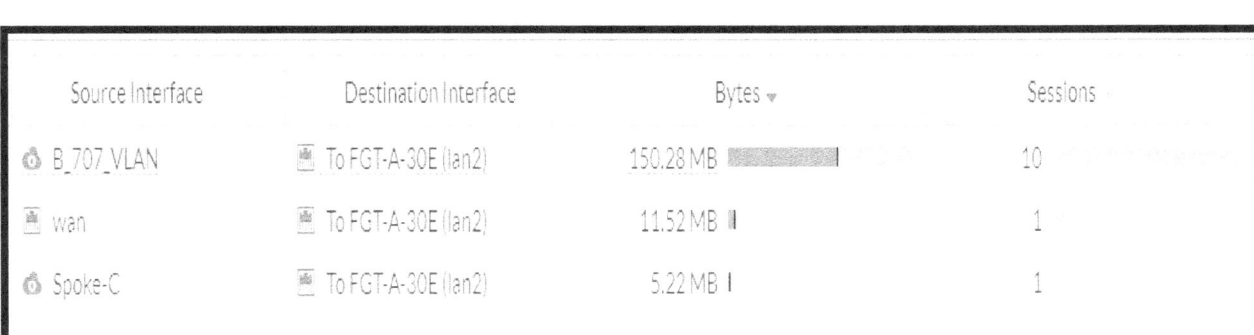

Chapter 1 | Introduction to FortiGate

can be used to view real-time sessions and security events. Pretty cool, right? *Image 1.6.2*

Image 1.6.2 provides an example of the source and destination interfaces and how many Bytes and Sessions are transversing these interfaces. This is a great place to check out when you are making your rounds through your network devices when checking for anomalies.

Image 1.6.3 – Network Configuration Menu

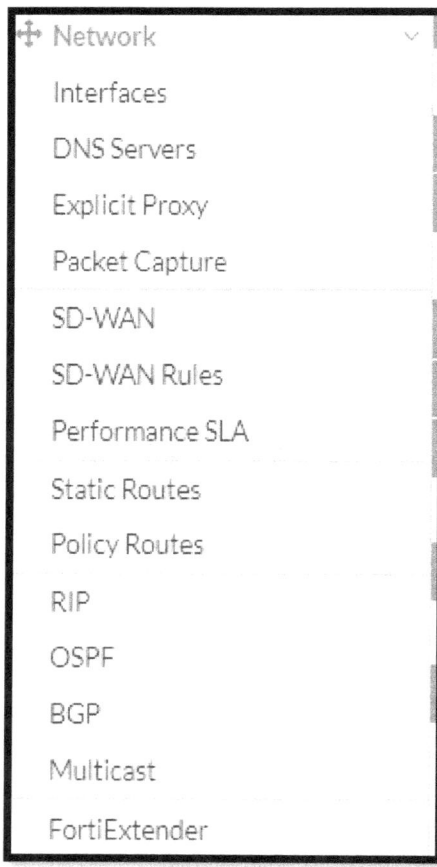

Network Menu

Next, the Network drop-down menu provides the configuration options for various routing features and network interface configuration options. We will work with the interface configuration section in this chapter for our basic setup. There is a lot of options here that we will be going over in our routing chapter! See *Image 1.6.3* for details.

System Menu

Next, is our System dropdown menu dropdown; this section provides the configuration options for various administrative functions for the local system. Some important things we have here are Administrator configuration, general system settings, FortiGuard settings, Replacement Messages, and Firmware. See *Image 1.6.4* for details.

Image 1.6.4 – System Config. Menu

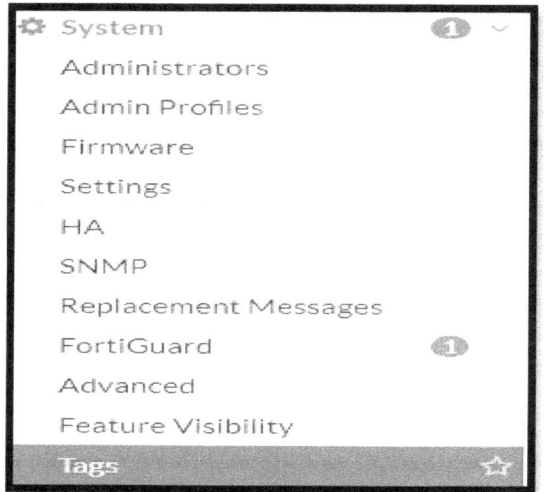

Chapter 1 | Introduction to FortiGate

Policy & Objects Menu

Next, we will cover the Policy and Objects dropdown menu. You will be working a lot in this section. This is where we define all our transit traffic rules and apply our security profiles. Essentially this is where all our security profiles come together, the Policy, which means what objects you need to build an IPv4 firewall policy (IP source, IP destination, ports, security profiles, etc..).We also build out Network Address Translation (NAT) objects here, as well as many more features we will be going over later on.

I say *Policy* here, but other vendors call this function an Access Control List (ACL). FortiGate does not use this term for its transit traffic rules but uses Policy instead. See *Image 1.6.5* for details.

Image 1.6.5 – Policy Configuration Menu

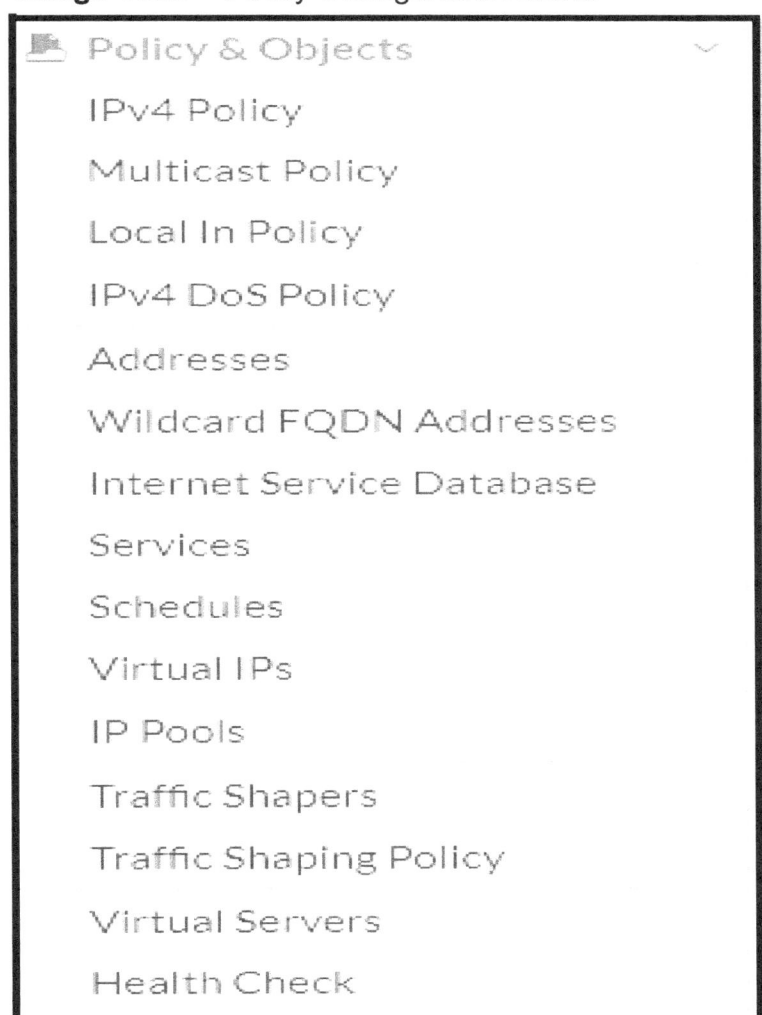

Chapter 1 | Introduction to FortiGate

Security Profiles

Next, we will take a look at our Security Profile dropdown menu. This is where all the magic happens. Within this configuration section, we find access to many of our security features that we can customize and build. Once built, we take these objects and reference them in our firewall policies! We go over most of these extensively in this book! See *Image 1.6.6* for details.

Image 1.6.6 – Security Profile Configuration Menu

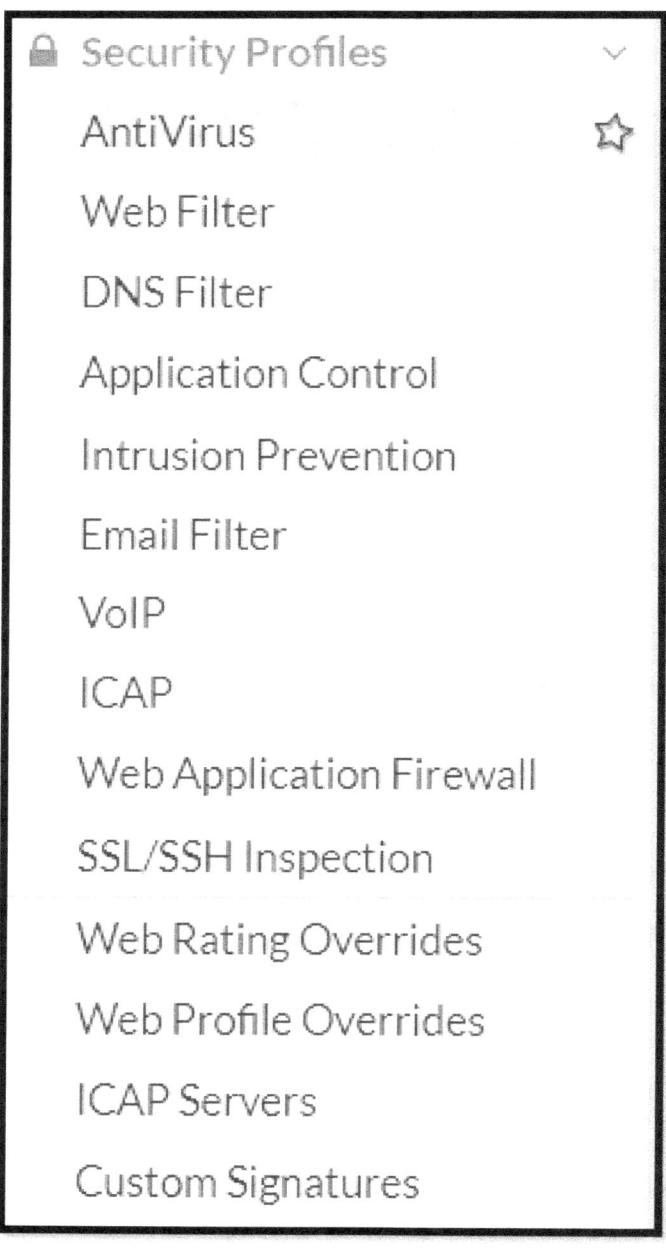

Chapter 1 | Introduction to FortiGate

VPN Menu

FortiGate has a vast amount of VPN settings. What makes the VPN technologies so powerful here is the SPU chips offloading ability. In this configuration section, there are options to configure the VPN features like SSL or IPsec. We also have other features like IPsec Wizard for quick IPsec VPN provisioning along with several templates. See *Image 1.6.7* for details.

Image 1.6.7 – VPN Configuration Menu

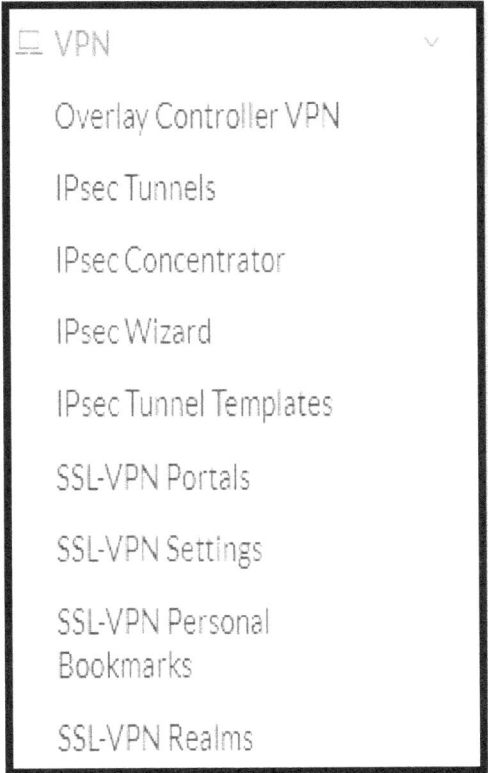

User & Devices Menu

In the User & Devices section, there are configuration options to create users and devices objects that would be referenced in firewall policies or authentication profiles. We also have options to make FortiGate an LDAP or Radius client that can be tied into things like VPN authentication. Lastly, there is our two-factor authentication, FortiToken. For details, see *Image 1.6.7*.

Image 1.6.7 – User & Device Configuration Menu

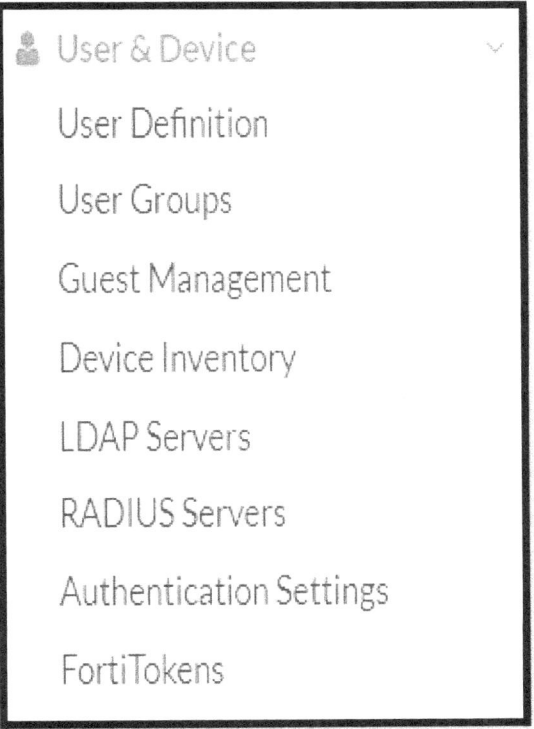

Chapter 1 | Introduction to FortiGate

WiFi & Switch Controller Menu

This section provides configuration options for CAPWAP for FortiAP management and FortiSwitch management. We build all the configuration profiles for SSID settings and security for managed access points. See *Image 1.6.8* for details.

Image 1.6.8 – Wifi & Switch Controller Menu

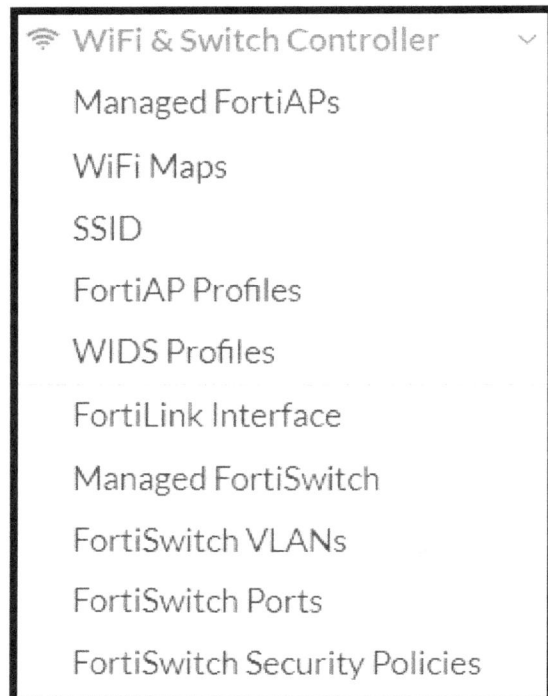

Log & Report Menu

Next is the Log & Report Section, In this section, you can view various logs and events. These logs can be pull from a FortiAnalyzer or FortiCloud, which means no need to store logs locally on your FortiGate! You can view your FortiCloud or FortiAnalyzer reports here as well, which

Image 1.6.9 – Log & Report Configuration Menu

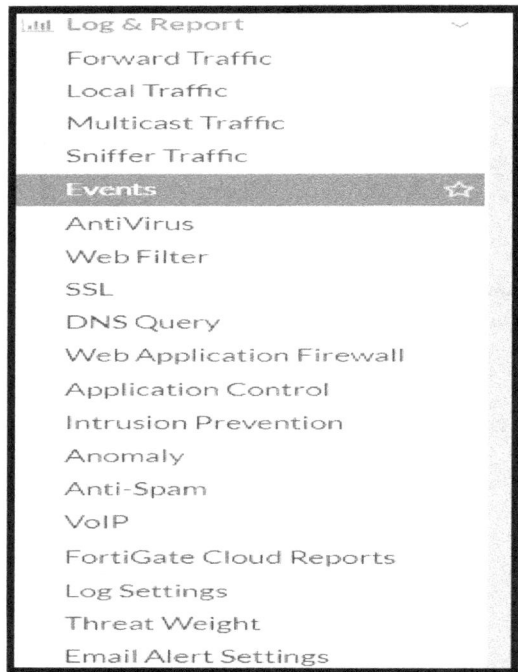

52 | P a g e

Chapter 1 | Introduction to FortiGate

is very convenient. We also can configure various log settings and alerting that we review in Chapter 7, the Logging chapter.

Monitor Menu

Lastly, we have our Monitor drop-down menu, and If you are troubleshooting or investigating an issue from the GUI, this is where you would start! This section provides real-time data for various firewall features like the routing monitor, which is the FortiGates routing table, and currently authenticated users. We could also look into our Security Fabric here as well; for example, if we had a compromised endpoint, we could take action! I recommend taking some time to look over these options in *Image 1.6.10*. We use these features throughout this book.

Image 1.6.10 – Monitor Menu

Chapter 1 | Introduction to FortiGate

Alright, folks, that concludes the tour of the FortiGate GUI! I hope it was helpful. There is much information in GUI navigation menus, and so please take some time and browse through these lists for yourself and just look around and explore the different options and write down your questions. We will be going over many of these configuration sections heavily in Part-I of this NSE4 study guide. If you're worried or confused about the amount of information here, don't be, this was just a quick introduction. I'm going to show you what you need to know to manage FortiGate firewalls and how to make them work effectively for you!

Intro to administrator access and permissions

Alright, so we got a handle on the FortiOS GUI navigation, next. Let's start looking at our admin accounts and how to set permissions on those accounts. When setting up a new FortiGate, take time, and think about how this user can take down the network? Or abuse his privilege. Should a junior analyst have the same permissions as a senior? Permissions are critical in operations. I've seen it many times where misconfigurations happen on a production network that results in downtime. Be sure to restrict permission on your FortiGate as needed!

In this section, I walk you through how to find your 'admin' account post login and change your password. Next, I go over the different types of Admin Profiles, which provide permissions to the admin users. Lastly, I'm going to go over how to set the password policy and how to change the management protocol port number!

We can do a lot in the GUI on a FortiGate, and you can become a good Fortinet engineer just using the GUI alone. However, if you want to become a great Fortinet engineer, you must master the CLI as well. This section goes over some basic configuration using the GUI, but note, there is a secret little command that will show the CLI output of your GUI configuration. Mostly everything you can do in the GUI, there is a CLI equivalent on FortiGate. So, I recommend you have a CLI session up while you are working in the GUI throughout this book. This way, you can get a feel for what is going on behind the scene on your FortiGate. Ok, so are you ready for the super-secret command? It is:

```
NSE4-PASS # diagnose debug cli 7
NSE4-PASS # diagnose debug enable
```

Okay, it might not be that big of a secret, but I still recommend having this debug running in the background while you work in the GUI to see all the CLI syntax!

Chapter 1 | Introduction to FortiGate

Configure Admin Password

After we initially login into a brand new FortiGate firewall, the first thing we need to do is configure a password on our 'admin' account and add a trust host configuration to it. In the GUI, let's do this by navigating to the '*System >Administrators*' tab. Next, expand down the 'System Administrator' with the '+' button. Next, right-click 'admin' user and select Edit. You should now see the below window:

Image 1.8 – Edit Administrator User

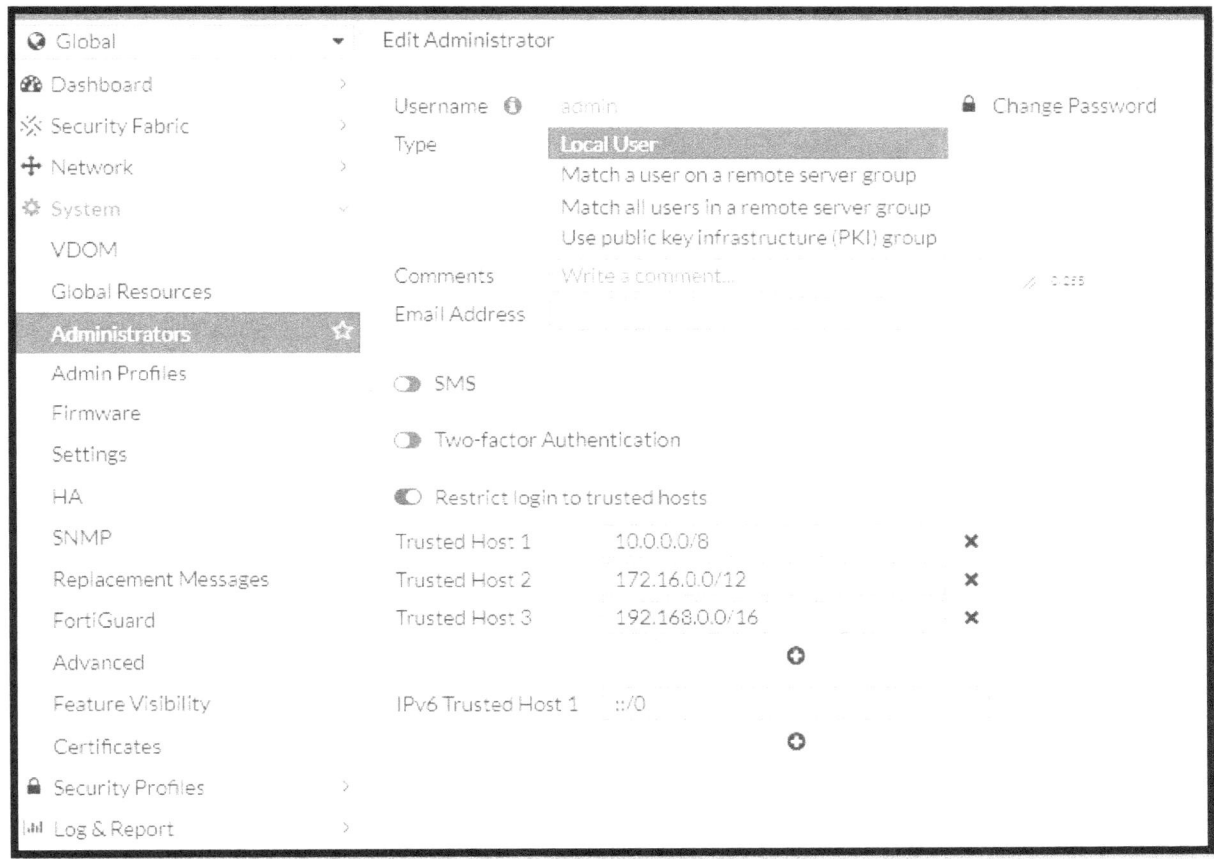

Let's go ahead and set a password for our built-in 'admin' account. Navigate to the 'Change Password' icon next to the username. Click it and set your password and hit OK. Once a password is configured, it is now time to lock down this account with Trust Host subnet ranges.

Trust Host Settings

Restricting login to trust hosts means you cannot login to an Admin account unless you are coming from a pre-defined IP subnet range or host. In our case, I will set up the RFC1918 address ranges as our trust host networks. This means anyone coming from a public IP address cannot access your admin account even if they have guessed the correct password and username. You may want to set single trust host IP here that is your bastion proxy used to manage your FortiGates to be even more secure. In short, configuring a trusted host on your admin accounts essentially prevents random login attempts to your device from across the Internet. It is highly recommended that you do this. You can see details on this configure in *Image 1.8* in the "Restrict Login to trust hosts" section.

> *Sometimes it is necessary to ping your public WAN interface from across the internet. The source IP's is random or unpredictable, then as a workaround you can create an 'PING' user, with no access at all, with no trusthost configured. This will allow ping to work.*

Admin Profiles

Next, let's go over the Admin Profiles. The default 'admin' account has the permission profile super_user. This account profile is built-in and cannot be deleted and provides the highest privileges on the FortiGate, which gives access to everything. At least one account should have the super_admin profile as it is required to add/remove administrator accounts. The second built-in Admin Profile that also cannot be deleted is the 'prof_admin' profile, which provides full access to certain VDOMs only and does not have access to global settings. Also, the permissions within prof_admin can be changed. Note that, the prof_admin profile does not have permissions to reset other admin passwords or change the account configuration of other admin accounts on the system.

We can configure new Admin Profiles as well on the local system by going to *'System->Admin Profiles' and select Create New.*

Chapter 1 | Introduction to FortiGate

Image 1.9 – Admin Access Permission Profile Example

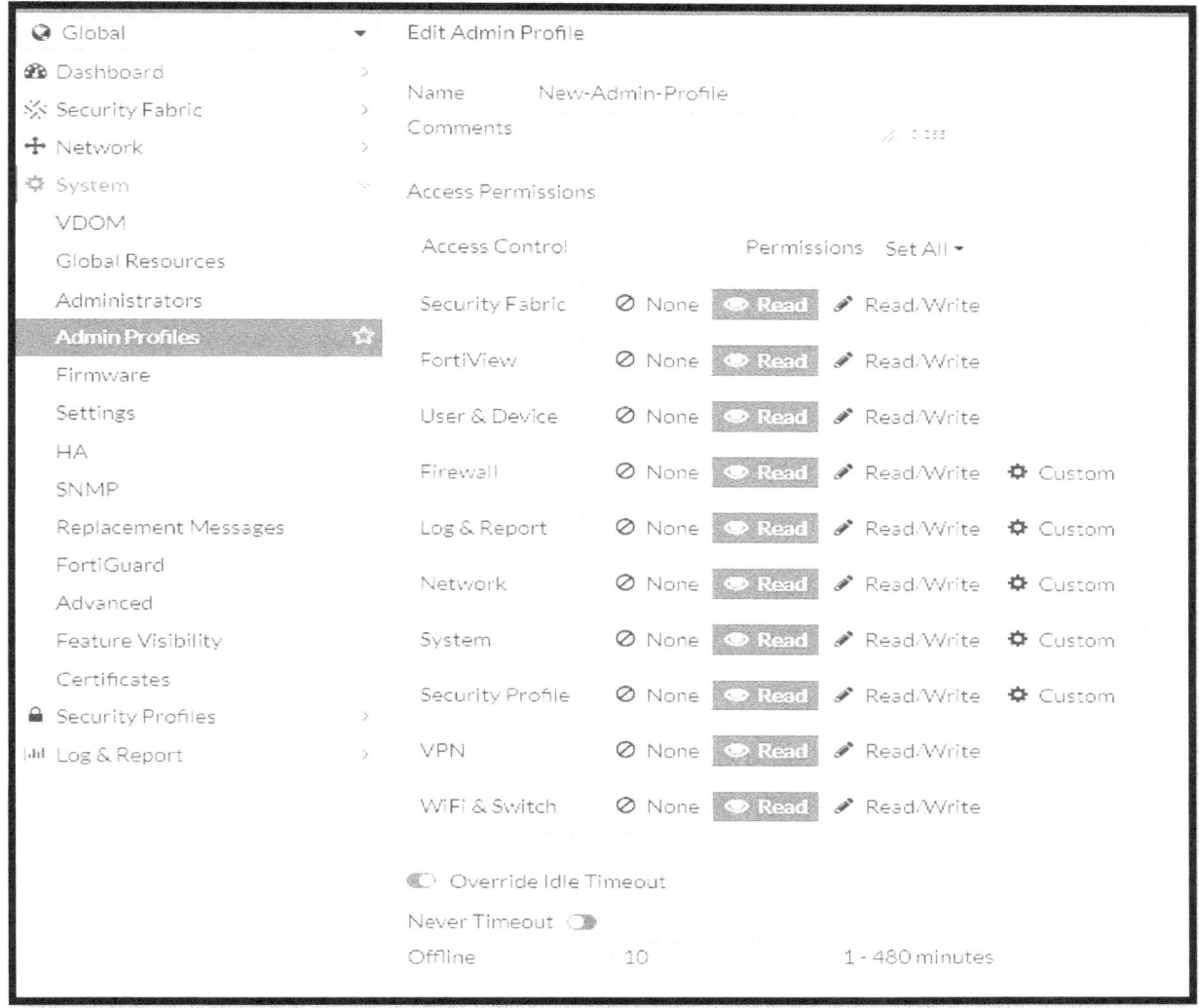

Here we can start customizing permission for our new custom Admin Profile. As seen in *Image 1.9*, we have a lot of granularity in 6.2 FortiOS in what we want to allow our admin users to access. For example, if we do not want certain admins to change firewall policies, then we would go to the Firewall Configuration options and select Read Only or None. This might be good for certain vendors that need limited access to your FortiGate.

Admin Override Idle Timeout

Another cool feature is the Override Idle Timeout shown at the bottom of Image 1.9, and if toggled on, this feature allows you to adjust the admin idle timeout value. This feature could be used within an NOC/SOC for extended GUI monitoring if you

Chapter 1 | Introduction to FortiGate

want only one user to never logout. This is a good feature if you need certain real-time monitoring visibility on a large screen that runs all the time.

Create Read-Only Administrator User

Moving on, once you have completed your new admin profile, 'New-Admin-Profile' for the root VDOM, we can now reference this object when creating a new admin account.

Navigate back to our admin windowpane via *System->Administrators* dropdown menu and select 'Create New'->Administrator icons.

> *You should be very restrictive who has accounts with the super_user permission profile. This account is equivalent to the root account on Linux devices.*

See Image 1.10, find the field Administrative Profile, and you can see where we have our newly create Admin Profile referenced here. We also need to set our password and what VDOM this Admin user has access to. Here we are going to set the root VDOM.

The 'New-Admin-Profile' Admin Profile we created is a custom profile and is more restrictive than our super_admin Admin Profile type, which has unrestricted access to global and VDOM level commands and settings.

As seen in *Image 1.10*, Read_Only_Admin admin only has read access to the 'root' VDOM. Since we have not covered VDOMs yet, here is a quick rundown. A VDOM stands for Virtual Domain and gives the ability to FortiOS to break away from just being one single firewall and into multiple virtual firewalls as needed, VDOMs are completely autonomous from other VDOMs and are dedicated virtual firewall with their own policies, objects, and routing scheme.

Chapter 1 | Introduction to FortiGate

Image 1.10 – New Administrator Account

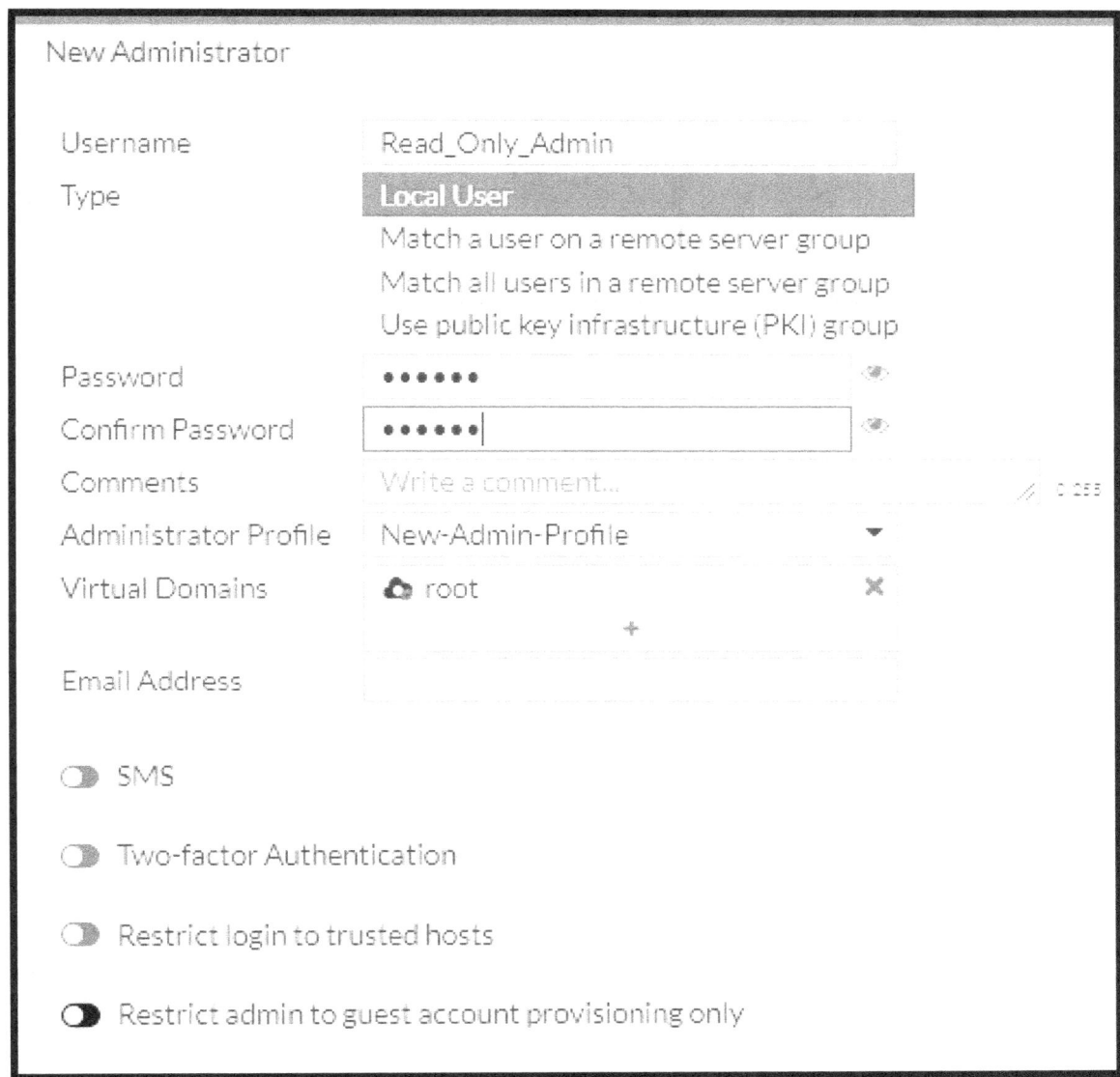

VDOMs are useful in Managed Security Service Providers (MSSPs) where a single FortiGate platform can serve multiple enterprise customers, and each customer has their own VDOM (virtual firewall). If you are familiar with Cisco ASA firewalls, then this concept is like their 'context' structure. If this doesn't make sense, don't fret, we will go over VDOMs in detail in chapter 5.

Chapter 1 | Introduction to FortiGate

Password Policy

The next topic we are going to cover is the password policy. FortiOS has password policy features to force users to set strong passwords and change them regularly. This feature is found via System->Settings->Password Policy section, *Image 1.11*. The

Image 1.11 – Password Policy FortiOS

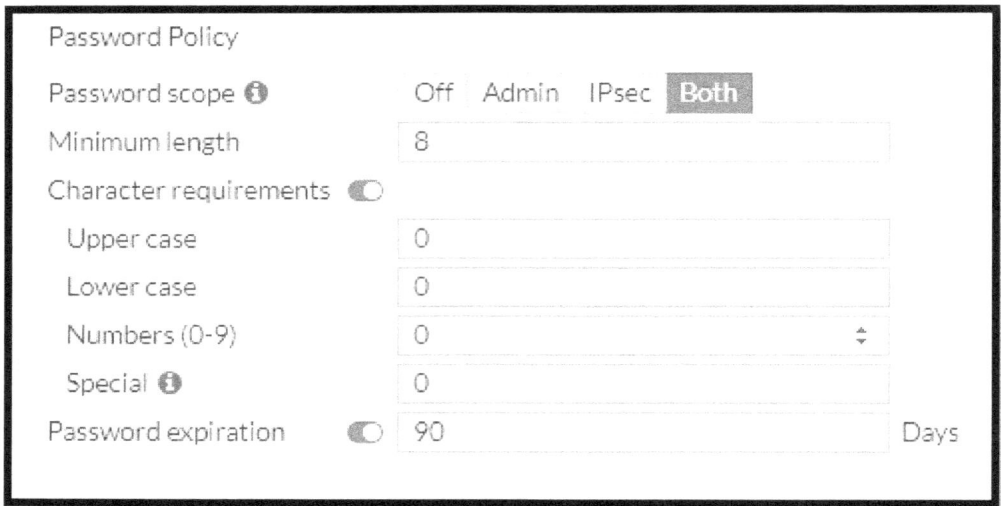

super_admin accounts have access to configure these password complexity requirements. For example, we could require our users to have a minimum password length and require them to use upper case, lower case, numbers, and special charters within their password. This section also gives the ability to set an expiration time that forces users to change their password, which is recommended. This policy can govern both Admin users and IPsec users.

The Password Policy is a good feature because users do not set a strong password by default most of the time. Along with strong passwords, we should also configure two-factor authentication.

Administrative Settings

The last topic I want to cover in this section is how we change the port for our management protocols. Meaning, by default, FortOS management access for HTTPS uses port 443, but we can change this to be something like 10443, and the same goes for any other management protocols. Our SSH management port we could change to 1022. We do this for many reasons; one being port 443 on the WAN interface conflicts with the SSLVPN; one of the listening ports must be changed here. Also, we apply security through obscurity by changing the default management port to something random to prevent malicious programs from brute-forcing our device. I know a simple port scan would show which port our

Chapter 1 | Introduction to FortiGate

management protocols are listening on, but this is one more step the attack must take. This feature is found via System->Settings->Administration Settings

Image 1.12 – Admin Access Settings

In

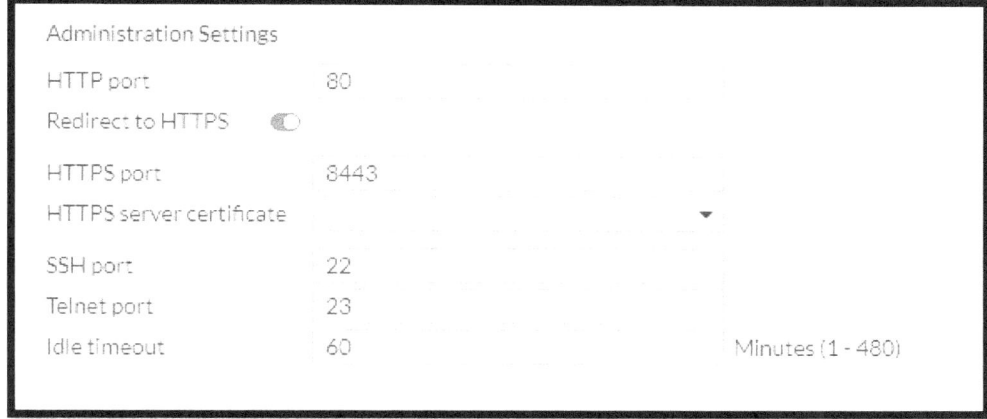

In summary, in this section, we explored how to find the Administrator configuration section in the GUI and change the admin password, create new admin accounts, and discuss the different types of Admin Profiles on FortiOS, which are super_user and prof_user. We also discussed the difference between these two types of accounts. We discussed the concept of VDOM on a high level, and lastly, I spoke a little about how to enforce good password practice on FortiOS using Password Policy. Lastly, we covered Administration access settings and how to adjust management ports, idle timeout, and concurrent sessions.

Within CLI you can list and disconnect admin users with:
 # get system info admin status
 # execute disconnect-admin-session <index_id>

Intro to the network interface

Ready to configure your first network connection with FortiGate? FortiOS is not only an amazing stateful UTM firewall, but it can also serve as a full-featured production router when in NAT mode. In this section, I'm going to introduce how to configure FortiOS to interact with the local network and go over the different management protocols we have to work with, and lastly, go over some basic static routing features.

Chapter 1 | Introduction to FortiGate

Network Interface Configuration

We can find our interfaces on the GUI via 'Network->Interfaces', and our interface settings in the CLI can be found under 'config system interface'. I will go over basic

Image 1.13 – Network Interface Windowpane

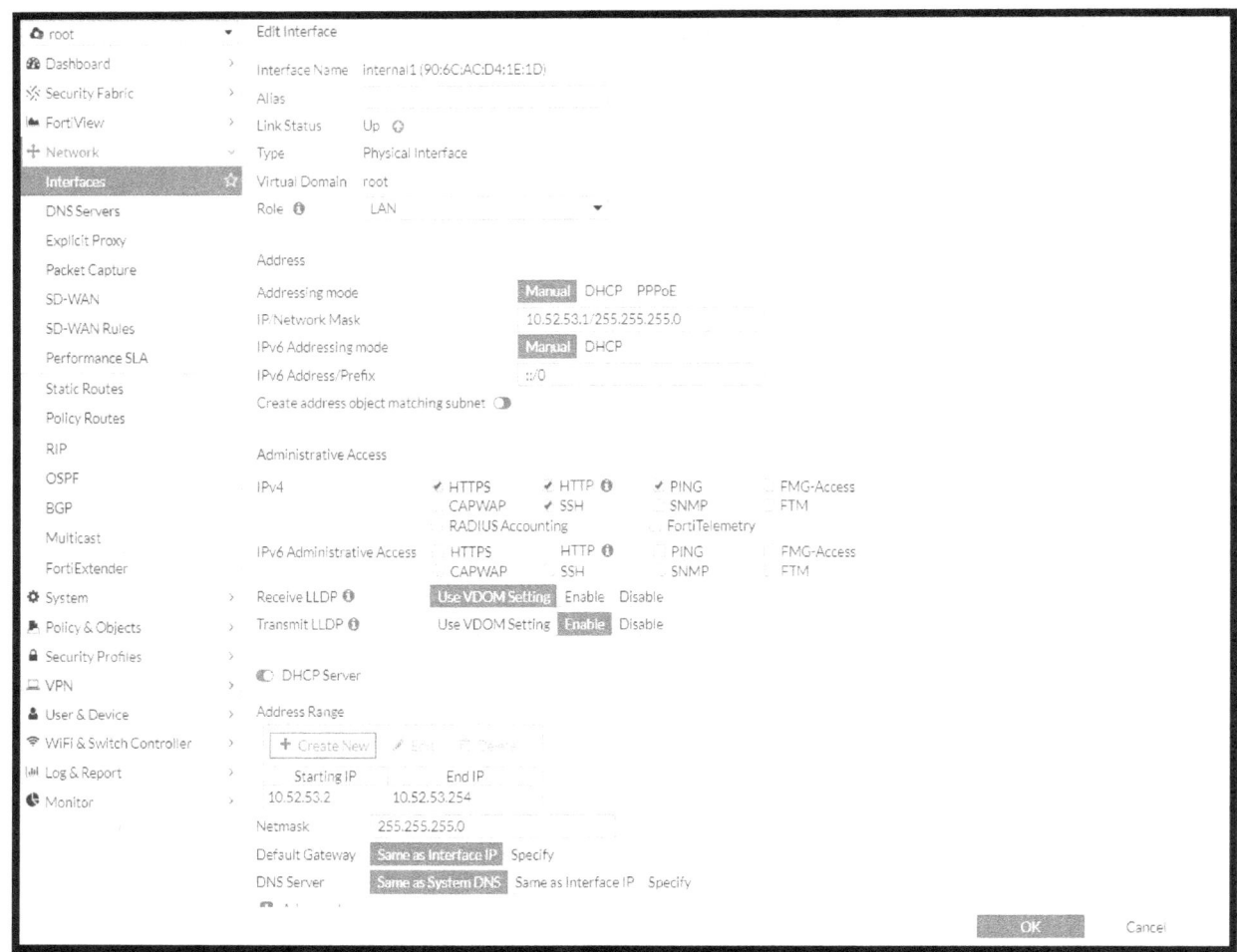

CLI navigation in the next section. We focus on the GUI interface IPv4 configuration for this section. Let's go ahead and select Interface 'Internal1' and select 'Edit.' The first thing we can see is the Interface name and the MAC address at the top; next is the Alias, which can be very useful by providing a detailed description of the interface. For example, INSIDE-LAN-FLOOR-3 here so we know exactly how this interface relates to the rest of the network.

Chapter 1 | Introduction to FortiGate

Moving on, we can see an array of options for interface Internl1. I have gone ahead and enabled the Administrative protocols on this interface, HTTPS, HTTP, PING, and

Image 1.13.1 – Administrative Access IPv4 Protocols

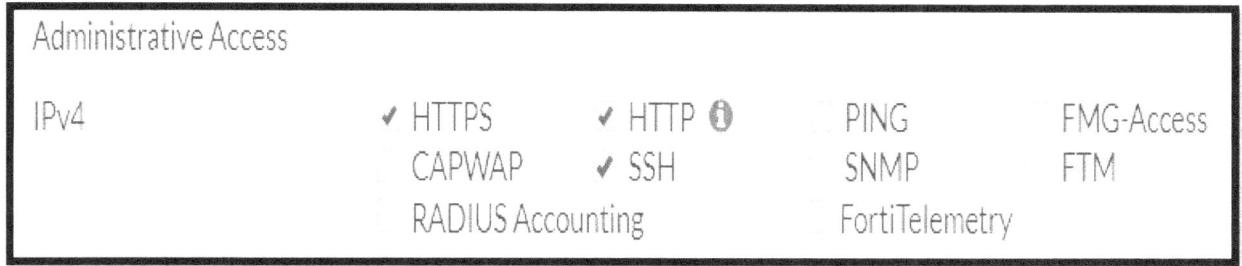

SSH. By default, telnet is disabled and is only available in the CLI. This section defines what protocols are allowed local-in access to FortiGate.

IPv4 Address Assignment

Let's go over the static IPv4 address assignment. I have configured the IP address of

Image 1.13.2 – IPv4 Static IP

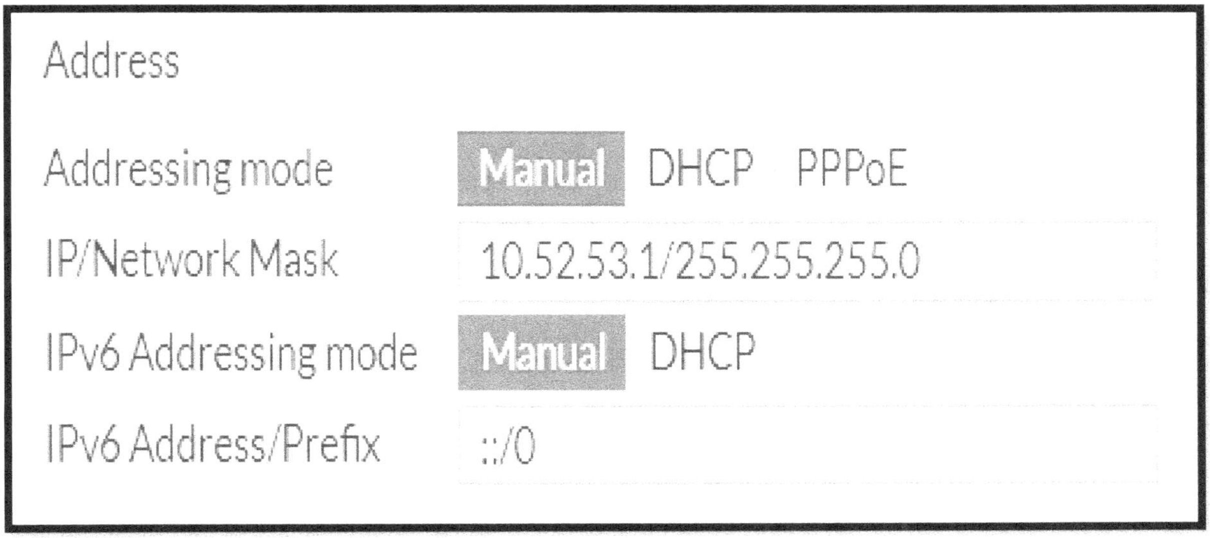

10.52.53.1/24 for interface Interal1. We can use this IP address for our management protocol access.

Chapter 1 | Introduction to FortiGate

We can now access Internal1 with one of our management protocols like HTTPS or SSH via 10.52.53.1, and we log in with the administrator account we created; this is considered local-in access, meaning network traffic is destined for the IP address assigned to the FortiGate itself. These access protocols are not global options; all device access protocols are enabled or disabled on an interface to interface basis. IPv4 and IPv6 management protocols are configured in separate sections. There are other protocols listed here not used for user management access but application protocol access that FortiGate can use for different purposes.

> *Device management protocols allowed on a interface does not enable global access for the protocol but is an interface to interface configuration option specific to only that interface.*

In NAT mode, all interfaces can be assigned an IP address and are required when an Interface is handling network traffic. FortiGate creates Local-out sessions with this IP address or could create source/destination NATs sessions using this IP address as well. A local-out session would be, for example, FortiGate reaching out to FortiGuard for updates itself. Transit traffic is traffic coming from another device communicating through the firewall, like a client Windows machine going to a web server on the internet.

The other choices we have aside from statically assigning an IP on our interface are to dynamically assign an IP via DHCP or PPPoE to the FortiGate interface.

Summary of Interface Access Protocols

Here is a quick overview of local-in protocol access we have on FortiGate, which are configured on a per-interface basis:

- Administration protocols
    - HTTP, HTTPS, PING, SSH, and TELNET
    - Protocols used by users to manage the FortiGate
- FMG-Access
    - This is for FortiManager access and is required if FortiGate is managed by FortiManager. The management protocol is called FGFM and uses TCP port 541. The local daemon process is called fgfmd.
- CAPWAP (Control and Provisioning of Wireless Access Points)
    - When this setting is enabled, port 5246 UDP is opened on the local interfaces and is used for the discovery of FortiAP's that FortiGate manages as a Wireless Controller.

Chapter 1 | Introduction to FortiGate

- SNMP (Simple Network Management Protocol)
    - With this setting enabled, FortiGate allows SNMP queries inbound to this interface. The default port and protocol for this service is UDP 161.
- FTM (FortiToken Mobile Push)
    - Used for two-factor authentication to communicate with the FortiToken Mobile push services server. The default port for this service is TCP 4433. Apple (APNS) and Google (GCM) provide the Push service for iPhone and Android, respectively.
- RADIUS Accounting
    - This access setting is needed if you create a Radius Signal sign-on (RSSO) agent on FortiGate or if Accounting information is required on the interfaces that face the RADIUS server. The default port for this service is UDP 1813.
- FortiTelemetry
    - This protocol is used between Different Fortinet products to create the Security Fabric. The default port and protocol for this service TCP port 8013.
- LLDP (Link Layer Discovery Protocol)
    - LLDP is a vendor-neutral layer two protocol and is mainly used by FortiGate in general device discovery, FortiClient Monitor, and simplifying the creation of the Security Fabric by FortiGate discovery.

Interface Role Feature

Next, notice the 'Role' features; here, we can select WAN, LAN, or DMZ. This is a mechanism to bring certain interface features into the GUI view of the interfaces

Image 1.14 – Interface Role Feature

related to those specific roles. If we select WAN, then we are given the option to provide estimated upstream bandwidth. These stats can be used in various places like MRTG (Multi Router Traffic Grapher) widgets on the dashboard and estimate WAN utilization. Here is the list of options that are removed when the interface is in the WAN role:

- Device Identification
- One-arm sniffer
- Dedicate to extension/FortiAP modes

Chapter 1 | Introduction to FortiGate

- DHCP server
- Security mode and Admission control

The Role of LAN provides the GUI interface page with focused settings for options like Admission control and captive portal. Please note that defining interface roles is not a requirement; the feature is only there to make it easier for administrators to configure important interface role-related options and prevent accidental misconfiguration.

Local-in firewall can be configured via CLI:
NSE4-PASS (root) # conf firewall local-in-policy
NSE4-PASS (local-in-policy) #

Interface DHCP Client Options

Furthermore, if this interface was required to be a DHCP client, then we could easily change our configuration by selecting the DHCP icon, and we would see options for DHCP parameters like retrieve a gateway IP, distance of gateway IP

Image 1.15 – Interface DHCP Addressing Option

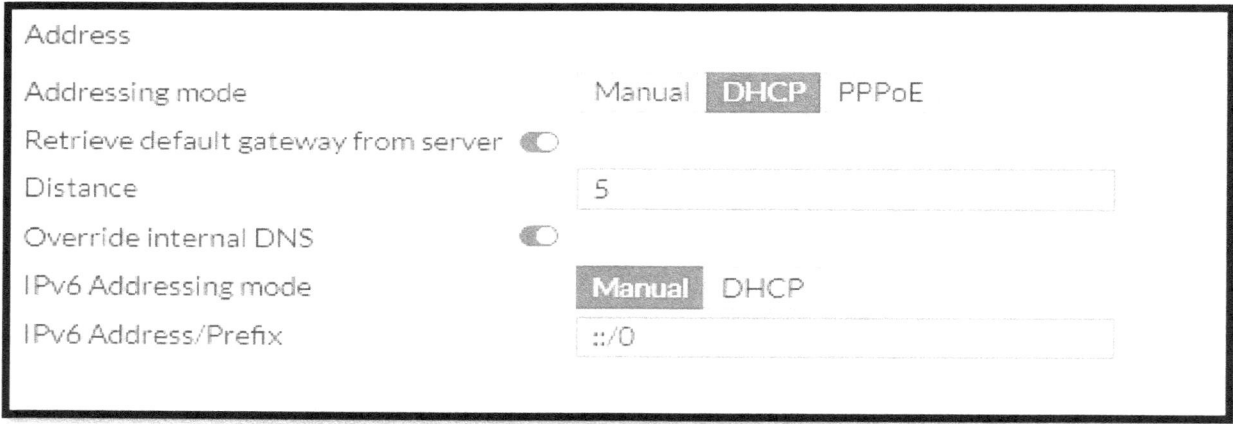

(Distance is the same as Administrative distance on CISCO IOS) and Override internal DNS.

Chapter 1 | Introduction to FortiGate

Image 1.16 – Interface PPPoE Address options

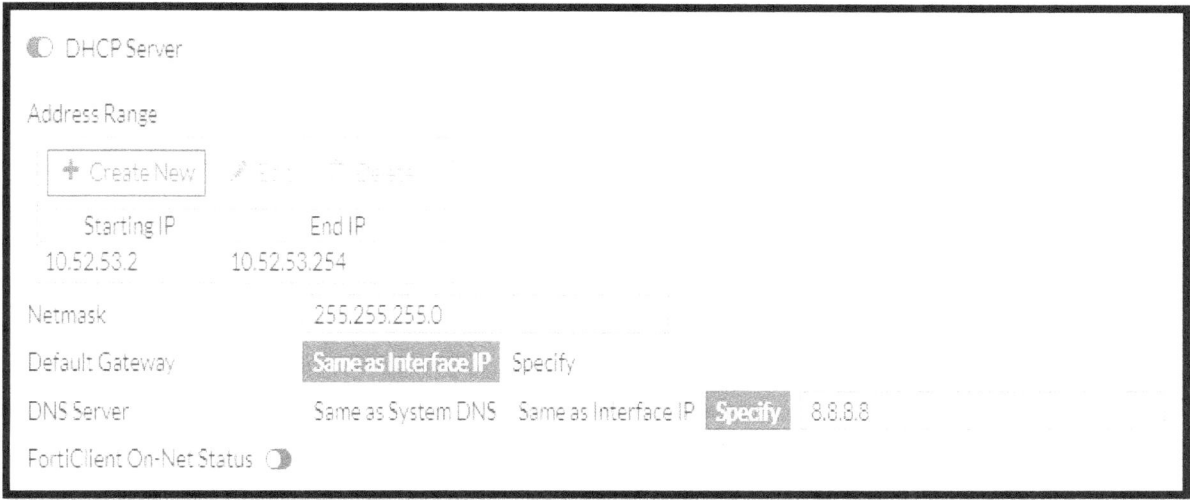

PPPoE Interface Addressing

Lastly, we have the option to use PPPoE to obtain a dynamic IP. PPPoE stands for Point-to-Point Protocol over Ethernet and is mainly used with DSL services. We have options like with DHCP to allow for a gateway IP, Distance, and DNS override. FortiGate supports many of RFC 2516 features like unnumbered IPs, initial discovery timeout, and PPPoE Active Discovery Terminate (PADT). PPPoE is configurable in GUI on desktop model FortGates like 30E, 50E, or 60E units, but for 1U rack space size, FortiGate models and up PPPoE must be configured in CLI.

DHCP Server Configuration

On every interface, there are options for a DHCP server; that's right; the essential protocol we need to dynamically serve IP information to clients looking to use the network is easily configurable at this same location. The DHCP server toggle is automatically enabled when you select LAN or Undefined role. The FortiGate interface GUI page populates the DHCP server values on its own using the IP and subnet values you configured for its interface, which makes it very easy and intuitive to deploy this service. In this example, *Image 1.17*, our IP Address Range values were auto-populated with 10.52.53.2-10.52.53.254, the first and last usable IP in the subnet. By default, the gateway IP is set to the IP configured on the physical interfaces, but we can specify a different one if needed. I have changed the default DNS IP from our internal DNS IP address to Google DNS server 8.8.8.8, so you can see how easy it is to change these values. The last option is for DNS, and we have configured the *Same as Interface IP*; this is used when FortiGate is configured to be a DNS server, which we touch on in a later chapter.

Chapter 1 | Introduction to FortiGate

DHCP Relay

Let's move into some of the DHCP advanced options. Firstly, let's talk about DHCP relay; this could be used when there is a centralized DHCP server that serves the

Image 1.18 – Interface DHCP Relay Option

entire organization and is not located on the local subnet where the DHCP client is located. To set this option, we toggled the Mode *Relay* and set the IP address of the DHCP server that FortiGate forwards all DHCP communication to coming from this interface, as seen in *Image 1.17*. Lastly, we have an option to specific here *Regular* or *IPsec* Type. IPsec type is used when an IPsec client is assigned an IP address by a centralized DHCP server instead of letting FortiGate assign these addresses. If this option is set, then when an IPsec client connects asking for an IP address via DHCP, then FortiGate proxies the DHCP communication between the centralized server and remote IPsec client. This section also provides some other DHCP options we could modify, like the NTP server, Time Zone, Next Bootstrap, and Server IP value. Lastly,

Chapter 1 | Introduction to FortiGate

we are able to customize even more here once we expand the Advanced+ options for DHCP, As seen in Image *1.19*.

Image 1.19 – DHCP Advanced Options

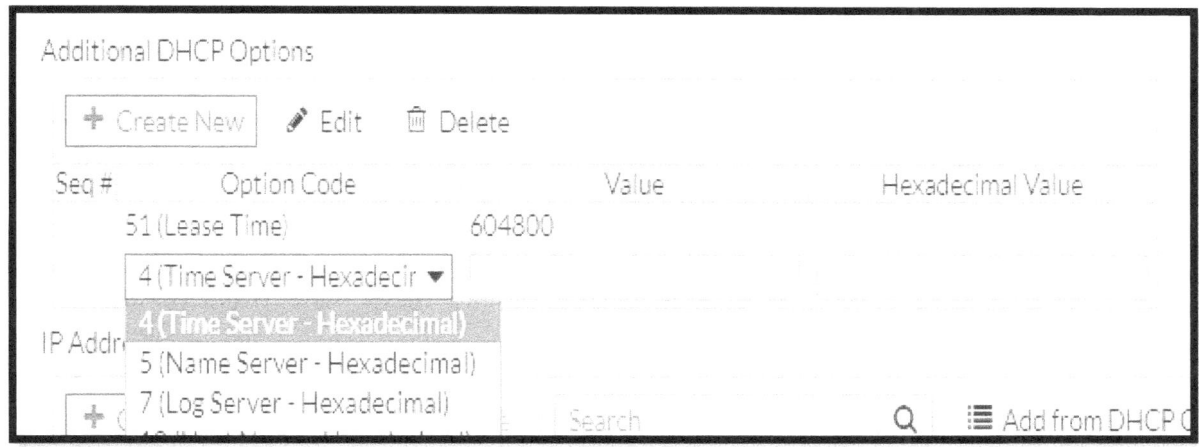

DHCP IP Address Assignment (Reservation)

The last DHCP server feature to go over is IP reservation or IP Address Assignment Rule. We use this feature when certain clients need to have a specific IP address.

Image 1.20 – DHCP MAC Reservation

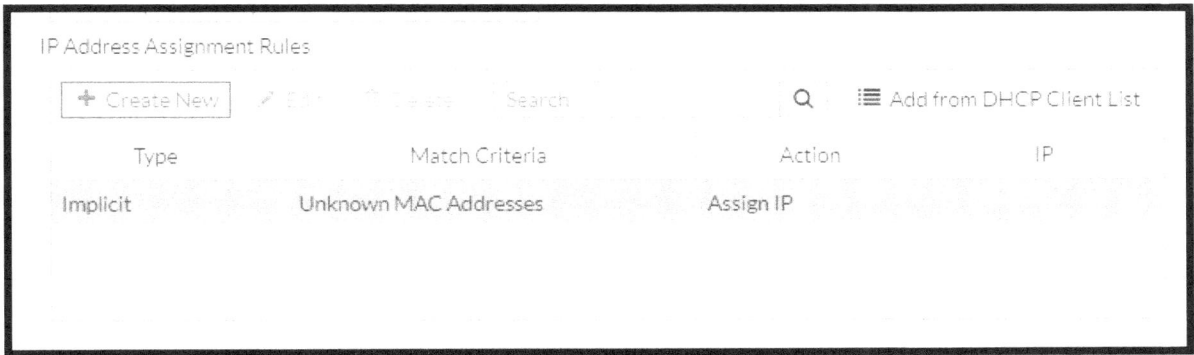

We can accomplish this by obtaining the client's MAC address and creating an IP Address Assignment Rule where we toggle the Reserve IP icon and enter the desired IP address; we wish the client to be given via DHCP.

Chapter 1 | Introduction to FortiGate

In this example, as seen in *Image 1.21*, I made up a MAC address of 11:22:33:44:55:66 and told FortiGate if you see this MAC address asking for an IP address via DHCP, then assign it 10.52.53.100. FortiGate does not assign this IP to any other client. Once you select OK, then a new entry is added to the IP Address Assignment Rules table, *Image 1.20*. We have several options regarding DHCP IP

Image 1.21 – MAC IP Assignment Rule

Assignment rules; we can also deny host based on MAC address or send a certain IP host to a DHCP relay server instead of local DHCP on the interface. Lastly, we can reserve IP by navigating to the *Add from DHCP Client List* menu, where we can select clients that currently have DHCP lease and map them to an IP address; and this feature makes it easy to obtain MAC address for the clients on your local network.

Static Routing

Alright, it's time to jump into some FortiGate IPv4 routing. To configure static routing in FortiGate GUI, navigate to Network->Static Routes. This is where we go to configure our default route. Most likely, this is going to be our Internet-facing port where FortiGate will go to obtain FortiGuard updates.

Look at Image 1.22; the first option we see is the 'Dynamic Gateway' toggle; if this option is enabled, then FortiGate declares its gateway IP for the default route will be received dynamically via DHCP or PPPoE on this interface. This setting can be used in SD-WAN when multiple interfaces receive a dynamic address that FortiGate needs to load-balance across.

Chapter 1 | *Introduction to FortiGate*

Image 1.22 –Configure Static Route

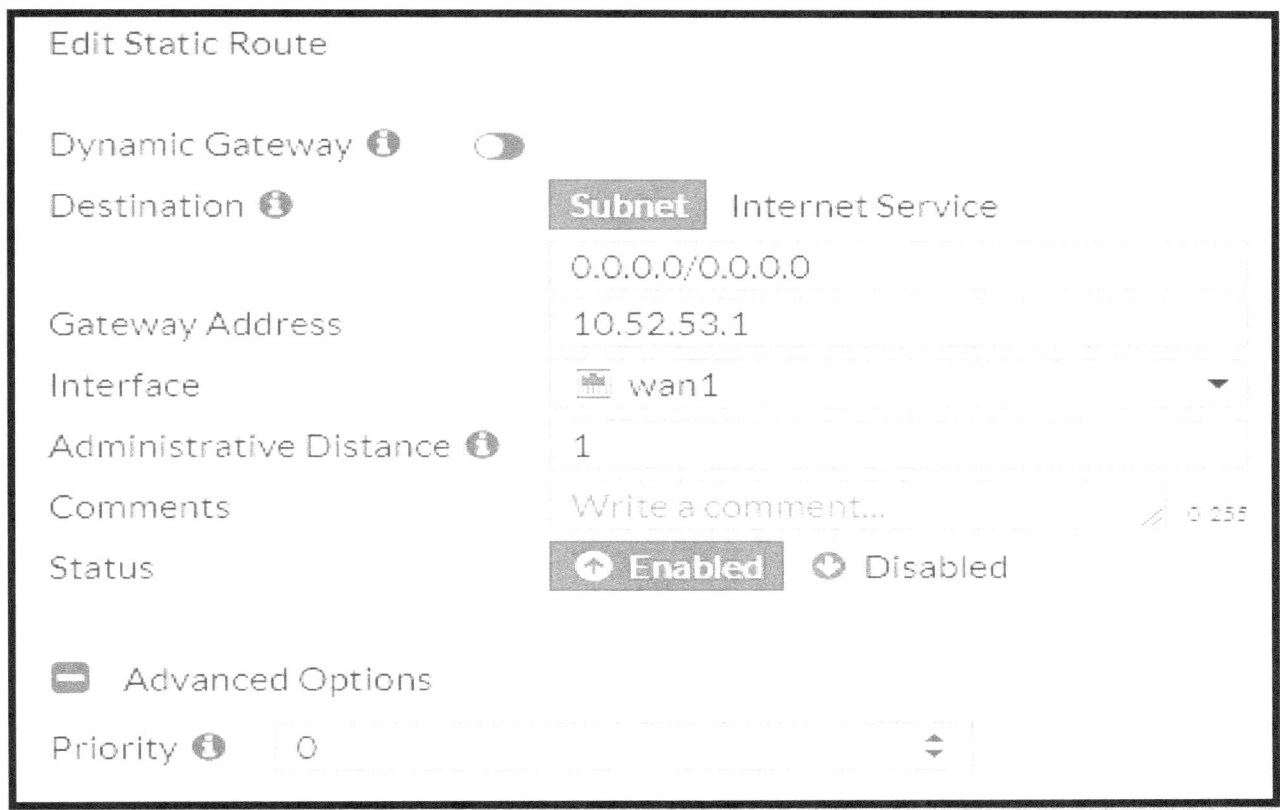

Next, we see our Destination IP configuration, we can manually configure our destination subnet, but we also can route Internet Services (IS) here. Internally, FortiGate Holds an Internet Service Database (ISDB) that is updated by FortiGuard, which is a pairing of destination IP addresses and port numbers that are mapped to well-known applications and services (DNS, Skype, Facebook..etc.). We talk more about ISDB in our routing chapter, but keeping it simple, and we will just configure all zeros for a default route.

Next, we must manually configure our next-hop gateway IP and bind this to an egress interface that holds the subnet of the next-hop IP, meaning 10.52.53.1 is within the directly connected subnet of wan1, which is 10.52.53.0/24.

> *If you do not see a static route in routing table, and interface is up, check and make sure next hop IP is within subnet of egress interface*

Moving on, next we look at Administrative Distance (also just called Distance in FortiOS). Distance is significant in IP routing when there are multiple routes to the same destination subnets. The preferred route is the one with the lowest Distance value. This local attribute allows for multiple backup routes to be placed in standby, and these are also called floating static routes; if the preferred route is removed from the routing-table, either upon link failure or routing update, FortiGate will then install a floating backup route into routing-table and continue to route traffic.

Next, we have the option of explicitly disabling a route if we do not wish to delete it from the config. This could be used for testing.

Lastly, under Advanced Options, we have Priority. Priority is a local attribute used when there are multiple static routes with an even Distance value, but one static route needs to be preferred over the other. This is necessary in some cases to overcome the Reverse Path Forward (RPF) checks or anti-spoofing feature on FortiGate that drops packets that ingress an interface where the route back or locally connected subnet for the source IP is indeed not that interfaces but another. FortiGate views this traffic as malicious by default. We dive deeper into this security mechanism in our routing chapter.

Intro to CLI and navigation

We have made it to the FortiGate Command Line Interface (CLI) section. The CLI can be intimidating for most people, and one reason for this is because every vendor is very different in how they implement their CLI solutions. FortiGate is no different, and its CLI structure is unique to itself.

I came from a Cisco background before I started working with FortiGate, and I was very confused about how FortiOS CLI was structured, but after working with FortiGate a while, I actually began to enjoy the FortiGate CLI much more than a Cisco CLI. Now I find it much more robust and intuitive. My advice here is to drop all expectations of a CLI before you go into this chapter so you can learn it from the ground up without judgment and have an open mind.

This chapter will give you a strong foundation on how to use FortiGate CLI and how it is structured, and by the end, you will feel much more confident when using it. I'll say again; you can become a good Fortinet engineer by just working in the GUI, but.. If you want to be a great one, then you must master the CLI. Let's get started by firstly showing you how to access the FortiGate CLI.

Connecting to the Command Line Interface (CLI)

With FortiGate, we have three ways to connect to the CLI:

- Serial Console Connection –

Chapter 1 | Introduction to FortiGate

- o console cable through your management computer using the provided RJ-45-to-DB-9 cable.
- o I highly recommend obtaining a USB to Serial Adapter (USB to DB9 Serial Cable). These can be found on many online retailers. This adapter makes it easy to obtain a console connection from a standard USB port.
- o Next, I recommend *Putty* for a serial terminal emulator application, and a couple of online searches should point you to a download for the application. There are many console or terminal emulator applications out there, so use what you are conformable with.
    - COM port settings required:

Table 1.1 – Console settings

Bits per second	9600
Data bits	8
Parity	None
Stop bits	1
Flow Control	None

- Network Management protocols
    - o You can use an SSH or Telnet client application to connect to FortiGate's network interface if the protocol is set to allow.
        - Putty is also a good basic SSH/Telnet client as well.
    - o We can use the FortiGates GUI Dashboard *CLI Console* Widget tool to gain CLI access as well.
        - This is good for quick configurations but not for troubleshooting and debugging.
- FortiExplorer
    - o This an application you can download that has the ability to interface with FortiGate via its local USB port.
    - o This tool can be found on the Fortinet website for download. www.fortinet.com

Chapter 1 | Introduction to FortiGate

FortiGate CLI Terminology

Let's start the tour of the CLI and get your feet wet! In this section, I go over FortiGate CLI terminology and some basic CLI commands, navigation, and structure. If you come from a Cisco background, as I did, then you are most likely going to be taken back by the FortiOS CLI structure. In general, a CLI is harder to use because it requires you to memorize various commands or command sets with specific syntax to accomplish your goals. The first thing you to notice with FortiGate CLI is that the configuration settings are structured into blocks of config, stanzas, and not one line like some other vendors. FortiGate stores configuration in a CMDB (Configuration Management Database) internally, which holds config settings in database tables, and we use the CLI interactive with these tables. If you are not familiar with database tables, then think of it as an excel spreadsheet with rows and columns

Image 1.23 – Command Structure

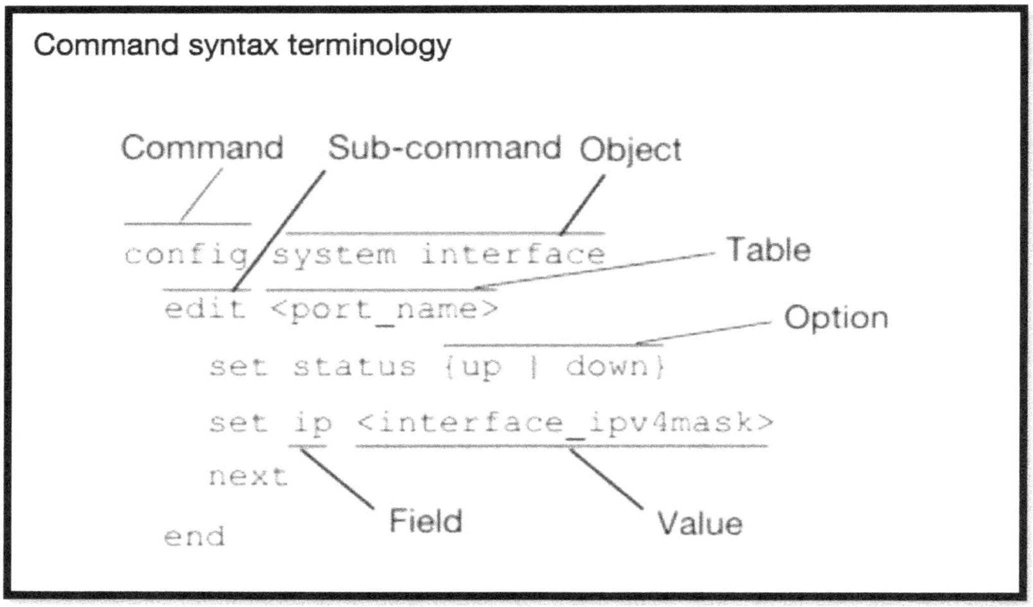

```
Command syntax terminology

        Command    Sub-command  Object
           /         /            /
        config / system interface        — Table
          edit <port_name>               — Option
          set status {up | down}
          set ip <interface_ipv4mask>
          next
                      Field          Value
          end
```

that hold values for FortiGate. FortiGate is an object-oriented operating system, meaning we must build CLI objects and then reference their function to interact with the underlying network. Here is the official Fortinet FortiOS command syntax terminology.

- Command (Top Level Command) — is the first word in a command line and steers an action that the FortiGate unit could perform. This can be config related, diagnostic related, or trigger a process like FortiGuard updates. We will go over top-level commands here soon.
- Sub-command — Each top-level command has sub-command(s) and forms a tree-like structure with branches that hold objects. After entering a top-level command, it then gives you options for its related sub-commands, which lets

Chapter 1 | *Introduction to FortiGate*

you steer toward what you are trying to accomplish. Most sub-commands have more even more sub-commands, but some don't; there is no requirement.
- Object — This is the last part of your completed CLI command. This part points to a table(s) and/or field(s). A valid command must be specific enough to indicate an individual CLI table pointed to by the Object.
- Table — An index of fields that are pair together with values. It could be viewed as a key pair in programming, but the field name contents are static and cannot be changed, but its related value is the variable that can be set. These values are referenced throughout FortiOS.
- Field — Fields are predefined static values within FortiOS that allow us to configure certain functions. For example, under our interface table, we have the field 'ip', here we assign a value of the IP address we want this interface to have. But we are unable to change this field.
- Value — This is the variable for the field within a table. This variable could hold things like numbers or letters. Many commands on FortiOS allow us to set multiple values, like the allowaccess field; we could set values like SSH, HTTP, or HTTPS. Certain fields require input to be a string or numeric values.
- Option — Has a pre-defined list of values or a fixed set of options for a field. User input is limited to the options presented

Sub-commands examples

As we get into some examples, I want to explain the CLI structure:

```
NSE4-PASS (root) #
```
Our FortiGate hostname here is NSE4-PASS, and we are in the root VDOM; the pound sign (#) indicates the beginning of our CLI. Next, let's talk about the importance of the Indentation within the configuration. This indicates a different context within CLI, and we are provided only CLI commands that relate to that specific context. For example:

```
NSE4-PASS (root) #config system interface
```

> *When typing a command or sub-command you can use the 'TAB' key to autocomplete it. TAB is your friend in the CLI.*

This is a fully qualified command with the top-level command being config and the sub-command being system and with an object that points to certain tables that hold config settings, interface. Once you submit this command to FortiGate via Return key, you descend into a CLI context that is focused on the different tables that hold interface configuration settings. The command prompt changes to indicate the name of the current scope. In the example below, the command prompt added

Chapter 1 | Introduction to FortiGate

(interface) to the command line. Also, within this context, FortiGate provides us a new specific command that allows us to interact with these tables. For example, if we issue the question mark "?" on the CLI, we see all the options we have available to us within this context:

```
NSE4-PASS (interface) #?
edit      Add/edit a table value.
delete    Delete a table value.
purge     Clear all table values.
get       Get dynamic and system information.
show      Show configuration.
end       End and save last config.
```

For example, the edit sub-command is only available after you issue a fully qualified command that descends you into a context that contains tables. Once in a table context, you receive access to new commands that interact with table entries. Next, if we wish to interact with internal1 table values, then we would issue edit <table>:

```
NSE4-PASS (interface) #edit internal1
NSE4-PASS (internal1) #?
config     Configure object.
set        Modify value.
unset      Set to the default value.
select     Select multi-option values.
unselect   Unselect multi-option values.
append     Append values to multi-option.
clear      Clear multi-option values.
get        Get dynamic and system information.
show       Show configuration.
next       Configure next table entry.
abort      End and discard last config.
end        End and save last config.
```

After we issue the questions mark "?" again, you can see as we descend into a specific table, we are giving certain CLI tools to interact with the table objects.

CLI *Show* Command

Let's discuss the show command so you can see what FortiGate was doing behind the scene when we were working in the GUI in the last chapter; remember internal1 interface?

```
NSE4-PASS (internal1) #show
config system interface
    edit "internal1"
```

Chapter 1 | Introduction to FortiGate

```
            set vdom "root"
            set ip 10.52.53.1 255.255.255.0
            set allowaccess ping https ssh http
            set type physical
            set snmp-index 29
        next
    end
```

When you issue the 'show' command at this level, this will not show all available settings but only the ones that have been changed from the defaults. If you wish to see all the available settings, you must issue the 'show full' command.

<u>Modify Table Values CLI</u>

To make changes to this table, and therefore interface internal1, we could use the follow sub-commands in this context set, unset, unselect, select and append. Let's go ahead and change the access protocols to this interface and only allow ssh access. To do this, will use the 'set' command with the field being 'allowaccess' and provide a value of 'ssh':

```
NSE4-PASS (internal1) # set allowaccess ssh
NSE4-PASS (internal1) # show
config system interface
    edit "internal1"
        set vdom "root"
        set ip 10.52.53.1 255.255.255.0
        set allowaccess ssh
        set type physical
        set lldp-reception enable
        set role wan
        set snmp-index 29
    next
end
```

The command has overwritten the prior values and replaced them with just 'ssh.' Note that the config setting change is not active until we commit them to a table. To do this, we simply issue the 'end' or 'next' command. The 'next' command descends you back one level into the interface table list where you could then 'edit' another interface. The 'end' command takes you all the way back to your original command prompt context here, but both will effectively make the setting change(s) active. If you wish to discard any change made while in the interface table context, you could issue the 'abort' command, this takes you back to the interface table list and keep prior config settings. Also worth mention here is the commands append, unset, purge, and get. The append command allows an admin to easily add value(s)

Chapter 1 | Introduction to FortiGate

to a field that allows multiple values while preserving the existing. In this case, we could add HTTP access without removing ssh:

```
NSE4-PASS (internal1) # append allowaccess http
NSE4-PASS (internal1) # show
config system interface
    edit "internal1"
        set vdom "root"
        set ip 10.52.53.1 255.255.255.0
        set allowaccess ssh http
        set type physical
        set lldp-reception enable
        set role wan
        set snmp-index 29
    next
end
```

Next, the unset command returns any field to its default value(s). Lastly, the get command pulls dynamic information from a table, which is sometimes useful for

Caution: purge cannot be undone. To restore purged tables, the configuration must be restored from a backup.

Caution: Do not purge system interface or system admin tables. purge does not provide default tables. This can result in being unable to connect or log in, requiring the FortiGate unit to be formatted and restored.

troubleshooting. The purge command will drop all tables within an object that contains tables. For example, this is useful when you desire to remove all firewall policies from a FortiGate VDOM.

<u>CLI Commands Edit, Delete, Move, Purge and Clone</u>

We have to work with a few more commands regarding tables are delete, move, and clone commands. We can find these commands available in our IPv4 transit policy tables; let's navigate to these firewall policies:

```
NSE4-PASS (interface) # edit internal1
NSE4-PASS (internal1) # end
NSE4-PASS (root) # config firewall policy
```

Chapter 1 | Introduction to FortiGate

```
NSE4-PASS (policy) #?
edit      Add/edit a table value.
delete    Delete a table value.
purge     Clear all table values.
move      Move an ordered table value.
clone     Clone a table entry.
get       Get dynamic and system information.
show      Show configuration.
end       End and save last config.
```
Our fully qualified command here is 'config firewall policy', with 'policy' being the object holding our IPv4 tables for transit traffic rules. We can create a new table for

> *A cool feature is 'edit 0', this will automatically create a new policy with the next available policy number.*

a firewall policy using the 'edit' command. We could specify a policy number, and if currently not in use, then FortiGate creates one; if in use, then FortiGate would go into policy configuration context, but once a number is selected, then we would descend into that table configuration either new or existing.

```
NSE4-PASS (root) # config firewall policy
NSE4-PASS (policy) # edit 101
new entry '101' added

NSE4-PASS (101) # show
config firewall policy
    edit 101
        set uuid 529c3d6a-235a-51ea-088a-def23999ee1f
    next
end
```

We used policy 101, and since we see 'new entry' after we enter this command, we can conclude the policy ID number is unused. Next, let configure a basic firewall policy to allow all traffic from interface internal1 to wan1, and let us be sure to perform a source NAT on our traffic as well since this is a public-facing port; we dig into all the policy details in our firewall policy chapter, for now, let's focus on the CLI commands:

```
NSE4-PASS (101) #show
config firewall policy
    edit 101
        set uuid 521552da-235c-51ea-0213-3cb7dfc5dd33
        set srcintf "internal1"
        set dstintf "wan1"
```

Chapter 1 | Introduction to FortiGate

```
            set srcaddr "all"
            set dstaddr "all"
            set action accept
            set schedule "always"
            set service "ALL"
            set nat enable
      next
end
NSE4-PASS (101) # next
```

After issuing the 'next' command, our settings are committed to the table in the object Policy and is an active configuration. Our command prompt is now at the Policy context level:

```
NSE4-PASS (policy) #
```

Now we are ready to go over those CLI commands mentioned previously, delete, move, and clone.

```
NSE4-PASS (policy) #delete 101
```

The delete command removes only the specified table referenced in the argument; here is 101. There is no warning here, so be careful when using this command. We could consider this to be a Resume' generating command! Also, when using this command, the requirement to delete a table, under any object that holds tables, is that it cannot be referenced somewhere else. If it is, then you will receive an error and must hunt down where this table is referenced. Fortigate makes this easy in the GUI, but there is also a CLI command we can use to find out if anything is referencing our table we want to delete. This command is:

```
NSE4-PASS (global) # diagnose sys cmdb refcnt show system.interface.name wan1
..
entry used by child table srcintf:name 'wan1' of table firewall.policy:policyid 101
..
```

If you wish to remove all firewall policy tables under the Policy context, then you would issue the purge command.

```
NSE4-PASS (policy) # purge
This operation will clear all table!
Do you want to continue? (y/n) n
```

And lucky for us, this command does give us a warning and a choice to confirm or abort the command with the 'y/n' option. I'm going to say no 'n'.

Another command that could be useful to us here is the 'clone' command. This command will let us duplicate a table and, in this case, an IPv4 firewall policy. This could be useful if we just need to change one or two settings for a new policy, instead of creating an entire policy from scratch; this is just a time saver.

```
NSE4-PASS (policy) # clone 102 to 101
NSE4-PASS (policy) # edit 102
NSE4-PASS (102) # show
config firewall policy
    edit 102
        set uuid a344cf06-2360-51ea-b11e-ca0673281bea
        set srcintf "internal1"
        set dstintf "wan1"
        set srcaddr "all"
        set dstaddr "all"
        set action accept
        set schedule "always"
        set service "ALL"
        set nat enable
    next
end
```
now we have a duplicate policy to allow us to create more specific firewall rules.

Lastly, here, let's talk about the 'move' command. We need this command because the order of the policy table matters. Like other vendor firewalls, access control entries (ACE) or access control list (ACL) are read from the top down when trying to match a rule or, in our case, a policy; there are some exceptions that we cover in the NAT chapter. When FortiGate receives new IPv4 transit communication, not local-in, it performs a policy lookup referencing the Policy object table list that holds our IPv4 transit policies, and it starts its evaluation from the top down in sequence.

The policy ID 101 does not matter, and it is just a label for the table; it is the order that matters. And finally, this is why the 'move' command is important. In the IPv4 firewall policy GUI page, you see sequence numbers, and then you see policy IDs. This is a little confusing. We discuss more in the firewall policy chapter. But for now, let's learn how to use the 'move' command.

<u>CLI Firewall Policy Move Example</u>

For example, say we wanted policy 102 to allow all traffic coming from internal1 to wan1 but limit the services allowed to be only HTTP, HTTPS, and DNS, and then we want to use policy 101 to block any other type of traffic. We would modify services in Policy ID 102:

```
NSE4-PASS (policy) # edit 102
NSE4-PASS (102) # set service HTTP HTTPS DNS
NSE4-PASS (102) # show
```

Chapter 1 | Introduction to FortiGate

```
config firewall policy
    edit 102
        set uuid a344cf06-2360-51ea-b11e-ca0673281bea
        set srcintf "internal1"
        set dstintf "wan1"
        set srcaddr "all"
        set dstaddr "all"
        set action accept
        set schedule "always"
        set service "HTTP" "HTTPS" "DNS"
        set nat enable
    next
end
NSE4-PASS (102) # next
```

Next, we need to deny all traffic coming from internal1 going to wan1

```
NSE4-PASS (policy) # edit 101
NSE4-PASS (101) # set action deny
NSE4-PASS (101) # next
NSE4-PASS (policy) #show
    edit 101
        set uuid 7f42be76-235e-51ea-7f7a-894f6d83472e
        set srcintf "internal1"
        set dstintf "wan1"
        set srcaddr "all"
        set dstaddr "all"
        set schedule "always"
        set service "ALL"
        set logtraffic disable
    next
    edit 102
        set uuid a344cf06-2360-51ea-b11e-ca0673281bea
        set srcintf "internal1"
        set dstintf "wan1"
        set srcaddr "all"
        set dstaddr "all"
        set action accept
        set schedule "always"
        set service "HTTP" "HTTPS" "DNS"
        set nat enable
    next
end
```

Note that we do not see 'set action deny' within policy 101 when we issue the show command. This is because **deny** is the default value of the *action* field and

Chapter 1 | Introduction to FortiGate

remember the show command will only show us non-default values. If you wish to see all values in a table, use show full or get. Alright, now we have our policies created, but they are indeed in the wrong order because once FortiOS starts evaluating traffic from *internal1* to *wan1*, policy 101 will be matched first, and all traffic will be dropped; this is not what we want. So let us change the firewall policy order with our move command:

```
NSE4-PASS (policy) # move 102 before 101
NSE4-PASS (policy) # show
    edit 102
        set uuid a344cf06-2360-51ea-b11e-ca0673281bea
        set srcintf "internal1"
        set dstintf "wan1"
        set srcaddr "all"
        set dstaddr "all"
        set action accept
        set schedule "always"
        set service "HTTP" "HTTPS" "DNS"
        set nat enable
    next
    edit 101
        set uuid 7f42be76-235e-51ea-7f7a-894f6d83472e
        set srcintf "internal1"
        set dstintf "wan1"
        set srcaddr "all"
        set dstaddr "all"
        set schedule "always"
        set service "ALL"
        set logtraffic disable
    next
end
```

Now the logic flow reads, all traffic coming from *internal1* going to *wan1* for HTTP, HTTPS, or DNS services then allow, else deny. Note that FortiGate has an implicit deny rule. Meaning, if no policy is configured to allow traffic explicitly then, FortiGate drops all traffic. In this example, I wanted to show you an explicit deny policy used wit the 'move' command.

CLI Tips and Tricks

There are a couple of useful commands that make navigating the CLI a little easier. The first one is grep. Grep is an awesome command, and it has been around for a long time. This command allows us to parse through the output on the CLI and present only what we are looking for. For example, we can find certain values within our firewall policies. Let's look for policies that allow HTTP

Chapter 1 | Introduction to FortiGate

```
NSE4-PASS (policy) # show | grep HTTP
        set service "HTTP" "HTTPS" "DNS"
```
Well, this doesn't help us much because there is no context. Let us feed grep the '-f' argument and gather some more useful output.

```
NSE4-PASS (policy) # show | grep HTTP -f
    edit 102
        set uuid a344cf06-2360-51ea-b11e-ca0673281bea
        set srcintf "internal1"
        set dstintf "wan1"
        set srcaddr "all"
        set dstaddr "all"
        set action accept
        set schedule "always"
        set service "HTTP" "HTTPS" "DNS"  <---
        set nat enable
    next
end
```
Now we have the context to which policies are allowing the HTTP services, and we can understand what is going on here in this policy. The '-f' in FortiOS displays the entire config stanza when a match is found.

Tablesize Command

The last thing I wanted to mention on this topic is the *tablesize* command. There are a software limit and hardware limit to how many objects can be created on FortiOS. There is a special command that displays how many objects that are allowed to be configured on your particular FortiOS firmware version. The CLI commands is:

```
NSE4-PASS # print tablesize
system.vdom: 0 0 10
system.datasource: 0 0 0
system.accprofile: 0 0 18
system.vdom-link: 0 0 0
system.switch-interface: 0 0 0
system.switch-interface:span-source-port: 0 0 0
system.switch-interface:member: 0 0 0
system.object-tagging: 0 256 256
..
firewall.address: 0 5000 5000
..
system.interface:ipv6:ip6-prefix-list: 32 0 0
..
```

Chapter 1 | Introduction to FortiGate

Here you see a list of tables that can contain objects. Take *firewall.address*, for example. This is the table that contains the Address Object values used on FortiOS. The three values after the table name (0 5000 5000) are the defined limits of the table, if any.

1. The 1st column value is the max entries per table Instance
2. The 2nd column value is the max entries per VDOM for all instances
3. The 3rd column value is the max entries allowed on a global level, for all VDOMs

The value of '0' here means no hard limit, meaning no software-defined limit and is only limited by hardware resources. These limits can change between Major Release Versions of FortiOS.

On a heavily utilized FortiGate, it would be wise to monitor how many objects you are using before the global limit is hit. For example, I've worked a case where a FortiGate blade, 5.2 FortiOS, hit the global limit for Address Objects, and the only way to increase this value was to upgrade to 5.4+ FortiOS, which the customer could not do.

General Administrative Task

In this section, we jump into some of our general maintenance and administrative requirements when working with FortiGate firewalls. We are going to touch on firmware management along with the software and hardware life cycle. Next, we will go over the FortiGate Configuration File and handling. We are going to review how to backup and restore these files on FortiGate. Lastly, we touch some on the password recovery method just in case you ever get locked out of your FortiGate.

This is a very important section because many Fortigate engineers don't know this and miss these foundational steps when they start their journey into Fortinet technologies. This is because it just not things you think about right away when you take over managing an operational FortiGate firewall. When you look at an active live firewall, you think of your security that is in place and the logs that are being generated. You do not think about the correct upgrade path and the structure of the FortiGate configuration file and the Lifecycle software/hardware. But no worries, we are going to take care of all these items in this section!

Firmware management

Fortinet is a very ambitious and competitive company when developing new features & methods to be used in cybersecurity and is considered a leader in most categories within the cybersecurity industry. Therefore, Fortinet has to constantly update FortiOS with new features and code fixes. I started working on FortiGate firewalls on 4.3 GA code base, and now we are up to 6.2, and 6.4 is coming soon. As you can

Chapter 1 | Introduction to FortiGate

see, FortiOS is always moving, changing, and adapting. That is why we need firmware management. You need to understand the Fortinet software life cycle and why it is important to stay up to date with the latest code. Note that firmware management is always a balance between stability and innovation.

Firmware Naming and Evolution

Let's go ahead and break down what the firmware numbers mean and let's use FortiOS **6**.2.3 GA as an example. The first number **6** is the Version number; the industry recognizes this as the beginning of a new code trunk in a software lifecycle. This allows Fortinet development teams to add new features, perform complicated bug fixes, and/or add new code frameworks. In software development, when many new code changes are added, this usually impacts the overall code stability, and what I mean by this is the likely hood of hitting a *bug* is higher. The term bug is lingo for a software defected or unexpected behavior in a software feature. So, in general, the latest software release or the "cutting edge" is considered the most unstable when compared to older firmware Versions, but this does not always hold true. Sometimes it just depends on the type of environment FortiOS is placed in. Therefore, it is very important to certify new firmware before placing it into production. You certify firmware by creating a lab environment that replicates the production in regard to features being used and traffic type and load.

The changes made between Versions (or code trunks) could be because of many reasons, but some common ones are new features to compete with other vendors or new methods are discovered that better handle certain security processing or network traffic. Also, the new Version could correct limitations in features, or new solutions are found for complex problems but require a full code redesign to be implemented. The Fortinet development team tries to limit major code changes until new firmware Versions are initiated to manage code stability. The next number is **.2,** which indicates a Major Release (MR) within a firmware Version within the software lifecycle. An MR has significant changes in code and behavior, and essentially, do not take it lightly when upgrading from 5.4.x GA to 5.6.x GA, for example, this is a major jump. The MR is reserved again for major changes, bug fixes, and new features. The difference between a new MR and Version is the significance of the changes regarding code stability.

Lastly, we get to the number .3 within 6.2.**3** GA, and this indicates the patch number. Once a new MR or Version of code is released into the 'wild' or publicly, for example, 6.2.0 GA, any problems Fortinet Quality issuance (QA) teams do not catch will be reported by customers to TAC (Technical Assistance Center) and will be evaluated by appropriate development teams. If a solution is found and the 'fix' is deemed acceptable to be added into the MR or Version, it was reported on, and it becomes part of a patch for that Version and MR. Patches are also reserved for vulnerability fixes as well. So as new vulnerabilities are discovered, Fortinet

Chapter 1 | Introduction to FortiGate

developers will add these fixes to patch releases as well with MR's. The 'GA' stands for *General Availability*, meaning publicly available. Once a stable build is found within, it becomes a GA version that Fortinet is obligated to support while it is within the supported code lifecycle. To recap, 6.2.3 GA, this means the 6th Version of FortiOS and 2nd Major Release (MR) within the Version, and 3rd patch within that MR that has been certified by Fortinet QA engineers to be GA, or publicly available, use.

Next, I'm going to show you where you go to download firmware for Fortinet products. We are going to go over the naming structure of the firmware image file. Then we are going to learn how to find what version of FortiOS your FortiGate is running and explain the build number in relation to GA code. Lastly, we will go over the upgrade and downgrade methods.

Where to Download Firmware

Fortinet allows you to download firmware for its products via the Fortinet One support portal located at https://support.fortinet.com. Note that a license is required to download firmware for your device. You should have created a user account at the very beginning of this book if not do so now. Once logged into Fortinet One, navigate to *Download > Firmware Image*.

Image 1.24 – *Support Portal Firmware Download*

Next, navigate to the drop-down menu under *Select Product* and Select your product. In our case, it will be FortiGate, which is the default selection. Next, click the Download tab on this page. This will bring you to an *Image File Path* that lists all the available Firmware versions for download. We want 6.2.3 GA, so we will select the v6.00 folder, then the 6.2 folders, and lastly, the 6.2.3 folder, which will present all 6.2.3 GA firmware available for download. You must select the firmware that matches the platform (50E, 60E ..etc.) or Virtual Machine (VM) type you are working with you else; you will receive an error.

Chapter 1 | Introduction to FortiGate

Firmware File Naming Scheme

We are working with a 60E FortiGate. Let's find this firmware. Here we are, the FortiGate 60E 6.2.3 GA firmware image:

Image 1.25 – Download Firmware Navigation

> *Within the firmware download directory you can also find the release notes for that code base and other useful reading regarding the release*

FGT_60E-v6-build1066-FORTINET.out

I'm sure your next question is, what is all this stuff in the file name? Well, let's go over it real quick. The reason for an explicit FGT_ in the file name is because there are other firewall types like FortiWifi platforms built-in wireless access points and virtual machines (VMs). FortiWifi model firmware is specified by FWF_ within the firmware name, and VMs are specified by FOS_ within the firmware name. Since we are not working with a VM or a platform with built-in wifi AP, then we need to choose FGT_ file type. For you note, a FortiWifi 60E firewall firmware image would look like:

FWF_60E-v6-build1066-FORTINET.out

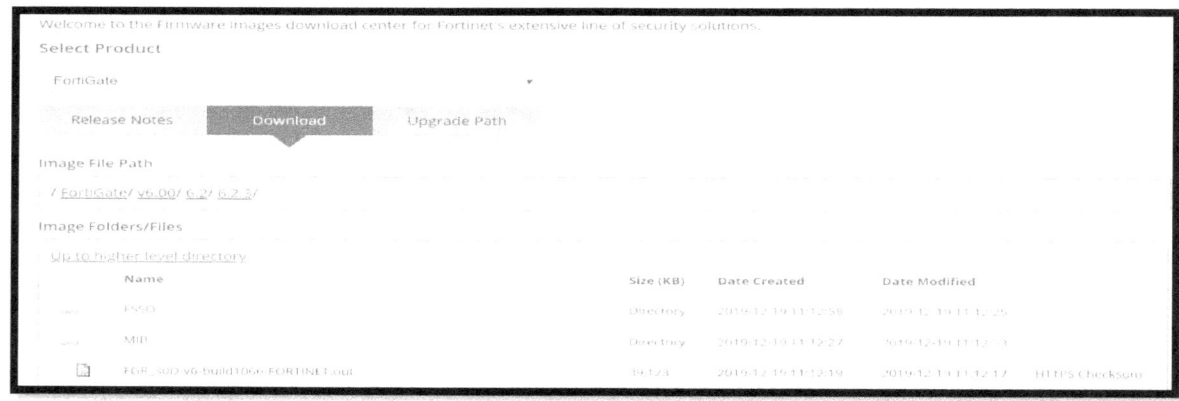

Next, let us look like the next part of the file name _60E-; this part, as I'm sure you guessed, indicates the platform model of the FortiGate. I will go over how to find your model firewall type here soon. Moving on, -v6- this indicates what Version the firmware is since we download 6.2.3 GA, then our Version is 6. Lastly, the -

Chapter 1 | Introduction to FortiGate

build1066- is most likely the most confusing part. We have firmware build 1066, and it has been considered by Fortinet to be the 6.2.3 GA release. Build numbers are created as developers work on code trunks resolving issues or adding features. To make more sense of this, let's take a look at 6.2.2 GA build number, which is 1010. This means Fortinet complied 56 FortiOS images between 6.2.2 GA release and 6.2.3 GA release. Each one of these images contained a new code that we call change orders that addresses problems within the code Version or MR. As change orders are added, new builds are compiled so QA engineers can perform different types of testing while maintaining code stability, and this cycle continues.

As time goes on, Fortinet's development teams determine when to release a new code patch to the public with the most current fixes. In this case, it was deemed build 1066 was most stable and suitable to be labeled a GA release. It is hard to correlate the build numbers to a GA releases, so I recommend when downloading firmware images and then create a folder structure with GA version names so to organize the build numbers within the structure or else it will get a little confusing when trying to find certain GA version if you place multiple build numbers within the same folder.

Lastly, you will see the -FORTINET.out part of the firmware image file naming scheme, this part the file is stamped with FORTINET so no one is confused where this masterpiece came from and the .out is a file formatted used in Unix based computing systems for executables and is an abbreviation form of "assembler output."

Alright were done with a file naming scheme (wiping sweaty eyebrows). I felt like that was a lengthy overview but necessary since we need to know what firmware .out file goes to what platform. Moving on!!

Upgrade and Download Firmware Management

Let's jump into the meat and potatoes of things, how to upgrade and downgrade FortiGate firmware. The actual function is straight forward. We can do this from the GUI or the CLI. But always, before you upgrade firmware at a minimum, review the release notes, which can be found here FortiGate Release Notes. Here you can find things like known issues, upgrade paths, and product integration.

Upgrade Path

Let's talk a little about the firmware upgrade path. This is very important when performing production FortiGates firmware upgrades. The path is defined as the multiple firmware jumps required to reach the desired code version. This path is certified by Fortinet development QA teams in the fact that FortiGate will retain the same functionality regarding its configuration. If this path is not following, then

Chapter 1 | Introduction to FortiGate

Fortinet TAC will not support any post-upgrade issues. To view supported upgrade path information:

- Go to https://support.fortinet.com .
- From the Download menu, select Firmware Images.
- Check that Selected Product is FortiGate.
- Click the Upgrade Path tab and select the following:
- >Current Product > Current FortiOS Version > Upgrade To FortiOS Version
- Click Go.

That being said, you are not restricted to follow upgrade paths; you can load any firmware at any time as long as the platform supports the code image, but if you do this, you might lose very important configuration settings and could lose access or even take down your network. When you are working in a controlled lab environment with a very simple configuration, you can skip firmware jumps; just don't expect your configuration to be maintained perfectly. If you see odd behavior after firmware upgrade and you didn't follow the upgrade path, perform a config backup and then a factory reset and restore the backup configuration file to recover. IF you still have a problem, perform a clean install by formatting and TFTP the firmware image to your device; we go over this later in this section.

Firmware Upgrade GUI

Image 1.27 – Finding Firmware on filesystem

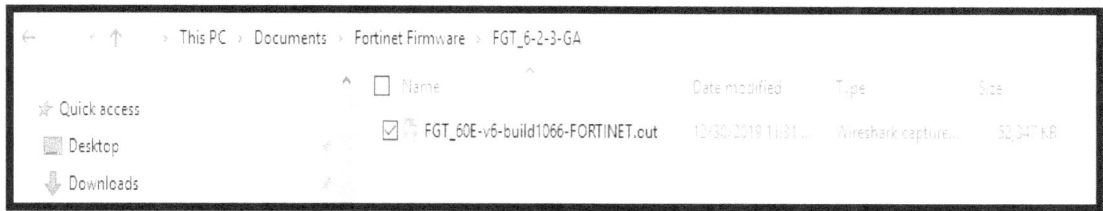

So, let's get started in the GUI to go System>Firmware and navigate to *Browse* under the *Upload Firmware* section. We can also upgrade firmware from FortiGuard

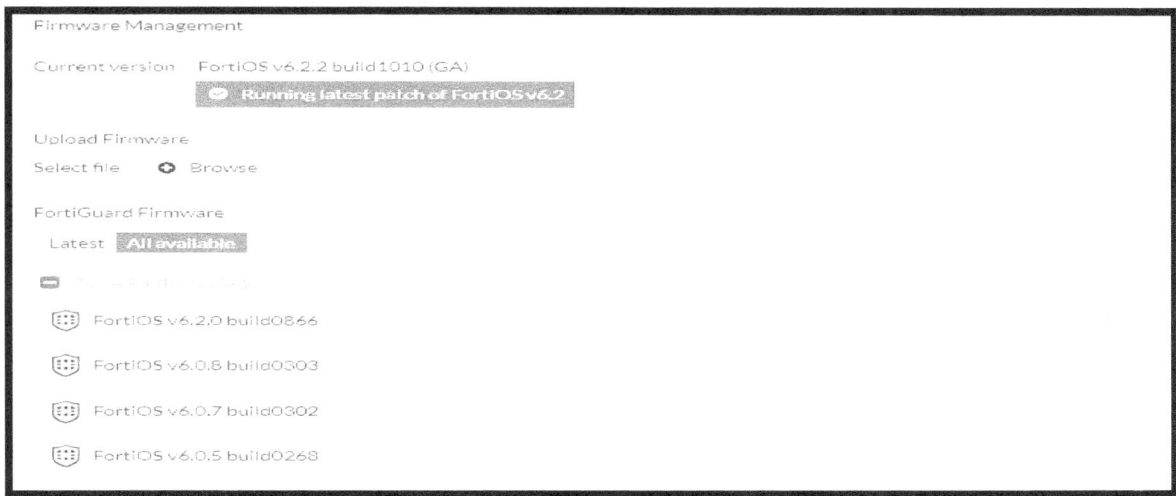

if the device has a valid support contract but, in this example, we use the firmware image downloaded earlier. This will give you a window pop up, and you will need to navigate to where you stored the previously downloaded 6.2.3 GA firmware image on your file system; find Image 1.27 for details.

Next, you will receive a warning to make sure that moving for 6.2.2 GA to 6.2.3 GA is supported (check release notes), which it is. To continue, click the 'Backup config and upgrade' button. This initiates the firmware upgrade from the GUI and grab a fresh configuration file backup as well. Now sit back and wait for the firmware to complete; this takes 5 to 10 minutes for smaller platforms. For large platforms, this takes 2-5 minutes. It is also good practice to have console access during the upgrade process just in case something goes wrong.

Firmware Upgrade CLI

Next, we can upgrade from the CLI using either flash, FTP, a management station, TFTP, or USB with the below commands:

Chapter 1 | Introduction to FortiGate

```
NSE4-PASS (global) # execute restore image ?
flash                Restore image from flash.
ftp                  Load image from FTP server.
management-station   Restore image from Management station.
tftp                 Restore image from TFTP server.
usb                  Restore image from USB disk.
```

Here is an example of how to FTP an image to FortiGate via CLI:

```
NSE4-PASS (global) # execute restore image ftp IMAGE_NAME.OUT 192.168.1.1 Username Password123
```

The last method we can use to upgrade FortiGate firmware is FortiManager. This book does not cover this method, but check out NSE5 FortiManager training if you wish to learn this.

Downgrading Firmware

Next, let's take a look at downgrading firmware. Sometimes this is necessary when a major bug is hit post-upgrade, and the best thing to do is just rollback. We use the same method to downgrade as we do to upgrade firmware. Select the desired firmware version and use one of the methods describe before to load the firmware to Fortigate. A warning will be presented that you are initiating a downgrade since the build or Version number is lower than what is currently running on FortiGate.

Please note that Fortinet does not support the downgrading of firmware; it is considered the best-effort. Since most of the time, a downgrade happens because of an unknown issue found post-upgrade. So, it would be expected to have a config backup on the prior firmware version. The most effective way to downgrade or rollback firmware is to:

- Upload your desired firmware image to FortiGate to initiate the downgrade.
- Next, once downgrade is complete and FortiGate reboots with original firmware, perform a factory reset.
    - #execute factoryreset
- Next, restore the original Configuration File taken from before the upgrade
    - This is assuming you took a backup.

Chapter 1 | Introduction to FortiGate

Firmware Upgrading Tips

In summary, evaluate your environment needs to see if upgrading to the latest firmware is the right move. Sometimes it is, sometimes, it might not be; every environment is different. Upgrading firmware is a big deal, treat it like one and please be sure to review the firmware release notes before proceeding with any production firmware upgrade. Also, if you have a lab to test out the upgrade process and new firmware, that would be even better! Here is an upgrade quick checklist guide that can help you decide if upgrading firmware is best and how to plan for it:

> *Post firmware upgrade you can run:*
> *#diagnose debug config-error-log read*
> *to show you any configuration loss*

- Do you understand the new version of the code? Release notes will have all this information.
    - Understand the differences and enhancements between the new code Version and the old.
    - Understand the impact of the upgrade regarding features in use
    - Are there any license changes in the new Version of code?
- What is the reason you need to upgrade?
    - Has it become of a software defect a.k.a bug that is impacting your environment?
    - Are you required to use a new security feature?
    - Are you impacted by a major vulnerability with no workaround ?
    - Are you losing vendor support on the current code?
- Write an upgrade plan or MOP (maintenance Operation Procedure)
    - This is a step by step guide for the entire operation from initial backup to post-upgrade regression testing of critical application and overall system evaluation.
- Schedule upgrade during off business hours
    - Schedule a maintenance window within enough time to complete all upgrade steps and perform regression testing outlined in MOP.
- Execute an upgrade plan
    - Document everything during the process and follow up with a summary report and send it to all parties of interest.

Product Life Cycle

All good things must come to an end. The same goes for cybersecurity products. As new methods are invented to serve better networks, cybersecurity needs others are decommissioned. This is the natural order of things. So, we must understand the life

Chapter 1 | Introduction to FortiGate

cycle of the products we work with. We have a software life cycle, and we also have a hardware life cycle when it comes to working with Fortinet products, so let's touch on these in this section

Software life cycle

Let's talk about the Fortinet software lifecycle. Once a new Version or MR becomes GA, then Fortinet supports that code trunk for 36 months. This means during this time, Fortinet development teams actively provide patches for the release until it reaches the End of Engineering Support Date (EOES), and then after this period for 18 months, Fortinet development teams only provide critical system and vulnerability fixes and considered "Must Fix' support. The next milestone for the software life cycle is the End Of Support Date (EOS). After this date, there is no

Image 1.28 – Software & Firmware Life Cycle

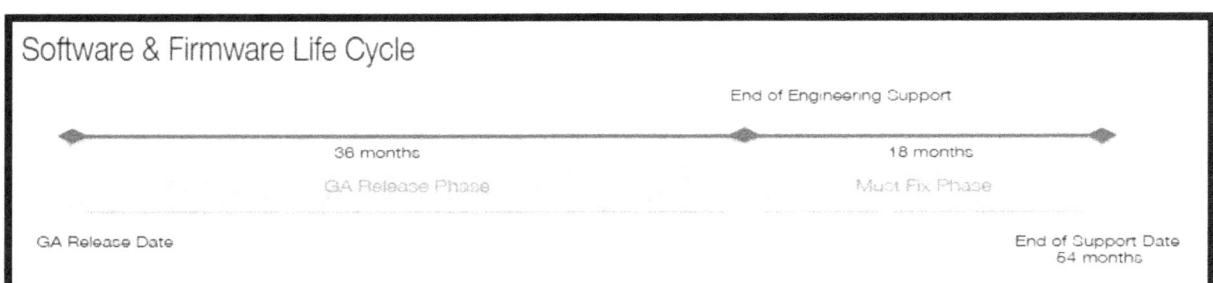

more improvement made on the code base, and Fortinet has no obligation to support it, meaning you cannot engage TAC on firmware issue that has reached EOS (they will tell you to upgrade). In Summary, once a new Version or MR becomes GA, then you have 54 months (4 ½ years) before you will have to move to a newer codebase. Please note, past the software EOS date, your FortiGate will continue to receive FortiGuard updates for things like IPS and AV as long as you have a valid contract on your FortiGate.

So, if you wish to run firmware that is past the EOS date, that's ok. Just know, you cannot engage TAC for help on Technical Assistant (TA) issues, and the code base will not receive any more patch updates that fix critical system issues and/or vulnerabilities. You can still submit RMA support cases because this process is related to hardware, not software. One example of a problem running EOS firmware is within PCI compliance environments where receiving vulnerability patches on firmware is a requirement to be PCI certified. Fortinet product lifecycles can be found via:

https://support.fortinet.com/Information/ProductLifeCycle.aspx

Chapter 1 | Introduction to FortiGate

Hardware lifecycle

Fortinet hardware appliances are called platforms, and once new platforms are designed and manufactured and released to the public eventually, they are given an End Of Order Date (EOO), a Last Service Extension Date (LSED) date, and End Of Support (EOS) date.

End Of Order (EOO) Date is fairly intuitive, meaning this is the cut off when you are able to purchase this hardware new and is no longer for sale. Fortinet will provide at least ninety days advance notice of any product about to enter the EOO date and will publish an End Of Life (EOL) notification. LSED, this is the cutoff date where you can renew a support contract or purchase additional security services for a platform. Fortinet will not allow services contracts to be extended past the EOS date. The LSED is twelve months before the EOS date. The EOS date is the final milestone for the product lifecycle. After this date, Fortinet will not sell, manufacture support, or improve the product. The EOS date is sixty months after the EOO date.

The Hardware EOS date is a lot more critical than the Software EOS date. Once the Hardware EOS date is reached, then your platform loses any FortiGuard Security subscriptions, and the platform hardware is no longer covered, meaning if a hardware failure occurs, then Fortinet is under no obligation to replace your hardware via RMA. Also, note older platforms cannot run newer firmware most the time.

Configuration File Management

Backups are critical to operations. Things do not always go as planned, and unforeseen things happen. Like a hardware failure or a disaster of some sort that takes down your firewall. Or maybe disk issues where you must format the disk. If anything like this happens and you do not have a configuration backup, the industry calls this, once again, a resume` generating event. Make sure to take backups and plenty of them to prepare for the unexpected because it is not always possible to reconfigure a FortiGate, for example, if there are hundreds or thousands of policies, it is just not feasible.

On FortiGate, we have many methods to backup the Configuration File. We can use the GUI or CLI. We can use scheduled auto-backups to an FTP or even better, if FortiGate is centrally managed by FortiManager then a config backup will be stored on FortiManager automatically. After this section, you should feel comfortable with performing config backups and restore procedures on FortiGate.

Chapter 1 | Introduction to FortiGate

Performing Configuration Backup

Let us go ahead and take a config backup from FortiGate. When FortiGate takes a backup of the active configuration, we only see values that have been modified

Image 1.29 – Config Backup location

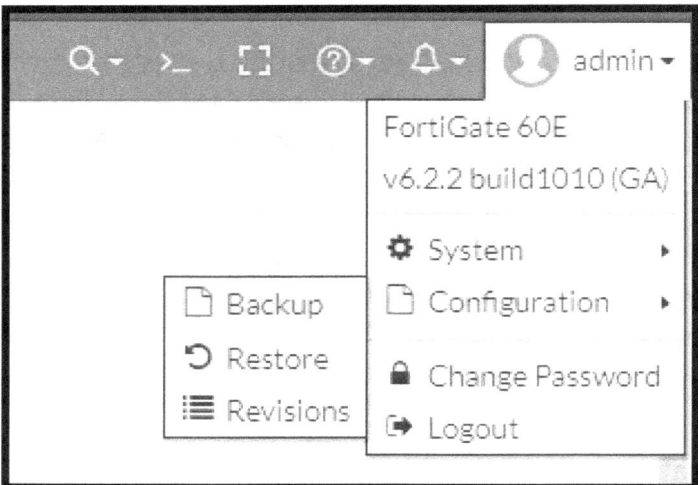

away from the defaults. If this didn't happen, the configuration would be more difficult to review and understand. By taking only the defaults, we are provided what is important. So that being said, it is good to know some of the default values

Image 1.30 – Backup System Configuration Windowpane

in FortiOS. I will highlight some important ones as we move forward in this book. But let's go ahead and find the location where we perform a configuration backup in the GUI, navigate to the upper right-hand corner and click the chevron icon next to the username and you will receive a context menu. Next, go to Configuration > Backup. Next, you will receive a screen to select Global or VDOM and backup to Local PC or USB as well as encryption options. I am going to leave mine to the defaults, Global-Local PC -No encryption.

Note that if you select the encryption toggle, the configuration file cannot be decrypted unless the password is provided along with the same model FortiGate the file was initially encrypted on. So, if you are working with TAC support and send

Chapter 1 | Introduction to FortiGate

them an encrypted configuration file with the password, then unless they have the same model FortiGate they cannot open it, which could cause your case to take longer to progress.

Configuration File Header Overview

Once you select OK, then the configuration file will be download to your PC. So navigate to the config file and open in a text editor and let us review some of the header information here:

```
#config-version=FGT60E-6.2.2-FW-build1010-191008:opmode=0:vdom=1:user=admin
#conf_file_ver=9357659998338613
#buildno=1010
#global_vdom=1
```

These header fields are important when restoring the Configuration File, so do not modify these fields; else, FortiGate could error out. Let's go over these values. The first line provides what platform the config backup came from FGT60E, along with the GA version, 6.2.2, and build number 1010. This backup was performed on a FortiGate with VDOMs enabled vdom=1, which is a global backup global_vdom=1.

The first line platform name must match the type of platform or model of FortiGate you will restore the configuration to. You can manually edit the first line to be able to restore this configuration to a 60D 6.0.8 GA FortiGate if so desired, for example, if we changed the first line to be:

```
#config-version=FGT60D-6.0.8-FW-build0303-191205:opmode=0:vdom=0:user=admin
```

Then a 60D FortiGate would accept this configuration backup and 'attempt' to restore the config. We would leave the rest of the header information; this way, the correct VDOM and OPMODE settings are applied. This method to migrate a configuration to a different platform is considered best-effort, and there will most likely be a lot of errors, especially in this case, since this backup of a different firmware MR and also a different platform. Most of the time, this method is useful when attempting to replicate a large production configuration on a lab device. Use this with caution.

Here is an example of Configuration File headers when we perform a backup on a certain VDOMs. The VDOM name here is 'Test-VDOM1' and would look like so:

```
#config-version=FGT60E-6.2.2-FW-build1010-191008:opmode=0:vdom=1:user=admin
#conf_file_ver=9392019736714613
#buildno=1010
#global_vdom=0:vd_name=Test-VDOM1/Test-VDOM1
```

Chapter 1 | Introduction to FortiGate

The next thing I want to touch on is how we can perform configuration revisions on FortiGate itself, which could be useful if your environment does not have a FortiManager. We do this via CLI:

```
#NSE4-PASS (global) # show ful | grep revision
    set revision-backup-on-logout enable
#end
```

These Configuration File revisions can be managed from the GUI or the CLI. The downside of this method is if all Configuration File revisions are kept on FortiGate, and something happens to its hardware, then there is no way to restore a new device. It is recommended to keep Configuration File backups in a remote location.

Password Recovery

It happens. Yes, you know what I am talking about, that embarrassing moment when you lock yourself out of your own FortiGate! It could happen for many different reasons, but at the end of the day, you need to obtain access, and you no longer have a correct username/password. Well, you are in luck, my friend, because there is a method to obtain access to a FortiGate using a special account called *maintainer*. The *maintainer* account is a back door to Fortigate essentially, and here is how you use it. Firstly, obtain a console connect; yes, this account only works via console connection. Next, once you receive a login prompt like so:

```
FGT60D4Q16XXXXXX login: maintainer
```

Next, you must enter the *maintainer* account name here. The maintainer password is different for every FortiGate because part of the password scheme is the device Serial Number. The device Serial Number can be found on the bottom of the platform or from the output of 'get system status'. Once we obtain our device Serial Number, we then pre-pend the letters bcpb to it, so we then have 'bcpbFGT60D4Q16XXXXXX'; this is our password. The username and password are case sensitive, the maintainer is all lower case, and the letters within the Serial Number are uppercase format while bcpb are lowercase format. It would look like this:

```
FGT60D4Q16XXXXXX login: maintainer
Password: bcpbFGT60D4Q16XXXXXX
```

And there is one more thing you should know, once the device is fully booted, you only have 14 seconds to enter in this account name and password, else FortiGate will not accept the maintainer login. So, my recommendation here is to place the username and password into a text editor first before attempting this procedure so you can easily copy and paste into the console connection before running out of time.

Chapter 1 | Introduction to FortiGate

Well, that pretty much covers how to use the maintainer account, but I'm pretty sure you are considered this feature actually exists and if it could be abused. Well, I'm sure it could be, so that's why there are protection measures we can perform on this account by disabling it globally via:

NSE4-PASS (global) # config system global
NSE4-PASS (global) # set admin-maintainer disable
NSE4-PASS (global) # end

Alright, problem solved, but I'm sure you have guessed the downside. Now, if you lose your login information, there is no way to login to this device. Now, if you try using the maintainer account, you will receive the following message on the console:

"PASSWORD RECOVERY FUNCTIONALITY IS DISABLED"

If this is the boat you are in, the only way to reclaim your device would be to perform a clean install by interrupting the boot cycle and TFTP, a new firmware image that will also format the device.

Formatting and loading firmware TFTP

In some instances, you will run into problems that will require you to format a FortiGate and reinstall firmware completely. The method here is called "Clean Install'. Some possible reasons for this are the one I just mentioned where you are locked out of you FortiGate, and the maintainer account had been disabled. Also, if the FortiGate runs into a disk issue and you start seeing system-level ext4 file system errors and/or the device is not behaving as expected. For example, rebooting randomly or CLI commands entered are failing to run, or general errors when attempting to make any sort of change on your FortiGate. When we perform a format, the process will mark all bad sectors on the disk and re-create the ext4 file system fresh, and then the TFTP firmware upload process will essentially provide a fresh factory install. Once the new firmware image is loaded, you would need to restore your Configuration File. Here is what you will need to accomplish this process:

- A console connection with a terminal application like Putty.exe
- A TFTP server
    - There are many TFTP server out there on the Internet, but I usually use pumpkin-2.7.3
- Copy FortiGate firmware image to TFTP root directory
- Must have an ethernet connection from the TFTP server machine to the internal interface on FortiGate. You will configure which port to use.
- Next, here are the steps to format and load the firmware image:
- Restart the FortiGate will connect to the console
- During the reboot process, you will see:

Chapter 1 | Introduction to FortiGate

> o Note you only have 3 seconds to press any key to interrupt the boot process

```
Please wait for OS to boot, or press any key to display configuration
menu........

[C]: Configure TFTP parameters.
[R]: Review TFTP parameters.
[T]: Initiate TFTP firmware transfer.
[F]: Format boot device.
[I]: System information.
[B]: Boot with backup firmware and set as default.
[Q]: Quit menu and continue to boot.
[H]: Display this list of options.
```

- Select the F key to Format device
- Once the FortiGate is formatted, it will reboot again and again, you will see the configuration menu and you must interrupt the boot process.
- Next, you must press C key to config TFTP parameters

```
Enter C,R,T,F,I,B,Q,or H:

[P]: Set firmware download port.
[D]: Set DHCP mode.
[I]: Set local IP address.
[S]: Set local subnet mask.
[G]: Set local gateway.
[V]: Set local VLAN ID.
[T]: Set remote TFTP server IP address.
[F]: Set firmware file name.
[E]: Reset TFTP parameters to factory defaults.
[R]: Review TFTP parameters.
[N]: Diagnose networking(ping).
[A]: Restricted mode setting.
[B]: Auto-boot resume time setting.
[Q]: Quit this menu.
[H]: Display this list of options.
Enter C,R,T,F,I,B,Q,or H: R
```

Image download port: Any of port 1 - 7
DHCP status: Disabled
Local VLAN ID: <NULL>
Local IP address: 10.52.53.2
Local subnet mask: 255.255.255.0

Chapter 1 | Introduction to FortiGate

Local gateway: 10.52.53.1
TFTP server IP address: 10.52.53.10
Firmware file name: FGT_60D-v5-build0718-FORTINET.out

- Once you have all your parameters configured to accomplish a TFTP upload of the firmware image, you must press Q key to return to the prior menu
- Lastly, if everything is correct with your cabling, TFTP server, firmware image placement, and FortiGate parameters here, push T Initiate TFTP firmware transfer.
- If successful, you will see a progress bar on your screen

I promise you, at some point in your career, working with FortiGate firewalls, you will need to perform this procedure, so be sure to set up a lab and practice. For example, if you think your hardware is 'bad' for whatever reason and you want to RMA the device, then most likely, TAC will require you to perform this operation first.

Initial Configuration and Services

FortiGate a lot of features, and some you may never use, and even more you are never going to hear of, but some features you will use on every deployment. So lastly, in this chapter, we look at some common initial FortiGate configuration and how-to set up some basic services like logging, management services, and SNMP on the FortiGate side. Let's get started!

Login Banner

Most organizations require all their devices to have a login banner. This requirement came from a legal case regarding a hacker who got caught but said nothing explicitly stated he could not access the system. He won. So, the industry learned a hard lesson; we must warn anyone attempting to access our device and present a disclaimer. We can configure this via the CLI or GUI, but first, we need to enable this feature:

```
NSE4-PASS (global) # config system global
NSE4-PASS (global) # set pre-login-banner enable
NSE4-PASS (global) # set post-login-banner enable
NSE4-PASS (global) # end
```

Next, you can find this feature in the GUI via System > Replacement Messages; next, navigate to the upper right-hand corner of the screen and click 'Extended View.' Now you can access the two login disclaimer messages. The first one is called *Post-*

Chapter 1 | Introduction to FortiGate

Image 1.31 – Login Banner Configuration Windowpane

login Disclaimer Message, and the second *Pre-login Disclaimer Message*. With the first message being presented to the user post login and the second pre logins, respectively. We can also configure this via CLI using the below commands:

NSE4-PASS (global) #config system replacemsg admin pre_admin-disclaimer-text

NSE4-PASS (pre_admin-discla~ext) # get
msg-type   : pre_admin-disclaimer-text
buffer   : PRE WARNING:
This is a private computer system. Unauthorized access or use
is prohibited and subject to prosecution and/or disciplinary
action. All use of this system constitutes consent to
monitoring at all times and users are not entitled to any
expectation of privacy. If monitoring reveals possible evidence
of violation of criminal statutes, this evidence and any other
related information, including identification information about
the user, may be provided to law enforcement officials.
If monitoring reveals violations of security regulations or
unauthorized use, employees who violate security regulations or
make unauthorized use of this system are subject to appropriate
disciplinary action.
header   : none
format   : text

NSE4-PASS (pre_admin-discla~ext) #end
You can update the contents of the disclaimer message via CLI or GUI. If using the CLI method, then you would tell use the following command and using quotations as a delimiter:

NSE4-PASS (pre_admin-discla~ext) #set buffer "This is my new message"
You can also update this message on the GUI by double-clicking Pre-login Disclaimer Message, and a text window is displayed on the bottom right-hand corner where you can edit the text content. Now when users attempt to access this FortiGate, they will be presented with a disclaimer. This is one of the more important steps to remember when provisioning new FortiGates.

Chapter 1 | *Introduction to FortiGate*

Basic Services

Most of the defaults on FortiGate work well for most environments, and the things you might expect you would need to configure initially, you do not, like an NTP server. By default, FortiGate uses FortiGuard NTP servers, but this can be modified in the GUI via 'System > Settings' and find the *System Time* section. Next, the first thing I will show you is how to set up logging, which is critical to operations. We can either set up Syslog, which runs on port 514 UDP by default, and these could be sent to a SIEM deployment, or we can also log to a FortiAnalyzer or both! In this example, I am going to show you how to set up logging to a FortiAnalyzer, which is a log aggregation device that has many features for in-depth log visibility. This setup is very common for FortiGate deployments FortiAnalyzer is covered in the NSE5 certification.

FortiAnalyzer Logging Configuration Example

To set up logging to FortiAnalyzer in the GUI we goto Log & Report > Log Settings; see Image 1.32.

Image 1.32 – FortiAnalyzer Config Windowpane

Here we can see an example of how we can configure FortiGate to send its logs to a FortiAnalyzer. We have several options, but right now, we will stick with the defaults, which are to buffer and send logs in bulk every 5 minutes using SSL encryption. We can make sure we have good connectivity to FortiAnalyzer by using our 'Test Connectivity' button. Once configured, hit Ok, and then you would need

Chapter 1 | Introduction to FortiGate

to navigate to your FortiAnalyzer and accept the FortiGate device before log would be stored there.

FortiManager Configuration Example

Moving right along, the next service we need to be sure to set up FortiManager central management service on FortiGate. FortiManager is useful if you are managing many firewalls and allow yous to use a single policy package for multiple

Image 1.32 – FortiManager Configuration Windowpane

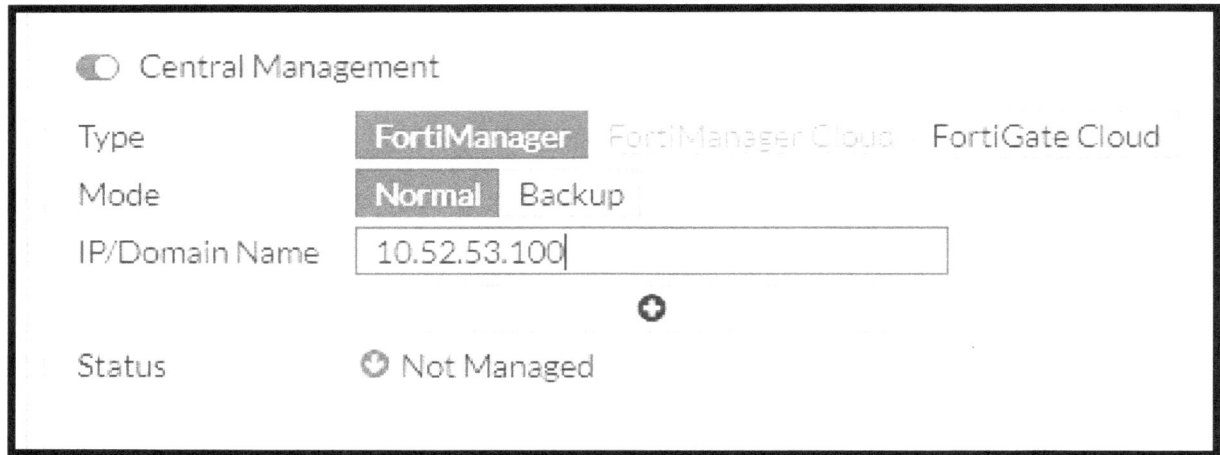

devices.

FortiManager is the single pane of glass for your Fortinet deployment and provides change management, audit compliance requirements, and workflow automation. To-Do this, we would use the GUI and navigate to Security Fabric > Settings and toggle Central Management and specify the IP address of our FortiManager. Also, here we have the option to point our FortiGate to FortiCloud for central management. This could be useful if you do not have very many FortiGates to manage.

SNMP Configuration Example

Lastly, let's take a look at SNMP. We can find this configuration on FortiGate in the GUI via System > SNMP. On this page, we can enable an SNMP agent that can accept queries from a Network Management Station (NMS) or send traps to one.

Chapter 1 | Introduction to FortiGate

Let's go ahead and configure SNMPv2 by navigating to the +Create New button. We also have SNMPv1 and SNMPv3 available as well. Next, we configure our NMS IP address, and here we Accept queries and send traps as well. We need to set our Community Name, which is essentially the pre-shared key that authenticates the NMS to this SNMP Agent. At the bottom of Image 1.33, it shows one SNMP Event, but we have many SNMP Events options to choose from. These options causes FortiGate to send SNMP Traps on certain system events to the NMS.

Image 1.33 – SNMP Configuration

Chapter 1 | Introduction to FortiGate

Chapter One Summary

That's it, and we are finished with chapter one! So, congratulations! A fantastic job making through! You are well on your way to becoming NSE4 certified and even better, an outstanding Fortinet engineer!

This chapter covered a lot of different content, but it was necessary to create a foundation to build your skill further. If you feel lost, do not sweat it, it is normal for most folks to read new material at least 3 times before it is retained. So, my advice is to go through, take your time, and read the chapter once more, take your notes, and study, study, study. The material will become 2nd nature to you. I promise.

To recap what we covered here, we went over the unboxing of the FortiGate and a basic setup overview. We also touched on FortiCloud. Next, we provided you the foundation of Fortinet licensing models, which encompasses FortiCare and FortiGuard. FortiCare entitlement is for hardware/software coverage and technical support essentially. FortiGuard delivers the most up to date security information to devices with active subscriptions, like FortiGates. We covered the Fortinet RMA process and Device Warranty overview.

Next, we went over high-level FortiOS design and platform SPU ASIC chips like the NP6, SoC3, and CP9. I explained the difference between NAT mode and Transparent mode FortiGate operations, and NAT is a layer-3 device while Transparent is a layer-2. We also got the chance to take a tour of many GUI and CLI features within these chapters, which gives you the foundation you need to start implanting some of this technology.

Lastly, we discussed the basic setup and administration of FortiGate. We discussed setting up the Admin account and interfacing with the local network and basic service configuration like logging to FortiAnalyzer and central management with FortiManager.

In Summary, it is critical for you to know this stuff before moving on! This is ground zero. Next, be sure to knock out those end of chapter questions while everything is still fresh in your mind!

Chapter 1 | Introduction to FortiGate

Chapter One Review Questions

1) Which SPU is responsible for SSL Encryption and Decryption?
   a) Security Processor (SP)
   b) System-on-a-Chip 3 Processor (SoC3)
   c) Content Processor (CP)
   d) Network Processor (NP)

2) What is the FQDN for FDN used by FortiGate for live security rating queries on FortOS 6.2+ ?
   a) securewf.fortiguard.net
   b) service. fortiguard.com
   c) service. fortiguard.net
   d) info.fortiguard.net

3) What is the FQDN for FDN used by FortiGate for live security rating queries on FortOS 6.0 and below?
   a) securewf.fortiguard.net
   b) service.fortinet.com
   c) service.fortinet.net
   d) info.fortiguard.net

4) What UTM features store have their own local database on FortiGate?
   a) AV
   b) AV and IPS
   c) AV, IPS and Web Filter
   d) AV, IPS, Web Filter and Spam Filter

5) A registered FortiGate with a valid FortiGuard subscription will receive weekly updates for local security databases by default.
   a) Tue
   b) False

Chapter 1 | Introduction to FortiGate

6) On Transparent mode FortiGate, it is required to assign an IP address to any interface that handles networking traffic.
   a) True
   b) False

7) Sessions that require flow-based security scanning can be offloaded to a Network Processor (NP) only if the platform model supports the Nturbo feature.
   a) True
   b) False

8) On FortiGate GUI default Dashboard, which widget holds information of serial number and current firmware version?
   a) FortiGate Cloud
   b) Security Fabric
   c) System Information
   d) Licenses

9) What is the back-door account that can be used for password recovery?
   a) admin
   b) root
   c) system
   d) maintainer

10) What feature restricts admin users' access to specified source IPs?
    a) Forti-access control
    b) Local-in policy
    c) Transit policy
    d) Trust-host

11) What is the default IP address and subnet assigned to lower-end FortiGate models by default?
    a) 192.168.1.1/24
    b) 192.168.1.254/24
    c) 10.1.1.1/24
    d) 192.168.1.99/24

Chapter 1 | Introduction to FortiGate

12) What is the default username and password on FortiGate?
    a) Username: admin   Password: fortinet
    b) Username: fortinet   Password: <password is blank>
    c) Username: root   Password: root
    d) Username: admin   Password: <password is blank>

13) Will the below firewall policy allow all network traffic from interface LAN to WAN1:
    a) True
    b) False

```
NSE4-PASS#config firewall policy
NSE4-PASS (policy) # show
    edit 101
        set srcintf "LAN"
        set dstintf "WAN1"
        set srcaddr "all"
        set dstaddr "all"
        set schedule "always"
        set service "ALL"
        set logtraffic disable
    end
```

14) Once a new code Version or MR becomes GA, how long does Fortinet support this codebase?
    a) As long as FortiGate has a valid Forticare license, the code base will be supported
    b) As long as FortiGate has a valid FortiGuard subscription, the code base will be supported
    c) Fortinet supports every code base for a total of 54 months
    d) Fortinet will support the code as long as the hardware has not reached the end of life.

15) What is FortiCare?
    a) FortiCare allows FortiGate to receive updates from FDN.
    b) FortiCare is a license that allows endpoints to be registered to the FortiGate
    c) FortiCare is an entitlement that is purchased for a single platform that allows for vendor support and hardware replacement
    d) FortiCare allows for vendor support through TAC but not hardware replacement; this requires a separate entitlement license.

Chapter 1 | Introduction to FortiGate

16) If you engage Fortinet regarding RMA case for a bad NIC on FortiGate with valid FortiCare entitlement, what will they ask for?
    a) The RMA team does not ask for further information and will replace the device
    b) The RMA team will stage the case with TAC, and TAC will require you to perform an HQIP test and/or perform a clean install
    c) The RMA team will ask you for your FortiCare contract number for processing
    d) The RMA team will ask you first perform a factory reset on your device before moving forward with RMA process

17) If you engage Fortinet TAC on a routing issue and your FortiGate is currently running firmware that is past End Of Support (EoS) Date. How will TAC be handling your routing issue?
    a) TAC will assist you on the routing issue and provide a recommendation
    b) TAC will request you upgrade to support firmware version before providing assistance on routing issue
    c) TAC will assist on any technical issue brought to them by customers regardless
    d) TAC only requires you provide a back configuration of your FortiGate before beginning their technical investigation

Chapter 1 | Introduction to FortiGate

19) If there are three firewall policy configured on FortiGate for transits traffic, the first policy has ID 25, the second policy has ID 14, and the third policy has ID 3, the FortiGate always evaluate firewall policies IDs from lowest to highest. In this case, policy ID 3 would be evaluated first.
20) True
21) False

22) What is the password to the maintainer account on FortiGate?
23) The password is bcpb
24) The password is Fortinet
25) The password is the FortiGate serial number
26) The password is 'bcpb'+ 'FortiGate serial number'

27) What is required for a clean install?
28) The maintainer account to be active and not disabled
29) The HQIP image for that platform model
30) Console access with the maintainer account and the HQIP image
31) Console access with a TFTP server, firmware, and console connection

32) What CLI command will display the FortiGate interfaces?
33) show interface
34) get interface
35) show system interface
36) system interface

Chapter 2 | Layer Two Technologies

NSE4 Blueprint Topics Covered

- Configuration of layer-2 VLANs
- Describe VLANs and VLAN tagging process
- Describe FortiOS Transparent Mode
- Configure FortiOS Transparent Mode settings
- Describe Transparent Mode Bridge Table
- Describe MAC forwarding
- Describe how to find MAC address on FortiOS
- Describe Forwarding Domains
- Describe and configure Virtual Switches
- Describe Spanning Tree Protocol
- Describe and Configure varous NAT Mode layer-2 protocols
- Describe and configure Layer-3 VLAN interface
- Describe Virtual Wire Pairing
- Describe and Configure VXLAN

Chapter 2 | Layer Two Technologies

FortiGate Layer-2 Technologies

Everyone has a favorite firewall mode they like to work on (or at least I do); some think network-based firewalls should be a layer-2 device, and others think they should be a layer-3 device, but at the end of the days, it really just depends on the network requirements. If the network requirements allow for either, then you can look at what features are offered within each operational mode. Me personally, I'm a routing guy at heart. I like routing protocols and VPNs. I feel like I'm in more control of the network traffic. Nevertheless, I've worked on plenty of Transparent FortiGate's within many carrier environments, and when they are set up correctly, they offer a solid line of defense to any network!

But let's not kid ourselves, Layer-2 is a vast subject with many protocols available, and entire books have been written just covering these topics. This chapter is not meant to be comprehensive in that I'm going to cover all FortiGate layer-2 technologies in depth because this book would be a little too thick! What this chapter does focus on is what you need to know to pass your NSE4 exam and what you need to know to build a strong foundation on FortiOS layer-2 technologies so to become an awesome Fortinet engineer!

I broke this chapter up into two major sections.

- NAT Mode at Layer-2
- Transparent Mode at Layer-2

In the first section, we will look at the different types of switch interfaces built into certain FortiGate models running NAT mode, and we also take a look at some common layer-2 protocols you will run into when working in NAT mode. And lastly, of course, we will look at layer-3 VLAN interfaces here as well.

The second section is fully dedicated to Transparent (TP) mode FortiGate. I'm going to show you how to deploy FortiGate in TP mode and then provide an overview of how TP FortiGate handles various layer-2 protocols. We also go over VLAN handling and forwarding domains here as well.

Put on your Layer-2 thinking cap!! because we have a whole lot to cover here... Let's get started!!

Chapter 2 | Layer Two Technologies

NAT Mode at Layer-2

It's time to explore layer-2 in NAT mode! One of the most popular layer-2 protocols is IEEE 802.3 Ethernet II. These standards are what you will most likely see when working with FortiGate and with most networks nowadays. So that being said, before we dive into some of the NAT Mode layer-2 features, I would like to review the Ethernet II frame standard and the switch MAC learning process. Note, I will be referring to Ethernet II and IEEE 802.3 standards as just Ethernet. This book does not go over the difference.

If you already know these topics, then feel free to skip ahead to the 'Interface Details' section, where we learn to locate the MAC address on FortiGate!

Ethernet Frame Overview

Ethernet, the story goes, in 1983, the Institute of Electrical and Electronics Engineers (IEEE) completed a project to standardize Local Area Network protocols. They drew up the 802.3 standard that governs the physical media requirements and the signaling structure itself. This is a big topic, and there are many standards

Image 2.0 – Ethernet II Frame

Preamble	SFD	Destination MAC	Source MAC	Type	Data and Pad	FCS
7 Bytes	1 Byte	6 Bytes	6 Bytes	2 Bytes	46-1500 Bytes	4 Bytes

within IEEE 802.3. In this section, we are going to focus on the Ethernet II frame header structure. We can see this in *image 2.0*. Here is a rundown on Ethernet header fields.

- Preamble
    - This is the first piece of communication between two devices that support Ethernet, which is 7 specific bytes that allows synchronization or clocking time slots between said devices.
- Start Frame Delimiter (SFD)
    - Once device synchronization is complete, this field indicates that the destination MAC address field begins with the next byte
- Destination MAC
    - This field indicates the Media Access Control (MAC) address for the receiving device
- Source MAC
    - This field indicates the MAC address for the sending device

Chapter 2 | Layer Two Technologies

- EtherType / Length
    - This field defines the next level protocol on the stack, which will most likely be IPv4 or IPv6, which are EtherTypes 0x0800 and 0x86DD, respectively.
        - Length vs. EtherType can be found in IEEE 802.3 Clause 3.2.6.
- Data and/or Pad
    - It contains the upper layer protocol header information and application data. The minimum length required here is 46 Bytes.
- Frame Check Sequence
    - This field contains a 32-bit Cyclic Redundancy Check (CRC) used to detect data corruption

I want to mention here that a MAC address is broken into two logical identifiers. The first 24 bits (high order bits or furthest to the left) will identify an organization or vendor, and this is called the OUI, which stands for Organizationally Unique Identifier. It is good to know that the OUI portion of the MAC is used by FortiOS to help with device identification on the network. We can easily look up MAC addresses and see who the vendor is, whether it be Fortinet, Cisco, or Checkpoint. Every firewall vendor should have its very own OUI. The second half (low order bits) of the MAC address is used to identify a device interface for that vendor uniquely.

MAC Learning and Forwarding

Before we get into specific FortiGate TP features, I want to provide a refresher on how Layer-2 switches general learn MAC address and forward Frames.

Layer-2 switches have a MAC forwarding database (FDB) that is dynamic in nature, which stores all visible MAC addresses on the network and map them to an interface/port. The switch uses this FDB to steer Ethernet frames to the correct egress port. A layer-2 switch learns MAC addresses from inspecting the source MAC address of ingress Ethernet frames and comparing it with the ingress port.

In this scenario, we have a switch with nothing yet stored in its MAC forwarding database. When the switch receives its first Ethernet frame to process, it will most likely have a destination MAC of FFFF:FFFF:FFFF:FFFF, which is a broadcast frame, and we will say the source MAC is 1111:2222:3333:4444, and this frame ingresses interface port1. The switch is going to do a couple of things here. Firstly, it recognizes it is a broadcast packet and forwards the frame out of every active interface except for the one it came in on, port1. Secondly, the switch parses the source MAC address and places it in its MAC FDB, and maps it to port1. The reason for this is so when the switch receives a response frame with a destination MAC address of 1111:2222:3333:4444, and it knows to forward the frame to the port1 interface. But if no entry is found in the FDB, the frame is treated like a broadcast, which causes network congestion.

Chapter 2 | Layer Two Technologies

Below is an example of a Transparent mode FortiGate MAC Forwarding Database (FDB), we go over this output in the coming up section.

```
FGT# diag netlink brctl name host root.b
show bridge control interface root.b host.
fdb: size=256, used=6, num=7, depth=2, simple=no
Bridge root.b host table
port  no  device  devname  mac addr              ttl      atributes
2     7           wan2     02:09:0f:11:22:33     0        Local Static
5     6           trunk_1  02:09:0f:44:55:66     0        Local Static
3     8           dmz      02:09:0f:77:88:99     0        Local Static
```

<u>Interface Details</u>

Alright, that covers our layer-2 foundation knowledge. The next thing we need to do is be able to find the MAC address on a FortiGate interface! There is a very useful CLI command that gives us these details; let's take a look.

To find interface details on our FortiGate Layer-3 interfaces, we issue the below command:

```
NSE4-PASS (global) # diagnose hardware deviceinfo nic wan1
Description       :FortiASIC NP6LITE Adapter
Driver Name       :FortiASIC NP6LITE Driver
Board             :60E
lif id            :0
lif oid           :64
netdev oid        :64
tx group          :1
Current_HWaddr    90:6c:ac:xx:xx:xx
Permanent_HWaddr  90:6c:ac:xx:xx:xx
========== Link Status ==========
Admin             :up
netdev status     :up
autonego_setting:1
link_setting      :1
speed_setting     :10
duplex_setting    :0
Speed             :1000
Duplex            :Full
link_status       :Up
============ Counters ===========
Rx Pkts           :689252177
Rx Bytes          :890790735557
Tx Pkts           :364166647
Tx Bytes          :64718543139
```

Chapter 2 | Layer Two Technologies

```
Host Rx Pkts      :53895641
Host Rx Bytes     :10876234322
Host Tx Pkts      :65743773
Host Tx Bytes     :9932117671
Host Tx dropped   :0
FragTxCreate      :0
FragTxOk          :0
FragTxDrop        :0
```

Take a moment to review this output. We are referencing this output in this section. This is also a great command to store away in the notebook because you use it a lot when troubleshooting network issues. This is one of the first commands I use to help identify any interface or network issues on FortiGate.

Link Health

The first part of the output I want to review is the 'Link Status' section. The first question to ask, is our interface up or operational?

..

Admin   :up
netdev status   :up
..

And yes, it is. The first field to look at is 'netdev status -> up', netdev represents the NIC driver Ethernet physical signaling which is considered to be layer one on the OSI model, and 'up' here states it has identified activity with a remote device, and this essentially means there is something alive on the other side of the wire and wants to communicate with FortiGate. If this field is ever down, then you are most likely dealing with a cut cable, bad interface, or something is not cabled as you expect because FortiGate does not recognize the physical signaling or something is very wrong with it.

Next, the fields 'Admin -> up' indicates the port is Administratively enabled within FortiOS configuration settings. If we explicitly disable this port in CLI, then this output would be 'Admin -> down'.

Note that FortiGate uses Auto MDI/MDIX, which means ports on FortiGate can detect if a connection requires crossover settings or not and adjust which NIC pins are used for transmitting and receiving signaling appropriately. This means you do not need to worry about using crossover cable vs. straight through. FortiGate figures it out for you.

By default, FortiGates interfaces will negotiate duplex and speed interface settings automatically with the remote side. We do have the option to hard code Ethernet

Chapter 2 | Layer Two Technologies

speed values to be 10Mbps, 100Mbps, or 1000Mbps on 60E.Next, let us find the link speed and duplex settings that were negotiated:

```
..
Speed             :1000
Duplex            :Full
..
```

We can determine FortiGate has successfully negotiated an ethernet speed of 1000Mbps, which is the max speed on this interface, meaning no link degradation, and the other side of this connection allows for 1000Mbps Ethernet speeds as well. Next, we find 'Duplex -> Full', here 'Full' means that the link can transmit and receive data simultaneously. If you see Duplex -> Half, then this could point to a damaged cable, a bad NIC, or extreme interference regarding the Ethernet cable. Half-duplex means each device must take turns sending data and receiving data; this is not what we want.

Locate MAC address

Next, with the same output, we can also find the 'burnt in' MAC address for the wan1 interface, which is the value of the Permanent_HWaddr field. This field contains the MAC address that is hard code onto the NIC itself by Fortinet. This cannot be changed.

```
..
Current_HWaddr    90:6c:ac:xx:xx:xx
Permanent_HWaddr  90:6c:ac:xx:xx:xx
..
```

I'm sure you are curious about the Current_HWaddr field vs. the Permanent_HWaddr field. The 'Current_HWaddr' is the active MAC address the interface is using, and this is the MAC address other devices on the network use. You can think of this as a logical MAC address, and yes, we can change this MAC address value. This procedure can be done in the CLI:

```
config system interface
edit "wan1"
set macaddr 90:6c:ac:11:22:33
next
```
Also, during High Availability (HA) operations, the Current_HWaddr becomes a special virtual MAC, which we cover in the HA chapter.

The last thing we can conclude from this output is our error counters. If you see odd behavior or packet loss, then check these counters. Note, that the output of this command is different for each platform.

Chapter 2 | Layer Two Technologies

```
============ Counters ============
Rx Pkts           :689252177
Rx Bytes          :890790735557
Tx Pkts           :364166647
Tx Bytes          :64718543139
Host Rx Pkts      :53895641
Host Rx Bytes     :10876234322
Host Tx Pkts      :65743773
Host Tx Bytes     :9932117671
Host Tx dropped   :0
FragTxCreate      :0
FragTxOk          :0
FragTxDrop        :0
```

> *Another command to show errors on interface is # fnsysctl ifconfig <interface name>*

Also, there is another useful command to display interface attributes like MTU and duplex, which is:

```
NSE4-PASS (root) #  get system interface physical
== [onboard]
        ==[dmz]
                mode: static
                ip: 10.159.8.1 255.255.255.0
                ipv6: ::/0
                status: up
                speed: 1000Mbps (Duplex: full)
..
```

I recommend tucking this one away in the notebook as well.

That wraps up our physical interface overview. Remember these commands when checking for basic interface and network health. You can find many different types of error counters here and low-level information regarding the directly connected network. The last topic to cover in this section is how MAC addresses related to virtual interfaces.

Virtual Interface MAC

FortiGate can have virtual interfaces attached to the physical interface. These virtual interfaces could be a Virtual Local Area Network (VLAN) interface or perhaps an IPsec virtual interface. By default, virtual interfaces inherit the parent interface

Chapter 2 | Layer Two Technologies

attributes like MAC address and Maximum Transmission Unit (MTU) settings. You can use the below command to find interface MTU:

```
 NSE4-PASS (global) # diagnose netlink interface list
..
if=dmz family=00 type=1 index=4 mtu=1500 link=0 master=0
ref=10  state=start  present  tx_sched  fw_flags=0  flags=up  broadcast
allmulti multicast

if=wan1 family=00 type=1 index=5 mtu=1500 link=0 master=0
ref=25 state=start present fw_flags=0 flags=up broadcast run allmulti
multicast
..
```

We can change the MTU by navigating in the CLI to FortiOS interface level configuration settings.

```
NSE4-PASS (root) # conf sys int
NSE4-PASS (interface) # edit wan1
NSE4-PASS (wan1) # set mtu-override enable
NSE4-PASS (wan1) # set mtu 1360
```

Also, another good thing to known since we are talking about MTU, is the Path MTU (PMTU) we can gather this by issuing the following command:

```
NSE4-PASS (global) # diagnose ip rtcache list | grep wan1 -A 1 -B 1
family=02 tab=254 vrf=0 vf=0 type=01 tos=0 flag=04000200
192.168.209.52@33(vsw.internal7)->10.10.10.10@5(wan1)
gwy=10.123.233.1 prefsrc=192.168.209.62
ci: ref=1 lastused=253 expire=0 err=00000000 used=1 br=0 pmtu=1500
```

The PMTU is the MTU for the entire transit path from source to destination, and knowing the PMTU is good for troubleshooting latency issues caused by IPv4 fragmentation.

For the NSE4 exam, remember that virtual interfaces inherit MTU and MAC addresses from the parent interface by default. That wraps up our MAC learning and forwarding sections. Next, we discuss NAT Mode Software and Hardware switch!

Software Switch & Hardware Switch

NAT Mode provides many layer-2 switch topology options for lower end FortiGate models. These terms at first may sound counter-intuitive because we are in NAT Mode, right? Which makes FortiGate operate as a layer-3 device. That being true, in this mode, we have the option to create and manage virtual switch interfaces on

Chapter 2 | Layer Two Technologies

certain platforms. We have two options, a Software switch or a Hardware switch. Let me first explain the Hardware Switch.

Hardware Switch Overview

The terms Hardware Switch and Virtual Switch are used inner changeability, but there is a difference. Every FortiGate platform comes with certain features specific to its model. The FortiGate models where we can build Virtual Switches already have certain ports bound to a physical switch chipset internally, and we cannot change this. But what we can do is take this physical switch layout and separate it out to meet our needs. Meaning, we can virtually separate the built-in physical switch. FortiGate gives us a lot of granularity when designing virtual switches and which ports can be part of any given virtual switch topology.

Let us take a FortiGate 60E; for example, this FGT comes with a preconfigured virtual switch for ports 1-7, meaning any devices connected to these ports can share a layer-2 environment and broadcast domain. Also, the virtual switch interface itself shares a single IP address, configuration options, and general functionality across all 7 ports in this example. The virtual switch can be viewed as a single layer-3 interface. All these interfaces within this virtual switch objected are treated the same and are expected to be on the same IP subnet unless using VLANs.

You can stack multiple VLAN interfaces on a single Virtual Switch interface

Furthermore, to make total sense here, ports 1-7 are also the physical hardware switch built into the 60E platform, and it just so happen by default ports 1-7 are used in one virtual switch configuration, but this does not have to be the case. We can move these ports out of this virtual switch and create new virtual switches! We can even let every port be a standalone interface. Our limitation here is we cannot use a port not already apart of the physical switch. In this 60E FGT example, it

Chapter 2 | Layer Two Technologies

Image 2.1 - Virtual Switch Example

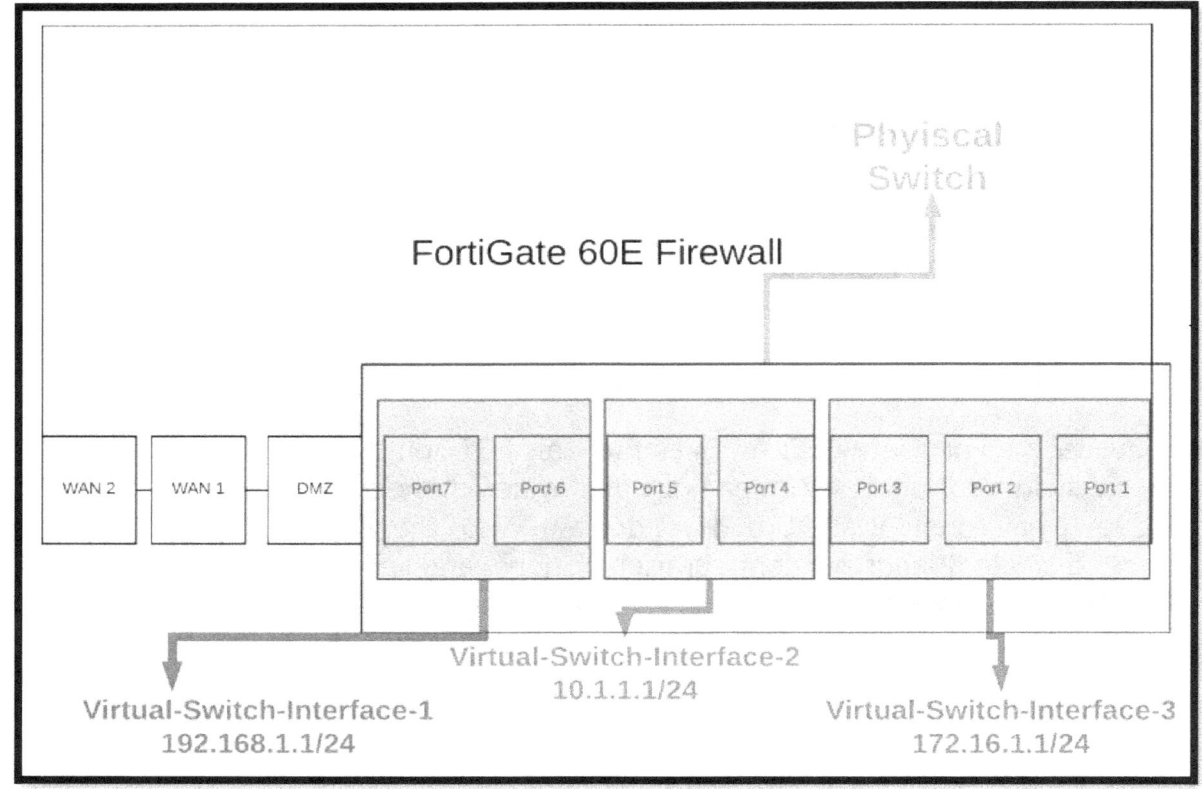

would be interfaces WAN2, WAN1, and DMZ that are independent of the built-in physical switch.

Another example of a virtual switch configuration can be seen in *image 2.1*. Here we have a diagram of the 60E FortiGate, let us first take a look at the built-in physical switch. This hardware switch chipset tie interfaces 1-7 together, which will be our choices to be used in the virtual switch object.

Image 2.1, we grouped ports Port7 and Port6 into a virtual switch object named *Virtual-Switch-Interface1* with IP and subnet of 192.168.1.1/24. Then we also grouped Port5 and Port4 into *Virtual-Switch-Interface-2* with IP and subnet of 10.1.1.1/24. Lastly, we grouped Port3, Port2, and Port1 into Virtual-Switch-Interface-3 with IP and subnet of 172.16.1.1/24. Now, this FortiGate has a total of three virtual switches, all having separate broadcast domains that function as three different single interfaces. Pretty cool, right?

Well, there are some limitations when creating virtual switch objects. For example, we lose the ability to map specific MAC addresses to a physical interface from a configuration standpoint; we can only see in the CLI the MAC to virtual switch interface mapping here because the port-to-mac address mapping table is handled in hardware and the kernel has no visibility here. The traffic on a hardware switch

Chapter 2 | Layer Two Technologies

will indeed be offloaded to the NPlite chip. Remember that traffic between interfaces within a virtual switch is not regulated by security policies, and we can only reference the virtual switch itself in a security policy. It's a tradeoff for convince. If you need layer-2 granularity and deep control in handling various layer-2 protocols, then I recommend deploying a FortiSwitch instead of using the built-in virtual switch feature.

Hardware Switch Configuration Example

We are going to configure the virtual switch in the CLI so you can visualize the underlying tables that hold these values, but we can indeed configure this in the GUI at Network > Interfaces > 'Create New' > Interface > Type > Hardware Switch. The first thing to look at is the physical switch that will be our base for this exercise.

```
NSE4-PASS (global) # show sys physical-switch
config system physical-switch
    edit "sw0"
        set age-val 0
    next
end
```

There is not much here in this section, but 'sw0' is indeed the base object for the next configuration. Right now, 'sw0' represents the physical switch that contains ports 1-7 on 60E FGT. Next, let's find our virtual switch configuration.

```
NSE4-PASS (global) # config system virtual-switch
NSE4-PASS (virtual-switch) #edit Vswitch-Int
NSE4-PASS (Vswitch-Int) # show ful
    edit "Vswitch-Int"
        set physical-switch "sw0"
        set span disable
        config port
            edit "internal3"
                set speed auto
                set status up
                set alias ''
            next
            edit "internal4"
                set speed auto
                set status up
                set alias ''
            next
            edit "internal5"
                set speed auto
```

Chapter 2 | Layer Two Technologies

```
                    set status up
                    set alias ''
            next
        end
    next
```

In my current configuration, I have ports internal3, internal4, and internal5 bundled into my virtual switch named 'Vswitch-Int". As you can see, the underlying physical switch is 'sw0'. Also, note, if you ever need to bring a single interface administratively down, this is the section you would perform that action, '*set status down*'. Now let's try to add an interface that is not apart of the physical switch, like WAN2.

```
NSE4-PASS (internal) # config port
NSE4-PASS (port) # edit
*All    members of physical switch sw0:

current members of internal

internal3
internal4
internal5

NSE4-PASS (port) # edit WAN2
WAN2 is not a member of physical switch sw0.
node_check_object fail! for name WAN2

value parse error before 'WAN2'
Command fail. Return code -501
```

As you can see, it failed as expected. And we have no options to add this interface to 'sw0' because it is dependent on the hard platform schematics. Next, we will give our virtual switch "Vswitch-Int" an IP address so you can see how all the induvial interfaces share configuration.

```
NSE4-PASS (global) # config sys int
NSE4-PASS (interface) # edit Vswitch-Int
change table entry 'Vswitch-Int'
NSE4-PASS (Vswitch-Int) # show
path=system, objname=interface, tablename=Vswitch-Int, size=4092
config system interface
    edit "Vswitch-Int"
        set vdom "root"
        set ip 172.25.20.1 255.255.255.0
        set allowaccess ping ssh
```

Chapter 2 | Layer Two Technologies

```
            set type hard-switch
            set alias "Virtual Switch Example"
            set device-identification enable
            set lldp-transmission enable
            set fortiheartbeat enable
            set role lan
            set snmp-index 46
    next
end
```

Here is what it looks like in the GUI, *image 2.2*.

Image 2.2 – Hardware Switch GUI

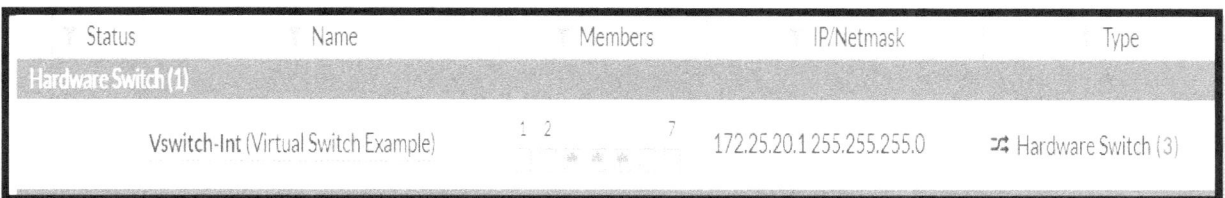

Just remember, if you want to create a new Hardware Switch interface, you must use the Virtual Switch Configuration.

Software Switch Overview

Now that we have an understanding of FortiGate NAT Mode Hardware Switch, let us move on to the Software Switch. I'll start by saying on a high level, you can think of these two features being the same regarding bundling interfaces into one virtual object, and by default, no policy governs traffic between the individual interfaces. A Software Switch, just like a Hardware Switch, interfaces share one configuration profile that has a single IP address, and all bundled interfaces share a single broadcast domain.

Now let's talk about the differences; this feature is very cool because it lets us break the rules of computer networking, kinda. We can pull the MAC table off of the Hardware Switch chipset and pull it into memory. Meaning, with this feature, we can bundle together any interface into a virtual software switch, and we are not limited to what interfaces are linked together on the backplane of the device.

For example, we can place the interfaces VLAN-15, internal5 port, and a WiFi network all nested in a newly created software switch. Yes, that is correct; if you have a FortiWiFI 60E platform, you can place your WiFI network, a single physical port, and a single VLAN interface into a single logical switch interface that shares a single broadcast domain. Pretty slick, right? Not saying that is a good idea to do of

Chapter 2 | Layer Two Technologies

course, but it's an option, and it lets you understand what we can do with this feature.

Now let's talk about why you shouldn't use this feature. When you pull the MAC table into running memory, we lose the ability to offload traffic to our specialized ASIC NP chips. Meaning, more load is put on the CPU, and the likely hood of maxing out our CPU cycles is much greater. Use this feature with caution and consider the network size and traffic load the FortiGate will handle. There are also some limitations regarding High Available (HA) and this feature as well.

<u>Software Switch Configuration Example</u>

I'm sure this is the part you have been waiting for, where we learn how to configure this! I'll show you the magic, lets hit the CLI and find our 'switch-interface object' which represents our Software Switch:

```
NSE4-PASS (switch-interface) # show
config system switch-interface
    edit "Software-SW-Int"
        set vdom "root"
        set member "LocalBridgeWifi" "internal5" "test-vlan-15"
    next
end
NSE4-PASS (global) # conf sys int
NSE4-PASS (interface) # edit Software-SW-Int
NSE4-PASS (Software-SW-Int) # show
config system interface
    edit "Software-SW-Int"
        set vdom "root"
        set ip 172.26.19.1 255.255.255.0
        set type switch
        set alias "Software Switch Example"
        set device-identification enable
        set lldp-transmission enable
        set role lan
        set snmp-index 43
    next
end
```

Chapter 2 | Layer Two Technologies

Here we used the object "config system switch-interface" to create a software switch table, and within that table, we reference our interfaces in the member field. Note, before you can bundle interface into a software switch, there can be no objects referenced to them. For example, they can not be used in a policy, used in static routing, or have a DHCP server associated with them. Once all object references are removed, you are free to bundle interfaces into one logical software switch interface.

> *..before you can bundle interface into a software switch there can be no objects referenced to them..*

Next here, just like the Hardware Switch, we configured an IP address and subnet for our switch interface Software-SW-Int. Now we are free to add objects like a DHCP server to the Software Switch interface Software-SW-Int or use this object in a firewall policy. For example, we could write a policy that limits certain traffic between our Software-SW-Int interface to our hardware switch Vswitch-Int.

Lastly, on Software Switch, there is a little command to force traffic between members to be evaluated by the Firewall Policy. By default, traffic is not evaluated. This command is found in the CLI under the Software Switch configuration:

```
NSE4-PASS (lan) # show full
config system switch-interface
    edit "lan"
        set vdom "root"
        set member "internal"
        set type switch
        set intra-switch-policy implicit
        set span disable
    next
end
```

For interface members transit traffic to be evaluated by the Firewall Policy Table, we must issue the following command:

```
config system switch-interface
    edit "lan"
      intra-switch-policy explicit
    end
```

Here are the CLI notes for the commands:

```
intra-switch-policy     Allow any traffic between switch interfaces or
require firewall policies to allow traffic between switch interfaces.
```

Chapter 2 | *Layer Two Technologies*

<u>Virtual Switch Summary</u>

Remember that there are limitations when using virtual switches, and they have limited features to control layer-2 traffic between switch interfaces. Also, they have limit visibility when it comes to the physical interface to MAC address mapping. They are used best in simple network deployments with few layer-2 requirements. Nevertheless, they are very useful and effective if deployed in the correct environment.

NAT Mode L2-Protocols

NAT Mode FortiGate interacts with many important layer-2 protocols for general operations. In this section, we are going to touch on some of these protocols like Address Resolution Protocol (ARP), Spanning Tree Protocol (STP), Link Aggregation Control Protocol (LACP), Link layer discovery protocol (LLDP), VLANs, and lastly, Virtual Wire Pairing.

<u>Address Resolution Protocol (ARP)</u>

ARP is a keystone protocol for IPv4 networks and is used to resolve known IPv4 addresses to unknown MAC addresses used in Ethernet frames. As FortiGate learns MAC addresses, it stores them in its ARP cache, which is a temporary dynamic table for mapping MAC addresses to IP addresses. FortiGate looks in this cache first and tries to obtain a MAC for an IPv4 address before sending an ARP request out to the LAN. We can find the ARP table with the following CLI command:

```
NSE4-PASS (root) # get system arp
Address              Age(min)   Hardware Addr        Interface
192.168.1.52         0          50:7b:44:11:22:33    vsw.internal7
10.159.8.2           0          60:38:44:11:22:33    dmz
192.168.1.247        0          90:6c:44:11:22:33    vsw.internal7
169.254.0.2          0          90:6c:44:11:22:33    internal7
192.168.1.7          0          18:66:44:11:22:33    vsw.internal7
10.123.1.1           0          90:6c:44:11:22:33    wan1
```

The EtherType for ARP is 0x0806. Can be used in sniffer debug:
#diagnose sniffer packet any "ether proto 0x0806"

From this table, we can gather known IPv4 addresses to MAC address mappings. We can also gather the egress interface for each entry. Lastly, we have an Age column,

Chapter 2 | Layer Two Technologies

and by default, an ARP entry will age out in 5 minutes to keep the latest network information.

FortiGate also holds a static ARP entry table as well. This could be useful in certain troubleshooting situations, and we access this table with CLI object arp-table:

```
config system arp-table
    edit 1
        set interface ''
        set ip 0.0.0.0
        set mac 00:00:00:00:00:00
    next
end
```

The last item to take note of is the ARP cache can be cleared with the following CLI command, which in turn, allows FortiGate to re-build a fresh ARP table.

```
NSE4-PASS (root) # execute clear system arp table
```

To this day, one of the first things I do when troubleshooting a network is to look in the ARP table so I can get a feel for the local Layer-2 environment.

Spanning Tree Protocol (STP)

The purpose of the IEEE 802.1d Spanning Tree Protocol (STP) is to prevent loops in a layer-2 environment. What I mean by this, if you cable a few switches in a ring and send them a broadcast Ethernet frame without running spanning-tree, then this frame continues to circle the network because, by default, a layer-2 switch floods a broadcast frame out all ports except the ingress port. Since there is no TTL in the field in the Ethernet header, the frame continues around the network way longer than we would like and will most likely bring down our switches once the CPU is maxed out. This is not a good day. Since we're not going to redesign Ethernet standards, STP was created to deal with this problem. Modern switches have the capability to detect broadcast storms and mitigate them.

Chapter 2 | Layer Two Technologies

This section is not meant to educate you on how STP works from the ground up but to show you what features FortiGate has regarding STP.

Image 2.3 – Broadcast storm

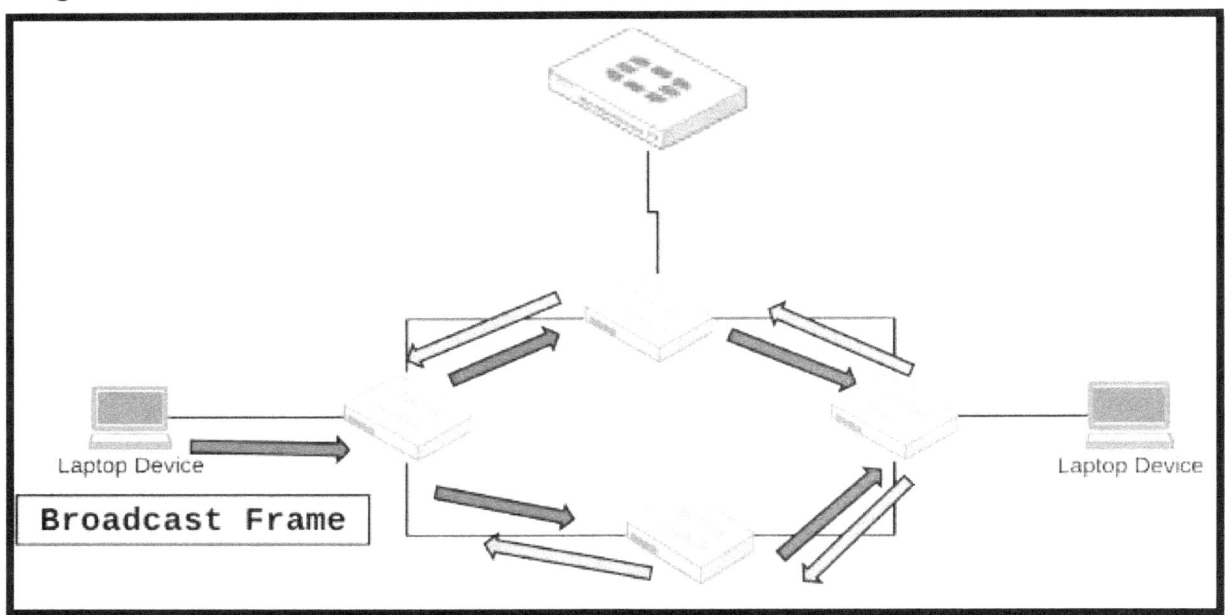

6.2 NAT Mode FortiGate Hardware switch, by default does not participate in spanning tree, and if you have a switch connected to a FortiGate Hardware Switch and its running STP on its directly connected port, then the switch marks the ports connected to FortiGate as discarding state and forwards traffic to another path.

On FortiGate, we have a couple of options here to deal with STP. The first being, we could forward STP traffic BPDUs (Bridge Protocol Data Units) to all other hardware switch interfaces, like a broadcast. By default, forwarding is disabled, and FortiGate drops STP traffic, be sure to account for this. Next, we could configure FortiGate to participate in STP. The last option would be to configure the remote switch interface to be an edge port if the topology allows it.

If we look under our Hardware Switch interface Vswitch-Int that we created, we can see the STP options. To forward STP traffic, we configure *"set stpforward enable"* but if we want our hardware switch to run STP with another switch actively, then we would enable it by configuring *"set stp enable"*.

Take a look at the default STP settings for the Hardware Switch Vswitch-Int CLI output for reference.

```
NSE4-PASS (root) #config system interface
NSE4-PASS (interface) #edit Vswitch-Int
NSE4-PASS (Vswitch-Int) # show ful | grep stp
        set stpforward disable
```

Chapter 2 | Layer Two Technologies

```
            set stp disable
            set stp-ha-slave priority-adjust
```

Take a moment to review this output.

STP configuration

Alright, moving into our STP configuration section, let's go ahead and enable STP on our hardware switch.

```
NSE4-PASS (Vswitch-Int) # set stp enable
NSE4-PASS (Vswitch-Int) # end
```

Next, I performed a simple test on our 60E FGT, where I cabled internal3 to internal4 so we can have some output with our next command. To see the current STP status on FortiGate issue CLI command "get sys stp list"

```
NSE4-PASS (root) # get sys stp list

bridge 'Vswitch-Int'  prio 32768  mac 90:6C:AC:33:22:11  vd 'root'
  root prio 32768  mac 90:6C:AC:33:22:11  cost 0
  port 'internal3'  role designated  state forward  cost 20000  edge no  rx 1    tx 245
  port 'internal4'  role backup      state listen   cost 20000  edge no  rx 245  tx 1
```

From reviewing this debug output, we can conclude that we are running Rapid STP (RSTP) since we see port roles as designated and backup for internal3 and internal4, respectively. By default, FortiGate will attempt to use rapid spanning first 802.1w and fall back to 802.1d as needed. Next, we can see our bridge priority at 32768 and our bridge MAC 90:6C:AC:33:22:11 (sanitized), which will be the source MAC address for our BPDU frames. Next, this FortiGate is indeed the root bridge. We know this because we see our own MAC as the MAC of the root bridge, '90:6C:AC:33:22:11 '. Next, for internal3, we can see it is in forwarding state with a cost of 2000. Lastly, we can see active traffic on the interfaces because the transmit and receive fields (tx and rx) are Incrementing. FortiOS gives us the ability to modify the STP values in the 'stp' CLI object. If FortiGate is actively participating in STP, then it might be necessary to adjust these values.

```
NSE4-PASS (root) # config system stp
NSE4-PASS (stp) # show ful
config system stp
    set switch-priority 32768
    set hello-time 2
    set forward-delay 15
    set max-age 20
    set max-hops 20
```

Chapter 2 | Layer Two Technologies

end

Take a moment to review this output.

In Summary, plan for STP when deploying FortiGate into a network topology, so to be sure traffic flows as expected.

Link Aggregation Control Protocol (LACP)

The next protocol to review is LACP, 802.3ad standard. Note this is commonly used protocol on FortiGate production networks, so be sure to know this protocol well. The purpose of LACP is to logically bundle together multiple physical interfaces to be viewed as one logical link on the network. The benefit of doing this is to obtain redundancy and more throughput. Once multiple links become part of LACP configuration, Fortinet calls this a LAG group, short for link aggregation group. A LAG group allows us to load balance traffic across multiple links, and STP does not block any single interface apart of a LAG group because it views it as one logical interface. Redundancy is accomplished because if one link goes down in the bundle, we have backups to use! Also, just recently was the LAG feature added to lower-end FortiGate E-Series models running 6.2 code.

It is good to know how LACP creates a functional LAG group, let's review. LACP sends Ethernet frames called Link Aggregation Control Protocol Data Unit (LACPDU) that have an EtherType of 0x8809, a destination MAC address of 01-80-C2-00-00-02, which is considered to be IEEE 802.3 "Slow Protocols Multicast Address", and the source MAC address is the first members interface MAC address. Some new terms to know within the protocol are Actor and Partner, which refers to the local participant of LACP. From the perspective of the local system, the Actor is self, and the Partner is the peer system or remote side of LACP communication. The Actor sends a frame every second when beginning negotiations down every member link to form an 802.3ad LAG. Also, know that each interface apart of a LAG Group is called a member.

Each side of the LAG sends values called a *key* and *sysid*. The key value is used to differentiate between local LAGs (LAG_1 , LAG_2, etc.) . The sysid value is used to uniquely identify devices useful when multiple devices form LAGs to a single unit. For regular LACP operations, these values are used internally to map interface members to the correct LAG group.

You can view LACP layer-2 traffic with CLI debug:
 # diagnose sniffer packet internal "ether proto 0x8809"

Chapter 2 | Layer Two Technologies

Luckily for us, on FortiGate, these values are negotiated in the background without user intervention but this is still useful to know about for troubleshooting purposes. Next, when two devices begin negotiating a LAG group, there are a couple of different settings we should know about.

- LACP Active Mode
    - A LAG group will actively send out LACPDU frames and try and negotiate a LAG with the remote side
- LACP Passive Mode
    - A LAG Group will not send LACPDU frames but will respond to them.
- Static Mode
    - A Lag group will not send or accept LACPDU frames, but locally, FortiGate will treat all members as bundled even if the remote peer members have issues. This configuration could potentially black hole traffic but could be useful in troubleshooting.

The next setting to know about is LACP 'speed'. The speed setting essentially means how fast an Actor or Partner sends LACPDUs to maintain their aggregation state, which is essentially a keep alive. We have the following options:

- LACP Fast
    - Will send LACPDU down each member every 1 second
- LACP Slow
    - Will send LACPDU down each member every 30 seconds

FortiGate allows for three consecutive LACPDU losses before marking a member as down. A member is marked as down by setting the expired flag in the LACPDU frame. If a member receives an expired flag or misses three consecutive keepalives, then the *synchronization* flag, *collecting* flag, and *distributing* flag states will be marked as *Out of sync, Collection Disabled*, and *Distribution Disabled*, respectively.

Now it is time to talk a little more about these LACP flags. To begin, we review some LACP CLI output on FortiGate by running a command to show us the LACP state. We are going to look at a LAG Group interface called *LAG_1*.

```
NSE4-PASS (root) # diagnose netlink aggregate name LAG_1
LACP flags: (A|P)(S|F)(A|I)(I|O)(E|D)(E|D)
(A|P) - LACP mode is Active or Passive
(S|F) - LACP speed is Slow or Fast
(A|I) - Aggregatable or Individual
(I|O) - Port In sync or Out of sync
(E|D) - Frame collection is Enabled or Disabled
(E|D) - Frame distribution is Enabled or Disabled
..
```

Take a moment to analyze this output.

Chapter 2 | Layer Two Technologies

We went over Active and Passive negotiation. We also went over Slow and Fast keep alive timers. The next LACP feature we look at is "(A|I) - Aggregatable or Individual", this flag lets us know if LACP allows an individual member to be part of a LAG Group. For example, if a member interface goes down physically, then this flag would be set to 'I', which stands for 'Individual' since it cannot be part of the LAG when an interface is in a downstate. We want to see the 'A' flag (Aggregatable) here, meaning the interface layer one protocol is up and also administratively up.

Next, "(I|O) - Port In sync or Out of sync" this flag indicates that a participant's physical port status is in sync with the system ID (sysid) and key (keyid) information being transmitted; this accounts for port flapping or members being move into or from the LAG Group interface. Essentially, the flag 'I' or 'Port In Sync' means the physical port driver software is in sync with the LACP process and accounts for the lag time between the process that is responsible for sending the single across the wire, and the high-level logic LACP provides. In a working state, this flag should be 'I'.

Next, let's talk about "(E|D) - Frame collection is Enabled or Disabled" Collection means a member is receiving data OK, and distribution means a member is sending data OK. These flags will be set to 'Enabled' or 'E' if the participants 'Port In sync' flag is 'I'.

Alright, now that we have a good understanding of the LCAP flags, we will review more LACP debug output on the CLI:

NSE4-PASS (root) # diagnose netlink aggregate name LAG_1

..

```
status: up
distribution algorithm: L3
LACP mode: active
LACP speed: slow
LACP HA: enable
aggregator ID: 1
ports: 1
actor key: 17
actor MAC address: 00:09:0f:AA:BB:22
partner key: 45
partner MAC address: 00:0d:66:AA:BB:40

slave: internal5
status: up
link failure count: 19
```

Chapter 2 | Layer Two Technologies

```
permanent MAC addr: 00:09:0f: AA:BB:22
actor state: ASAIDD <- DISABLED
partner state: ASIODD <- OUT OF SYNC / DISABLED
aggregator ID: 2

slave: internal6
status: up
link failure count: 2
permanent MAC addr: 00:09:0f:CC:DD:11
actor state: ASAIEE
partner state: ASAIEE
aggregator ID: 1
```

Once again, take a moment or two to analyze this out.

Here you can see what a good LACP state looks like and a bad one. For internal5, we see the partners' flags are ASIODD, which means our partner port is out of sync, and therefore, collection and distribution are disabled. The remote port will not be sending or receiving any traffic.

```
actor state: ASAIDD <- DISABLED
partner state: ASIODD <- OUT OF SYNC / DISABLED
```

Next on interface internal6, we can see a good operational state with flags being ASAIEE:

```
actor state: ASAIEE
partner state: ASAIEE
```

This means all is well; the FortiGate and partner ports are in sync and are sending and receiving traffic OK. This is always good news. Now that we understand the LACP flag states. Next, I want to talk about the LACP load balancing algorithms we have to work with on FortiOS and why they are required.

<u>LACP Load Balancing</u>

Firstly, when creating LAG Groups, each member is always given an index value. For example, if we have 4 members in our LAG group, which are internal1, internal2, internal3, and internal4. Then they would be indexed like so:

$$\text{Index 0 -> internal1}$$

$$\text{Index 1 -> internal2}$$

$$\text{Index 2 -> internal3}$$

Chapter 2 | Layer Two Technologies

Index 3 -> internal4

FortiGate can load balance on the different links within a LAG by using a hash value calculated from header information from a packet. The hash generated from the header is then taken and ran through a function that maps the packet to one of the member index values, which is the interface the packet egresses.

We have three algorithms to choose from, L2, L3, and L4. Firstly, the 'L2' algorithm means the hash is generated from Layer-2 Ethernet header information like source and destination MAC addresses. The 'L3' algorithm means the hash is generated from layer-3 information like IPv4 or IPv6 source and destination information. 'L4' means the hash is generated from layer-4 information like UDP/TCP source and destination port numbers.

I'm sure you are wondering why this is necessary. The reason behind this is to create randomness, and we are provided these three options to account for unique situations. For example, suppose we have a client with a static IP and a server with static IP, and these machines make up 90% of the traffic on a four-member LAG. In that case, it doesn't make sense to set our load balancing algorithm to L3 because the source and destination IP never changes, meaning the hash is the same every time, and therefore every single packet in this communication is mapped to the same member index and not distributed across any of other 3 members. For this situation, it would make more sense to use the 'L4' algorithm because at least the source port is known to be random and provides more randomness, so communication is distributed across all four members in the LAG. This allows us to effectively utilize the bandwidth of all members of the LAG Group. The below command can be used to give us what member a certain packet egresses:

```
NSE4-PASS (root) # diag netlink aggre port LAG_1 src-ip 1.2.3.4 dst-ip 5.6.7.8
port internal3
```

The above command could be useful when troubleshooting certain network traffic transversing a LAG interface. This section wraps up LACP theory, it is time to move on to the configuration piece of this section.

Configure LACP

To configure a LAG on FortiGate is very simple. We need to find our 'interface object' and create a new table. We name this LAG 'LAG_1'. Let's do this in the CLI real quick:

```
NSE4-PASS (root) # config system interface
NSE4-PASS (interface) # edit LAG_1
NSE4-PASS (LAG_1) # show
```

Chapter 2 | Layer Two Technologies

```
config system interface
    edit "LAG_1"
        set vdom "root"
        set ip 192.168.168.1 255.255.255.252
        set allowaccess ping https http
        set type aggregate
        set member "internal3" "internal4"
        set alias "LAG Example"
        set device-identification enable
        set lldp-transmission enable
        set role lan
        set snmp-index 45
        set lacp-speed fast
    next
end
```

As you can see, we create a LAG group interface just like we would create or edit any other interface by navigating to our interface object in the CLI "config system interface". I've bolded the important settings in our interface config; we need to set the *type* to *aggregate* and next assign members to it, which are *internal3* and

Image 2.3 – LAG Interface GUI

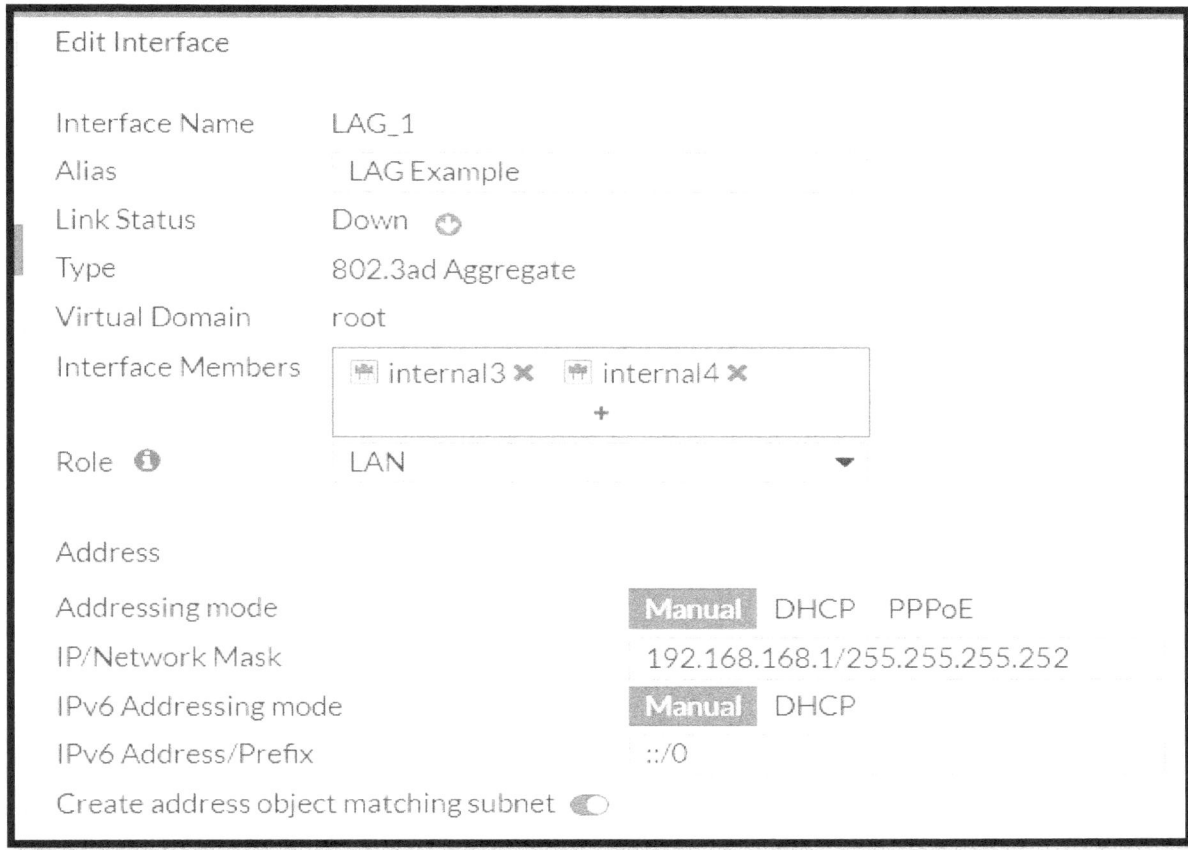

Chapter 2 | Layer Two Technologies

internal4. The LACP default settings are Mode Active, and Speed is slow. I've changed the speed to fast so to detect failures more quickly. Here is what it looks like in the GUI now, see image 2.3.

That wraps up the LACP section. I know this was a lengthy section, but I wanted to be sure I spent plenty of time here since this is a protocol you will most likely work with often. At some point in your networking career working with FortiGates, someone will ask you to create or troubleshoot this protocol, I promise you!

Redundant Interface Type

I'm not going to go into great detail on the Redundant interface Type, but you should know what it is and why it exists for the NSE4 Exam. The interface type operates similarly to LACP, but instead of all interfaces actively forwarding traffic, with a Redundant interface, only one member forwards at any given time. If the active interface fails for whatever reason, then the next member becomes active and starts forwarding traffic. You can think of this interface as having passive hot standby interfaces. The Redundant interface type is sometimes used in certain Hight Availability (HA) topologies.

Link Layer Discovery Protocol (LLDP)

LLDP is like the swiss army knife in computer networking. Many different processes using the information gathered by this protocol to learn about the local network environment and then use that information for another purpose. In our case, when working with FortiGate, we use this feature to help discover local devices and then use that information in a security-related way.

LLDP is a vendor-neutral layer-2 protocol to find device neighbors and obtain attributes about those neighbors. LLDP sends Protocol Data Units (LLDPDU) with destination MAC address being 01-80-C2-00-00-0E, which is a multicast address that 802.1D-compliant devices do not forward. LLDP has an EtherType field of 0x88cc. LLDPDU is made of type-length-value (TLV) structures that hold the below mandatory variables:

Mandatory variable attributes that are transmitted via LLDPDU:

- End of LLDPDU
    - Specifies the end of the LLDP Ethernet frame
- Chassis ID
    - Each firewall has a unique Chassis ID
- Port ID
    - Identifies the port from where the LLDPU was sent or the transmitting port

Chapter 2 | *Layer Two Technologies*

- TTL
    - How long in seconds the LLDPDU information is retained from a peer device

Image 2.3 – LLDPDU Ethernet Frame

Destination MAC	Source MAC	Ethertype	Chassis ID TLV	Port ID TLV	Time To Live TLV	Optional TLVs	End of LLDPDU TLV

Essentially, this layer-2 protocol allows FortiGate to discover local devices and gather various details about them. Next, let's talk more about how this information is useful to us. Well, firstly, LLDP is one tool that FortiOS uses to help build its device inventory list. The CLI output below from the 'diagnose user device list' command is an example of a remote FortiGate that was discovered. We can see attributes were given to these devices through information obtains by LLDP. Let's take a look at the output below.

```
NSE4-PASS (root) # diagnose user device list
..
  vd root/0  90:6c:ac:AA:BB:CC  gen 1893   req OUA/34
    created 77071s  gen 1892  seen 76531s    gen 1748
    ip 172.25.20.1  src lldp
    hardware vendor 'Fortinet'  src lldp  id 68
    type 'Router'  src lldp  id 68
    family 'FortiGate'  src lldp  id 68
    os 'FortiOS'  src lldp  id 68
    hardware version '60E'  src lldp  id 68
    software version '6.2.2 Build 101'  src lldp  id 68
    host 'FortiGate-2'  src lldp
..
```

Chapter 2 | *Layer Two Technologies*

Here we can see a lot of information obtained through LLDP, and we can gather this by looking at the 'src lldp' notation in the output. We can find information on the hardware, operating system, device type, or event software version! FortiOS then

Image 2.4 – Device Inventory GUI Page

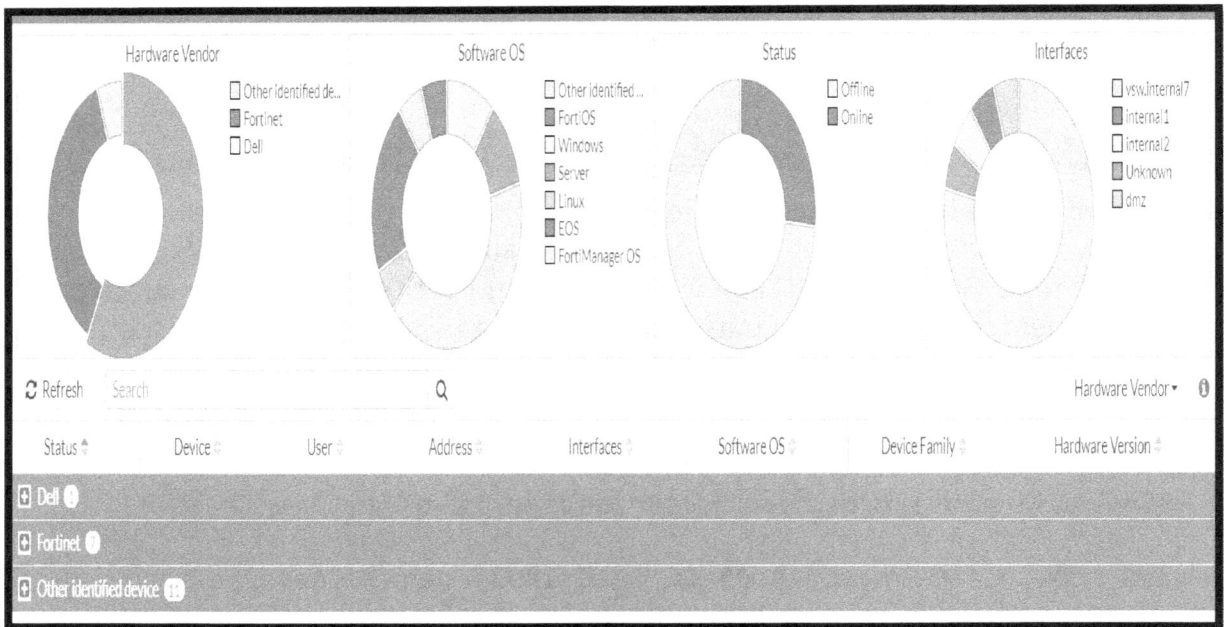

uses this information to make nice-looking charts for us to use in the GUI, see *image 2.4*. Note that all this information was not gathered solely by LLDP but various other sources as well to create the charts shown in *image 2.4*.

Configure LLDP

We can configure LLDP transmission on an interface level, VDOM level, or global level. Let us first take a look at the global settings:

```
NSE4-PASS (global) # show ful | grep lldp
    set lldp-reception disable
    set lldp-transmission disable
```

In global, lldp settings are set to disable by default. Let us now take a look at the VDOM LLDP settings.

```
NSE4-PASS # config global
NSE4-PASS (global) # config system global
NSE4-PASS (settings) # show ful | grep lldp
    set lldp-reception global
    set lldp-transmission global
```

Chapter 2 | Layer Two Technologies

By default, the VDOM settings reference the global settings, but this can, of course, be modified. We have the below options under the VDOM settings.

```
NSE4-PASS (root) # config system settings
NSE4-PASS (settings) # set lldp-reception ?
enable     LLDP reception for this VDOM.
disable    LLDP reception for this VDOM.
global     Use the global LLDP reception configuration for this VDOM.
```

As you can see, we can enable or disable per VDOM, which will override the global setting configuration. Lastly, we can enable LLDP on a per-interface basis as well. Let's take a look at our LAG_1 interface we configured earlier:

```
NSE4-PASS (root) # conf sys int
NSE4-PASS (interface) # edit LAG_1
NSE4-PASS (LAG_1) # show ful | grep lldp
    set lldp-reception vdom
    set lldp-transmission enable
```

By default, the interface LLDP ingress settings reference the VDOM configuration and, by default, is explicitly enabled for egress LLDP traffic. You should know, explicit LLDP interface configuration overrides VDOM level configuration, and VDOM configuration overrides global settings.

You should have a good idea of what LLDP is and how FortiOS uses the protocol. Next, we look at how FortiGate uses LLDP to help create the Security Fabric!

Leverage LLDP to Simplify Security Fabric Negotiation

An awesome feature FortiGates have the Security Fabric, which allows them to "*see*" and connect to each other on the local network. By creating this connection, an avenue is opened to share topology information or security information that all devices participating in the Security Fabric can reference. LLDP is the tool that simplifies the creation of the Security Fabric and lets FortiGate essentially auto-discover each other.

With two FortiGates that share a local network segment and each interface facing the shared segment has LLDP enabled for receive and transmission. The downstream FortiGate receives a GUI pop-up informing the administrator they can connect to an upstream Fortigate, which provides the IP address. All of this happens just because two FortiGates have LLDP enabled. To accept a Security Fabric join request, goto Security Fabric > Settings, which finalizes the configuration. This wraps up the LLDP sections, moving on to VLANs and VLAN interfaces!

Chapter 2 | Layer Two Technologies

VLAN Layer-3 Interface

A VLAN interface is a virtual interface (or logical) on FortiGate. So before we dive into the details of the VLAN interface, you should know there are many types of virtual interfaces that FortiGate can have. From a logic standpoint, we can create policies, add routing statements, configure interface settings, or configure services like DHCP on virtual interfaces just like we can on any physical interface in FortiOS NAT Mode. One of the most popular virtual interfaces that are used is VLANs.

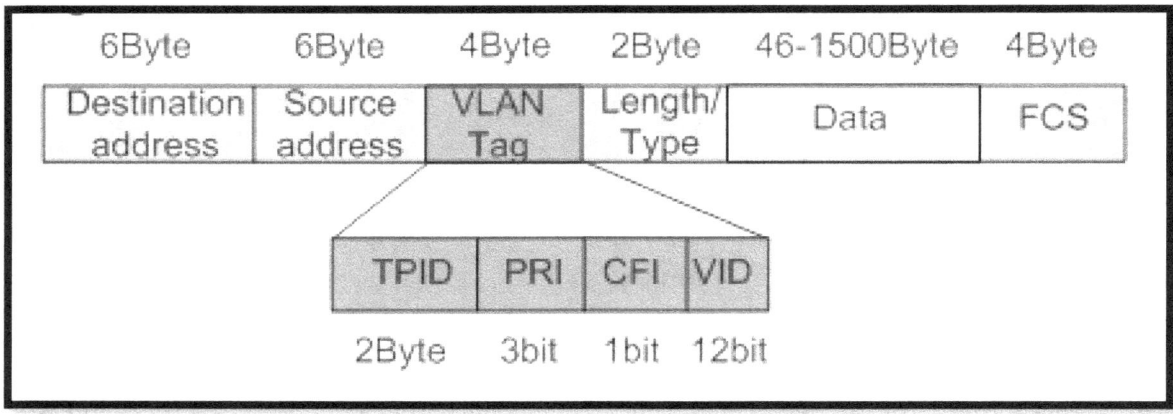

Virtual Local Area Networks (VLANs) Overview

An 802.1q VLAN Tag contains a VLAN ID, which is a 12-bit tag that is inserted into the Ethernet frame header used to logically separate layer-2 environments. The EtherType of an 802.1q frame is 0x8100. The 12 bit VLAN ID provides a theoretical total of 4096 VLANs on a single physical interface. VLAN Interfaces in NAT Mode essentially allows us to separate layer-2 broadcast domains, which gives us potentially a better security posture and better network performance. Each VLAN should be giving its own IP subnet in most cases. There are cases where we stack different VLANs on the same physical interface that all have the same subnet, but this requires VDOMs or subnet overlap to be enabled.

In general, on a layer-2 switch, we can assign physical ports to a certain VLAN by configuring it to be an Access port. Any traffic inbound to this port is given a VLAN ID, you can think of this as a pass to the local network, and this traffic can only be forwarded out other Access ports configured with the same VLAN ID or across a Trunk port that allows that particular VLAN. A Trunk port is a type of port that actively inserts the VLAN tag into an Ethernet frame before sending it onto the wire. The VLAN ID given to a frame depends on which port that frame originally ingressed. Meaning, if the frame ingressed an Access port configured for VLAN 50, then the Trunk port would need to allow VLAN 50 across it. If it does, then the switch would send the frame down the Trunk port with VLAN-ID of 50. Note that un-marked

Chapter 2 | Layer Two Technologies

frames (no VLAN tag) are considered to be apart of Native VLAN. VLANs give us much control over layer-2 networks by providing tools to segregate the network logically.

By default, network devices using VLANs on a layer-2 switch cannot talk to one another. It is required to introduce a router or layer-3 device to bridge this communication between different VLANs. This is where our NAT Mode FortiGate comes into play. On FortiGate, we configure its internal LAN interface to have stacked VLAN interfaces. This simply means we have more than one VLAN layer-3 interface on a single physical interface. When I say VLAN layer-3 interface, this means we can assign the logical VLAN interface an IP address and subnet mask, which respond to ARP requests. Therefore, when FortiGate does a route lookup on a packet and if it matches a VLAN subnet, it will then tag the frame with the associated VLAN ID before sending it out the physical interface. Once the switch receives this tagged frame on its trunk port, it then looks at its configured Access ports and sees if there is a matching VLAN ID for the ingress frame and, if so, will forward the frame out the port.

Creating VLAN Interface

Next, we create a VLAN interface on FortiGate! Let us jump into the CLI and navigate to our interfaces. In this example, we use the physical internal4 interface.

```
NSE4-PASS # config vdom
NSE4-PASS (vdom) # edit root
current vf=root:0
NSE4-PASS (root) # config system interface
NSE4-PASS (interface) # edit internal4
NSE4-PASS (internal4) # show
config system interface
    edit "internal4"
        set vdom "root"
        set type physical
        set snmp-index 44
    next
end
```

Now we can see our default attributes for our internal4 physical interface. It is in the root VDOM, and its type is physical and snmp-index 44. Our goal is to configure VLAN interface 150 with IP address and subnet mask of 10.159.57.1/24 and give it PING and SSH access.

```
NSE4-PASS (interface) #    edit "New-VLAN-150"
new entry 'New-VLAN-150' added
NSE4-PASS (New-VLAN-150) #set vdom "root"
NSE4-PASS (New-VLAN-150) #set ip 10.159.57.1 255.255.255.0
```

Chapter 2 | Layer Two Technologies

```
NSE4-PASS (New-VLAN-150) #set allowaccess ping ssh
NSE4-PASS (New-VLAN-150) #set device-identification enable
NSE4-PASS (New-VLAN-150) #set role lan
NSE4-PASS (New-VLAN-150) #set snmp-index 46
NSE4-PASS (New-VLAN-150) #set interface "internal4"
NSE4-PASS (New-VLAN-150) # set vlanid 150
NSE4-PASS (New-VLAN-150) # show
config system interface
    edit "New-VLAN-150"
        set vdom "root"
        set ip 10.159.57.1 255.255.255.0
        set allowaccess ping ssh
        set device-identification enable
        set role lan
        set snmp-index 46
        set interface "internal4"
        set vlanid 150
    next
end
NSE4-PASS (New-VLAN-150) # next
```

That's it! We have just created a brand new VLAN interface named New-VLAN-150. If you look at the settings here, you can see we had to reference which interface we wanted to stack this VLAN interface onto, specify our VLAN ID, and provide an IP address and subnet mask. Also, you might notice we had to specific our VDOM, which is root. We can map this VLAN interface to any VDOM on the device. This is useful in multitenant environments like MSSPs. Before moving on to our next section, take a look at our VLAN New-VLAN-150 in Image 2.5. You could have just as easily performed this in the GUI via Network->Interfaces->Create New-> Type VLAN.

Chapter 2 | Layer Two Technologies

Image 2.5 – VLAN Interface

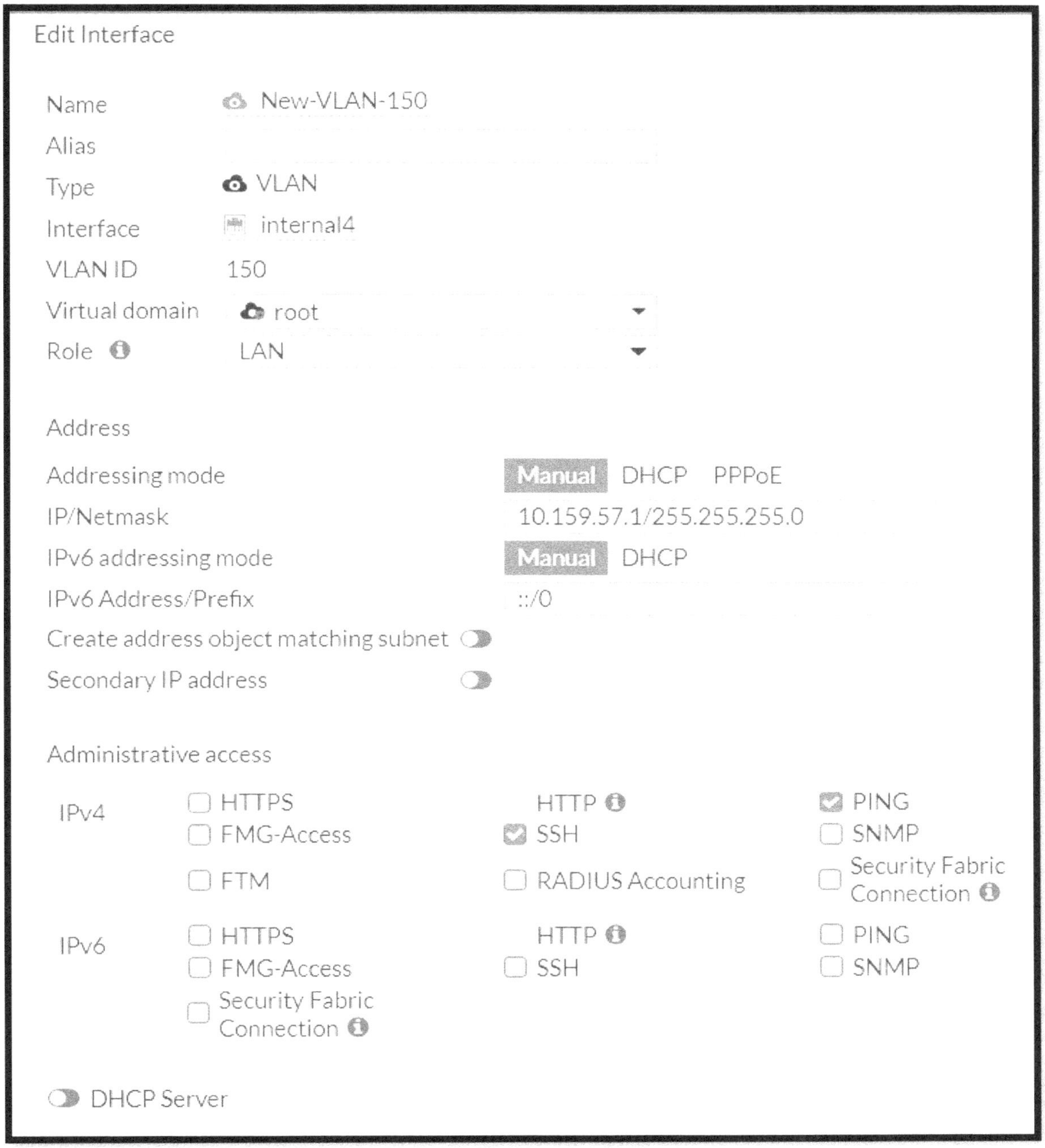

```
Edit Interface

  Name              New-VLAN-150
  Alias
  Type              VLAN
  Interface         internal4
  VLAN ID           150
  Virtual domain    root
  Role              LAN

  Address
  Addressing mode          Manual   DHCP   PPPoE
  IP/Netmask               10.159.57.1/255.255.255.0
  IPv6 addressing mode     Manual   DHCP
  IPv6 Address/Prefix      ::/0
  Create address object matching subnet
  Secondary IP address

  Administrative access
         ☐ HTTPS              HTTP            ☑ PING
  IPv4   ☐ FMG-Access         ☑ SSH           ☐ SNMP
         ☐ FTM                ☐ RADIUS Accounting   ☐ Security Fabric Connection

         ☐ HTTPS              HTTP            ☐ PING
  IPv6   ☐ FMG-Access         ☐ SSH           ☐ SNMP
         ☐ Security Fabric Connection

  ◯ DHCP Server
```

At the bottom of *Image 2.5*, you see we can configure a DHCP server for this VLAN as well, and have access to many other general interface settings. Now that we have created our layer-3 VLAN interface, I want to go over how to create firewall policies between VLANs!

Chapter 2 | *Layer Two Technologies*

Create Policy Between VLANs

I will create another VLAN named OUT-VLAN-160 stacked on the internal4 to be used in our firewall policy. This time I'm going to use the GUI to configure a firewall policy. Navigate to Policy & Objects > IPv4 Policy > Create New. You should see the below page, *image 2.6*.

Take a moment to analyze the firewall policy in Image 2.6.

Image 2.6 – IPv4 Firewall Policy

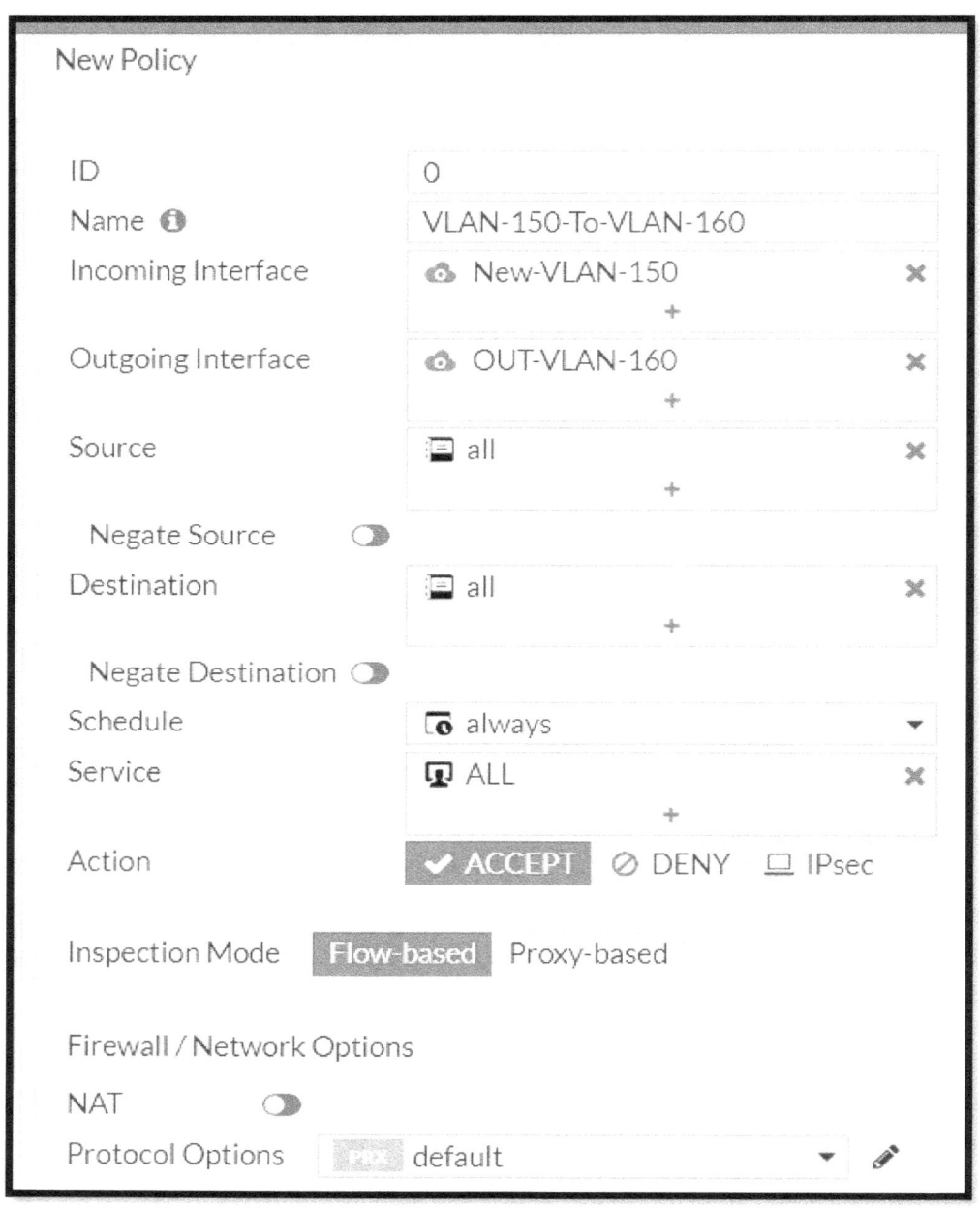

Chapter 2 | Layer Two Technologies

I specified policy 0, so it would use the next available policy ID. I configured to allow New-VLAN-150 VLAN Interface to communicate with OUT-VLAN-160 VLAN interface. I said I want any source and any destination IP with any service to be allowed, always in this firewall policy. I also disabled NAT, which is enabled by default. This policy only allows communication sourced from VLAN 150 going to VLAN 160. This policy does not allow traffic to source from VLAN 160 to communicate with devices on VLAN 150. Lastly, here, we look at this policy in the CLI. Let's find our policy.

```
NSE4-PASS (root) # conf firewall policy
NSE4-PASS (policy) # show | grep OUT-VLAN-160 -f
config firewall policy
    edit 87
        set name "VLAN-150-To-VLAN-160"
        set uuid 138c9c5c-3893-51ea-baf5-014fc9b2ada4
        set srcintf "New-VLAN-150"
        set dstintf "OUT-VLAN-160" <---
        set srcaddr "all"
        set dstaddr "all"
        set action accept
        set schedule "always"
        set service "ALL"
    next
end
```

We go over firewall policies in heavy details in a later chapter, I just wanted to show how easy it is to reference a VLAN interface in a firewall policy and given an overview of this process. That covers our layer-3 VLAN interfaces. You should now have a good idea of how VLAN interfaces work on FortiGate and how to configure them.

VLAN Forward Setting

In NAT Mode, by default, VLANs stacked on the same physical interface will not forward ARP traffic to all other VLANs. The command that controls this is under the physical interface level configuration:

```
(wan1) # show ful | grep vlan
        set vlanforward disable
```

With vlanfoward disable, each VLAN on the physical interface can only send traffic within its same VLAN. This prevents any cross-talk between VLANs and ARP. If vlanforward is enabled, then VLAN traffic is forward between all VLANs that share a single interface.

Chapter 2 | Layer Two Technologies

LLDP-MED Voice VLAN Auto-Assignment

The next item we are going to discuss is LLDP-MED. The first question to ask is, what is LLDP-MED? Well, LLDP-Med is an extension of LLDP 802.1AB, and it is published by the Telecommunications Industry Association (TIA). The *Med* stands for Media Endpoint Devices. The protocol was designed to support VOIP devices and the discovery of these devices like softphone or IP phones. Next question, why do we need it? We need it to dynamically discover voice devices or applications and map them to their own VLAN, a Voice VLAN! This is important so we can better manage our VoIP related traffic. This protocol saves the administrator the burden of manually having to do this. So let's talk about the frame structure for LLDP-MED. The extension includes Type-Length-Value fields so to store custom variables about different devices or applications. The LLDP-MED TLVs extension fields include:

- LLDP-MED Capabilities
  - This field lets endpoints see the capabilities of the Fortigate
- Network Policy
  - Allows both the FortiGate and endpoints to advertise VLAN configuration and associated layer-2 and layer-3 attributes. The endpoint can contact FortiGate and obtain its VLAN number then starting its call control SIP communication.
- Power Management
  - Allows FortiGate and endpoints to provide power information for like PoE connections.
- Inventory Management
  - Allows endpoint to transmit details about its self like firmware, serial number, manufacturer, model or hardware attributes
- Location
  - Lets FortiGate provides physical location information to an IP phone, for example.
    - Civic location information: This TLV can send and postal information like a street address
    - ELIN Location Information: which is the location of a call which is determined by the Emergency Location Identifier number ELIN used by the public safety answering point (PSAP)

The FortiGate sends out regular LLDP frames to the layer-2 network, and any VOIP devices running LLDP-MED responds with its attributes. Once FortiGate receives this response frame, FortiGate identifies the device or application as VoIP or phone-related and proceeds to give it its very own VLAN to communicate on!

Chapter 2 | Layer Two Technologies

Voice VLAN Auto-Assignment Configuration

Now that we know a little bit about LLDP-MED and how it works, next, I show you how we can configure this feature on FortiGate. In this example, I use our prior VLAN interface configuration, VLAN 150, and make this a voice VLAN for IP phone that connects to this LAN.

The first thing we need to do is add a DHCP server to VLAN Interface New-VLAN-150. We can do this in the CLI via:

```
config system dhcp server
    edit 7
        set forticlient-on-net-status disable
        set dns-service default
        set default-gateway 10.159.57.1
        set netmask 255.255.255.0
        set interface "New-VLAN-150"
        config ip-range
            edit 1
                set start-ip 10.159.57.2
                set end-ip 10.159.57.254
            next
        end
    next
end
```

Next, we need to create our LLDP network-policy object in the CLI. This is used to map a device or application to a certain VLAN using LLDP-MED:

```
config system lldp network-policy
edit "1"
config voice
set status enable
set tag dot1q
set vlan 150
end
next
end
```

LLDP-MED now sends TLV variables of dot1q and vlan-id 150 to the voice device or application, but we still need to map this network-policy object to the physical interface where the VLAN interface is configured, which is internal4. We also need to double-check that lldp reception and transmission settings are enabled.

```
config system interface
    edit "internal4"
        set vdom "root"
```

Chapter 2 | *Layer Two Technologies*

```
        set type physical
        set lldp-reception enable
        set lldp-transmission enable
        set lldp-network-policy "1"
        set snmp-index 44
    next
end
```
We used the command 'set lldp-network-policy "1"' to map our network-policy object to the physical interfaces. Now LLDP uses this information to tell VoIP devices or applications on LAN running LLDP-MED what VLAN they should be using. We also made sure this interface is indeed sending and receiving LLDP communication, which it is. That's it! Now voice traffic should use VLAN 150. Next, if we wanted to, we could prioritize this VLAN using a traffic shaper or QoS!

Virtual Wire Pairing

The last section to cover for layer-2 NAT mode is *Virtual Wire Pairing*. This feature makes a lot of sense in the right situation. This feature takes two interfaces and bounds them together to create an exclusively dedicated transit path between the inside LAN and the outside environment. Meaning, we could take port1 and port2 and create a Virtual Wire Pairing that would say any traffic ingress to port1 can only egress port2, and traffic that ingresses port2 can only egress port2. When this process happens within a Virtual Wire Pairing, if traffic is approved by FortiGates security policies, there is no route lookup; there are no MAC address table lookups either because there is only one choice where to send the traffic. You can think of this as a dedicated virtual switch circuit pass through or an ad-hoc transparent mode interface pairings.

There is a couple of reasons to do this. Firstly, we could use this feature to extend a broadcast domain were rebuilding the IP schema is not feasible. Also, there are certain situations where MAC addresses change a lot, which causes havoc for stateful firewalls. For example, in server farms with load balancing involved or VRRP, we could see the ingress MAC address being different from the egress MAC address frame for a related session. To overcome this issue, we can use Virtual Wire Pairing because there is no MAC table lookup because we know traffic will be symmetric, frames come in one interface, and out there other and vice versa.

Chapter 2 | Layer Two Technologies

You should note that once two interfaces are bonded together into a Virtual Wire Pairing, no other interface on FortiGate can communicate with the Virtual Wire Pairing because it's a dedicated path in the network. Also, within Virtual Wair Pairing, policies can only be created between interfaces between the two interfaces. Also, know we can even use LAG or Redundant interface types within a Virtual Wire Pairing.

> *Do not implement Virtual Wire Pairing without out-of-band management. You will loose access to your FortiGate. All traffic is forwarded to the paired interface.*

Virtual Wire Pairing Configuration

To create a Virtual Wire Pairing on FortiGate is very simple. Let's navigate to our CLI object 'virtual-wire-pair:

```
config system virtual-wire-pair
    edit "VW_Pair_Int"
        set member "internal5" "internal6"
        set wildcard-vlan disable
    next
end
```

Chapter 2 | Layer Two Technologies

Here we created a Virtual Wire Pairing named VW_Pair_Int for interface internal5 and internal6. By default, the Virtual Wire Pairing allows all VLANs. If wildcard-vlan is enabled, this is essentially a VLAN white list or an allowed range. Once enabled, we are given an option to allow VLANs through the virtual-wire-pair itself, or we can explicitly filter within a firewall policy. To configure this for all traffic on the pair, in general, we would configure the following settings:

Image 2.7 – Virtual Wire Pairing Example

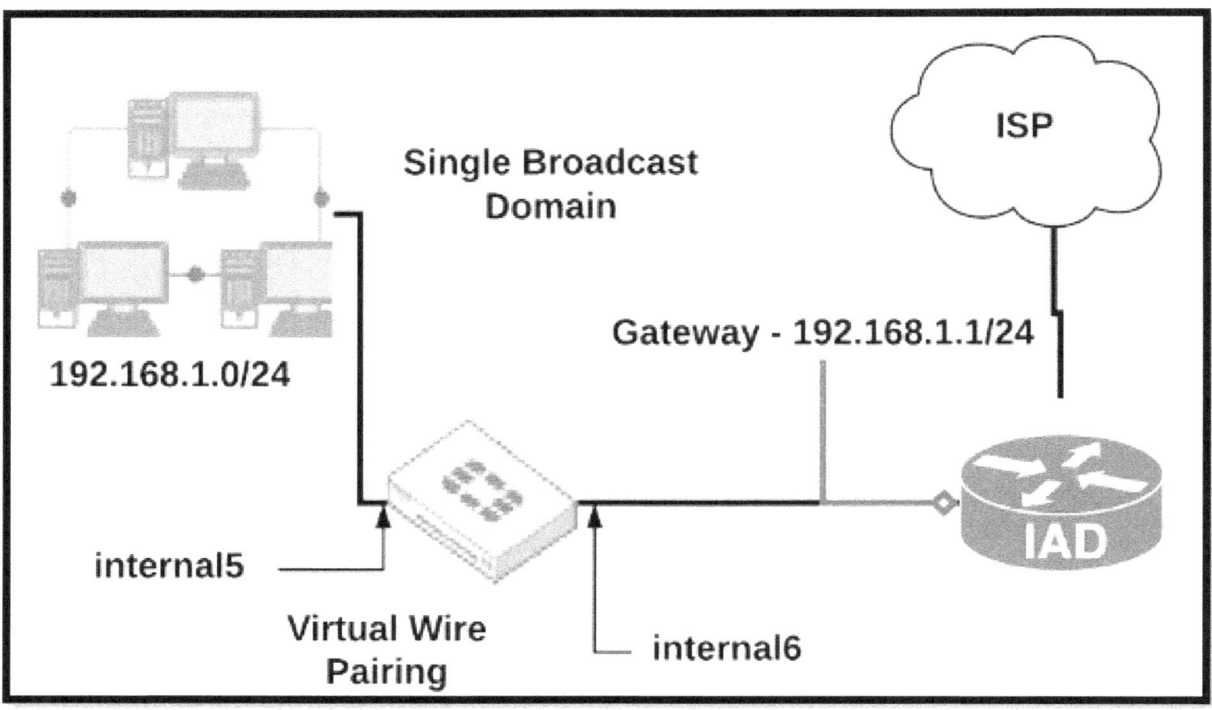

```
config system virtual-wire-pair
edit "VW_Pair_Int"
set wildcard-vlan enable
set vlan-filter 10-20
end
```

In this example, only VLANs 10 through 20 are allowed to pass on the Virtual Wire Pairing. Lastly, we would need to configure a policy to allow all bi-directional traffic:

```
config firewall policy
    edit 88
        set name "Any-Any"
```

Chapter 2 | *Layer Two Technologies*

```
            set uuid 3e2cfece-3948-51ea-3a0a-906c2d654983
            set srcintf "internal5" "internal6"
            set dstintf "internal5" "internal6"
            set srcaddr "all"
            set dstaddr "all"
            set action accept
            set schedule "always"
            set service "ALL"
    next
end
```

Take a moment to analyze this policy.

We must specify both interfaces in source and destination interface fields to allow everything on this Virtual Wire Pairing. Also, we must allow all services and always. Lastly, we could easily stack multiple policies here to be more restrictive to meet network requirements, just place the more restrictive policies above this one.

Virtual Extensible LAN (VXLAN)

The last topic I am going to cover in NAT Mode is VXLAN. VXLAN is outlined in RFC 7348. VXLAN is a protocol used to encapsulate a regular Ethernet frame within a layer-3 IP packet. The encapsulated Ethernet frame is also given a transport protocol of UDP that uses port 4789, see Image 2.7. below.

Image 2.7.1 – VXLAN Frame

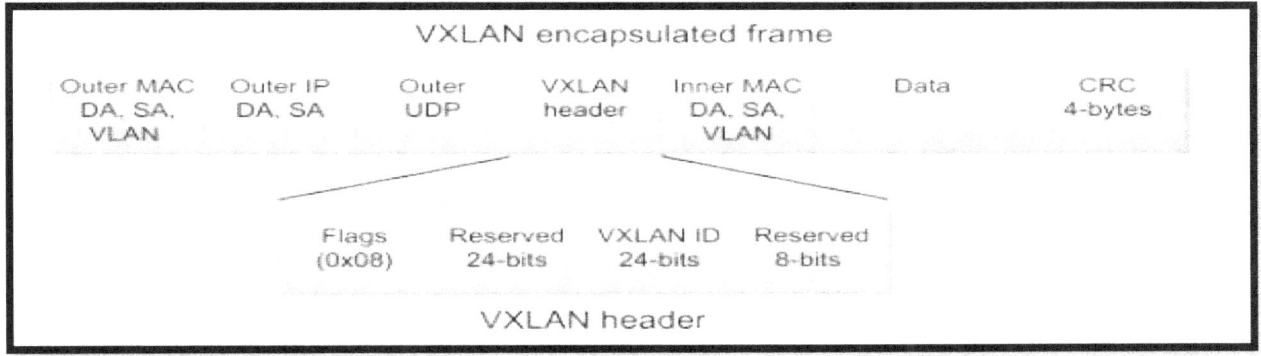

The reason for the creation of the VXLAN standard was to address the limitation of the 802.1Q 12-bit VLAN ID field, which limits networks to 4094 VLANs per interface. VXLAN addresses this limitation by using a 24-bit identifier field, which theoretically allows for over16 million VXLANs. Devices that terminate or encapsulate Ethernet frames with VXLAN standards is called a VXLAN Tunnel Endpoint (VTEP). A VTEP can be a virtual interface or a physical interface. Here is a CLI example:

Chapter 2 | Layer Two Technologies

```
NSE4-PASS (VXLAN-1) # show ful
config system vxlan
    edit "VXLAN-1"
        set interface "wan1"
        set vni 200
        set ip-version ipv4-unicast
        set dstport 4789
        set remote-ip "10.52.123.2"
    next
end
```

In this example, wan1 is the VTEP using a VXLAN ID of 200 and connecting to remote VTEP at 10.52.123.2. Lastly, diagnostic can be performing via CLI using the below commands:

```
NSE4-PASS (root) # diagnose sys vxlan fdb
list    Display VXLAN forwarding DB.
stat    Display VXLAN forwarding DB statistics.
```

NAT Mode Layer-2 Summary

That covers it for NSE4 layer-2 NAT Mode! We went over many layer-2 protocols that you will interact with when managing FortiGate in NAT Mode and are on the NSE4 exam. We analyzed the physical interface layer-2 output. We touched on Ethernet, ARP, Spanning Tree Protocol, LACP, LLDP, LLDP-MED, VLANs, and Virtual Wire Pairing. For these technologies, I provided an overview of how they work and how to implement them with FortiGate. There is much more to know, but this section provides you a solid foundation to build from and the tools you need to pass your NSE4 Exam. In our next section, we focus on FortiGate Transparent Mode!

Transparent Mode at Layer-2

It's Transparent (TP) Mode time! In the 2nd half of this chapter, we cover some major features of TP FortiGate. The NSE4 exam covers mostly NAT Mode topics, but you are expected to know some of the basic features of TP Mode as well.

In this section, I'm going to go over how to provision a new TP FortiGate in a network and step through the conversion process from NAT Mode. I'm going to go through frame handing and MAC learning and forwarding. I cover VLAN trunking. I also cover forwarding domains, which are most likely a new concept to you.

Transparent Mode Overview

I touched on TP Mode in chapter one, but here is a refresher on what it is. TP Mode FortiGate is built to forward traffic based on Ethernet frame header information and, more specifically, Ethernet II Mac addresses. FortiGate TP does not forward

Chapter 2 | Layer Two Technologies

communication base on packet IP address header information via route lookups. TP uses something called a Forwarding Database (FDB), and each VDOM has one of these tables. I'll be going over this more later on.

The reason to use TP Mode FortiGate is within a network where the IP addressing scheme cannot be modified, but security inspection on traffic is required. TP Mode does not respond to ARP requests on the network except for its management IP address. Note, there cannot be IP addresses assigned to the physical interface on a TP Mode FortiGate. Also note, even though FortiGate is steering traffic based on layer-2 information, it does not mean TP FortiGate is a layer-2 device only. TP Mode, you can still do full layer-7 application UTM security inspection and have most features available that you would find in NAT Mode.

Transparent Mode Provisioning

Since we know some about how TP Mode operates, let us go ahead and convert our NAT Mode FortiGate to TP Mode. I'm going to move over to my 60D lab FortiGate change it to TP Mode via CLI:

```
NSE4-LAB-60D # conf sys settings
NSE4-LAB-60D (settings) # set opmode transparent
NSE4-LAB-60D (settings) # set manageip 10.52.53.2
NSE4-LAB-60D (settings) # set gateway 10.52.53.1
path=system, objname=settings, size=464, sz_attr=1
This operation might change settings of vap interfaces, virtual switches, software switch interfaces, managed switches, ppp vdom-link, loopback interfaces, interface auto-ipsec allowaccess and wccp-cache-engine.
Do you want to continue? (y/n)y
```

This logs you out, but you should be able to log back in fairly quickly if your IP and gateway information is correct. You might be wondering now how you manage access or restrict access to FortiGate. It is the same way as NAT mode. Management protocol access is dependent on the 'allowaccess' setting under the physical ingress interface.

What we have just configured is In-Band Management. Meaning, our management traffic must transverse the same path as all other data communication. So if the network loses access to the local gateway, we will be unable to manage this device if that is our only management method.

In this configuration, we must explicitly set the opmode to transparent, and then we are required to provide a manageip value and a gateway value. Once these variables are filled, then FortiOS accepts the configuration change. This might take a few moments for FortiGate to reconfigure itself for Transparent Mode operation. After it

Chapter 2 | *Layer Two Technologies*

completes the transition, the FortiGate packet steering mechanism has changed from IP header information to Ethernet header information. Also, we have lost the ability to configure IP addresses on physical and logical interfaces.

Transparent Mode Networking

The FortiOS Transparent Mode section is focused on how Ethernet frames are handled by TP Mode FortiGate. I'm going to provide a refresher on layer-2 MAC learning and then jump into the different types of MAC addresses and how they are forwarded within TP FortiGate. Let's get started!

Layer-2 MAC learning Overview

Now that we have our FortiGate in TP Mode configured, let us review how MAC addresses are learned and how frames are forwarded.

 The first thing to discuss is MAC learning. Since TP Mode forwards Ethernet frames using the Forwarding Database (FDB), then how is it populated??...Step a little closer, and I'll tell you...*whispering* the source MAC address of Ethernet frames.

Let's walk through a scenario together; if the FDB is empty on TP FortiGate when it receives its first Ethernet frame, then it is most likely going to be a broadcast frame, which means the destination MAC is all F's -> FFFF:FFFF:FFFF:FFFF which simply represents all bits turned on in hexadecimal. This tells TP FortiGate, the sender of this frame has no idea how to get to where it wants to go from a layer-2 perspective. Also, this is mostly an ARP request since ARP is helpful mapping IP addresses to MAC addresses and all... Let's say it is an ARP request.

Once the ingress Frame is fully buffered into memory, FortiOS parses the source MAC address from the Ethernet header information. Next, this source MAC address is mapped to the port in which the frame had just entered. For example, If the source MAC is AA:BB:CC:DD:EE:FF and the inbound port was port1, then the first FDB dynamic MAC entry will be something like *Table 2.1*.

Table 2.1 – Forwarding Database Port to MAC Mapping Example

Port Name	MAC Address
Port1	AA:BB:CC:DD:EE:FF

Note, this is not exactly what the FortiGate FDB looks like on FortiOS, but this is the general idea behind it. Next, FortiGate floods the frame to every active port within its forwarding domain, since it is an ARP broadcast. Now since we have a MAC entry in the FDB, if there is a return frame replying to AA:BB:CC:DD:EE:FF ARP request

Chapter 2 | Layer Two Technologies

with an ARP reply, then once the frame is buffered in memory, FortiGate is going to perform two major functions. The first being, parse the source MAC address of the return frame and add the source MAC to an interface mapping within its FDB. Secondly, FortiGate is going to parse the destination MAC address out of the Ethernet header (AA:BB:CC:DD:EE:FF) and compare that with its active entries within its FDB. And guess what happens if FortiGate finds a match? It will then transmit the frame down the related mapped interfaces, and in our case here, it is Port1. This is basic TP Mode Ethernet frame handling and FDB management.

By default, in TP Mode, MAC to port mappings within the FDB has a lifetime of 300 seconds, which is 5 minutes. Once aged out, FortiGate drops the entry and relearns it if needed; this is how FortiGate keeps the most up-to-date information for its MAC to Port mappings.

Transparent Mode Bridge Forwarding Table Overview

Now that we have had a refresher on how to frame forwarding and MAC learning works within TP FortiGate. Next, we reviews the actual FDB for the root VDOM. To do this, we navigate to the CLI and run the below command to present this information.

```
NSE4-LAB-60D # diagnose netlink brctl name host root.b
show bridge control interface root.b host.
fdb: size=2048, used=12, num=12, depth=1
Bridge root.b host table

port  no  device  devname    mac addr              ttl    attributes
 10    8          internal2  90:6c:ac:49:59:38      0     Local Static
 10    8          internal2  90:6c:ac:d4:1e:1f     15     Hit(15)
 11    9          internal3  90:6c:ac:49:59:39      0     Local Static
  5   10          internal4  90:6c:ac:49:59:3a      0     Local Static
  2    5          wan1       90:6c:ac:d4:1e:1d      0     Hit(0)
  6   11          internal5  90:6c:ac:49:59:3b      0     Local Static
  4   18          internal   90:6c:ac:49:59:34      0     Local Static
  7   12          internal6  90:6c:ac:49:59:3c      0     Local Static
  1    4          dmz        90:6c:ac:49:59:35      0     Local Static
  8   13          internal7  90:6c:ac:49:59:3d      0     Local Static
  2    5          wan1       90:6c:ac:49:59:36      0     Local Static
  3    6          wan2       90:6c:ac:49:59:37      0     Local Static
```

Take a moment to review this output and generate some questions you might have.

This output describes one Forwarding Database (FDB). Each VDOM has its own FDB. The first values I will point out are the devname and 'mac addr' columns. The

Chapter 2 | *Layer Two Technologies*

values held within these fields are where we can find the MAC addresses learned by FortiGate and what ports they are mapped to. For example, take a look at the below row:

```
10      8       internal2       90:6c:ac:d4:1e:1f       15      Hit(15)
```

We can tell that MAC 90:6c:ac:d4:1e:1f was learned on internal2 port, so in turn, this is our MAC to port mapping. If TP FortiGate receives this MAC within the destination field within an Ethernet frame, then it will, therefore, be forwarded out internal2. Next, take a look at the next column headers bolded below:

```
port no device  devname         mac addr                ttl
attributes
```

'device' value in this column is the interface index values held in FortiOS used for various operational functions and is simply a FortiOS interface attribute (an important one). To find this index value, run the following command:

```
# diagnose netlink interface list
..
f=wan1 family=00 type=1 index=5 mtu=1500 link=0 master=0
ref=28 state=start present fw_flags=0 flags=up broadcast run allmulti
multicast
..
```

Now go use your elite analytical skills and find the row that contains the wan1 interfaces and see if you can find the '5' value in the FDB output above. Next, look at 'devname'; this column contains the port name. Next, the value is 'ttl' and as I stated earlier, entries in the Forwarding Table will age out every 5 minutes so to keep the most up to date information about the network. This field tells how long the entry has been held within the FDB. Lastly, look at the 'attributes' column; this field could contain two different values, Hits or Local Static. Hits mean the MAC address was learned from a remote device on the LAN, and Local Static indicates the MAC address for the local interface on FortiGate itself.

Unicast MAC Frame Forwarding

Processing Ethernet frames with an explicit unicast source and destination MAC address defined, meaning not broadcast or multicast MAC, then FortiOS notes the ingress port of the Ethernet frame and performs a lookup for the destination MAC address to find the egress interface using the FDB. Once the interface pairing for the communication is defined, then Layer-3 and layer-4 header information are parsed out. FortiGate firstly takes the source and destination IP address and UDP/TCP destination port information and takes this information and attempts to

Chapter 2 | Layer Two Technologies

find an active session in the session table. If no session matches, then FortiOS then attempts to find a firewall transit policy to match starting from top to bottom.

Next, if a match is found and the action of Policy is to 'ACCEPT' then FortiOS isolates this traffic stream for security inspection, meaning if Security Profiles like Web Filter or IPS is referenced in the Policy, then these security modules are engaged which perform their own functions which could allow or deny traffic based on user criteria. If everything checks out with the security inspection, then the frame is forwarded with the original source and destination MAC address of the frame, and a session is created within the session table.

The session table is very important and is what makes FortiOS a stateful firewall. The session table stores active session information and keeps track of source and destination MAC addresses, IP addresses, and ports. The reason for this is to allow return traffic back through the FortiGate without having to define an explicit firewall policy, which is what stateless firewalls must do, which can get very complicated. We go over our session table thoroughly in our routing chapter but to show the session table on FortiGate, run the below command:

```
NSE4-LAB-60D # diagnose sys session list

session  info:  proto=6  proto_state=02  duration=9  expire=0  timeout=3600
flags=00000000 sockflag=00000000 sockport=0 av_idx=0 use=4
origin-shaper=
reply-shaper=
per_ip_shaper=
class_id=0 ha_id=0 policy_dir=0 tunnel=/ vlan_cos=255/255
state=local nds
statistic(bytes/packets/allow_err): org=60/1/0 reply=88/1/1 tuples=2
tx speed(Bps/kbps): 6/0 rx speed(Bps/kbps): 9/0
orgin->sink:   org    out->post,    reply    pre->in    dev=16->5/5->16
gwy=0.0.0.0/10.52.53.2
hook=out dir=org act=noop 10.52.53.2:19389->192.168.209.54:541(0.0.0.0:0)
hook=in dir=reply act=noop 192.168.209.54:541->10.52.53.2:19389(0.0.0.0:0)
pos/(before,after) 0/(0,0), 0/(0,0)
misc=0 policy_id=0 auth_info=0 chk_client_info=0 vd=0
serial=0002121f tos=ff/ff app_list=0 app=0 url_cat=0
rpdb_link_id = 00000000
dd_type=0 dd_mode=0
npu_state=00000000
no_ofld_reason:   local
```

Take a moment to analyze the above output and write down your questions. I hope I will answer all of them in the next chapter, but for now, you should understand the general operations of MAC learning and frame forwarding. Next, we are going to talk about a few exceptions and configuration options around layer-2 traffic.

Chapter 2 | Layer Two Technologies

ARP Broadcast Handling

By default, ARP broadcast frames are flooded out all ports except the ingress port without needing an explicit firewall policy to allow the traffic. ARP is the foundation for general layer-2 operations, and FortiOS must forward this protocol so to obtain general layer-2 communication between devices on LAN. The MAC learning process relies heavily on the source MAC address on ARP packets to populate the Forwarding Database. We can disable this functionality if required. To perform this configuration change, we would navigate to the ingress interface and find the setting arpforward and set it to disable. See the below example:

```
NSE4-LAB-60D (wan1) # show ful | grep arp
    set arpforward disable
```

The above configuration forces FortiGate to drop ARP broadcast. If you need to look for ARP packets on FortiGate, then you can run the sniffer debug command. Here is the command you would use:

```
NSE4-LAB-60D # diagnose sniffer packet any "ether proto 0x0806"
interfaces=[any]
filters=[ether proto 0x0806]
25.664230 arp who-has 10.52.53.254 tell 10.52.53.1
25.664313 arp who-has 10.52.53.254 tell 10.52.53.1
25.664447 arp reply 10.52.53.254 is-at 90:6c:ac:ee:1e:ff
25.664488 arp reply 10.52.53.254 is-at 90:6c:ac:ee:1e:ff
```

This is why it is good to know the EtherType for common protocols like ARP, which is 0x0806, so to easily debug traffic as needed.

Broadcast Frames Handling

Next, regarding Ethernet broadcast frames in general, meaning frames with EtherType's other than 0x0806 (which is ARP), FortiGate will drop these frames by default. If you wish to change this behavior, then you must specify this setting within the interface level configuration, which is broadcast-forward enable.

```
NSE4-LAB-60D (wan1) # show ful | grep broad
    set broadcast-forward disable
```

If we enable the broadcast-forward setting on the interface, then all Ethernet broadcast frames are forward out of every interface except the ingress interface within the forwarding domain without the need for a transit firewall Policy.

Chapter 2 | Layer Two Technologies

Multicast Frames Handling

Frames with destination multicast MAC addresses are not forwarded by default. Routing protocols are one such example that utilizes these MAC addresses or certain streaming media protocols. FortiGate allows for the configuration of multicast transit policies to explicitly allow this type of traffic to pass. Also note, multicast MAC addresses may be forwarded if the multicast-skip-policy setting is enabled. This setting can be found under VDOM settings via:

```
NSE4-LAB-60D (settings) # show ful | grep multicast
    set multicast-skip-policy disable
```

If this setting is enabled, then FortiGate forwards frames to all interfaces except the incoming interface within a single forwarding domain.

STP BPDU Handling

Bridge Protocol Data Unit (BPDU) frames are not forwarded through TP FortiGate by default. To forward these frames, then *stpforward* would need to be enabled on the interface level. We can do this in the CLI via:

```
NSE4-LAB-60D (wan1) # show ful | grep stp
      set stpforward disable
```

If enabled, then STP is flooded out all interfaces within the same forwarding domain except the ingress interface.

Non- Ethernet frames Handling

TP FortiGate mainly works with Ethernet II frame types. However, if a situation arises where other layer-2 protocols need to be forwarded through FortiGate, then we would need to explicitly allow this because, by default, FortiGate will drop these frames. The setting to enable is l2forward and again is on the interface level:

```
NSE4-LAB-60D (wan1) # show ful | grep l2
      set l2forward disable
```

Once this is enabled, this setting flood non-Ethernet II communication out all interfaces except the ingress interface within a single forwarding domain, and this would be required, for example, to forward LLDP frames.

Forwarding Domains

All you folks coming from a Cisco background are most likely going to be shocked by this feature. TP Mode FortiGate has reshaped the idea around broadcast domains. If

Chapter 2 | Layer Two Technologies

you learned Cisco before Fortinet technologies like me, then you know we separate broadcast domains by implementing VLANs, right? Well, that is not true when working with TP FortiGate. Broadcast domains are define using forwarding domains with TP Mode. Meaning, we could have many different VLANs, and physical portals share one broadcast domain as long as they are all a part of the same forwarding domain. By default, all interfaces on TP FortiGate share the forwarding domain '0'. We can see this setting on the interface level.

```
NSE4-LAB-60D (wan1) # show ful | grep forward-domain
        set forward-domain 0
```

All Forwarding Domain values within a VDOM must be unique. This is because every VDOM has a single bridge forwarding database. By creating separate Forwarding Domains and mapping VLANs within the Forwarding Domain, we can accomplish learning the same MAC address in different VLANs, and this is called Inner VLAN Learning (IVL). Let's go ahead and place our internal2 and wan1 interface within Forwarding Domain 100.

```
NSE4-LAB-60D # config system interface
NSE4-LAB-60D (interface) # edit wan1
NSE4-LAB-60D (wan1) # set forward-domain 100
NSE4-LAB-60D (wan1) # next
NSE4-LAB-60D (interface) # edit internal2
NSE4-LAB-60D (internal2) # set forward-domain 100
NSE4-LAB-60D (internal2) # end
```

Now only devices attached to wan1 and internal2 can communicate with one another because they are within forwarding domain 100. Also, we can only create firewall policies between interfaces that share the same forwarding domain. An error is given if you attempt to set interfaces from different forwarding domains. *Image 2.8* is the error present if attempted.

Image 2.8 – Forwarding Domain Policy Error

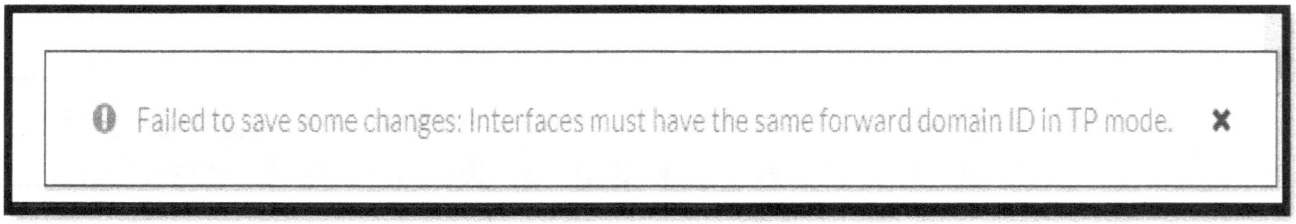

> ❶ Failed to save some changes: Interfaces must have the same forward domain ID in TP mode.   ✕

In Summary, Forwarding Domain is the feature that restricts layer-2 to a logical LAN within FortiGate TP Mode. We work more with forwarding domains in the next section when working with VLANs.

Chapter 2 | Layer Two Technologies

VLANs in Transparent Mode

In this section, we are going over VLAN handling and will be discussing things like trunking, VLANs within Forwarding Domains, VLAN forwarding, and VLAN translation.

VLAN Access and Trunking

A VLAN trunk interface is a physical interface with stacked VLANs associated with it. Meaning, VLAN tagged Ethernet frames are allowed to be received and sent on the physical interface. On TP FortiGate, to create a layer-2 trunk interface, we must define a layer-2 VLAN interface and associate it with the physical interface. This is similar to the same method we used to define layer-3 VLAN interfaces in NAT Mode, but in TP Mode, we do not define an IP address. For layer-2 VLAN interfaces, it is required to associate the VLAN to a Forwarding Domain.

To help explain this concept better, I will be going through a configuration example using an Access port and a VLAN Trunk on TP FortiGate. Remember, an Access port is a physical interface that receives untagged VLAN frames (regular Ethernet frames) and associates the traffic with a particular VLAN, and trunk sends and receives tagged frames. To accomplish this task, we utilize the Forwarding Domain feature and associate the two.

Image 2.9 - Forwarding Domain

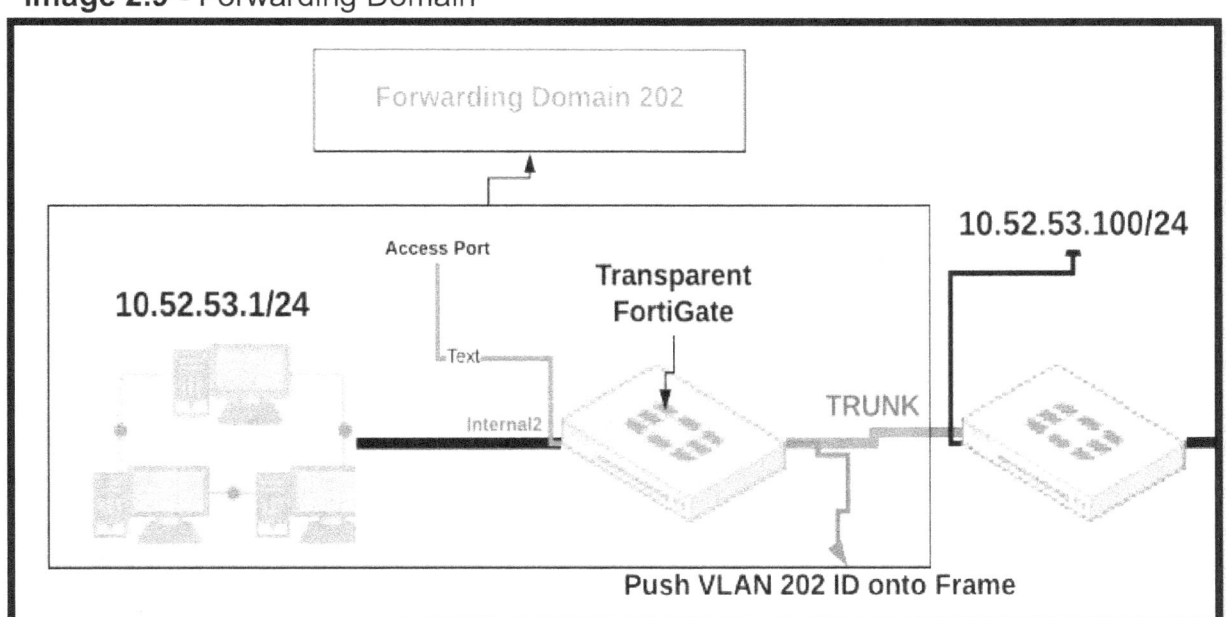

Take a moment to review *Image 2.9*.

We are going to set up a small lab outlined in Image 2.9 to demonstrate these features. In the lab, the source IP is 10.52.53.1/24, which is acting as our client PC

Chapter 2 | Layer Two Technologies

machine, and the destination IP is 10.52.53.100/24, which is the gateway for the LAN. We are testing PING traffic through a TP FortiGate to the LAN gateway.

The first step is to create a VLAN interface. Next, we configure the 202 Forwarding Domain to encompass interface internal2 (Access Port) and the VLAN interface on the trunk port. Finally, we configure firewall policies to allow traffic from the access port to the trunk port.

Internal2 interface is the Access Port that excepts untagged traffic, and wan1 is the Trunk port where a VLAN ID is inserted into Ethernet frames before transmitting them across the wire. The VLAN Interface on wan1 is Trunk_VLAN_202. Remember, the VLAN interface is the CLI object that performs the tagging function of egress frames and the accepting of ingress frames.

Both the Access port and VLAN interface exclusively share the Forwarding Domain 202. Note, Forwarding Domains restrict MAC learning between certain interfaces and creates separate broadcast domains. VLANs do not create separate layer-2 broadcast domains within TP Mode FortiGate. It is best practice to keep related VLAN objects and the Forwarding Domain the same value, and this is so the configuration is easy to read and troubleshoot if needed. Next, we are going to start the configuration outlined in *Image 2.9* by navigating to the CLI. The first thing to configure is our VLAN interface Trunk_VLAN_202 on the wan1.

```
NSE4-LAB-60D (Trunk_VLAN_202) # show
config system interface
    edit "Trunk_VLAN_202"
        set vdom "root"
        set forward-domain 202
        set device-identification enable
        set role lan
        set snmp-index 5
        set interface "wan1"
        set vlanid 202
```

Image 2.10 – Layer-2 VLAN Interface

Here is what this layer-2 VLAN interface looks like in the GUI, *Image 2.10*. As you can see, the layer-2 VLAN interface is virtually stacked on top of the wan1 interface, which now makes it a Trunk port. Let's review some of these values under the Trunk_VLAN_202 interface. We set the Forwarding Domain to be 202 by using

Chapter 2 | Layer Two Technologies

the forward-domain command under the interface level settings. Next, we specified the physical interface to be wan1 and, lastly, specified the vlanid to be 202. This means wan1 accepts ingress VLAN frames with VLAN ID 202. Also, wan1 inserts VLAN ID 202 into the frame if the destination MAC address matches an entry in the MAC Forwarding Database within the Forwarding Domain 202 that egress wan1.

Next, we place interface internal2 within the Forwarding Domain as VLAN interface Trunk_VLAN_202. This is, so machines on LAN connected to internal2 can communicate only over VLAN 202 on wan1 Trunk port.

```
config system interface
    edit "internal2"
        set vdom "root"
        set allowaccess ping
        set type physical
        set forward-domain 202
        set snmp-index 13
    next
end
```

Now, these two interfaces are logically bounded together and allows transit traffic because they now share the same Forwarding Database and broadcast domain. Next, we must configure firewall policies to allow bi-directional traffic to flow between VLAN interface Trunk_VLAN_202 and physical interface internal2. Remember, FortiGate is mainly a firewall but acting as a switch, policies are always required.

```
config firewall policy
    edit 1
        set name "internal2-wan2-vlan202"
        set srcintf "internal2"
        set dstintf "Trunk_VLAN_202"
        set srcaddr "all"
        set dstaddr "all"
        set action accept
        set schedule "always"
        set service "ALL"
        set fsso disable
    next
    edit 2
        set srcintf "Trunk_VLAN_202"
        set dstintf "internal2"
        set srcaddr "all"
        set dstaddr "all"
        set action accept
        set schedule "always"
```

Chapter 2 | *Layer Two Technologies*

```
            set service "ALL"
            set fsso disable
            set comments "Reverse of internal2-wan2-vlan202"
    next
end
```

Lastly, we perform a Proof of Concert (PoC) to be sure that traffic ingress to internal2 egresses Trunk_VLAN_202 when 10.52.53.1 issues PING to 10.52.53.100. To do this, we use a special command set:

```
#diagnose debug reset
#diagnose debug enable
#diagnose debug flow filter addr 10.52.53.100
#diagnose debug flow trace start 200
```

This command set, when issued on the CLI, will present all traffic destined for IP 10.52.53.100, which is the gateway in our case. Next, let's go through the debug output:

```
..
msg="vd-root    received    a    packet(proto=1,    10.52.53.1:50226->10.52.53.100:2048) from internal2. type=8, code=0, id=50226, seq=0."

msg="allocate a new session-0002464b"
msg="Allowed by Policy-1:"
msg="send out via dev-Trunk_VLAN_202, dst-mac-90:6c:ac:d4:1e:1f"
..
```

Take a moment to scan through the above output. Note, I cleaned this up a little, so it is easier to read. From the debug, we can see our PING ingresses internal2, allowed by Policy 1, and sent out the Trunk_VLAN_202 VLAN interface. It doesn't say it explicitly here, but the egress frame conforms to 802.1q and contains a VLAN ID 202. A packet capture would show this, just trust me on that one!

At this point in time, we could add more VLANs to our wan1 Trunk port by simply performing the same VLAN interface configuration and just changing the object name and the VLAN ID, to easy!

VLAN Translation

The next topic we are going to discuss is VLAN Translation. TP Mode FortiGate gives the ability to bridge communication for different VLANs within the same Forwarding Domain. For example, a frame can ingress on VLAN 101 on Port1 and egress on VLAN 202 on Port2 by design. This is possible because Forwarding Domains is what is solely responsible for containing layer-2 network traffic, and not VLANs.

Chapter 2 | Layer Two Technologies

Let's walk through this configuration. We are going to use prior topology. Interface internal2 is the ingress for vlan 101, and wan1 is the egress for vlan 303. The source IP is Server-A @ 172.15.19.1/24 and gateway address 172.15.19.100 on layer-3 VLAN interface 303. Let's jump into the CLI.

```
NSE4-LAB-60D (Trunk_VLAN_303) # show
config system interface
    edit "Trunk_VLAN_303"
        set vdom "root"
        set allowaccess ping https ssh snmp http
        set forward-domain 500
        set device-identification enable
        set role lan
        set snmp-index 7
        set interface "wan1"
        set vlanid 303
    next
NSE4-LAB-60D (interface) # edit INSIDE_VLAN_101
NSE4-LAB-60D (INSIDE_VLAN_101) # show
config system interface
    edit "INSIDE_VLAN_101"
        set vdom "root"
        set allowaccess ping https ssh snmp http
        set forward-domain 500
        set device-identification enable
        set role lan
        set snmp-index 14
        set interface "internal2"
        set vlanid 101
    next
end
```

Let's review this configuration. Here we created two new layer-2 VLAN interfaces INSIDE_VLAN_101 and Trunk_VLAN_303. INSIDE_VLAN_101 is built off of internal2, and Trunk_VLAN_303 is built off of 303. Next, internal2 now accept and forward VLAN 101 frames, and wan1 now accept and forward VLAN 303 frames. Both VLANs 101 & 303 are both apart of Forwarding Domain 500. *Image 2.11* gives a visual of the topology. Note, the internal2 interface is effectively now a trunk port since it is accepting tagged VLAN frames.

We issue a PING from Server-1, which pushes VLAN 101 onto the frame. Internal2 accepts VLAN 101 PING and map it to Forwarding Domain 500. MAC lookup on FDB directs the frame to egress wan1 on VLAN 303. Here we will see VLAN translation where TP FortiGate is changing VLAN IDs in transit layer-2 communicate.

Next, we will perform a PoC and PING the gateway @ 172.15.19.100 on VLAN 303 from Server-A @ 172.15.19.1 on VLAN 101. We are going to use the same diagnose flow debug command set as before:

```
msg="vd-root    received    a    packet(proto=1,    172.15.19.1:55745->172.15.19.100:2048) from INSIDE_VLAN_101. type=8, code=0, id=55745, seq=0."
msg="allocate a new session-000277fe"
msg="Allowed by Policy-3:"
msg="send out via dev-Trunk_VLAN_303, dst-mac-90:6c:ac:d4:1e:1f"
msg="vd-root    received    a    packet(proto=1,    172.15.19.100:55745->172.15.19.1:0) from Trunk_VLAN_303. type=0, code=0, id=55745, seq=0."
```

Image 2.11 – VLAN Translation

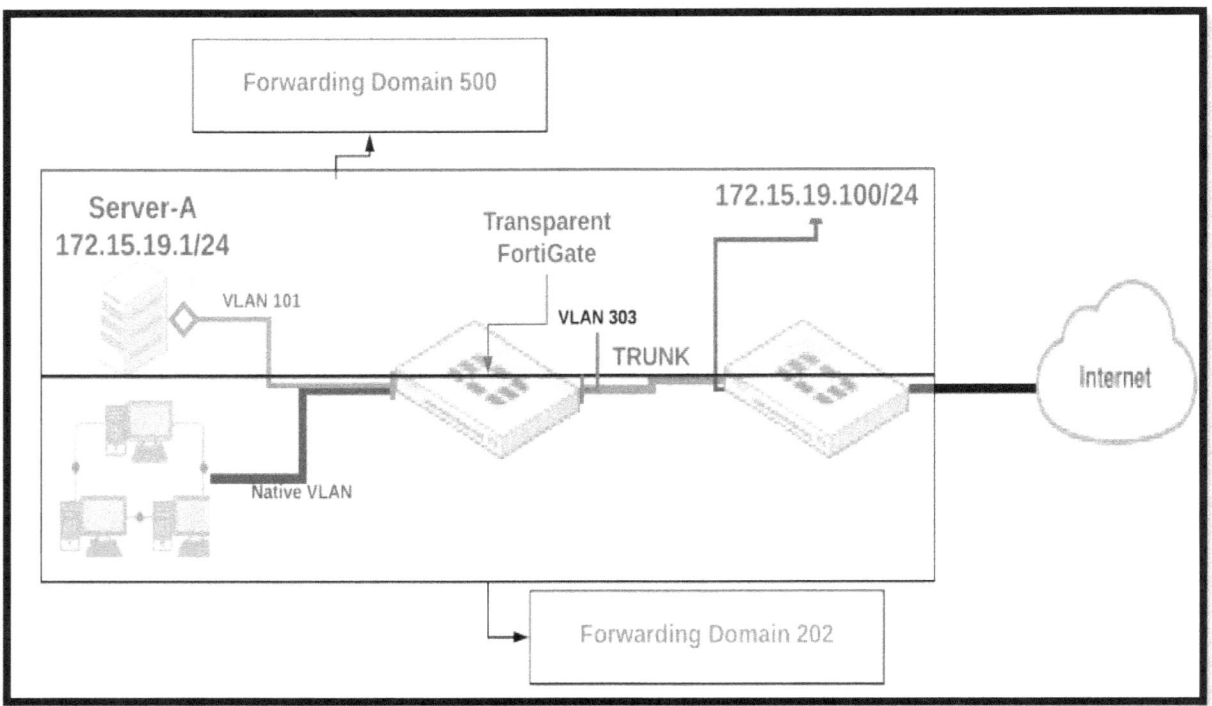

From the debugs, we can see that a PING packet tagged with VLAN 101 ingresses INSIDE_VLAN_101 interface and is allowed by policy 3 and then egresses on VLAN 303 on interface Trunk_VLAN_303. We can confirm the communication is good, and VLAN translation took place.

VLAN Forwarding

The last thing we are going to talk about on VLANs is about the interface level setting vlanforward. The command is disabled by default in 6.2 FortiOS. See below.

Chapter 2 | Layer Two Technologies

```
NSE4-LAB-60D (wan1) # show ful | grep vlan
    set vlanforward disable
```

But know, In earlier FortiOS code versions, this command was enabled by default, and in general, it is misunderstood. So, the question is, what happens if you enable this command under your interface settings? A couple of things will happen. The first thing is on is all VLAN traffic that ingresses the physical interface, or logical layer-2 VLAN interfaces, will now be forwarded to all other VLANs and ports within the Forwarding Domain without the need for a firewall. This would allow devices on separate VLANs within a Forwarding Domain to communicate.

The next thing you should know is by default TP FortiGate drops any unknown VLAN ID traffic, meaning FortiGate does not have an explicit VLAN layer-2 interface configured for the ingress VLAN ID. When you enable vlanforward on the physical interface, this behavior changes. The frame with the unknown VLAN ID will now be forwarded to all other VLANs and physical ports within the Forwarding Domain.

Remember that this is a method to allow devices on different VLANs to communicate without an explicit firewall policy. Most of the time you would want to create a separate Forwarding Domain for each VLAN and not allow VLAN cross talk on a Layer-2 level but bridge this traffic at a layer-3 device so as to have more tools to manage the communication.

In summary, when vlanforward is enabled, known and unknown VLAN traffic is forwarded to all other interfaces within a Forwarding Domain without the need for a policy.

Chapter 2 | *Layer Two Technologies*

Summary

Alright, you made it! This wraps up the FortiGate layer-2 chapter. In this chapter, we review FortiGate NAT Mode and Transparent Mode and how they interacted with the layer-2 environment. We discussed general MAC learning and forwarding. We reviewed interface details like the MAC address and virtual MAC. We discussed ARP in NAT Mode.

We discussed various layer-2 protocols like Spanning Tree, LACP, LLDP, and 802.1q and discussed how to configure them on FortiGate. We discussed the Virtual Wire Pairing Feature and how to configure it as well.

We reviewed Transparent Mode FortiGate and how to convert from NAT Mode to TP Mode. We reviewed different types of frame forwarding like Unicast MAC, ARP, Broadcast, Multicast, and BPDUs. We talked about TP Mode VLAN handling and went over Access and Trunk ports and how to configure them. We talked about VLAN translation and VLAN Forwarding.

This chapter has prepared you to pass the layer-2 and transparent mode sections of the NSE4 exam. Also, you have insight now on FortiGate layer-2 operations so to help you properly deploy FortiGate's in your environment. The last thing to do is to answer the questions for this chapter. Remember to study and practice, and this stuff will become second nature!

Chapter 2 | Layer Two Technologies

End of Chapter Two Questions

1) What attributes does a virtual interface inherit from the parent interface?
    a. MAC Address
    b. Mac Address and MTU
    c. MAC address, MTU and Duplex/Speed
    d. All virtual interface attributes must be explicitly defined.

2) What command would present the MAC address for the wan1 interface on FortiGate?
    a. get system information interface wan1
    b. show system status wan1
    c. diagnose hardware deviceinfo nic wan1
    d. diagnose sys device list root wan1

3) Software Switch and Hardware Switch interfaces both have the ability to offload traffic to ASIC.
    a. True
    b. False

4) From output from 'diagnose hardware deviceinfo nic', What field shows the active MAC address for the physical interface?
    a. Permanent_HWaddr
    b. Status
    c. Current_HWaddr
    d. ACTIVE_MAC_ADDR

5) Which CLI object holds the configuration for the Hardware Switch?
    a. switch-interface
    b. virtual-switch
    c. hardware-switch
    d. hardware-interface

6) What CLI object allows the configuration for a Software Switch?

Chapter 2 | Layer Two Technologies

    a. switch-interface
    b. virtual-switch
    c. hardware-switch
    d. hardware-interface

7) By default, how longs will FortiOS retain a cached ARP entry?
    a. 30 seconds
    b. 1 minute
    c. 5 minutes
    d. ARP entries are perpetual

8) In NAT Mode, a hardware-switch will run STP by default.
    a. True
    b. False

9) In NAT Mode, what command will show current STP status on FortiGate
    a. diagnose stp status
    b. get stp status
    c. get sys stp list
    d. diagnose sys stp list

10) What are the main benefits of LACP?
    a. Gain information from other LAN devices
    b. loop prevention
    c. logical divide layer-2 LAN
    d. Redundancy and throughput

11) What are the LACP flags set for an operational state where members are apart of the LAG and forwarding traffic and receiving traffic?
    a. ASAODD
    b. ASAIDE
    c. ASAIDD
    d. ASAIEE

12) What separates broadcast domains on a TP Mode FortiGate?
    a. VLAN

Chapter 2 | Layer Two Technologies

  b. VLANFORWARD
  c. Forwarding Domain
  d. Firewall Transit Policy

13) Review the below output. What is the MAC address of the wan1 interface?

```
NSE4-LAB-60D (global) # diagnose netlink brctl name host root.b
show bridge control interface root.b host.
fdb: size=2048, used=11, num=14, depth=3
Bridge root.b host table
port no device   devname mac addr                ttl     attributes
  13     29      INSIDE_VLAN_101 90:6c:ac:49:59:38   0       Local Static
  10     8       internal2       90:6c:ac:49:59:38   0       Local Static
   2     5      wan1    90:6c:ac:d4:1e:1f          25      Hit(25)
..
   2     5      wan1    90:6c:ac:49:59:36           0      Local Static
```

  a. 90:6c:ac:49:59:36
  b. 90:6c:ac:d4:1e:1f
  c. 90:6c:ac:49:59:35
  d. 90:6c:ac:49:59:38

14) What protocol resolves IP address to MAC address?
  a. LACP
  b. LLDP
  c. ARP
  d. STP

15) What protocol assist in dynamically assigning voice devices and voice applications to a certain VLAN?
  a. LLDP
  b. LACP
  c. ARP
  d. LLDP-MED

16) Interfaces apart of a Virtual Wire Pairing have exclusive communication, and no other interface can communicate with them.
  a. True
  b. False

Chapter 2 | Layer Two Technologies

17) The interface level setting vlanforward, if enabled, will forward all VLAN traffic to all other VLANs sharing parent interface.
    a. True
    b. False

18) In FortiGate TP Mode, ARP broadcast by default is forwarded without a firewall policy.
    a. True
    b. False

19) What is the FDB?
    a. A table that holds VLAN information
    b. A table that transit policies
    c. A table that is used for IP routing
    d. A table used for Ethernet frame forwarding

20) In TP Mode, VLANs create separate broadcast domains.
    a. True
    b. False

Chapter 3 | Layer Three Technologies

NSE4 Blueprint Topics Covered

- Configuration of Static Routes
- implementation of Policy-Based Routes
- Control traffic for well-known Internet Services
- Interpret the FortiOS Routing Table
- Understand FortiOS anti-spoofing mechanism
- Implement route failover and floating route
- Understand ECMP
- Recognize active route vs standby route vs inactive routes
- Use built in sniffer and diagnose flow debug tools,
- Understand Session Table Entry.

Chapter 3 | Layer Three Technologies

FortiOS Layer Three Technologies

For a firewall, the FortiGate has very robust routing features, and in many cases, these features allow us to merge the routing and security needs into one device. I'm excited to go over this chapter because routing is the heart of network security and one of my favorite subjects. If traffic cannot transverse the network to its destination, then we cannot secure it. It is as simple as that functionality first and then security.

In this chapter, we are going to discuss FortiOS layer-3 routing capabilities. I'm going to start with a refresher on general IP routing so we can make sure we are on the same page. I'll touch on the IPv4 and IPv6 theory. Then we jump into the specifics of what FortiOS can do regarding IP routing. Also, I go over the FortiOS Route Table with you and the route lookup process. Also, in this chapter, I go over IP packet processing so you can understand the logic behind the scenes. I'll be discussing the Reverse Path Forwarding(RPF) feature and the session table, which are very important topics.

After we gain a strong foundation on FortiOS IP packet handling, the next topic we are going to jump into static routing, where I provide configuration examples and a general overview of the feature. Also, here we talk about some of the advanced FortiOS routing features like ECMP. Lastly, we discuss Policy Based Routing (PBR), Internet-Service routing, Link Monitoring, and the Dynamic Gateway features on FortiOS. We have plenty to cover, so let's get started!

Chapter 3 | Layer Three Technologies

IP Routing Overview

What is IP routing? And why do we need it? Well, firstly, let's first talk about the Internet Protocol (IP) address; this is a logical value within the IP header that network devices use to represent themselves on a LAN subnet.

The term IP Routing is the function of referencing the destination IP address within the packet header against a device's (router) routing table so a decision can be made of where a packet will be transmitted. IP routing only takes place when a device wants to communicate with an IP address outside of its own local subnet because, as you should know, to communicate within a LAN only, this is handled by layer-2 Ethernet switches. Essentially, the IP Address is the value that allows different LAN subnets to be connected logically referenced to as internetworking, which makes up the Internet. There are two versions of IP currently in use on today's networks, IP version 4 (IPv4) and IP version 6 (IPv6. I'm going to talk a little about each here.

IPv4 Review

IPv4 was invented back in the 1970s and was introduced to the public in 1981. IPv4 addresses have 32-bit values and provide around 4.3 billion unique IP addresses. As it stands, all the address space has been allocated, and there is no available IP space left to be allocated, and this was a major drive for IPv6.

Image 3. 1 – IPv4 Header

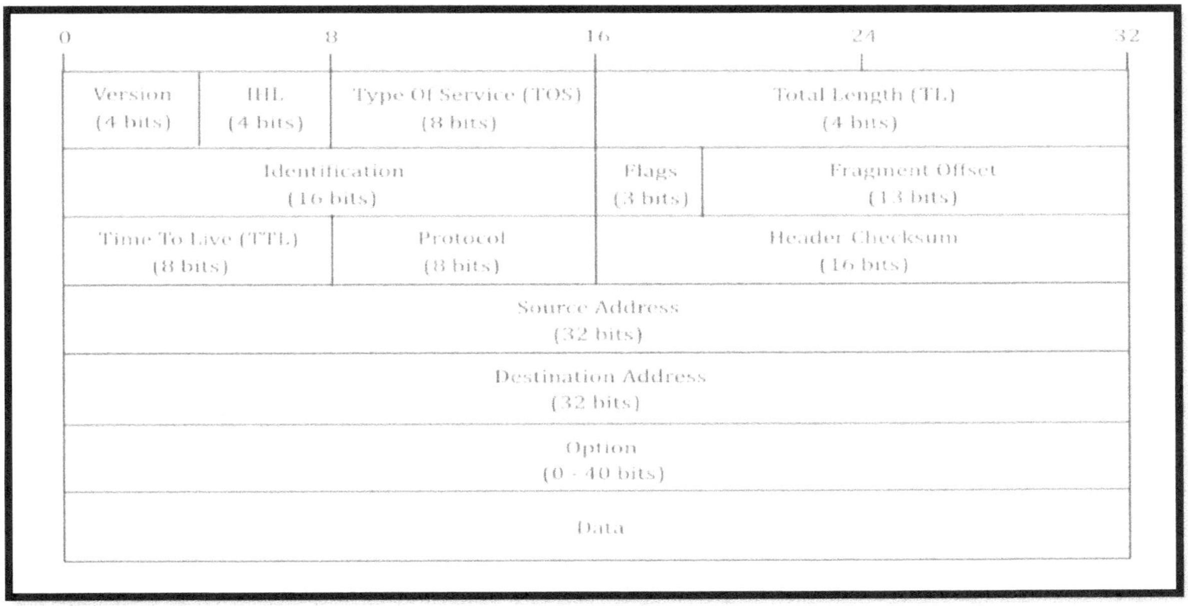

Version (4 bits)	IHL (4 bits)	Type Of Service (TOS) (8 bits)	Total Length (TL) (4 bits)
Identification (16 bits)		Flags (3 bits)	Fragment Offset (13 bits)
Time To Live (TTL) (8 bits)	Protocol (8 bits)	Header Checksum (16 bits)	
Source Address (32 bits)			
Destination Address (32 bits)			
Option (0 - 40 bits)			
Data			

The IPv4 header is encapsulated by the layer-2 header, which is why IPv4 is considered a layer-3 protocol. The main fields we are going to focus on within the

Chapter 3 | Layer Three Technologies

IPv4 header are the source and destination IP address as well as the protocol number here in this chapter. I want to stay focused on the routing function. Take the time to review the IPv4 header in *image 3.1* on the next page. Next, I want to provide a quick rundown on all the fields within the IPv4 header.

<u>IPv4 Header Review</u>

This section covers all the fields within the IPv4 header. If you already know this, please feel free to skip this part.

1) Version
    a. This field is always equal to 4 in IPv4.
2) Internet Header
    a. This field holds the length of the IPv4 header
3) Type of Service (ToS)
    a. An 8-bit field that specifies differentiated services (DSCP); this field is marked and referenced by devices for classification to perform Quality of Service (QoS) functions, which provides priority processing.
4) Total Length
    a. A 16-bit field and specifies the entire length of the datagram, which is the header and data
5) Identification
    a. A 16-bit field that is used for packet reassembly if fragmented
6) Flags
    a. A 3-bit field that determines if a packet is allowed to be fragmented or not and to help control fragmentation reassembly. This field contains the DF bit (don't fragment)
7) Fragment Offset
    a. A 13-bit field that is used to reassemble fragmented IPv4 packets. Fragmentation takes place if the packet size is large, then the MTU on the egress interface
8) Time To Live
    a. An 8-bit field that is used to prevents a packet from looping the network forever. This is accomplished by decrementing this field by one every hop, and once this field reaches zero, then the packets are discarded, and ICMP TTL expired in transit can be sent to the source.
9) Protocol
    a. An 8-bit field that defines the next layer protocol being used, for example, if TCP is being used as the transport protocol, then the protocol value in this field would be 6.
10) Header Checksum
    a. A 16-bit field that is used for error checking regarding header information. This is done by generating a checksum against the IPv4

Chapter 3 | Layer Three Technologies

> header before transmitting the packet, and each router will generate this same checksum value and compare it with the original value. If mismatch, then the packet will be dropped.

11) Source IP Address
    a. A 32-bit field to logical identify the device that sent the packet
12) Destination IP Address
    a. A 32-bit field to logical identify the device to receive the packet
13) Options
    a. Not typical or required but can be used to indicate certain handling requirements

Now that we understand the fields available within the IPv4 header, the next item to discuss is the different types of IPv4 Addresses.

<u>IPv4 Address Types</u>

IPv4 offers a few different methods of packet types; they are:

1) Unicast
   a. A term used to describe IP communicates where one host sends information to another host. In this case, there is only one sender and one receiver.
2) Broadcast
   a. A term used to describe IP communication where one host sends information to all hosts within the same IP subnet. The Broadcast IP is where all host bits are turned on.
3) Multicast

Chapter 3 | Layer Three Technologies

    a. A term used to describe IP communicates where one host sends a stream of information to a specific group of subscribers. Multicast is managed by protocols like Internet Group Management Protocol (IGMP) and Protocol Independent Multicast (PIM)

Image 3.1.1 – Multicast Addresses

Multicast Address	Usage
224.0.0.1	All Hosts
224.0.0.2	All Routers
224.0.0.5	All OSPF Routers
224.0.0.6	OSPF DRs
224.0.0.9	RIPv2 Routers
224.0.0.10	EIGRP Routers
224.0.0.13	PIMv2
224.0.0.18	VRRP Devices
224.0.0.19-21	IS-IS Routers
224.0.1.1	Multicast NTP

<u>RFC 1918</u>

This is one of my favorite interview questions. Can you tell me the RFC 1918 address space? And believe it or not, many network engineers cannot do this. Know this, and don't let your interview end prematurely. RFC 1918 outlines the IPv4 address space that is considered private or non-routable on the Internet. This space is available for anyone to use within their enterprise network. Below is the private address space:

    1) 10.0.0.0   - 10.255.255.255 (10/8 prefix)
    2) 172.16.0.0 - 172.31.255.255 (172.16/12 prefix)
    3) 192.168.0.0 - 192.168.255.255 (192.168/16 prefix)

Chapter 3 | Layer Three Technologies

APIPA

Automatic Private IP Addressing (APIPA), defined in RFC 3927 and the network reserved for APIPA usage is 169.254.0.0/16. If you ever see this IP configured on one of your machine clients, then I would recommend checking out your DHCP server because there might be a problem. A machine is given this IP when it does not have a static IP assigned and was not able to obtain an IP via DHCP.

Loopback Address

The 127.0.0.0/8 IP space was received for local use only and is non-routable on the Internet. A good initial to see if a client machine TCP/IP protocol stack is functioning properly is to ping the loopback address 127.0.0.1.

IPv6 Review

IPv6 was created to address the limitations of IPv4. The most obvious is the larger address space provided by IPv6, which is 128-bits in length for source and destination. The length of an IPv6 Address offers an immense range of possible unique IP space. With IPv6, every device on the internet could have its very own public IP; this cancels the technical requirement for NAT, but some organizations still perform NAT to help hide their internal IP space for security reasons. Also, you will find the need to use DNS with IPv6 addresses because the bit length makes them challenging to reference by themselves. Meaning if you ever try to type in a full 128-bit hex value, the probability to mistype is high.

3. 2 – IPv6 Header

Version	Traffic class	Flow label	
Payload length		Next header	Hop limit
Source address			
Destination address			

Also, you should know IPv6 provides simplified headers, and the idea behind this was to create faster packet processing in general. There is no broadcast on IPv6 subnets because it uses multicast instead. There is no ARP, but a function called neighbor discovery is used to find other IPv6 nodes on the LAN. Below is an example of the

Chapter 3 | Layer Three Technologies

IPv6 header in *image 3.2*. The NSE4 does not focus on IPv4 or IPv6 theory but does expect you to be able to configure IPv6 network functionality and IPv6 policies, which we will cover in this chapter.

IPv6 Packet Header

1) Version
   a. A 4-bit value that specifies the IP version which is 6 or 0110
2) Traffic Class
   a. An 8-bit value which is similar to the IPv4 ToS field. This field is to give packets label so a router can give priority to individual packets over others
3) Flow Label
   a. This field is A 20-bit value and allows the sender to mark this field with a unique value so routers can identify related traffic flows. A Flow Label of zero is used to indicate packets not part of any flow.
4) Payload Length
   a. A 16-bit field that tells the router how information much the packet contains in its payload. If a payload is larger than 65,535, then the Payload Length Field will be set to 0, and the jumbo payload option is used in the Hop-By-Hop options extension IPv6 header.
5) Next-Header
   a. An 8-bit value field indicates the Extension Header used or the Upper layer protocol being used, which are the same values as IPv4
6) Hop-Limit
   a. An 8-bit value field that is the same as the TTL field in IPv4 and is used for loop prevention. This field is decremented by one for each hop through a network. Once this field reaches zero, it is discarded.
7) Source Address
   a. A 128-bit value that identifies the sender of the IP packet
8) Destination Address
   a. A 128-bit value that identifies the intended receiver of the IP packet

IPv6 Address Types

Just like IPv4 has different address types, so does IPv6. There are three types to discuss here.

1) Unicast Address Type
   a. This address represents a single source and destination communicating. This is the routable address assigned to a NIC.
2) Anycast Address Type

Chapter 3 | Layer Three Technologies

   a. This address could represent multiple destinations, and multiple machines could have the same address assigned to their NIC. Packets sent to this address are forwarded to the nearest destination by a router. This is used by distributed services for redundancy.
3) Multicast Address Type
   a. This address represents a certain group of nodes. Nodes can subscribe to a multicast stream and unsubscribe. This is a one to many types of communication that is popular with streaming media.
4) Link-layer Address Type
   a. This is a non-routable IP space used only within a LAN. IPv6 Link-Local address is generated automatically using FE80::/64 as the network space and the MAC address for the host bits.
   b. Link-Local addresses are similar to the IPv4 APIPA addresses

<u>IPv6 Neighbor Discovery Protocol (NDP)</u>

IPv6 uses NDP for many functions. This is a layer-2 protocol that uses link-local addresses to transverse the LAN. IPv6 uses NDP to discover other IPv6 nodes on the LAN, similar to how ARP is used in IPv4 networks. Also, this protocol is used for the IPv6 dynamic address assignment. NDP defined five different types of ICMPv6 communication. These are:

1) Router Solicitation
   a. ICMPv6 Type 133
   b. Router Solicitation message is used to locate routers on the LAN.
2) Router Advertisement
   a. ICMPv6 Type 134
   b. Used by routers to advertise their presence and other attributes. This is also used as a response to the Router Solicitation message.
3) Neighbor Solicitation
   a. ICMPv6 Type 135
   b. Used by a node to find the link-layer address of neighboring devices on a LAN. Also used to verify if neighbors are reachable.
4) Neighbor Advertisement
   a. ICMPv6 Type 136
   b. Used by a node to respond to Neighbor Solicitation Messages
5) Redirect
   a. ICMPv6 Type 137
   b. Used by routers to inform the host that there is a better gateway on the LAN.

Chapter 3 | Layer Three Technologies

IPv6 Interface Configuration

You are required to know how to configure an IPv6 address on FortiOS. To do this, you must go to the interface level settings and then use the 'config ipv6' sub-command, which descends you into the IPv6 interface settings. Goto the CLI to configure this:

```
config system interface
    edit "wan1"
        set vdom "root"
        set ip 192.168.209.247 255.255.255.0
        set allowaccess ping https ssh snmp http telnet fgfm radius-acct probe-response capwap
        set type physical
        set alias "TEST"
        set role wan
        set snmp-index 2
        config ipv6
            set ip6-address 2001:db7::1/96
            set allowaccess ping https ssh snmp http
        end
    next
end
```

Once within the IPv6 context, and one of those commands is *ipv6-address*. This command allows us to assign an IPv6 address to the wan1 interface. In the above example, we have just configured a dual-stacked interface, meaning it runs IPv4 and IPv6 simultaneously.

Stateless Address Autoconfiguration (SLAAC)

SLAAC is an IPv6 feature that allows devices on an IPv6 network to receive an IPv6 address automatically. This works like DHCP on IPv4 networks. SLAAC is built into IPv6 and is defined by RFC 2462. Router Advertisement is used for IPv6 addresses assigned in SLAAC. The FortiGate configuration is:

```
config system interface
    edit "wan1"
        set vdom "root"
        set ip 192.168.1.247 255.255.255.0
        set allowaccess ping https ssh snmp http telnet fgfm radius-acct probe-response capwap
        set type physical
        set alias "TEST"
```

```
            set role wan
            set snmp-index 2
            config ipv6
                set ip6-address 2001:db8::1/32
                    set ip6-send-adv enable
                    config ip6-prefix-list
                        edit 2001:db7::/64
                            set autonomous-flag enable
                            set onlink-flag enable
                        next
                    end
                end
        next
    end
```

FortiGate IP Routing

This is an exciting section where you are going to learn the inner workings of how FortiGate handles IP packets. Meaning, we are going to look at the FortiOS Routing Table and the route selection process. Then we will move into the Session Table and break that down. By the end of this section, you should feel confident about how FortiOS makes routing decisions and stores routing information. So not wasting time, let us jump into the meat and potatoes of things, the Routing Table!

Routing Table Overview

The Routing Table is where all the magic happens. This table contains all active routes FortiOS recognizes and is the foundation for packet routing decisions. A routing table entry has four major components.

The first major component is the Route Type. This is indicated by a single letter on FortiOS at the beginning of the entry. The first Route Types I'm going to talk about are Static and Connected. Static is marked with an 'S', and Connected is marked with a 'C'. A static route is one that is submitted through the static route configuration table located in the CLI via '*#config router static*', *and* a Connected Route is entered by configuring a physical or logical interface under interface tables located in CLI via 'config system interface'. The rule is, if the interface is considered UP and operational and has an IP address and subnet configured, then it is located within the FortiOS route table.

The next major component of a Route Entry is the destination subnet or host. When FortiOS receives a packet, the destination IP is parsed out of the IP header and

Chapter 3 | Layer Three Technologies

compared against these destination subnet values that are within the various route entries so to find an egress interface to send the packet out.

Within a Route Entry, a destination subnet is also called an IP Prefix, which is a subnet or aggregation of IP space. To create an IP Prefix, you must pair network bits of an IP address with a subnet mask value. A subnet mask is required so FortiOS can perform an exclusive OR (XOR) function against the 32-bit IP address that basically identifies which bits are the network bit and which are the host bits.

For example, a destination subnet in a Route Entry could be 10.1.2.0/24. Here the network bits are represented in decimal as '10.1.2', and the subnet mask is 255.255.255.0 represented by CIDR (Classless Inter-Domain Routing) notation /24. Together they specify the destination network to match. Essentially, this means this Route Entry wants to match the first three high order bytes in the destination IP. For example, a destination IP of 10.1.2.59 would match this destination Route Entry, but 10.2.1.59 would not.

The next major component of a Route Entry is the egress physical or logical egress interface. This must be specified on FortiOS, and the egress interface must be up and operational for the route to be considered active by the routing table.

Moving on, the next Major Component of a route entry is the next-hop IP address. FortiOS performs an ARP request for the gateway (next-hop) IP out the egress interface to obtain a destination MAC address for Ethernet for LAN transit. This IP gateway address must fall within a directly connected subnet of the egress interface for the route to be valid.

The last major component of a route entry is a metric. There are different terms used for this value in different routing protocols or even in different vendors. But essentially, in general, a metric is a value that FortiOS users prefer one route over another when multiple route entries exist with the same destination. For example, if we have two static routes with the same destination of 10.1.2.0/24 and one is directed out wan1 and the other out wan2, then the metric is evaluated. If the route pointed out wan1 has a lower metric value, then it is preferred and will be an active route. Within *Table 3.1* is a generic example of a Route Entry displaying the five components we just discussed.

Table 3.1 – General Route Entry Example

Route Type	Destination IP	Metric	Egress Interface	Next Hop
Static	10.2.2.0/24	10	wan1	10.123.123.1/24

Chapter 3 | Layer Three Technologies

IPv4 Routing Table and Monitor

Now it's time to take a look at the actual FortiOS routing table since you have a general idea now what to expect. We are going to go over two commands here:

1) get router info routing-table all
2) get router info routing-table database

Both these commands display FortiOS route entries. It is important to know the difference between these commands. The first command above here presents the active or live routing table. The second command shows the entire route database, which presents all known routes regardless if they are active or not.

Let's look at the output of the 'get router info routing-table all' command and view the active routing:

If a static route does not show up in the routing table then check your egress interface status and check next hop IP; It should fall within the egress interface subnet.

```
NSE4-PASS (root) # get router info routing-table all
Routing table for VRF=0
Codes: K - kernel, C - connected, S - static, R - RIP, B - BGP
       O - OSPF, IA - OSPF inter area
       N1 - OSPF NSSA external type 1, N2 - OSPF NSSA external type 2
       E1 - OSPF external type 1, E2 - OSPF external type 2
       i - IS-IS, L1 - IS-IS level-1, L2 - IS-IS level-2, ia - IS-IS inter area
       * - candidate default

S*      0.0.0.0/0 [5/0] via 10.123.233.1, wan1
S       7.7.7.7/32 [10/0] is a summary, Null
S       10.0.0.0/8 [10/0] is directly connected, Fortinet_ph1
C       10.3.3.0/24 is directly connected, DC-1-303-vlan
S       10.3.3.100/32 [10/0] is a summary, Null
C       10.4.4.0/24 is directly connected, DC-2-304-vlan
S       10.9.16.0/20 [10/0] is directly connected, Fortinet_ph1
C       10.20.30.1/32 is directly connected, vlan
C       10.52.53.0/24 is directly connected, internal1
C       10.123.233.0/30 is directly connected, wan1
..
```

Take a moment to review this output and generate some questions.

Chapter 3 | Layer Three Technologies

Let us analyze this output. Firstly, find the default route, which is the route packets take if there is no explicit match in the routing table.

```
S*       0.0.0.0/0 [5/0] via 10.123.233.1, wan1
```

The default route is indicated by two attributes the '*' and the destination being quad 0's (0.0.0.0/0), which is a match all statement for IPv4 packets. The Route Type here is Static, which is indicated by the capital 'S' furthest to the left. The Gateway IP is 10.123.123.1, and the egress interface is wan1. Lastly, here we see the metrics '[5/0]' for the route. On FortiOS, a static has two metrics Distance and Priority. The first value represents the Distance, and the second value represents the Priority. Only static routes have the Priority metric attribute. The next route type to discuss is Connected. Let's find one in the routing table:

```
C        10.123.233.0/30 is directly connected, wan1
```

Connected routes are indicated by the capital 'C'. From this output, we can conclude that the wan1 interface is up and operational because we see it here in the routing table. We can also conclude that wan1 holds the subnet 10.123.233.0/24. The last thing here to put together is that the Gateway IP for the default route 10.123.233.1 falls within the 10.123.233.0/24 subnet. Once again, this is a requirement for the route to be considered valid and to be placed in the active routing table.

The next to command to review here is:

```
#get router info routing-table database.
```

Let's take a look at this output:

```
NSE4-PASS (root) # get router info routing-table database
Routing table for VRF=0
Codes: K - kernel, C - connected, S - static, R - RIP, B - BGP
       O - OSPF, IA - OSPF inter area
       N1 - OSPF NSSA external type 1, N2 - OSPF NSSA external type 2
       E1 - OSPF external type 1, E2 - OSPF external type 2
       i - IS-IS, L1 - IS-IS level-1, L2 - IS-IS level-2, ia - IS-IS inter area
       > - selected route, * - FIB route, p - stale info

S    *> 0.0.0.0/0 [5/0] via 10.123.233.1, wan1
S       0.0.0.0/0 [10/0] is directly connected, Fortinet_ph1
                  [10/0] via 1.2.3.4, wan1
                  [10/0] is a summary, Null
..
```

Chapter 3 | Layer Three Technologies

```
S         6.6.6.6/32 [10/0] via 192.168.1.254, lan inactive
S      *> 7.7.7.7/32 [10/0] is a summary, Null
```

The Route Database provides all the possible routes, as well as the inactive ones. Let review this output, starting with all the possible default routes:

```
S      *> 0.0.0.0/0 [5/0] via 10.123.233.1, wan1
S         0.0.0.0/0 [10/0] is directly connected, Fortinet_ph1
                    [10/0] via 24.182.60.129, wan1
                    [10/0] is a summary, Null
```

There are four default routes configured on this FortiGate. FortiOS has chosen the one that egresses out wan1 via 10.123.233.1 because it meets all the requirements for a route to be active and has the lowest Distance value meaning it is the most preferred. The route that is indeed active in the Forwarding Information Database (FIB) is indicated by the ' *> '. The FIB is built from the best active routes and is what the kernel uses to route packets. Next, take a look at an inactive route:

```
S         6.6.6.6/32 [10/0] via 192.168.1.254, lan inactive
```

This is a route that had been configured via 'config router static' table but did not meet the requirements to be deemed as active. If we investigate further, we would either find that the 'lan' interface is down or 192.168.1.254 next hop does not fall into the 'lan' directly connected subnet interface subnet.

It is important to know for the NSE4 exam, as well as being a good Fortinet engineer, how to identify an active route and the difference between the Routing Table and the Route Database. For completeness, you can also view the Routing Table in the GUI via 'Monitor > Routing Monitor'. See image 3.3 for details.

Image 3.3 – GUI Route Monitor (Routing Table)

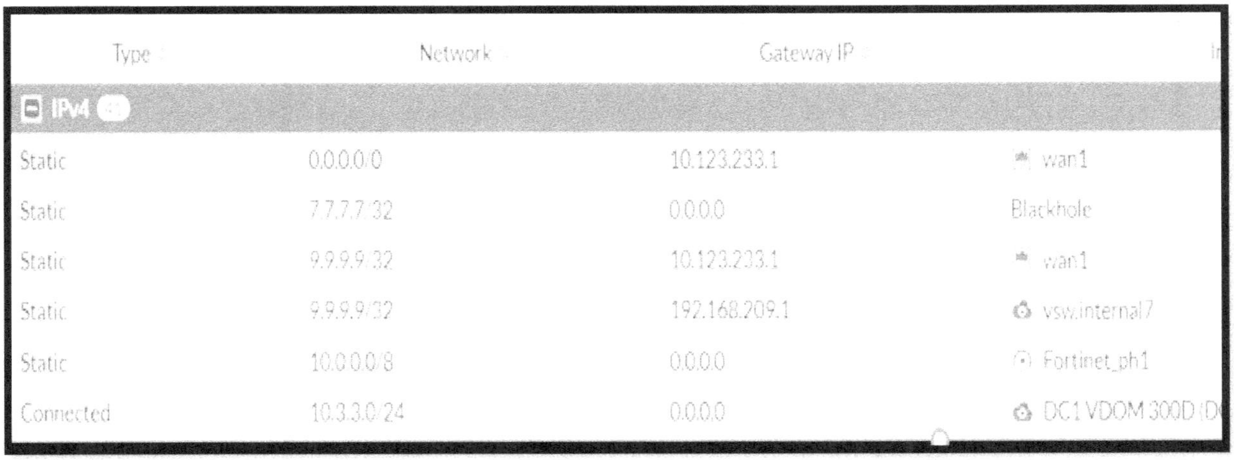

Type	Network	Gateway IP	
IPv4			
Static	0.0.0.0/0	10.123.233.1	wan1
Static	7.7.7.7/32	0.0.0.0	Blackhole
Static	9.9.9.9/32	10.123.233.1	wan1
Static	9.9.9.9/32	192.168.209.1	vsw.internal7
Static	10.0.0.0/8	0.0.0.0	Fortinet_ph1
Connected	10.3.3.0/24	0.0.0.0	DC1 VDOM 300D

Chapter 3 | Layer Three Technologies

Forwarding Information Database (FIB)

The FortiOS kernel holds its own routing table and references this when steering packets to their egress interfaces. Sometimes it is useful to view directly what the kernel is using to make decisions. We can gather this output from the below CLI command:

```
NSE4-PASS (root) # get router info kernel | grep wan1
tab=255  vf=0   scope=253  type=3  proto=2   prio=0   0.0.0.0/0.0.0.0/0-
>10.123.233.0/32 pref=10.123.233.2 gwy=0.0.0.0 dev=5(wan1)
..
tab=254  vf=0   scope=0    type=1  proto=11  prio=0   0.0.0.0/0.0.0.0/0->0.0.0.0/0
pref=0.0.0.0 gwy=10.123.233.1 dev=5(wan1)
..
```

FortiOS IPv6 Routing Table

Part of the NSE4 requirements is to understand basic IPv6 routing. The first thing to do is to turn on the feature. If in VDOM mode, go to the Global context and then 'System > Feature Visibility > Core Features > IPv6.'

Image 3.3.1 - IPv6 Feature

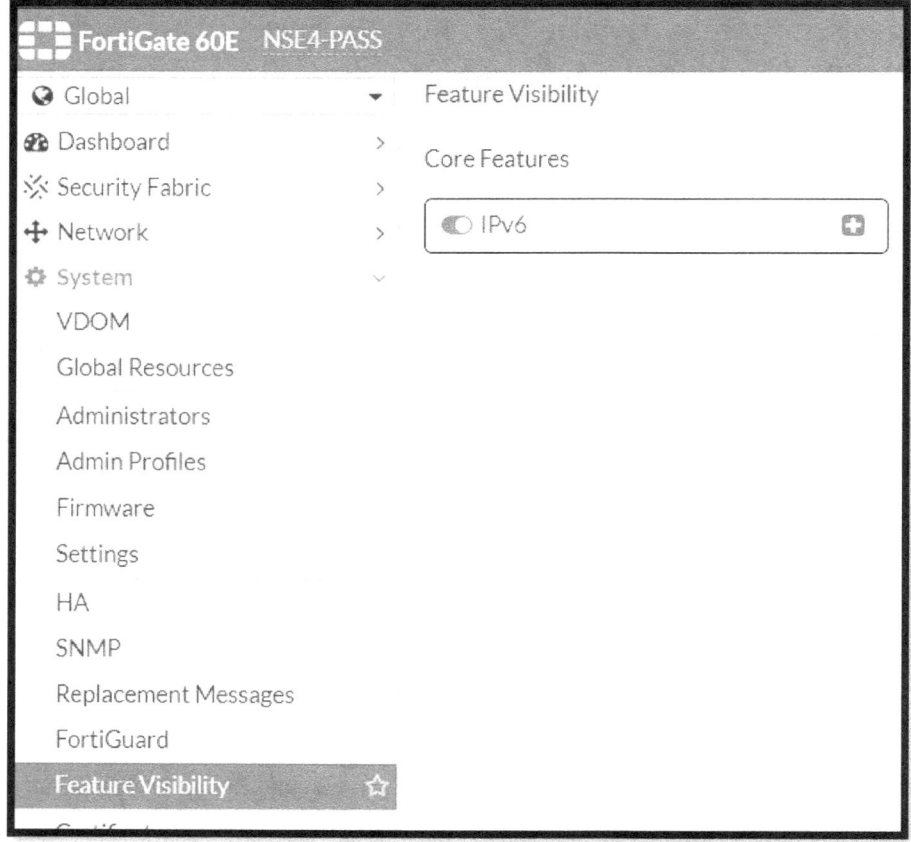

Chapter 3 | Layer Three Technologies

Next, to view the IPv6 routing table, issue the following command:

```
NSE4-PASS (root) # get router info6 routing-table
IPv6 Routing Table
Codes: K - kernel route, C - connected, S - static, R - RIP, O - OSPF,
       IA - OSPF inter area
       N1 - OSPF NSSA external type 1, N2 - OSPF NSSA external type 2
       E1 - OSPF external type 1, E2 - OSPF external type 2
       I - IS-IS, B - BGP
       * - candidate default
Timers: Uptime
C       ::1/128 via ::, root, 03w4d23h
C       2001:db8::/32 via ::, wan1, 00:00:02
C       fe80::/10 via ::, wan1, 00:00:02
```

Lastly, to configure an IPv6 Static Route, issue the below commands:

```
NSE4-PASS (0) # show
config router static6
    edit 1
        set dst 11::22/128
        set gateway 2001:db8::2
        set device "wan1"
    next
end
```

> *Most IPv6 CLI configurations are similar to IPv4 and most commands you just appending a '6' to specify IPv6.*

Route Attributes and Selection

Now that we have a handle on how to read the Routing Table and the difference between active and inactive routes, we can now talk more about route selection and route attributes.

I'm going to walk through the high level of how FortiOS makes routing decisions when there are no policy routes. When a packet ingress a network interface, FortiOS parses the destination IP address out of the header. The first thing FortiOS does is compare this IP with its own assigned IP information to see if this Local-In Traffic,

Chapter 3 | Layer Three Technologies

meaning the packet is destined for the FortiGate itself, or Transit Traffic, meaning FortiGate needs to forward the packet onward to its final destination. In this example, I will be going over Transit Traffic; the first thing FortiOS will do is compare the destination IP with its directly connected interface subnets, and if the destination IP falls within one of these subnets, then this is considered the last leg of the IP Routing journey of a packet, and from here Ethernet is used to forward the packet to its final destination. Hence, FortiOS would ARP for the destination IP, and if a response is received, then it would send a unicast Ethernet frame to the switch with the received destination MAC address that maps to the destination IP address.

Next, If the destination IP does not match a directly connected interface subnet, then the next function FortiOS performs is to look at the rest of the active route entries in its Routing Table. The rule here is the most specific destination subnet (IP Prefix) wins. For example, if there are three active route entries in the Routing Table that match the destination IP of 10.1.1.249, like so:

10.0.0.0/8 → Port1

10.1.0.0/16 → Port2

10.1.1.0/24 → Port3

Then FortiOS evaluates these statements and chooses to transmit the packet out Port3 because the Route Entry has a destination subnet that is more specific than the other Route Entry matches that point out Port2 and Port1.

Another example I'll show here, if I add a static route for 10.1.1.249/32, which is a host route, and pointed out Port1, then this would override the 10.1.1.0/24 route because, once again, it is more specific.

> *You can perform route lookups in the CLI via:*
> *#diagnose ip proute match <destination_ip_address> <source_ip_address> <interface_name> <protocol> <destination_port>*

In summary, FortiOS looks at directly connected subnets to forward a packet, but if no match, then FortiOS evaluates the rest of the Routing Table, and the most specific match will be preferred.

<u>Distance Route Attribute</u>

The next scenario is, what happens if we have multiple Route Entry matches with the same destination subnets? For example:

Chapter 3 | Layer Three Technologies

1) 10.1.1.0/24 → Port1
2) 10.1.1.0/24 → Port2

In this situation, where there is not a more specific route, we use an attribute called Distance to be the tiebreaker. Some other vendors call this route attribute Administrative Distance, but it's only Distance on FortiOS. The default Distance value is different for every Route Type. The rule is, the lowest Distance value is preferred. *Table 3.2* provides all the default Route Type Distance values on FortiOS:

Table 3. 2 – FortiOS Default Distance

Route Type	Default Distance
Directly Connected	0
DHCP Gateway	5
Static	10
eBGP	20
OSPF	110
RIP	120
iBGP	200

So essentially, if FortiOS held two Active Routes with the same destination subnet, for example, one Static Route and one OSPF Route, the Static Route would be preferred because it has the lowest Distance value.

Priority Route Attribute

The next route attribute is Priority, which is only an attribute of Static Routes. Priority is used when FortiOS has two Static Routes with matching destinations subnets and matching Distance values. In this case, Priority is the tiebreaker. The rule states that the route with the lowest Priority value is preferred. You might be wondering what the reason is behind this attribute. Let me explain.

For example, if there are two Static routes with matching destination subnets, but one has a lower Distance value, so to be preferred; therefore, only one route would be active in the routing table.

With Priority, if we keep both the Distance values the same but only lower the Priority value, then both routes will stay active in the routing table, and the backup route is used to accept ingress traffic of source IP that matches the route entry. The reason behind this is to overcome something call Reverse Path Forward check (RPF Check), which is designed to drop spoofed IP traffic. Let's review an example of this in the CLI:

```
NSE4-PASS (root) # get router info routing-table  all
```

Chapter 3 | Layer Three Technologies

```
Routing table for VRF=0
Codes: K - kernel, C - connected, S - static, R - RIP, B - BGP
       O - OSPF, IA - OSPF inter area
       N1 - OSPF NSSA external type 1, N2 - OSPF NSSA external type 2
       E1 - OSPF external type 1, E2 - OSPF external type 2
       i - IS-IS, L1 - IS-IS level-1, L2 - IS-IS level-2, ia - IS-IS
inter area
       * - candidate default
..
S       10.10.10.0/24 [10/0] via 10.52.53.2, internal1, [2/0]
                      [10/0] via 192.168.1.1, internal7, [3/0]
..
```

In this example, destination 10.10.10.0/24 has two Route Entries with the same Distance value 10, but with different Priority values. The Route Entry with Gateway IP of 10.52.53.2 and egresses internal1 has a Priority of 2, and the Route Entry with Gateway IP of 192.168.1.1 and egresses internal7 has a priority of 3.

Let me explain what these statements mean, ingress traffic with IP destination of 10.10.10.x is routed out internal1 next hop 10.52.53.2 because of the preferred Priority value. The other Route Entry with the egress interface of internal7 states if traffic ingresses internal7 with a source IP of 10.10.10.x It will not drop the traffic but proceed with route lookup, but if this route was removed, traffic would be dropped by RPF, this discuss this point further.

Reverse Path Forwarding (RPF)

Since we know, Priority is used to overcome the RPF check, in this section, I'm going to discuss with you the details of RPF.

RPF is simply an anti-spoofing mechanism. The rule states, if a source IP ingress an interface that does not fall within the subnet range assigned to the interface or doesn't have an active route back for source IP facing the ingress interface, then the packet will be dropped. Hence why we have a tool like Priority to overcome this. Take a moment to review *Image 3.3.3*.

Chapter 3 | Layer Three Technologies

Image 3.3.3 – RPF Example Diagram

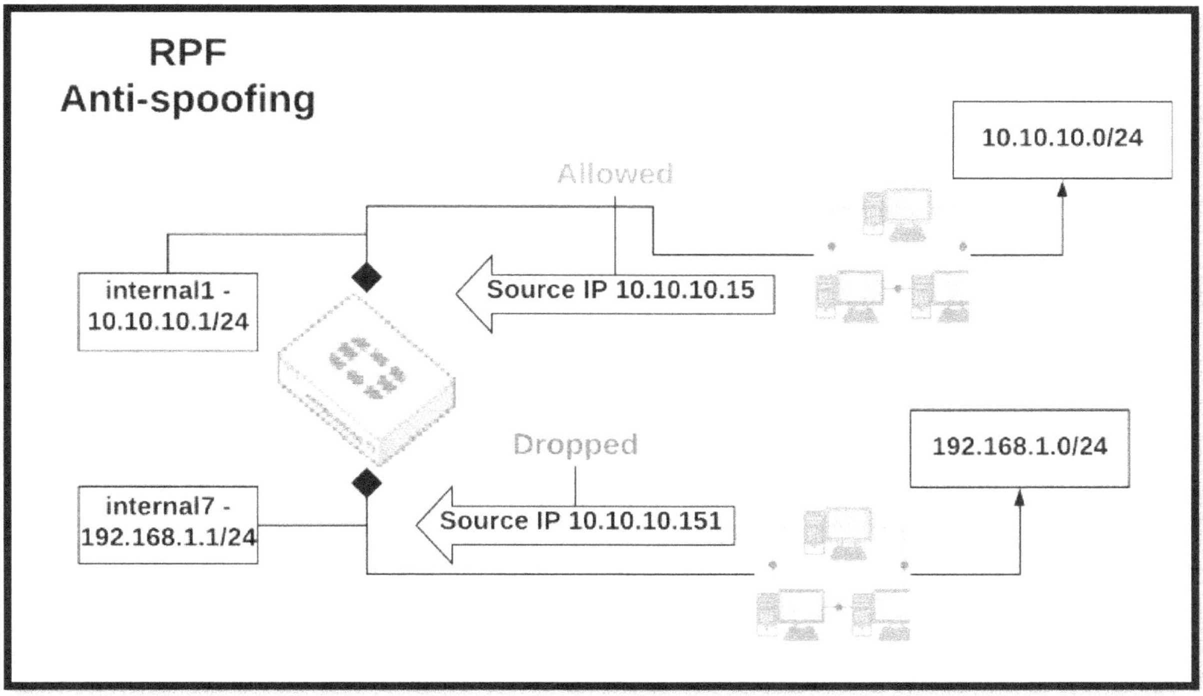

There are two different modes for RPF, strict and loose. Strict state the ingress interface must be the best route back to the source IP. Loose states, there must be at least a possibility to route back to the source with the current routing information. This is also called the feasible path.

1) RPF Strict
    a. a route lookup is made for source IP, and the packet is dropped if the ingress interface does not match the same interface as the route lookup.
2) RPF Loose (feasible)
    a. This mode FortiOS not only considered the best route, but all other Active Routes attached to the ingress interface are also checked, and if one matches the source IP, then the packet will be accepted

For example, with RPF loose setting, if you have a default route associated with an interface, then it will accept all unknown ingress source IP addresses because the default route makes it feasible to reach the source IP.

You should also know the default setting is RPF loose. This setting is found in the CLI via:

```
NSE4-PASS (root) # config sys settings
NSE4-PASS (settings) # show ful | grep strict
    set strict-src-check disable
```

Chapter 3 | Layer Three Technologies

The setting that controls this behavior is found under *config sys settings, and to enable strict* RPF checks, and then you must set the following field to enable, *# set strict-src-check enable.*

When troubleshooting RPF when the drop condition is met, then a message will show up in the diagnose flow debug. Here is an example:

```
NSE4-PASS (root) # id=20085 trace_id=97 func=print_pkt_detail line=5501 msg="vd-root:0 received a packet(proto=1, 9.9.9.9:512->8.8.8.8:2048) from vsw.internal7. type=8, code=0, id=512, seq=0."
id=20085 trace_id=97 func=init_ip_session_common line=5666 msg="allocate a new session-00447d92"
id=20085 trace_id=97 func=ip_route_input_slow line=2252 msg="reverse path check fail, drop"
id=20085 trace_id=97 func=ip_session_handle_no_dst line=5750 msg="trace"
id=20085 trace_id=98 func=print_pkt_detail line=5501 msg="vd-root:0 received a packet(proto=1, 9.9.9.9:512->8.8.8.8:2048) from vsw.internal7. type=8, code=0, id=512, seq=1."
```

Next, let's review the routing table and check for a route to the source address 9.9.9.9:

```
NSE4-PASS (root) # get router info routing-table all
..
S    9.9.9.9/32 [10/0] via 10.123.233.1, wan1, [5/0]
..
```

In the debug, we see the msg="reverse path check fail, drop" and that the packet is ingress on vsw.internal7. The routing table has a route for 9.9.9.9/32, but it points out wan1 and not vsw.internal7. Therefore, RPF Check dropped the packet.

Next, we are going to add a host route that points back to vsw.internal7 but adjust the Priority, so the route is less preferred than the route that points out wan1. Now, let's check the routing table again:

```
    S    9.9.9.9/32 [10/0] via 10.123.233.1, wan1, [5/0]
                    [10/0] via 192.168.209.1, vsw.internal7, [10/0]
```

The newly configured a route back to the ingress interface vsw.internal7 for 9.9.9.9/32 and set Priority to 10 while the Priority is set to 5 for the wan1 route. With these route statements FortiOS will still route traffic out wan1 but now will accept traffic ingress on vsw.internal7. Review debugs below:

```
NSE4-PASS (root) # id=20085 trace_id=112 func=print_pkt_detail line=5501 msg="vd-root:0 received a packet(proto=1, 9.9.9.9:1024->8.8.8.8:2048) from vsw.internal7. type=8, code=0, id=1024, seq=0."
id=20085 trace_id=112 func=init_ip_session_common line=5666 msg="allocate a new session-0044bcf3"
```

Chapter 3 | Layer Three Technologies

```
id=20085 trace_id=112 func=vf_ip_route_input_common line=2596 msg="find a route: flag=00000000 gw-10.123.233.1 via wan1"
id=20085 trace_id=112 func=fw_forward_handler line=771 msg="Allowed by Policy-59: SNAT"
```
From the debug messages we can conclude that the packet with source IP 9.9.9.9 ingresses vsw.internal7 but this time was allowed through to be processed by firewall policy 59.

The last thing I'm going to talk about RPF check is how to disable it. To completely disable this feature, then asymmetric routing would need to be enabled, or we can disable it at the interface level settings. We perform this config change in the CLI via:

```
NSE4-PASS (root) #  conf system settings
NSE4-PASS (settings) # set asymroute enable
or

NSE4-PASS (interface) # edit vsw.internal7
NSE4-PASS (vsw.internal7) # set src-check
enable     source IP check.
disable    source IP check.
```

By default, these commands are disabled. It is not good practice to enable asymmetric routing. Most of the time, it is only used for troubleshooting. When asymmetric routing is enabled, security scanning and ASIC offload do not work effectively.

In Summary, be aware of the RPF Check feature on FortiOS when designing a firewall solution for your network. And if you are having reachability problems, then run your diagnose flow debug command to check to see if it is causing the issue.

Session Table

We have discussed the Routing Table, how a route is selected, route attributes, and RPF Check so far in this chapter. The next topic that ties this all together is the Session Table. This is a fairly big topic because there are a lot of fields to go over, but no worries, I am going to step through them one and explain each one.

The Session Table is what makes FortiOS a stateful device. Meaning, once a packet is evaluated, and an egress interface is found, and the traffic can pass via Firewall Policy, then an entry in the Session Table is created. Some basic information that is stored in this entry is thing source and destination IP and port numbers. Also, the Session Entry tracks NAT operations and security features that evaluates the traffic. The Session Table is the mechanism that allows a returning packet back through the firewall without an explicit firewall policy, allowing it to do so.

Chapter 3 | Layer Three Technologies

Once one packet is evaluated and allowed by the Firewall Policy Table, then all subsequent packets apart of that communication matches the same Session Entry instead of being evaluated against the Firewall Policy Table again. A match is determined by the five items within the packet header information.

1) The source and destination IP addresses
2) The TCP/UDP source and destination port numbers
3) The Layer-3 protocol (ESP, IPv4, IPv6.. etc.)

The Session Table entry describes how the packet should be handled. Meaning, it states if NAT needs to be applied or if security features need to be applied to the packet, for example. All these decisions were made when processing the very first packet of the session, and the rest of the packets apart of the session will be handled the exact same way. When the session terminates, or a session becomes idle for too long, the Session Table entry is removed. To view the total of sessions within a VDOM issue CLI command:

```
NSE4-PASS (root) # get sys session status
The total number of IPv4 sessions for the current VDOM: 150
```

Next, to see a high-level session summary list issue the CLI command:

```
NSE4-PASS (root) # get sys session list
PROTO    EXPIRE SOURCE              SOURCE-NAT          DESTINATION         DESTINATION-NAT
tcp      3538   192.168.209.7:57655  10.123.233.2:57655  13.226.232.75:80    -
tcp      3562   192.168.209.52:61437 10.123.233.2:61437  216.58.197.142:443  -
```

This command is useful when wanting to obtain a quick snapshot of what type of traffic FortiGate is processing. For example, we could count how many open FortiGuard sessions are being handled via CLI command:

```
NSE4-PASS (root) # get sys session list | grep :8888 -c
38
```

which is 38 here. We could also use this command to look for a specific source/destination IP addresses.

FortiOS Clearing Sessions

Sometimes it is useful for troubleshooting to clear out Session Entries within the Session Table. To do this, you would use the following CLI command:

Chapter 3 | Layer Three Technologies

```
#diagnose sys session clear
```

> *If you issue CLI command:*
> *#diagnose sys session clear*
> *This will drop all session including routing protocols*
> *if a filter is not used.*

Next, there are also options here to configure a filter on which sessions you are interested in viewing or wanting to clear. To configure a session filter, you would issue the below CLI command(s):

```
NSE4-PASS (root) # diagnose sys session filter dst 8.8.8.8
NSE4-PASS (root) # diagnose sys session filter
session filter:
        vd: any
        sintf: any
        dintf: any
        proto: any
        proto-state: any
        source ip: any
        NAT'd source ip: any
        dest ip: 8.8.8.8-8.8.8.8
        source port: any
        NAT'd source port: any
        dest port: any
        policy id: any
        expire: any
        duration: any
        state1: any
        state2: any
```

UDP Session Table Entry

To view full Session Table Entries on FortiOS, we need to issue the following CLI command:

```
NSE4-PASS (root) # diagnose sys session filter dst 8.8.8.8
NSE4-PASS (root) # diagnose sys session list
```

session info: proto=17 proto_state=01 duration=64 expire=115 timeout=0 flags=00000000 sockflag=00000000 sockport=0 av_idx=0 use=5
origin-shaper=
reply-shaper=
per_ip_shaper=
class_id=0 ha_id=0 policy_dir=0 tunnel=/ helper=dns-udp vlan_cos=0/255

Chapter 3 | Layer Three Technologies

```
state=dirty may_dirty ndr npu app_valid
statistic(bytes/packets/allow_err): org=62/1/1 reply=99/1/1 tuples=3
tx speed(Bps/kbps): 0/0 rx speed(Bps/kbps): 1/0
orgin->sink:     org      pre->post,     reply     pre->post    dev=34->5/5->34
gwy=10.123.233.1/192.168.209.7
hook=post dir=org act=snat 192.168.1.7:58382->8.8.8.8:53(10.123.233.2:58382)
hook=pre dir=reply act=dnat 8.8.8.8:53->10.123.233.2:58382(192.168.209.7:58382)
hook=post dir=reply act=noop 8.8.8.8:53->192.168.1.7:58382(0.0.0.0:0)
src_mac=18:66:da:21:68:xx
misc=0 policy_id=59 auth_info=0 chk_client_info=0 vd=0
serial=004516dd tos=ff/ff app_list=6000 app=16195 url_cat=0
rpdb_link_id = 00000000 ngfwid=n/a
dd_type=0 dd_mode=0
npu_state=0x001008
npu info:   flag=0x00/0x00,  offload=0/0,  ips_offload=0/0,  epid=0/0,  ipid=0/0,
vlan=0x0000/0x0000
vlifid=0/0, vtag_in=0x0000/0x0000 in_npu=0/0, out_npu=0/0, fwd_en=0/0, qid=0/0
no_ofld_reason:  redir-to-ips
total session 11
```

Note that I had to use a filter command because if I did not, the output would be very large. The Session Table is very large most of the time, so use your filter. I know this is a lot of output and most likely looks a little confusing, well don't worry because it is. 😊

However, It is very important to understand this information if you work with FortiGates, so we are going to break this output downline by line. Let the fun begin!

`session info: proto=17 proto_state=01 duration=64 expire=115 timeout=0`

Line one, let's break this down. The 'proto' field means protocol, which is the layer-3 protocol value. The 17 here indicates UDP. Some other common protocol values to know are 1 and 6, which are ICMP and TCP, respectively. Next, the proto_state field tracks the current state of the upper-layer protocol. For example, since this is a UDP session, the state is '01', which means FortiOS has indeed seen a reply packet to the initial outbound request, and '00' would mean no reply. Even though UDP is a stateless protocol, there will still be a Session Table Entry for all UDP communication.

Table 3. 3 – UDP Protocol 17 State Values

State	Value
UDP Reply not seen	00
UDP Reply seen	01

..

duration=64 expire=115 timeout=0

Chapter 3 | Layer Three Technologies

..

The next fields to touch on are *duration, expire,* and *timeout*. The *duration* field is the time past in seconds after the creation of the session. The *expire* field is an idle count down timer and will reset every time a packet passes through the session entry. Lastly, the *timeout* field is how long a session can be idle before the session is removed from the Session Table; this field is used for TCP and SCTP. The UDP default timeout is 180 seconds.

TCP Session Table Entry

Next, we compare this line to a TCP Session Entry.

..

```
session   info:   proto=6   proto_state=11   duration=913   expire=3557 timeout=3600
```

..

We can tell this is a TCP session because of *proto=6,* which indicates protocol 6; the session has been alive for 913 seconds and will expire in 3557 seconds with an idle timeout configured to be 3600, which is the default for TCP. The next thing I want to touch on here is the TCP proto_state field. This field keeps track of the TCP state, which is more complex than UDP. The value of 11 here means the client and server-side of the TCP connection is in the established state. There are two values here 10=client and 01=server. FortiOS keeps track of the communication for both directions, and this is why two flags are required.

This might be a little confusing currently, so let me elaborate. The proto_state field contains two digits; the one on the left represents the client, and the one on the right represents the server. The possible values for each digit here are 0-9. Table 3.4 contains what each value represents regarding the bi-directional TCP connection and the associated default Expiry Timer for each state.

Table 3. 4 – Session Table proto_state value and Expire Timer

TCP State	Proto_state value	Default Expire Timer
NONE	0	10 Seconds
ESTABLISHED	1	3600 Seconds
SYN_SENT	2	120 Seconds
SYN_RECEIVED	3	60 Seconds
FIN_WAIT	4	120 Seconds
TIME_WAIT	5	1 Seconds
CLOSE	6	10 Seconds

Chapter 3 | Layer Three Technologies

CLOSE_WAIT	7	120 Seconds
LAST_ACK	8	30 Seconds
LISTEN	9	120 Seconds

It is good to know these TCP states in relation to this table when troubleshooting sessions in FortiOS. Moving on to the next part of the output:

```
origin-shaper=
reply-shaper=
per_ip_shaper=
```

I know we have not talked about traffic shapers yet, but essentially, a Traffic Shaper object is something that we can use to police certain traffic so it will not exceed a certain bandwidth or session threshold. These fields will indicate if there is a Traffic Shaper applied to the firewall Policy that allowed the traffic and what type of Traffic Shaper it is. The next line is:

```
class_id=0 ha_id=0 policy_dir=0 tunnel=/ helper=dns-udp vlan_cos=0/255
```

In 6.2.2 GA, you can configure class IDs. The purpose of this is to associate a Traffic Shaping Policy object with the Traffic Shaper Profile entries. Next, ha_id is used in High Availability operations. *policy_dir=0* is the field that represents the direction of the traffic, 0 is the original direction, and 1 is the reply direction. 'tunnel=/' this field points to a VPN tunnel the traffic is using. Next, 'helper=dns', this field points to any Session Helpers the traffic is using. A session helper is a function that adjusts application data values and creates PIN hole Session Entries for traffic like SIP or FTP. A PIN hole session is an expected port; the return traffic should hit that is different than the original outbound source port. Most of the time, this modification is needed when NAT is performed on the application traffic because certain applications were not meant to be NAT'ed when initially created.

Next, '*vlan_cos=*' , this points to any Cost of Service values being used in the communication, which is a field within the Ethernet header that is used to categorize traffic.

```
state=dirty may_dirty ndr npu app_valid
```

Next, look at 'state=' field. This is an important one to know. This field could contain many values that describe how the traffic in a session is being handled. Review Table 3.5 and take the time to know the meaning of these flags.

Table 3. 5 – Session Entry State Field Possible Values

State Flags	Details

Chapter 3 | Layer Three Technologies

may-dirty	Session marked with this flag when packet is allowed by firewall policy and is a place holder to mark the session as dirty in the future, which causes a re-evaluation of the policy.
dirty	When a route changes or policy changes, all sessions with may-dirty flags are then marked as dirty. The dirty flag indicates the next packet must be reevaluated against firewall policy and/or route lookup.
npu	The session goes through an acceleration ASIC like an NP6.
npd	The session is blocked from hardware acceleration
npr	The session is eligible for hardware acceleration
rem	The session is allowed to be reset in case of memory shortage for example if the device hit conserve mode
eph	The session is ephemeral, meaning TCP/UDP one way traffic
oe	The session is part of IPsec tunnel (from the originator)
re	The session is part of IPsec tunnel (from the responder)
local	The session originated from FortiOS itself which is local-out
br	The session is bridged meaning vdom is in transparent mode
redir	The session is redirected to an internal FGT proxy
wccp	The session is intercepted by wccp process which is Web Cache Communicate Protocol
nlb	The session is using a load-balanced VIP
log	The session is being logged, for example, Syslog or FortiAnalyzer
os	The session has traffic shaper on the origin direction
rs	The session has Traffic Shaper in the reply direction
ndr	The session is inspected by IPS engine
nds	The session is inspected by IPS anomaly which is DDoS security function
auth	The session is subject to authentication like FSSO
block	The session was blocked by IPS inspection
ext	The session is handled by a session helper
app_ntf	The session matched a policy entry that contains "set block-notification to enable."

I realize this is a big table, and it will take time for you to understand each one of these. I recommend taking this table and place it somewhere easy to reference.

Most of these values are intuitive, but I'll go over some of the important ones that may not be. Let's talk about may-dirty and dirty. All session entries that are allowed by a transit firewall policy are given the flag may_dirty. This simply marks what session should be re-evaluated if a policy change occurs or a route change occurs. If this happens, then may_dirty sessions add the dirty flag. This means the next packet that matches the session is completely re-evaluated, so the most up-to-date information can be applied to the session. This is useful because if you add or remove security features from a policy, FortiOS accounts for that. Also, if a route

Chapter 3 | Layer Three Technologies

change and the session might need to use a different egress interface, which could mean a different policy with different security features, the dirty flag solves these problems by telling FortiOS to re-process any packets that match the Session Entry and see if there are any new requirements when handling any subsequent packets in the flow. The next line to go over is:

```
..
statistic(bytes/packets/allow_err): org=62/1/1 reply=99/1/1 tuples=3
..
```

These fields are fairly intuitive. They provide packet and byte count bi-directionally. This is useful to see if packets are actively using a particular Session Entry.

```
..
tx speed(Bps/kbps): 0/0 rx speed(Bps/kbps): 1/0
..
```

These fields provide the bits and kilobits per second this session entry is passing.

```
..
orgin->sink: org pre->post, reply pre->post dev=34->5/5->34
..
```

These fields might not be so intuitive, but this indeed shows the ingress and egress interface of the session traffic flow.

1) The *org pre->post* are related to *34->5/*
2) The *reply pre->post* are related to */5->34*

Let's break down 34->5/ first. These are interfaces indicated by their index values. These index values can be found from the output of the CLI command diagnose netlink interface list.

```
NSE4-PASS (root) # diagnose netlink interface list | grep index=34 -A 1 -B 1
if=vsw.internal7 family=00 type=1 index=34 mtu=1500 link=0 master=0
ref=75 state=off start fw_flags=b800 flags=up broadcast run multicast
..
NSE4-PASS (root) # diagnose netlink interface list | grep wan1 -A 1 -B 1
if=wan1 family=00 type=1 index=5 mtu=1500 link=0 master=0
ref=132 state=off start fw_flags=8000 flags=up broadcast run multicast
--
```

The *orgin->sink* field states, the original traffic flow ingresses vsw.internal7 and egresses wan1, and the reply traffic flow ingresses wan1 and egress vsw.internal7. The next line to look at is,

```
..
gwy=10.123.233.1/192.168.1.7
..
```

Chapter 3 | Layer Three Technologies

the field *gwy* holds the value of the Gateway IP of the original traffic flow, which is 10.123.233.1 and also the return traffic flow Gateway IP, which is 192.168.1.7. Next is the NAT mapping information:

```
1) hook=post dir=org act=snat 192.168.1.7:58382->8.8.8.8:53(10.123.233.2:58382)
2) hook=pre            dir=reply            act=dnat            8.8.8.8:53-
   >10.123.233.2:58382(192.168.209.7:58382)
3) hook=post dir=reply act=noop 8.8.8.8:53->192.168.1.7:58382(0.0.0.0:0)
```

The first line here shows that 192.168.1.7 will be SNAT'ed to 10.123.233.2. Then on line 2, the *hook=pre dir=reply* means the reply traffic before any NAT function and what to expected ingress. FortiOS would expect to receive 10.123.233.2 on port 58382. Lastly, line 3 shows what the egress packet will look like post Destination NAT function takes place, which will be the original source IP of 192.168.1.7 using port 58382 to receive DNS reply traffic.

Next, we have *src_mac=18:66:da:21:68:xx*. This is fairly intuitive; this is the MAC address of 192.168.1.7. This is the machine that originated the communication and is directly connected to FortiOS, meaning the machine's MAC address will be used in the Ethernet header as the destination MAC address field. Moving on, take a look at:

```
..
 misc=0 policy_id=59 auth_info=0 chk_client_info=0 vd=0
..
```

Here we see the field *policy_id*, which contains policy ID 59, which is the policy that was associated with initially allowing the traffic to pass through FortiGate. This information could be useful in troubleshooting situations. Next is auth_info, which states if the session is using authentication within the policy or not. if 1 here, then the session is using some sort of authentication if 0 then is not.Next line:

```
..
serial=004516dd tos=ff/ff app_list=6000 app=16195 url_cat=0
..
```

The *serial* number field is used to assign each session a unique number used to identify sessions uniquely. Next, the *tos* field, which is currently set to override ToS values in packets using this session entry. FortiGate has the ability to mark ToS values in packets used in QoS. Next!

```
..
rpdb_link_id = 00000000 ngfwid=n/a
..
```

rpdb stands for Routing Policy Database. If the traffic was using a Policy Route instead of the regular Routing Table, then this field would have a value pointing to the PBR entry in the Policy Base Route Table, but this session is not using a policy

Chapter 3 | Layer Three Technologies

route. We will talk more about policy routing shortly. Next, *ngfwid* is used to associate traffic with NGFW features on FortiOS. Essentially, this is just a different method to apply security scanning features to traffic. Almost there!

```
..
npu info: flag=0x00/0x00, offload=0/0,
..
```

The field *flag* and *offload* are important to know because this tells us if the session is offloaded to the hardware ASIC. In this case, since we see all 0's here, this indicates this session is not offloaded. Before the slash is the original direction and after the slash is the reply direction of the traffic, (orginal_direction)/(reply_direction). Next, let's compare this with a session that is indeed offloaded to the hardware ASIC:

```
..
npu info: flag=0x81/0x81, offload=8/8
..
```

If a session is handed off to an NP6 or NP6lite, then the *offload* field value would be 8/8. Every NP will have a different value here. The *flag* field would be 0x81 for non-IPsec traffic and 0x82 for IPsec traffic. Here is a complete list of possible offload values for each type of NP chip.

Table 3. 6 – Session offload Field Value and Details

Session offload field values	Details
1/1	Network Processor 1 (FA1)
2/2	Network Processor 1 (FA2)
3/3	Network Processor 2
4/4	Network Processor 4
5/5	XLR ASIC Chip
6/6	Network Processor lite 4
7/7	XLP ASIC Chip
8/8	Network Processor 6

Table 3. 7 – Session flag Field Value and Details

Session flag Field Values	Details
0x81	Non-IPSEC or regular traffic.
0x82	IPsec traffic.

The important thing to take away from this part of the session output is the ability to recognize if a session if indeed offloaded to the NP or not. Lastly here:

Chapter 3 | *Layer Three Technologies*

```
..
no_ofld_reason:   redir-to-ips
..
```

This is a newer field that was added in a recent version of FOrtiOS that explicitly provides details on why a particular session is not offloaded to the NP.

<u>Dirty Session Handling Settings</u>

There are some options within FortiOS on how to handle dirty Session Entries. Remember, a Session Entry will add the Dirty flag if there is a firewall policy change or a routing change, and the next packet that matches the Session Entry will need to be re-evaluated by the CPU. In asymmetric environments combine with ECMP, this could overload certain CPUs because traffic will go back and forth between the NP and the CPU.

We change this behavior in the CLI via:

```
NSE4-PASS (root) # config system settings
NSE4-PASS (settings) # set firewall-session-dirty
check-all              All sessions affected by a firewall policy
change are flushed from the session table. When new packets are recived,
they are re-evaluated by stateful inspection and re-added to the session
table.

check-new              Established sessions for changed firewall
policies continue without being affected by the policy configuration
change. New sessions are evaluated according to the new firewall policy
configuration.

check-policy-option    Sessions are managed individually depending on
the firewall policy. Some sessions may restart. Some may continue.
```

There are three options here:

    1) *check-all*
        a. This means all session will be marked as dirty when a policy or routing change occurs and will be re-evaluated when a new packet is received. This is the default setting.
    2) *check-new*
        a. Only newly created sessions are evaluated against the modified policies or upon route change. This does not modify any existing session after any policy change.
    3) *check-policy-option*
        a. This option means the behavior is handled on a per firewall policy bases.

Chapter 3 | Layer Three Technologies

If check-policy-option is select, then a configuration option within the firewall policy will be available.

```
NSE4-PASS (86) # show ful | grep dirty
NSE4-PASS (root) # conf firewall policy
NSE4-PASS (policy) # edit 86
NSE4-PASS (86) # set firewall-session-dirty
check-all     Flush all current sessions accepted by this policy. These sessions must be started and re-matched with policies.
check-new     Continue to allow sessions already accepted by this policy.
```

That wraps it up for the Session Table overview. At this point, you should have a strong understanding of what the Session Table is and how to interpret the output. Nice work. In this next section, we are going to look at some routing examples and FortiOS routing features!

FortiOS Routing

Static Routing

The most basic and essential configuration on NAT Mode FortiGate is the Static Route entry. In some networks, all that is required on FortiGate one default static route and nothing more. I've already touched on how to configure static routes in chapter one, but I still want you to take a look at the static default route on FortiGate.

```
NSE4-PASS (static) # show | grep wan1 -f
config router static
..
    edit 71
        set gateway 10.123.233.1
        set device "wan1"  <---
    next
..
```

This is what a basic static default route looks like in the CLI. Notice the only thing that indicates this is indeed a default route is the absence of a destination network in the output. This is because the 'show' command does not display default table values. If we performed a 'show full', we could indeed see the expected quad 0's (0.0.0.0/0) that indicates a match all default route.

```
NSE4-PASS (static) # edit 71
change table entry '71'
NSE4-PASS (71) # show ful | grep dst
        set dst 0.0.0.0 0.0.0.0
        set dstaddr ''
```

Chapter 3 | Layer Three Technologies

This is something to be aware of when studying for the NSE4 exam and working on production networks. Also, be aware of the Route Entry attributes, which are:

1) Device (egress interface)
2) Destination (The destination Network)
3) Distance (or metric used for route preference)
4) Gateway (Next-hop IP address for route)
5) Priority (Another metric for static routes only)

Named Address Object Route

FortiOS can use different objects as the destination network within a Static Route Entry; if you are new to FortiOS, then you might not know how to create things like an Address Object and how to reference them, so let's go over this real quick.

To create an Address Object in the GUI navigate to 'Policy & Objects > Addresses > Create New Dropdown > Address'.

Image 3. 8 – Create Address Object

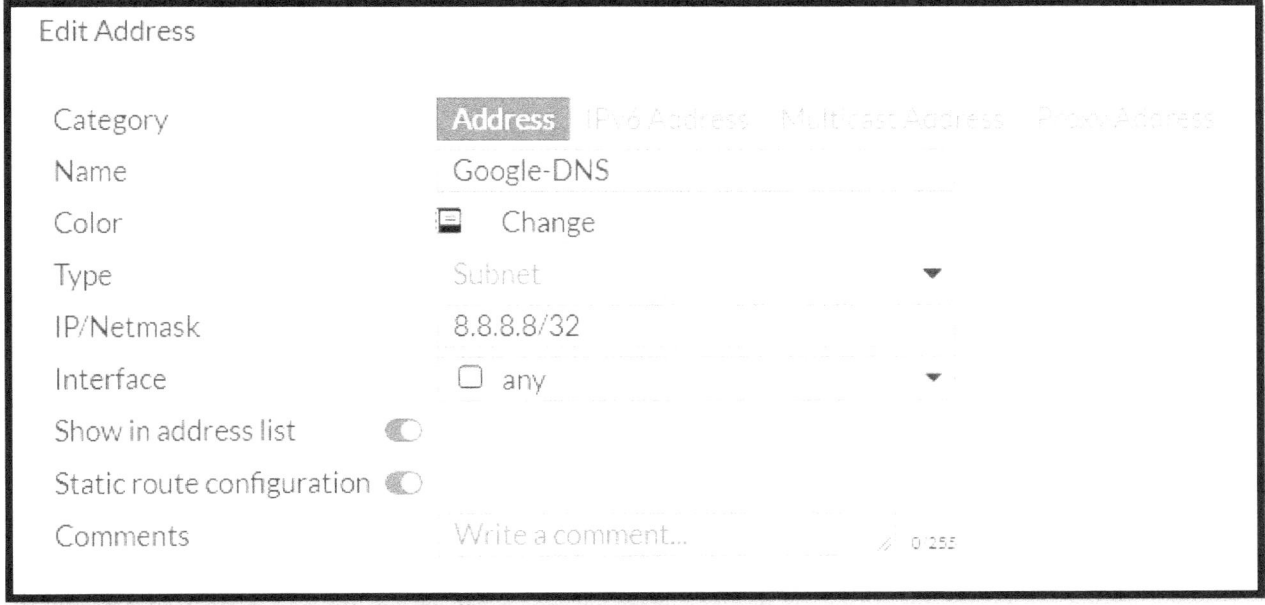

Here I am creating an Address Object for Google DNS, which is 8.8.8.8/32, since this is going to be used in a Static Route, then you must toggle on 'Static route configuration'. Here is what this looks like in the CLI:

```
NSE4-PASS (Google-DNS) # show
path=firewall, objname=address, tablename=Google-DNS, size=860
config firewall address
```

Chapter 3 | Layer Three Technologies

```
    edit "Google-DNS"
        set uuid 5b823b9a-49da-51ea-3889-a1e44341b9a7
        set allow-routing enable
        set subnet 8.8.8.8 255.255.255.255
    next
end
```

> *Remember to use your 'diag debug cli 7' command to view the CLI output of any GUI configuration*

You can think of objects like this as well as Service Objects, VIP Objects, or Security Profile Objects as something you build on your workbench. These objects are not live or active whatsoever when you create them (the exception are VIPs used in central-nat). They are just tools for you to reference in different parts of your configuration. Some objects can be referenced in the Firewall Policy Table, and others can be referenced in authentication functions. But here, we are going to reference our shiny new Address Object within our Static Route entry!

Next, navigate to the GUI Static Route configuration via 'Network > Static Routes > Create New Dropdown > IPv4 Route' and check out all the different destination types available. We use 'Named Address' in this example.

Image 3. 9 – Named Address Static Route

Chapter 3 | Layer Three Technologies

Here is what the CLI configuration would look like:

```
0: config vdom
0: edit root
0: config router static
0: edit 0
0: set gateway 10.123.233.1
0: set device "wan1"
0: set dstaddr "Google-DNS"
0: end
0: end
```

Using Address Objects and Object Groups could be useful when managing many static routes. This feature provides the ability to create one large Address Group that references many Address Objects that can be easily removed or added to the configuration, which in turn would add and remove Static Route Entries.

FQDN Static Route

Fully Qualified Domain Name (FQDN) is a DNS record with an associated IP address. In this next example, we are going to use the FQDN www.fortinet.com within our Static Route entry. The first step in accomplishing this is firstly to create an FQDN Address Object. Let us navigate back to 'Policy & Objects > Addresses > Create New Dropdown > Address' and create this.

Image 3.10 – GUI FQDN Address Object

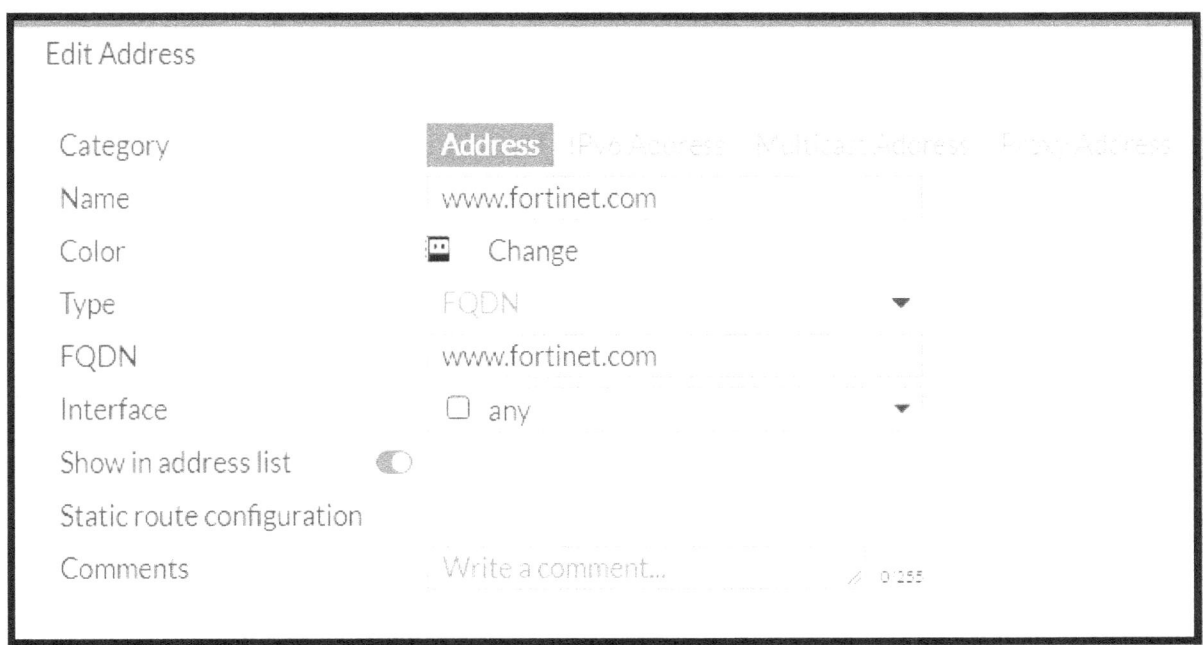

Chapter 3 | Layer Three Technologies

Here is the CLI equivalent of the GUI configuration in Image 3.10:

```
0: config firewall address
0: edit "www.fortinet.com"
0: set allow-routing enable
0: end
```

Next, take this object and reference it into the Static Route configuration, image 3.11:

Let me explain how FQDN routing works. Be sure to know that by just configuring a Static Route FQDN route does not route traffic by application data or HTTP host header information. FortiOS still uses IP information to reach www.fortinet.com. This is accomplished by firstly, FortiOS performs a DNS lookup on www.fortinet.com. If it is resolvable, then the IP address received will be injected into the Routing Table as a Static Route entry. That being said, for this route to work as expected, the source client machine and FortiGate should be resolving to the same IP address. To see what FortiGate resolved www.fortinet.com to we can issue the below commands:

Image 3.11 – FQDN Static Route

```
NSE4-PASS (global) # diagnose test application dnsproxy 6
worker idx: 0
vfid=0 name=www.fortinet.com ver=IPv4 timer running,  min_ttl=40:25,
cache_ttl=0 , slot=-1, num=1, wildcard=0
```

Chapter 3 | Layer Three Technologies

```
            52.52.208.2 (ttl=60:51:51)
NSE4-PASS (root) # diagnose firewall fqdn list
List all FQDN:
www.fortinet.com: ID(107) ADDR(52.52.208.2)
```

From this information, we can cross-reference the routing table with the resolved IP address and see the Static Route Entry.

```
NSE4-PASS (root) # get router info routing-table all | grep 52.52.20
S       52.52.208.2/32 [10/0] via 10.123.233.1, wan1
```

Here we can see the resolved IPv4 route was injected into the Routing Table. FortiOS will periodically query its assigned DNS server to resolve the FQDN address objects up to 32 IP entries per FQDN. it is also possible to increase the lifetime for the cached DNS IP for www.fortinet.com in the CLI:

NSE4-PASS (www.fortinet.com) # show

```
config firewall address
    edit "www.fortinet.com"
        set uuid 1503be7c-49d1-51ea-4c6d-1e48e0129ae7
        set type fqdn
        set allow-routing enable
        set fqdn "www.fortinet.com"
        set cache-ttl 86400      ←
end
```

Example of Floating Static Route

The next type to know about for the NSE4 exam is a floating static route. This is a fairly straight forward concept. A floating route is essential for a backup route. For example, If I have two WAN interfaces wan1 and wan2, and I have a default route pointing out wan1, and if I want my traffic to go out wan2 upon wan1 failure, then I would configure a static default route with a higher distance of say 250 for this to happen. Below is what the Routing Database would look like:

NSE4-PASS (root) # get router info routing-table database

```
Routing table for VRF=0
Codes: K - kernel, C - connected, S - static, R - RIP, B - BGP
       O - OSPF, IA - OSPF inter area
       N1 - OSPF NSSA external type 1, N2 - OSPF NSSA external type 2
       E1 - OSPF external type 1, E2 - OSPF external type 2
       i - IS-IS, L1 - IS-IS level-1, L2 - IS-IS level-2, ia - IS-IS
inter area
```

Chapter 3 | Layer Three Technologies

```
         > - selected route, * - FIB route, p - stale info

S       0.0.0.0/0 [250/0] via 10.25.69.1, wan2 inactive
S    *> 0.0.0.0/0 [5/0] via 10.123.233.1, wan1
```

As you can see, the active default route is pointing out wan1 since it has a more preferred Distance of 5, and there is an inactive floating default route pointing out wan2 with a Distance of 250, which is not in the Routing Table. The floating route will only become active if the wan1 interface goes down, which will result in the default route facing out wan2 to become active and, therefore, route traffic out wan2.

Static ECMP Routing

The next FortiOS routing feature to discuss is Equal Cost Multi-Path (ECMP). This is a method FortiOS uses to load-balance traffic across different paths. ECMP is activated when there are multiple routes with the same destination subnets that also have equal Distance and Priority values within the Routing Table.

For ECMP eligibility, routes must be injected by the same source. When I say source, I mean the same Routing Protocol or Static Route entries. For example, ECMP would not take place if there were an OSPF route and a Static route with the same destination network.

ECMP is available for the following Route Types:

1) Static
2) OSPF
3) BGP

For your NSE4 exam notes, for routes to be considered ECMP eligible, the following attributes must be the same:

1) Destination Subnet
2) Distance
3) Metric
4) Priority (Static Routes only)

Note, the default load-balancing algorithm is based on source IP and that all traffic from the same source will take the same path. In this example, I will be using static routes to demonstrate load balancing ECMP. I will configure two Static Route that is destined to 8.8.8.8/32 with the same Distance and Priority. Let's check out the Routing Table:

```
NSE4-PASS (root) # get router info routing-table  all
..
S       8.8.8.8/32 [10/0] via 192.168.1.72, vsw.internal7
```

Chapter 3 | Layer Three Technologies

```
                [10/0] via 10.123.233.1, wan1
..
```

After I create these routes, when we look in the Routing Table, there are two entries for 8.8.8.8/32. One that points out wan1 and one that points out vsw.internal7. Both Static Routes are active within the Routing Table because they have equal Distance and Priority, which creates an ECMP situation, and FortiOS effectively load-balances traffic destined for 8.8.8.8/32 between these two interfaces.

Next, the different load-balancing methods are:

1) Source IP (default)
    a. Meaning the Session from the same source IP will use the same route. This keeps sessions on an asymmetric path.
2) Source and Destination IP
    a. Meaning, Sessions with the same source and destination IP will use the same route. This also will keep sessions on an asymmetric path.
3) Weighted
    a. Meaning, Session will be distributed base on the weight value of SDWAN members. FortiOS will distribute sessions with different destination IPs by generating a random value with a probability of selecting one route over another based on the weight value.
4) Usage or Spillover
    a. Meaning a defined kbps rate threshold is set on the interfaces, and when the volume reaches the threshold for a single path only, then FortiOS use a different route.

These options are found in the CLI via:

```
60F-NSE4-PASS (settings) # set v4-ecmp-mode
source-ip-based         Select next hop based on source IP.
weight-based            Select next hop based on weight.
usage-based             Select next hop based on usage.
source-dest-ip-based     Select next hop based on both source and destination IPs.
```

For ECMP *weight-based* load-balancing, it is required to configure a weight value under the interface or the static route:

```
60F-NSE4-PASS (settings) # set v4-ecmp-mode weight-based
60F-NSE4-PASS (settings) # end
60F-NSE4-PASS # conf sys int
60F-NSE4-PASS (interface) # edit wan1
60F-NSE4-PASS (wan1) # set weight
weight    Enter an integer value from <0> to <255>.
..
```

Chapter 3 | Layer Three Technologies

```
60F-NSE4-PASS (0) # show
config router static
    edit 1
        set gateway 192.168.209.62
        set weight 100
        set device "wan1"
    next
end
```

Also, additional configuration is required if using *usage-based* (spillover) ECMP is used. This setting is also under the interface.

```
60F-NSE4-PASS (settings) # set v4-ecmp-mode usage-based
60F-NSE4-PASS (settings) # end
60F-NSE4-PASS # conf sys int
60F-NSE4-PASS (interface) # edit wan1
60F-NSE4-PASS (wan1) # set spillover-threshold
spillover-threshold    Enter an integer value from <0> to <16776000>.
```

In summary, ECMP provides redundancy and possible increased throughput. Note that SD-WAN features can be more effective when using ECMP. This wraps things up for our static routing section; next on the docket is Dynamic Routing!

Dynamic Routing Overview

Let me be clear on the goals of this section. I will only be providing a high-level overview of what dynamic routing protocols are offered in FortiOS and some cliff notes on each one. This section is in no way whatsoever a comprehensive chapter covering Dynamic Routing protocols and how to use them on FortiOS. The NSE4 Exam does not require in-depth knowledge of these protocols. The Fortinet NSE7 exam is where a deep dive into each of these protocols are provided.

Let's begin with a simple question, how is dynamic IP routing accomplished? It is accomplished by the various network-based protocol standards that were designed to share IP prefix information by forming neighbor relationships so to advertise known networks. These networks could be directly connected interfaces or explicitly specified networks in some cases.

All the routes discovered via routing protocols are evaluated by FortiOS, and the best route for each destination is then injected into the Routing Table. Metric is used to determine the best route within the same Routing Protocol. Also, Metric has different terms per Routing Protocol.

When a routing protocol neighbor is lost, all routes received from that neighboring device are then removed from the Routing Table, and it is then possible to re-route

Chapter 3 | Layer Three Technologies

traffic towards a new path. The ability to dynamically recover from topology change is one of the many reasons routing protocols are attractive to use, especially when managing large networks, because there comes the point when it is not feasible to manage a network with static routing alone. Let's go ahead and start the tour on what Dynamic Routing protocols are available on FortiOS.

Advanced Routing Feature Visibility

The first thing to know about FortiOS Dynamic Routing is how to turn the feature on so we can have GUI level configuration access to the underlying protocols. To do this, we navigate in the GUI to 'System > Feature Visibility> Advanced Routing' and click the toggle icon to enable it, and select Apply.

Image 3.12 – Advanced Routing Feature

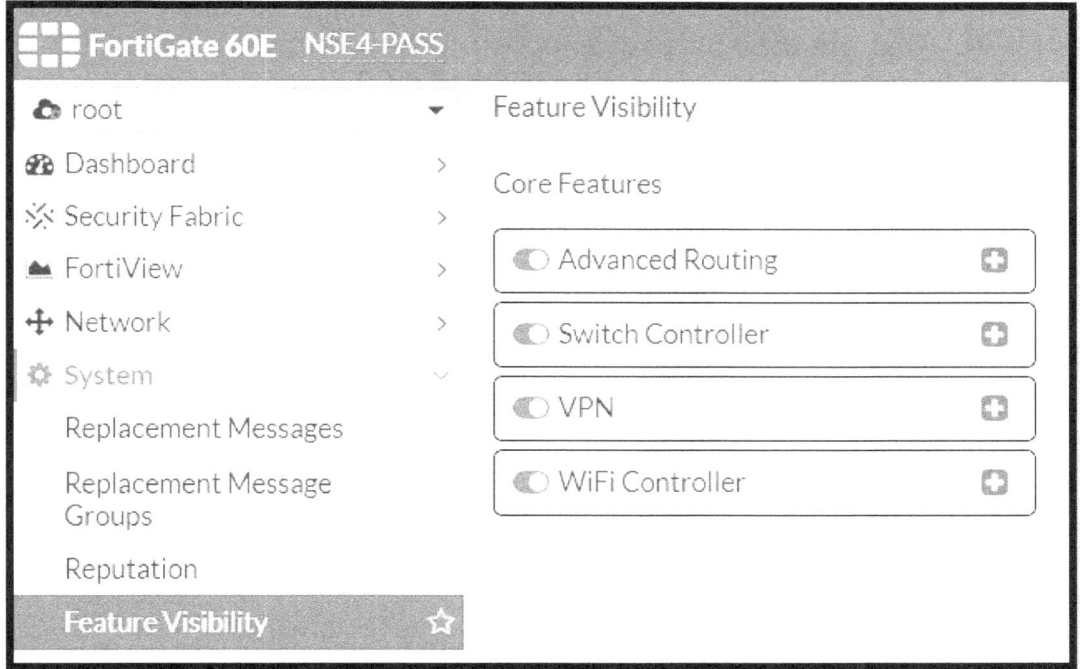

Border Gateway Protocol (BGP)

BGP-4 is available on FortiOS. The protocol was initially released in 1995 and was defined in RFC 1771 and has been replaced by a more recent standard, RFC 4271. BGP is the only routing protocol using TCP for transport on port 179. BGP is a very granular protocol and is the routing protocol I've worked with the most within my career. BGP is highly customizable and is the routing protocol Internet core routers use to share thousands of subnet blocks with each other.

Chapter 3 | Layer Three Technologies

The first thing to know about BGP is the BGP/TCP connection between two devices is referred to as a peering relationship, and each device is considered to be a BGP peer (or speaker). The next thing to know is that there are two different operational modes for BGP iBGP and eBGP, which are internal and external BGP, respectively. This operational mode is dependent on the Autonomous System (AS) number a BGP peer is locally assigned in comparison with the remote BGP peer AS number. If both BGP peers have the same AS number, then the operational mode is iBGP, and if different, BGP operational mode is eBGP. So, in other words, iBGP operations mean the AS number between the two peers are the same. eBGP operations mean the AS number between peers is different. Lastly, BGP has many values used as a Metric(s) regarding path selection. For example, eBGP mainly uses the AS Path attribute, which is a list of all the AS's the IP Prefix has been shared through, which is called the AS Path. The IP Prefix with the shortest path list wins. One of the metric values for iBGP is Local Preference, and this value is only shared with iBGP peers. The higher Local Preference value is preferred. There are many….many other metric values for BGP that are used for path selection. We cover these in the NSE7. Be sure to know the default Distance values for eBGP and iBGP Route Types.

1) iBGP
    a. Distance 200
2) eBGP
    a. Distance 20

Next, you should know where to configure BGP in FortiOS GUI to do this, navigate to 'Network > BGP' as seen in *image 3.13*.

Chapter 3 | Layer Three Technologies

Image 3.13 – BGP GUI Configuration Windowpane

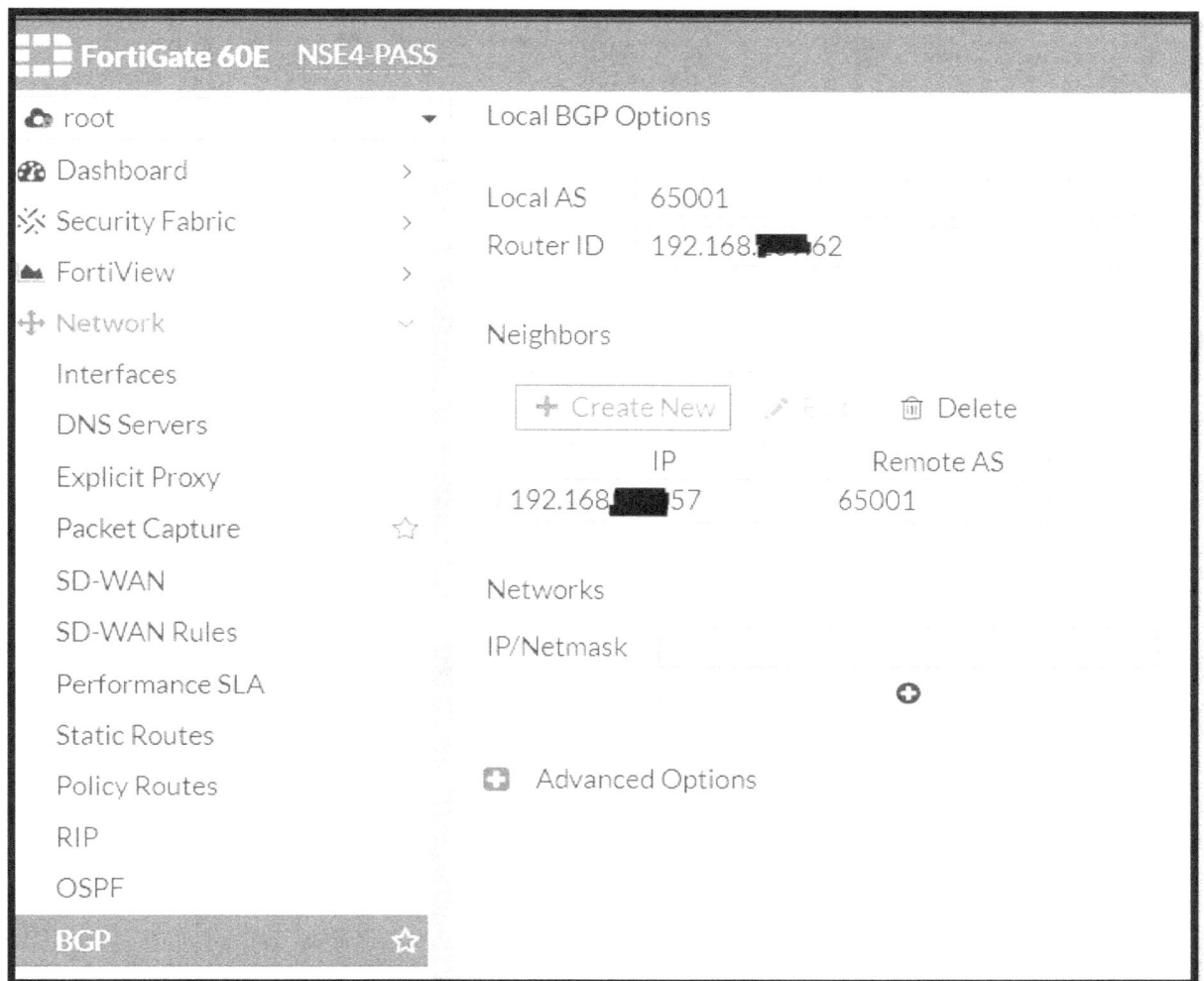

Here we can see a basic BGP configuration. We must specify the local AS, Router ID, which is like a name for the device in BGP. Next, configure a remote neighbor peer and its AS number. In the CLI, BGP configuration is found at #config router bgp.

Open Shortest Path First (OSPF)

The next Dynamic Routing protocol to touch on that FortiOS supports is OSPF. OSPF uses the Dijkstra's algorithm or Shortest Path First (SPF) algorithm, which was created by Edsger W. Dijkstra in 1956. OSPF is a popular interior gateway routing protocol (IGRP) that connects devices within a single AS or a single Enterprise network. This protocol is a link-state protocol, which means each device within an OSPF domain shares its interface attributes with each other, and each device determines the best path by running the SPF algorithm against the shared information. Each device essentially has a complete map of the OSPF Domain. The

Chapter 3 | Layer Three Technologies

metric in OSPF is called Cost. Also, know that the OSPF Domain can be divided into areas so as to achieve greater scalability.

You can use sniffer to see OSPF traffic:
NSE4-PASS (root) # diagnose sniffer packet any 'proto 89' 4

OSPF is known for its fast convergence times, meaning how fast OSPF can account for network topology changes and update the routing table to accommodate the newer topology. Also, OSPF is known for fast adjacency times, meaning how fast an OSPF neighbor relationship can be formed.

Know that OSPF is a layer-3 protocol, and its protocol number is 89 and uses a multicast address to find neighbors on direct connect LANs. The default Distance for OSPF is 110. The GUI configuration for OSPF is located at 'Network > OSPF'; see image 3.14 for details.

Image 3.14 – OSPF GUI Configuration Windowpane

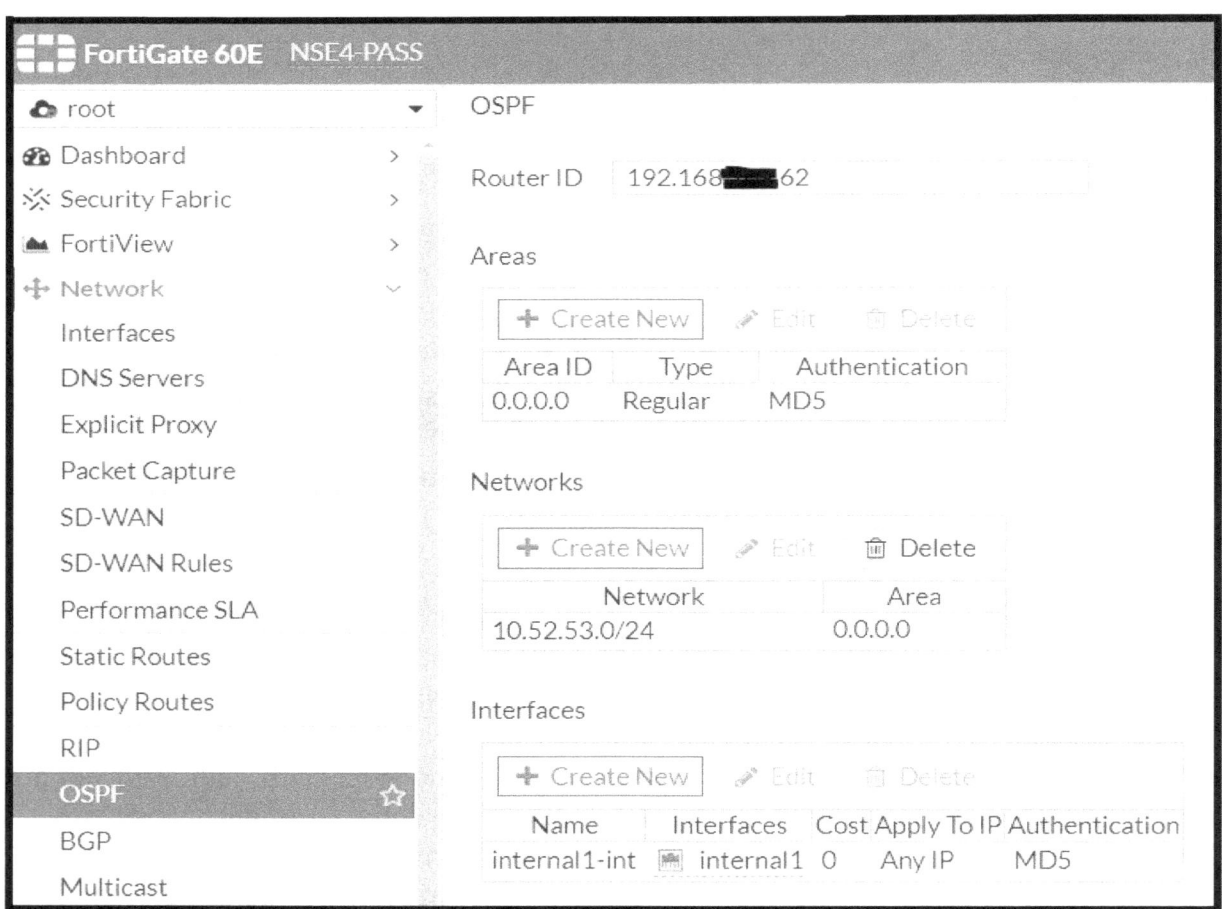

Chapter 3 | Layer Three Technologies

Let me go over *Image 3.14* with you. Once again, we have a router-ID, which is essentially the name of a device participating in the OSPF Routing Protocol within an OSPF Domain. Next, we have defined the area, which is area 0.0.0.0, which is just called Area Zero, but it is good to know this is actually a 32-bit value. Next, under Networks, this network value actually defines what local interfaces on FortiGate will run OSPF, meaning send and receive OSPF adjacency information. Meaning, internal1 interface assigned IP address falls with 10.52.53.0/24; therefore, internal1 sends and receive OSPF communication.

```
NSE4-PASS (root) # show sys int internal1
config system interface
    edit "internal1"
        set vdom "root"
        set ip 10.52.53.1 255.255.255.0
        set allowaccess ping https ssh snmp http telnet fgfm radius-acct probe-response fabric ftm
        set type physical
        set snmp-index 29
    next
end
```

Lastly, under the Interfaces configuration portion is where the OSPF interface attributes can be modified, like Cost.

Routing Information Protocol (RIP)

RIP is a protocol that is not widely used anymore, but we still have the option on FortiOS to run it. Some background, RIP is a distance-vector routing protocol meaning it does not share information on the interface like link speed. It only knows about its local information and next-hop value for defined routes. The RIP metric is defined by hop count, meaning how many physical devices ways of the original device that advertised the network subnet is.

RIP creates a neighbor relation using UDP as transport on port 520. RIP shares its entire routing table at defined intervals, which could consume large portions of bandwidth if the routing table is large – the default Distance for RIP on FortiOS 120. You can find the GUI RIP configuration section via 'Network > RIP'.

Dynamic Routing Summary

This was a really hard section to write, and I'm not being sarcastic. I love routing protocols, and I wish I could have just nerd'ed out and fill these pages with many details of OSPF and BGP and provide many examples, but at the end of the day, the NSE4 does not cover routing protocols like this. You really just need to know a very

Chapter 3 | Layer Three Technologies

high level of what they are. The NSE7 is where we get to have some real fun with these and break them down, and you can see just how effective the FortiGate is as a full-featured router! Moving on, in the last part of this chapter, I will be going over the many different FortiOS routing features we have to work with and show you how to use them.

FortiOS Routing Features

Let's be honest; FortiGate is a full-featured router as well as a security device. In this section, I'm going to be going over some really cool features we have to work with on FortiOS. I'm going to talk first about Policy Based Routing (PBR) and how to configure and use it. Next, I'm going to talk about the FortiOS Internet-Service Database and how we use it in our routing statements. Lastly, I'm going to touch on the Dynamic Gateway feature we have available to us in what it is and how to use it. Here we go!

Policy-Based Routing (PBR)

PBR and no, not the beer. I'm talking about Policy Based Routing. So, what is it? Well, PBR essentially allows us to break the rules of the Routing Table. As you know, FortiOS parse out the destination IP address of a packet and references the Routing Table to find the next-hop IP and egress interface for the packet. That being said, PBR, on the other hand, lets us parse out many other attributes of packet header information and allows us to make routing decisions based on this *other* information.

Next, why do we need it? One word, granularity. PBR provides us the tools to match the full conditions of an entire packet to generate a route decision. We could match anything from ingress/egress interfaces to source and destination IP pairings and level 4 transport protocols with any port number.

The first thing is first, find the PBR configuration section in FortiOS GUI via 'Network > Policy Route > Create New IPv4 Route'; see *image 3.15*.

CLI command to show PBR Table:
 # diagnose firewall proute list

Here is the CLI equivalent:

```
config router policy
..
    edit 3
        set input-device "vsw.internal7"
```

Chapter 3 | Layer Three Technologies

```
            set src "192.168.1.7/255.255.255.255"
            set dst "8.8.8.8/255.255.255.255"
            set protocol 1
            set gateway 10.52.53.2
            set output-device "internal1"
        next
end
```

Image 3.15 – Policy Based Route Configuration Windowpane

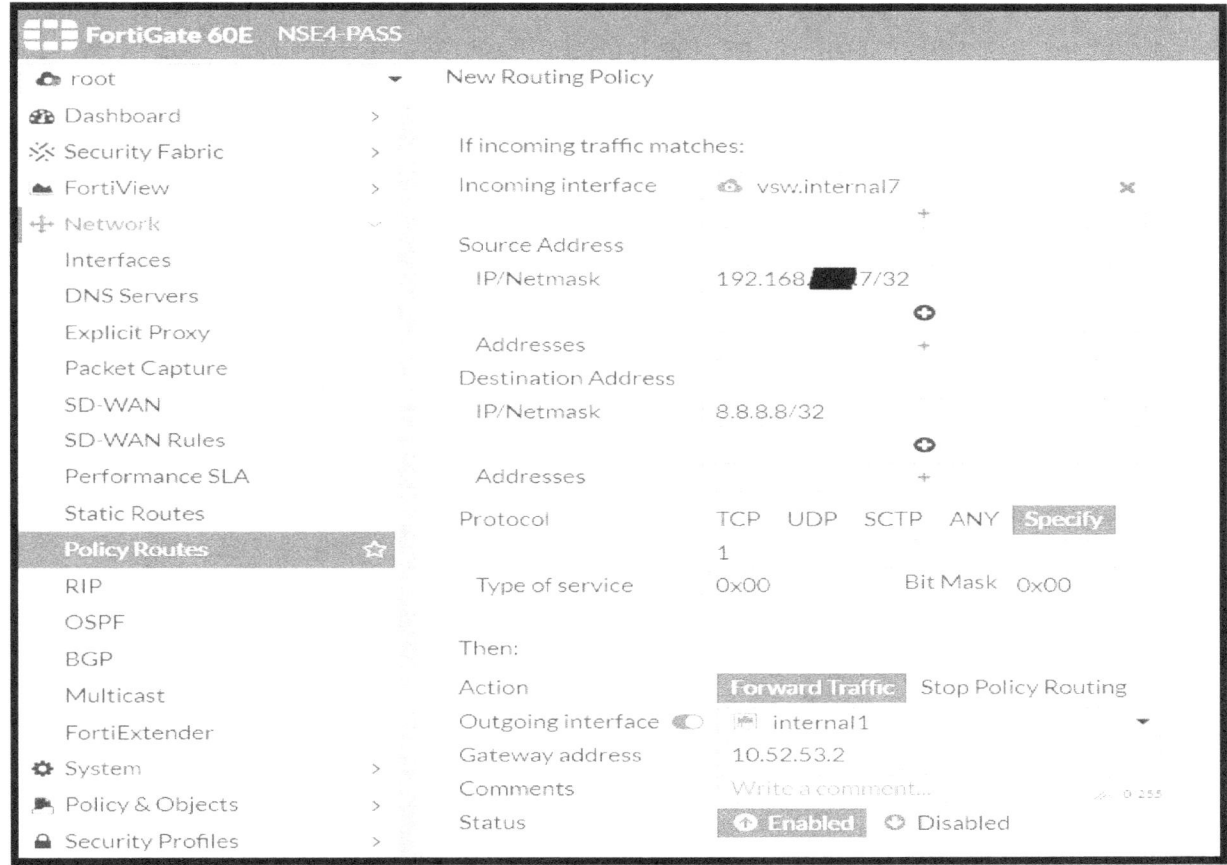

Let's step through these PBR configuration options. This rule state that if a packet is received on vsw.internal7 with source IP being 192.168.1.7 and destination IP 8.8.8.8 and is PING (protocol 1) THEN route this traffic to internal1 with next-hop being 10.52.53.1.

Policy Route Table

Next, let's review the PBR in the CLI:

```
NSE4-PASS (root) # diagnose firewall proute list
list route policy info(vf=root):
```

Chapter 3 | Layer Three Technologies

```
id=3 dscp_tag=0xff 0xff flags=0x0 tos=0x00 tos_mask=0x00 protocol=1
sport=0:65535 iif=34 dport=0-65535 oif=8 gwy=10.52.53.2
source wildcard(1): 192.168.209.7/255.255.255.255
destination wildcard(1): 8.8.8.8/255.255.255.255
hit_count=0 last_used=2020-02-10 14:02:04
```

This is what a PBR Table Entry looks like. Fairly intuitive, we can see this is for the root VDOM; this is the 3rd PBR configured, we are not matching on any ToS, but we are matching on protocol 1, which is PING. The *source wildcard* and *destination wildcard* are the source and destination IPv4 addresses being matched, respectfully. Lastly, we can see the hit count, meaning how many times this PBR has been used and the last time it has been used.

Note that ingress packets are evaluated against the PBR Table first before the regular Routing Table on FortiOS. If you see odd behavior in your routing on FortiGate, then remember to check for PBR.

Internet-Service Routing

The next topic we are going to discuss is routing with the Internet Service Database (ISDB). The first question, what is ISDB? ISDB is an internal database that is

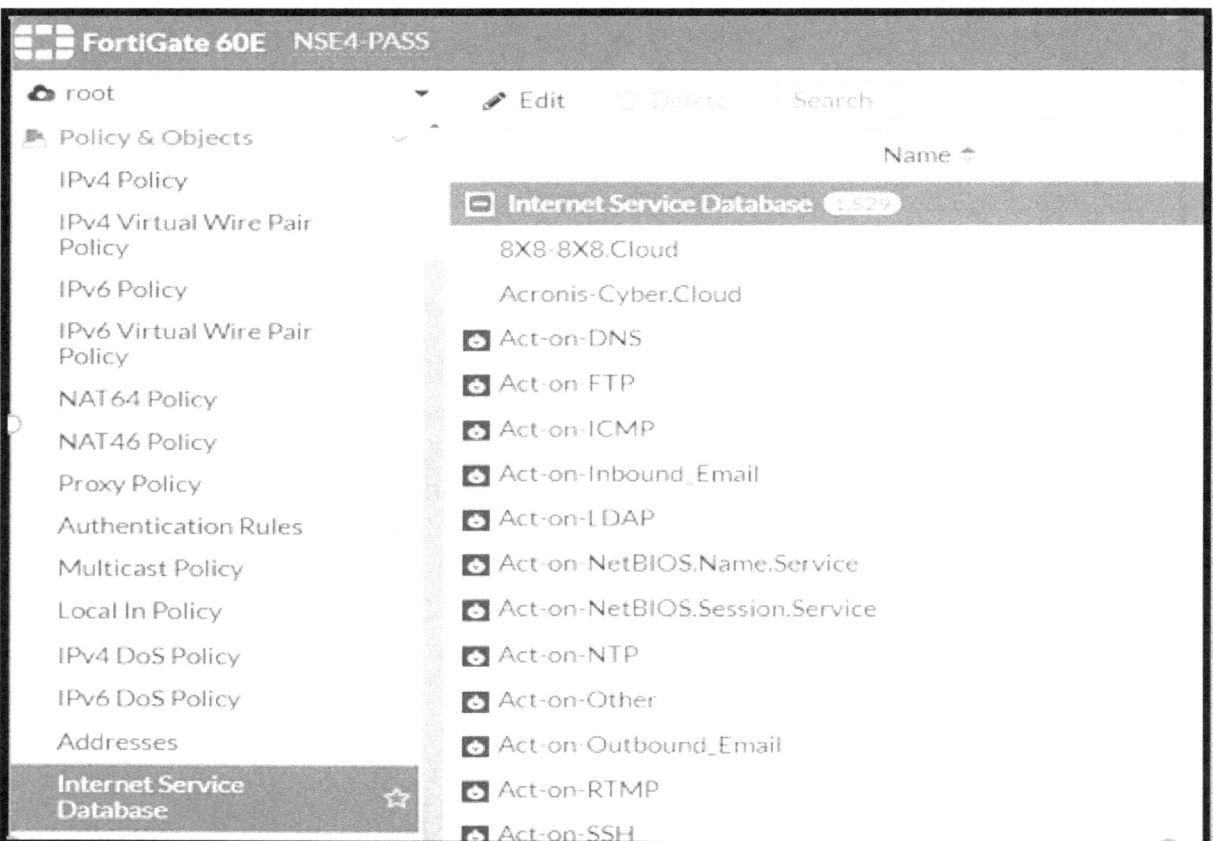

Chapter 3 | Layer Three Technologies

dynamically updated by FortiGuard. This database contains IP Prefix, Port, and Protocol, and these attributes are mapped to well-known services like Skype, Facebook, Amazon, Apple, or Citrix. To view this database on FortiOS in the GUI goto 'Policy & Objects > Internet Service Database', see *Image 3.15* for details.

Image 3.15 – ISDB Route Example

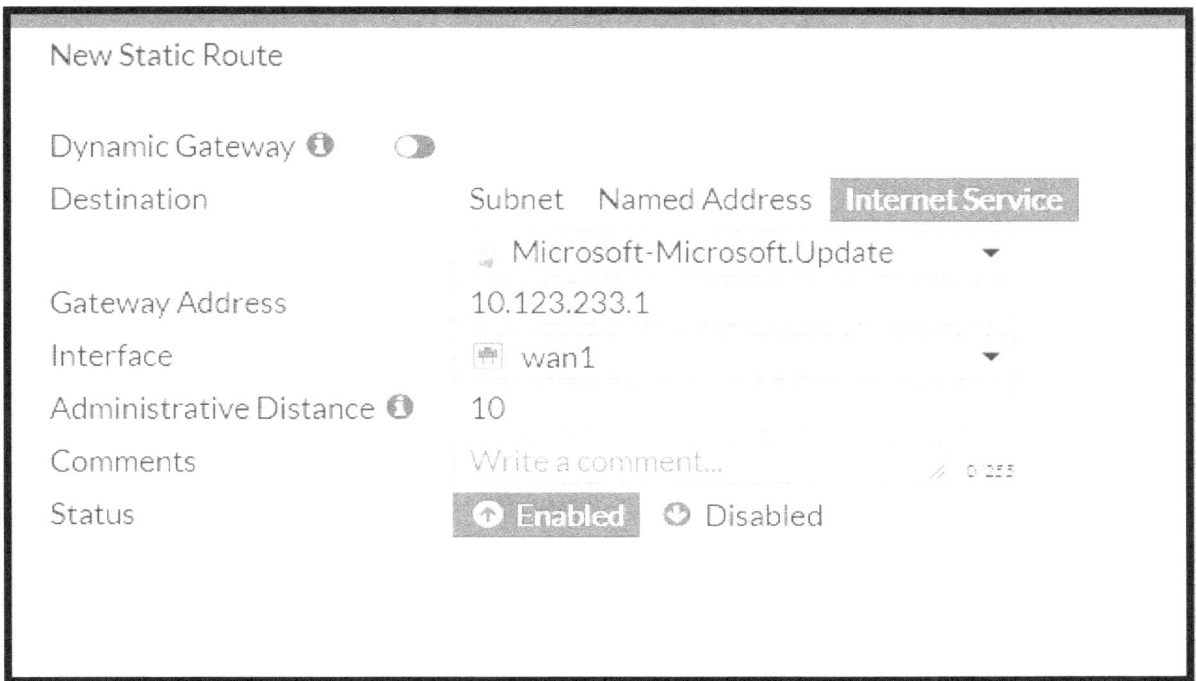

Since we now know what ISDB is, let use it. In this example, we are going to use an ISDB entry within a Static Route Entry. In this example, we are going to explicitly route Microsoft Update traffic, which could easily be a dedicated circuit. To do this, we navigate to: 'Network > Static Routes > Create New', see image 3.16.

Here is the CLI equivalent:

```
NSE4-PASS (root) # 0: config vdom
0: edit root
0: config router static
0: edit 0
0: set gateway 10.123.233.1
0: set device "wan1"
0: set internet-service 327793
0: end
0: end
```

Chapter 3 | Layer Three Technologies

On the backend, FortiOS installs a PBR with the values referenced in ISDB object 327793, which maps to Microsoft Update.

```
NSE4-PASS (root) # diagnose firewall proute list
list route policy info(vf=root):
..
id=2113929296  static_route=80  dscp_tag=0xff  0xff  flags=0x0  tos=0x00
tos_mask=0x00    protocol=0    sport=0:0    iif=0   dport=1-65535   oif=5
gwy=10.123.233.1
source wildcard(1): 0.0.0.0/0.0.0.0
destination wildcard(1): 0.0.0.0/0.0.0.0
internet service(1): Microsoft-Microsoft.Update(327793)
hit_count=11 last_used=2020-02-10 16:06:57
..
```

Here is our routing information, but still no IP/Port information. To extract the ISDB routing information for Microsoft Update you would need to issue the following command in the CLI for the ISDB ID 327793, but since this output is too large, I am going to use FortiGuard ISDB ID as an example:

```
NSE4-PASS (global) # diagnose internet-service id 1245324
Internet Service: 1245324(Fortinet-FortiGuard)
Version: 00007.00442
Timestamp: 202002101136
Number of IP ranges: 84
45.75.200.64-45.75.200.95  geo_id(22668)  black  list(0x0)  proto(6)
port(21 25 80 443 541 990 8000 8888-8890)
```

This is one example of FortiGuard IP, protocol, and port bindings. This information under the ISDB entry is what creates the PBR's. In summary, FortiOS gives the ability to route related subnet, protocol, and port pairings associate with popular applications and services. This can be done by referencing an ISDB id entry within a static route.

<u>Dynamic Gateway</u>

On FortiOS, we can receive a Dynamic Gateway via setting up an interface as a DHCP client and receiving interface configuration attributes like a gateway address from a DHCP server. This is commonly used for WAN links facing your ISP and in SDWAN deployments. To set this up first thing to do is set wan1 as a DHCP client:

```
config system interface
    edit "wan1"
        set vdom "root"
        set mode dhcp
        set allowaccess ping https ssh snmp http telnet fgfm
```

Chapter 3 | Layer Three Technologies

```
            set type physical
            set role wan
            set snmp-index 1
    next
end
```

By default, Dynamic Gateway routes have a Distance of 5, but this can be easily modified if multiple DHCP client interfaces exist on FortiGate, and one needs to be preferred over another. The Dynamic Gateway route is injected into the Routing Table as a Static Route:

```
FGT60FTK19031239 # get router info routing-table  all
..

S*      0.0.0.0/0 [5/0] via 192.168.209.62, wan1
C       192.168.209.0/24 is directly connected, wan1
```
Next, many attributes can be modified regarding attributes received from the DHCP server and to see these options; we navigate to the wan1 interface; see *Image 3.16*.

Image 3.16– Wan1 DHCP Client Interface

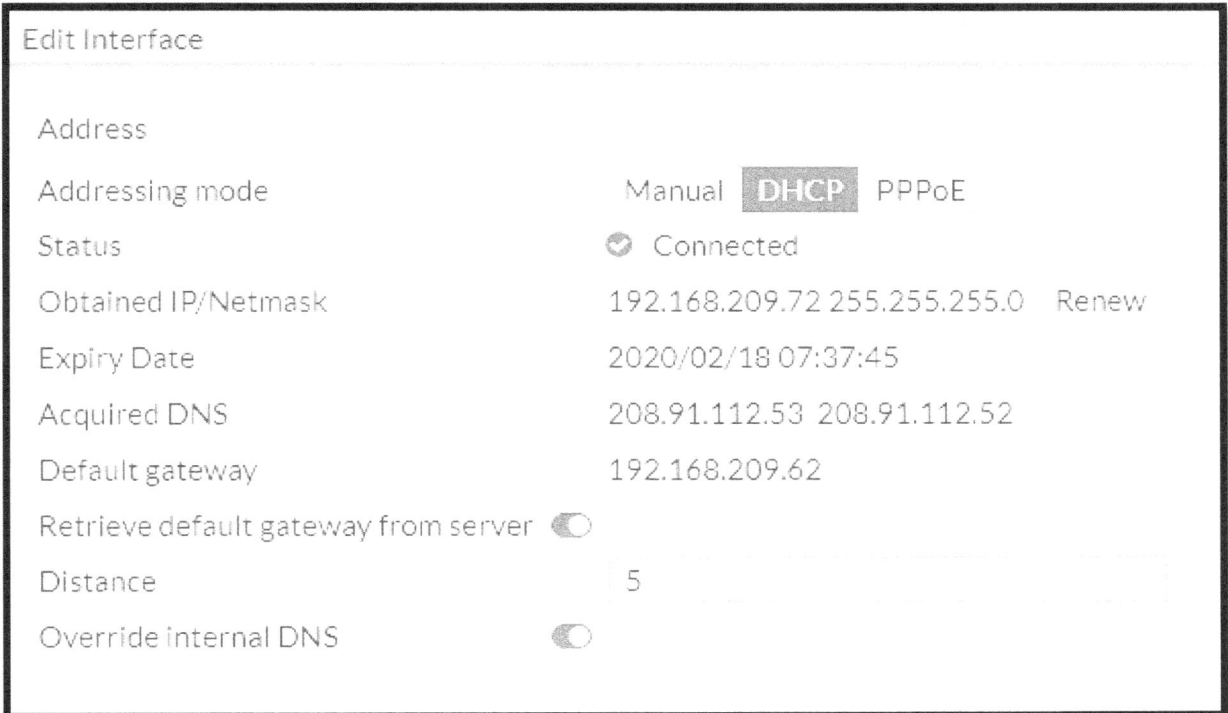

Here you can see that there are a few options, one is not to receive a gateway address via DHCP and another to adjust the Distance if needed. We can also see

Chapter 3 | Layer Three Technologies

here that FortiGate received an IP of 192.168.209.72 and DNS server IP addresses. That pretty much wraps it up for Dynamic Gateway Route Entry, moving on!

Link Monitor

The last routing feature to go over in this chapter is Link Monitor. This feature is essentially a mechanism to detect path failure on FortiOS and re-route traffic accordingly. Link Monitor can be configured to send probes down interfaces to a known good reachable location, and if the probes fail to return then, Link Monitor can be configured to remove all routes associated with the egress interface.

Note that the Link Monitor feature has been removed from the GUI because 6.2 is more focused on combining this feature into SDWAN in general. But if SDWAN is not used in your environment, we can still use this feature in the CLI. Let's walk through this configuration.

```
60F-NSE4-PASS (link-monitor) # show
path=system, objname=link-monitor, tablename=(null), size=3352
config system link-monitor
    edit "Link-mon"
        set srcintf "wan1"
        set server "8.8.8.8"
        set gateway-ip 192.168.209.62
    next
end
```

This is the most basic form of a Link Monitor configuration. What this configuration states is that FortiOS will send PING probes out wan1 with destination for 8.8.8.8 with a local gateway address of 192.168.209.62. If 5 PING's receive no response, then remove all routes associated with wan1.

To understand this better we are going to review the full output of 'Link-mon':

```
60F-NSE4-PASS (Link-mon) # show ful
config system link-monitor
    edit "Link-mon"
        set addr-mode ipv4
        set srcintf "wan1"
        set server "8.8.8.8"
        set protocol ping
        set gateway-ip 192.168.209.62
        set source-ip 0.0.0.0
        set interval 500
        set failtime 5
        set recoverytime 5
        set ha-priority 1
```

Chapter 3 | Layer Three Technologies

```
        set update-cascade-interface enable
        set update-static-route enable
        set status enable
    next
end
```

Let's walk through this configuration; the next thing I want to touch on here is the protocol. By default, the probe used by Link-Monitor is PING. This can be changed to:

1) ping   link monitor.
2) tcp-echo   TCP echo link monitor.
3) udp-echo   UDP echo link monitor.
4) http   HTTP-GET link monitor.
5) twamp   TWAMP link monitor.

PING is most commonly used, but there are other benefits using other methods that we will discuss in our SDWAN chapter. The interval that probes are sent down wan1 is every 500 msec:

```
60F-NSE4-PASS (Link-mon) # set interval
interval    Enter an integer value from <500> to <3600000> (default = <500>).
```

Next, *failtime* is how many probes can be lost before wan1 is considered down and *recoverytime* is how many successful probes must be received before the link is then again considered up and good, and routes are then again added back to the Routing Table.

```
60F-NSE4-PASS (Link-mon) # set
failtime                    Number of retry attempts before the server is considered down (1 - 10, default = 5)
recoverytime                Number of successful responses received before server is considered recovered (1 - 10, default = 5).
```

The next setting is *ha-priority*, which is related to the HA remote IP monitor which is used to trigger a failover event. *The related HA setting is:*

```
config system ha
..
set pingserver-failover-threshold 10
..
```

The next setting is *update-cascade-interface*; this is a useful setting because we can have FortiOS shutdown another interface if this link-monitor goes into the failed

Chapter 3 | Layer Three Technologies

state. For example, we could configure to shutdown wan2 as well if wan1 goes down.

```
config system interface
    edit "wan1"
        set vdom "root"
        set mode dhcp
        set allowaccess ping https ssh , http
        set fail-detect enable
        set fail-detect-option detectserver link-down
        set fail-alert-method link-failed-signal
        set fail-alert-interfaces "wan2"
        set type physical
        set role wan
        set snmp-index 1
    next
end
```

The last configuration setting I want to touch on here is *update-static-route*. If this setting is enabled when Link Monitor fails, then all routes associated with the source interface, which is wan1, will be removed from the routing table. If the setting is disabled, then routes will remain in the Routing Table. This provides granularity to accommodate network requirements. Lastly, to see the status of the Link-Monitor probe, we could issue the following CLI diagnose command:

```
60F-NSE4-PASS # diagnose sys link-monitor status
Link Monitor: Link-mon, Status: alive, Server num(1), Flags=0x1 init,
Create time: Tue Feb 11 08:25:45 2020
Source interface: wan1 (5)
Gateway: 192.168.209.62
Interval: 500 ms
  Peer: 8.8.8.8(8.8.8.8)
        Source IP(192.168.209.72)
        Route: 192.168.209.72->8.8.8.8/32, gwy(192.168.209.62)
        protocol: ping, state: alive
                Latency(Min/Max/Avg): 8.683/11.599/9.148 ms
                Jitter(Min/Max/Avg): 0.029/2.591/0.437
                Packet lost: 0.000%
                Number of out-of-sequence packets: 0
                Fail Times(0/5)
                Packet    sent:    8976,    received:    7206,
Sequence(sent/rcvd/exp): 8977/8977/8978
```

Note that the industry is moving away from using just Link-Monitor and moving more towards using the SDWAN, which indeed uses the same methods described in this

Chapter 3 | Layer Three Technologies

section to detect link failure or degradation. This wraps things up for FortiOS routing features. The last thing to cover in this chapter is troubleshooting!

FortiOS IP Diagnostic

Being NSE4 certified requires you to be able to perform basic IP routing troubleshooting on FortiGate networks. There are a few commands that help us with this. I've already touched on a few of them so far in this book, but this section lets us officially review them!

Sniffer

The first command I want to talk about is the diagnose sniffer command. This command is essentially TCPDUMP rebranded by Fortinet. If you are familiar with using TCPDUMP, then you are ahead of the curb here, but if not, that's ok. Just know, a lot of the TCPDUMP commands can be used within the Sniffer debug.

The CLI command to run to display network information is:

```
60F-NSE4-PASS # diagnose sniffer packet wan1
interfaces=[wan1]
filters=[none]
0.988850 arp who-has 192.168.209.55 tell 192.168.209.62
0.990487 192.168.209.72 -> 8.8.8.8: icmp: echo request
0.999363 8.8.8.8 -> 192.168.209.72: icmp: echo reply
```

This is the most basic form of the command. If we do not provide any options or filters here and specify a certain interface and in this case, wan1, then sniffer will display all and any packets received by the FortiOS. We could have easily not bonded this command to a particular interface by specifying 'any' instead of wan1, which will display all traffic from any interface.

```
60F-NSE4-PASS # diagnose sniffer packet any
interfaces=[any]
filters=[none]
```

This could be a lot of output, so be careful when issuing this command in a production environment without any filters on any interface. The sniffer displays if any packets were not captured and where dropped by the kernel. This could be because the sniffer was trying to intercept too much data. We can see this when we exit out of the sniffer debug:

```
..
1.520443 192.168.209.72 -> 8.8.8.8: icmp: echo request
1.529361 8.8.8.8 -> 192.168.209.72: icmp: echo reply
^C
```

Chapter 3 | Layer Three Technologies

```
24 packets received by filter
0 packets dropped by kernel
```
Here we see we captured a total of 24 packets and dropped none. And note, to exit sniffer debug, you must enter Ctrl+C. Next, let's look at some sniffer filter examples.

```
60F-NSE4-PASS # diagnose sniffer packet any 'host 8.8.8.8'
interfaces=[any]
filters=[host 8.8.8.8]
0.590467 192.168.209.72 -> 8.8.8.8: icmp: echo request
0.599178 8.8.8.8 -> 192.168.209.72: icmp: echo reply
```
Here we appended 'host 8.8.8.8' filter. This tells FortiOS we only want to see any packets with a source or destination of 8.8.8.8. Next, we can filter on port numbers as well. In this example, we will look for DNS traffic:

```
60F-NSE4-PASS # diagnose sniffer packet any 'port 53'
interfaces=[any]
filters=[port 53]
1.460519 192.168.209.72.3481 -> 208.91.112.52.53: udp 35
1.486795 208.91.112.52.53 -> 192.168.209.72.3481: udp 414
```

Note that by issuing the filter 'port 53' this captures UDP or TCP ports. We could specify UDP packets only by issuing the filter 'udp port 53', and the same goes for TCP. We could easily look for IPsec traffic using 'esp' within the filter as well. Next, we could combine these filters to narrow down what traffic we are looking for by using IP, port, and protocol:

```
60F-NSE4-PASS # diagnose sniffer packet any 'host 192.168.209.72 and host 208.91.112.52 and udp port 53'
interfaces=[any]
filters=[host 192.168.209.72 and host 208.91.112.52 and udp port 53]
18.170516 192.168.209.72.1645 -> 208.91.112.52.53: udp 27
```

We do this by using the 'and' conditional statement within our filter. The next import filter is the ability to look for certain EtherTypes. This provides the ability to look at different layer-3 protocols. For example, to find ARP packets:

```
60F-NSE4-PASS # diagnose sniffer packet any 'ether proto 0x0806'
interfaces=[any]
filters=[ether proto 0x0806]
1.282800 arp who-has 192.168.209.57 tell 192.168.209.62
```

The next important field to discuss when using the sniffer debug command is the verbosity level. We have a total of six verbosity levels. Each one will display different parts of the packets of interest. These options will provide the ability to display:

Chapter 3 | Layer Three Technologies

1) IP Headers
2) Packet payload
3) Ethernet Headers
4) Interface Name

If no verbosity is set, then the default is level one, which only shows IP Header information. This is set after the filter, and to use level six, the command would look like:

```
60F-NSE4-PASS # diagnose sniffer packet any 'host 8.8.8.8' 6
```
Here is a full list to verbosity to information mappings:

1) Verbosity Level One
    a. Display: IP Headers
2) Verbosity Level Two
    a. Display: IP Headers and Packet Payload,
3) Verbosity Level Three
    a. Display: IP Headers, Packet Payload, and Ethernet Headers
4) Verbosity Level Four
    a. Display: IP Headers, Interface Name
5) Verbosity Level Five
    a. Display: IP Headers, Packet Payload, and Interface Name
6) Verbosity Level Six
    a. Display: IP Headers, Packet Payload, Ethernet Headers, and Interface Name

The most common verbosity level to use other than one is four and six. Four because sometimes it is useful to see the ingress and egress interface a packet is taking. And Level Six because this verbosity level can be converted into a PCAP file, which then can be opened by a packet analyzer like Wireshark.

You can convert sniffer capture with verbosity level 6 to a PCAP with a tool called fgt2eth.exe found via: https://kb.fortinet.com/kb/documentLink.do?externalId=11186

The next setting to discuss is the count and by default is 0, meaning no limit. You can explicitly set the number of packets you wish to capture with the sniffer command after you set the verbosity level. For example, if you want to capture three packets at verbosity level six, then your command would look like so:

```
60F-NSE4-PASS # diagnose sniffer packet any 'host 8.8.8.8' 6 3
```

The last setting is the timestamp format. There are possible options.

Chapter 3 | Layer Three Technologies

1) option 'a' is UTC time
2) option 'l' is local time
3) no options set, meaning time will be relative to the start of the sniffer

The most common value to set is UTC time, which is 'a'. So in this last example, to set the verbosity level to six and capture three packets in UTC time, the command would be:

```
60F-NSE4-PASS # diagnose sniffer packet any 'host 8.8.8.8' 6 3 a
```

For reference here is the complete syntax for the sniffer command:

```
#diagnose sniffer packet <interface> <filter> <verbose> <count> <Timestamp format>
```

1) filter syntax
   a. [[src|dst] host<1st IP Address>] and/or [[src|dst] host<2nd IP Address>] [[arp|ip|gre|esp|udp|tcp] [port value]]

Traffic offloaded to NP will not show up on a sniffer debug, be sure to disable offload and clear sessions before debugging traffic

---

GUI PCAP

FortiOS provides a very convenient GUI feature that offers a method to generate PCAP's using filters. Let's explore this, in the GUI navigate to 'Network > Packet Capture > Create New,' and you should see the same as *image 3.16*.

Image 3.16 — GUI Packet Capture Filter

New Packet Capture Filter	
Interface	wan1
Maximum Captured Packets	4000
Filters	⬤
Host(s)	8.8.8.8
Port(s)	
VLAN(s)	
Protocol	17
Include IPv6 packets	⊙
Include Non-IP Packets	⊙

Chapter 3 | Layer Three Technologies

On this GUI page we can configure our filter, which is looking for the IP 8.8.8.8 using UDP, which will most likely be DNS traffic. After we complete our filter configuration next, we must right-click the object and click Start within the pop-up context menu, as seen in *image 3.17*.

Once you see packets hit your filter and you are satisfied with the count, you may click Stop and then Download.

Image 3.17 – Start Capture GUI

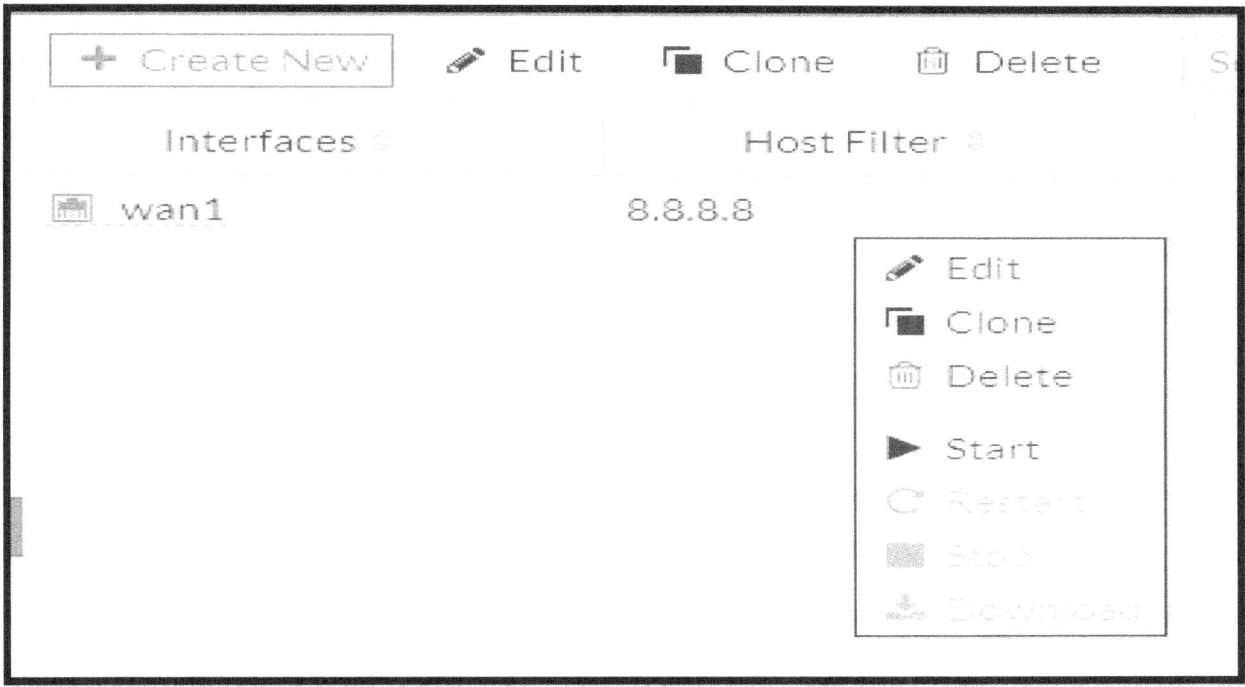

Diagnose Flow Debug

This is one of my favorite debugs, and I found it very useful when I worked at an MSSP managing FortiGate firewalls for customers. If you ever have issues, this is usually the first debug I use to understand the problem. This debug shows you the inner workings of the kernel processing packets through FortiGate. The first thing to review is the filter to use with this debug.

```
60F-NSE4-PASS # diagnose debug flow filter
clear      Clear filter.
vd         Index of virtual domain.
proto      Protocol number.
addr       IP address.
saddr      Source IP address.
daddr      Destination IP address.
port       port
```

Chapter 3 | Layer Three Technologies

```
sport      Source port.
dport      Destination port.
negate     Inverse filter.
```

The filter is reasonably intuitive to use. Before we start the debug trace, we need to be sure the filter is configured to catch only the traffic we are looking for. The best way to do this is to key onto a source and destination IP as well as a port number. In this example, the filter will be configured to look for the source IP of 192.168.209.7 and a destination IP of 8.8.8.8 and PING, which is protocol 1. Let's jump into the CLI and configure this.

```
NSE4-PASS (root) # diagnose debug flow filter saddr 192.168.209.7
NSE4-PASS (root) # diagnose debug flow filter daddr 8.8.8.8
NSE4-PASS (root) # diagnose debug flow filter proto 1
NSE4-PASS (root) # diagnose debug flow filter
        vf: any
        proto: 1
        Host addr: any
        host saddr: 192.168.209.7-192.168.209.7
        host daddr: 8.8.8.8-8.8.8.8
        port: any
        sport: any
        dport: any
NSE4-PASS (root) #
```

Now that we have our diagnose flow filter setup, we can set some parameters for the flow debug:

```
NSE4-PASS (root) # diagnose debug flow show iprope enable
show trace messages about iprope
NSE4-PASS (root) # diagnose debug flow show function-name enable
show function name
NSE4-PASS (root) # diagnose debug console timestamp enable
```

These functions provide more information when initiating the trace flow debug. The iprope will show what policies FortiOS is trying to match the packet against until a match is found unless the implicit deny is hit, meaning no match. The last thing to do is to start the debug flow.

```
NSE4-PASS (root) # diagnose debug flow trace start 10
NSE4-PASS (root) # diagnose debug enable
```

In this case, the flow trace will match 10 IPv4 packets. To match IPv6 packets, you would need to adjust the filter and use start6 instead of start.

```
NSE4-PASS (root) # diagnose debug flow trace
```

Chapter 3 | Layer Three Technologies

```
start      Start trace.
stop       Stop trace.
start6     Start IPv6 trace.
stop6      Stop IPv6 trace.
```

The output of this command would be like so:

```
2020-02-11  16:59:58  id=20085  trace_id=6  func=fw_forward_handler line=771 msg="Allowed by Policy-59: SNAT"
2020-02-11  16:59:58  id=20085  trace_id=6  func=ids_receive  line=289 msg="send to ips"
2020-02-11  16:59:58  id=20085  trace_id=6  func=__ip_session_run_tuple line=3286 msg="SNAT 192.168.209.7->10.123.233.2:60417"
2020-02-11  16:59:59  id=20085  trace_id=7  func=print_pkt_detail line=5501 msg="vd-root:0 received a packet(proto=1, 192.168.209.7:1->8.8.8.8:2048) from vsw.internal7. type=8, code=0, id=1, seq=759."
2020-02-11  16:59:59  id=20085  trace_id=7  func=resolve_ip_tuple_fast line=5581  msg="Find an existing session, id-0012b15b, original direction"
```

This output can seem intimidating, but this output holds valuable information. Take time to run through this output and generate some questions. The first line of the output is where we see the traffic was allowed to pass through the FortiGate via Policy 59. We can also conclude that within this point was a SNAT function and that there is an IPS sensor on this policy. Also, we can see protocol 1 with source 192.168.209.7 and a destination of 8.8.8.8. This is a lot to remember, so let me recommend that you create a small script to store away as a template and reference when you need to run the diagnose flow debug on FortiGate. Here is an example of my script template I keep in my notes:

========Diag Flow Script Template=========

```
diag debug dis
diag debug reset
diag debug flow filter clear
diag debug flow sh con en
diag debug flow sh func en
diag debug console timestamp en
diag debug flow filter addr xxxx
diag debug flow show iprope enable
diag debug flow trace start 5000
diag debug en
=======================================
```

Chapter 3 | Layer Three Technologies

adjust as needed. while we are script template let me provide another one to also allow you to quickly view sessions in the Session table:

=============Session Script Template================

```
diag debug reset
diag debug ena
diag sy session filter clear
diag sy session filter src x.x.x.x
diag sy session filter dst x.x.x.x
diag sy session filter dport xx
diag sy session list
```
===

Adjust as needed. This wraps up the IP diagnostics section. With these tools, you should have the ability to troubleshoot FortiGate firewalls and pass the NSE4 exam!

Chapter 3 | Layer Three Technologies

Summary

Chapter Three... Done! You have now been immersed in FortiOS Routing. Nice work. In this chapter, we covered many different routing topics, but we started with a quick overview of IPv4 and IPv6 and then moved onto the Routing Table overview. Next, we discussed the Route Entries and their associated attributes, which are Priority and Distance.

The next important thing we discussed is the Reverse Path Forwarding (RPF) feature on FortiOS. RPF is essentially an anti-spoofing mechanism, and we discussed how it is important to account for this feature when designing networks. I also provided instructions on how to turn this feature on or off. We had a chance to review the Session Table entry, and as you saw is quite extensive, but we took the time to walk through it line by line since it is very important to understand the output.I discussed FortiOS routing and provided details and examples on static routing and provided a high-level overview of dynamic routing protocols. The NSE4 doesn't require you to have in-depth knowledge of the dynamic routing protocol because these topics are covered in the NSE7 exam.

We had the opportunity to go over the different routing features FortiOS offers. For example, we reviewed Policy Based Routing, Internet-Service routing, and Link-Monitor features.

The last thing we reviewed in this chapter was FortiOS IP diagnostics, which is essential when managing FortiGate production networks. You will run into problems, so be sure to practice with the tools that help you solve those problems.

As always, it is essential you understand this chapter before moving on since IP routing is the foundation of computer networking. If you do not understand how packets move through the network and how to troubleshoot issues, then you are going to have a very hard time trying to secure that same network. Review and study, study, study! The more you work with FortiOS routing, the more 2nd nature it will become! Since all this is information is fresh in your mind, go ahead a knockout those end-of-chapter questions to be sure you understand everything we have gone over in this chapter. -Cheers

Chapter 3 | Layer Three Technologies

Chapter Three Review Questions

1) What command is used to present all route entries?
    a. get router info routing-table all
    b. get router info routing-table database
    c. get router info routing-table summary
    d. diagnose ip kernel rtcache

2) What is RFC 1918?
    a. The standard that describes IPv4 CIDR
    b. The standard that describes IPv4 classful addressing
    c. The standard that describes IPv4 Private IP space
    d. The standard that describes IANA address allocation

3) What is the default Distance for Static Routes?
    a. 0
    b. 1
    c. 5
    d. 10

4) What is the default Priority for Static Routes?
    a. 0
    b. 1
    c. 5
    d. 10

5) What is the Distance for the following route?

    S   9.9.9.9/32 [10/0] via 10.123.233.1, wan1, [5/0]

    a. 0
    b. 1
    c. 5
    d. 10

Chapter 3 | Layer Three Technologies

6) What is the Priority for the following route?

S   9.9.9.9/32 [10/0] via 10.123.233.1, wan1, [5/0]

   a. 0
   b. 1
   c. 5
   d. 10

7) What table is responsible for keeping track of transit traffic allowed by Firewall Policy?
   a. Firewall Policy Table
   b. Session Table
   c. Kernel Routing Table
   d. Routing Table

8) What is the anti-spoofing mechanism on FortiOS called?
   a. Anti-Spoofing
   b. Firewall Policy
   c. RPF
   d. DDoS Policy

9) Which Sniffer verbosity level only prints IP Headers and Interface Name?
   a. 1
   b. 3
   c. 4
   d. 6

10) PBR references the Routing Table to make forwarding decisions.
    a. True
    b. False

11) What does ISDB stand for?
    a. Internal System Database
    b. Inside System Database
    c. Internet Service Database
    d. Internet System Database

Chapter 3 | Layer Three Technologies

12) What is the default Distance for OSPF Route Type?
    a. 0
    b. 1
    c. 10
    d. 110

13) RPF Strict requires a feasible route back to the source not to drop a packet.
    a. True
    b. False

14) Regarding Session Table output, what does 'proto=17 proto_state=01' indicate?
    a. The Session Entry manages traffic for PING traffic and is expecting a return echo-reply packet
    b. The Session Entry manages traffic for a TCP connection that is in the half-open state.
    c. The Session Entry manages traffic for a UDP connection where a reply has been seen
    d. The Session Entry manages traffic for a UDP connection, and no reply has been seen yet.

15) Regarding Session Table output what does 'orgin->sink: org pre->post, reply pre->post dev=34->5/5->34' indicate?
    a. The Session Entry has 34 active connections using it.
    b. The Session Entry has seen 34 outbound packets and 5 reply packets
    c. The Session Entry original traffic flow ingress interface of index 34 and egress of interface of index 5.
    d. The Session Entry original traffic flow ingress interface of index 5 and egress of interface of index 34.

16) What command displays only the active FortiOS routes?
    a. get router info routing-table all
    b. get router info routing-table database
    c. diagnose ip route summary
    d. get ip route ipv4 summary

Chapter 3 | Layer Three Technologies

17) Which of the following attributes must be equal for routes to be considered for ECMP?
    a. Destination Subnet, Distance, Metric, and Priority
    b. Distance and Priority
    c. Destination Subnet and Distance,
    d. Destination Subnet, Distance, and Metric

18) What is the FIB
    a. Forward Internet-Service Database
    b. Forwarding Information Base
    c. First-out Interface Database
    d. Forwarding Interface Base

19) What marks an active route in the Routing Database?
    a. >*
    b. *
    c. >
    d. active

20) What CLI command displays the PBR Table?
    a. diagnose ip firewall route
    b. diagnose firewall proute list
    c. diagnose firewall route list
    d. get router info routing-table database

Chapter 4 | Firewall Policy and NAT

NSE4 Blueprint Topics Covered

- Identify components in Firewall Policy
- Describe how traffic matches Firewall Policy Entries
- Configure Firewall Policy Logging
- Describe Policy GUI list views
- Describe Policy ID's vs Policy Sequence numbers
- Described where objects are referenced
- Explain Name restrictions on Firewall Policies
- Perform Firewall Policy re-ordering
- Describe NAT and PAT
- Explain different configuration modes for NAT
- Configure and Describe SNAT and DNAT VIPs
- Troubleshoot NAT issues

Firewall Policy and NAT Introduction

We have made significant progress so far on our journey of learning FortiOS and obtaining your NSE4 certificate! In this chapter, we are going to dive into the Firewall Policy and Network Address Translation (NAT). I've already touched on Firewall Policies some throughout this book, but in this chapter, we are going to focus on and dive a little deeper into the subject, and a big part of the Firewall Policy is handling various NAT functions, which I guarantee you will work with if managing a FortiGate firewall infrastructure.

In this chapter, you can expect discussions and examples on the Firewall Policy Table. We review Firewall Policy functions, which include policy matching, policy logging, and configuration. I also discuss how to lookup policies using the GUI search feature and go over naming restrictions. Lastly, we touch on Policy Entry in detail and how to reference external objects to build a complete Firewall Policy Entry.

Next, once we complete the Firewall Policy section, we begin our discussion around FortiOS NAT. I review general NAT theory and then move into the different types of NAT and how to use them on FortiOS. In this section, you are going to learn some new terms, which are VIPs, IP Pools, Central NAT, NAT64, and NAT46 Translation.

By the end of this chapter, you should have a solid understanding of how FortiOS Firewall Policies work. Also, you should understand NAT and know how to reference NAT objects within the Firewall Policy itself. Lastly, you should be confident in troubleshooting fundamental NAT issues on FortiOS. Let's get started!!

Chapter 4 | Firewall Policy and NAT

Firewall Policy

We start simple; what is a Firewall Policy? On FortiOS, a Firewall Policy is an entry within the Firewall Policy Table that is designed to match network traffic and then do something with it. Once matched, FortiOS can be configured to drop or allow traffic and apply secure scanning or authentication.

The Firewall Policy Entry is where the magic happens. This is where most of the security features and advanced functionality on FortiOS come together. The objective is to isolate traffic streams and then apply various security features to the traffic flow. See Image 4.1 for a quick snapshot of all the features and functionality that's within the Firewall Policy.

Image 4. 1 – Firewall Policy Visual

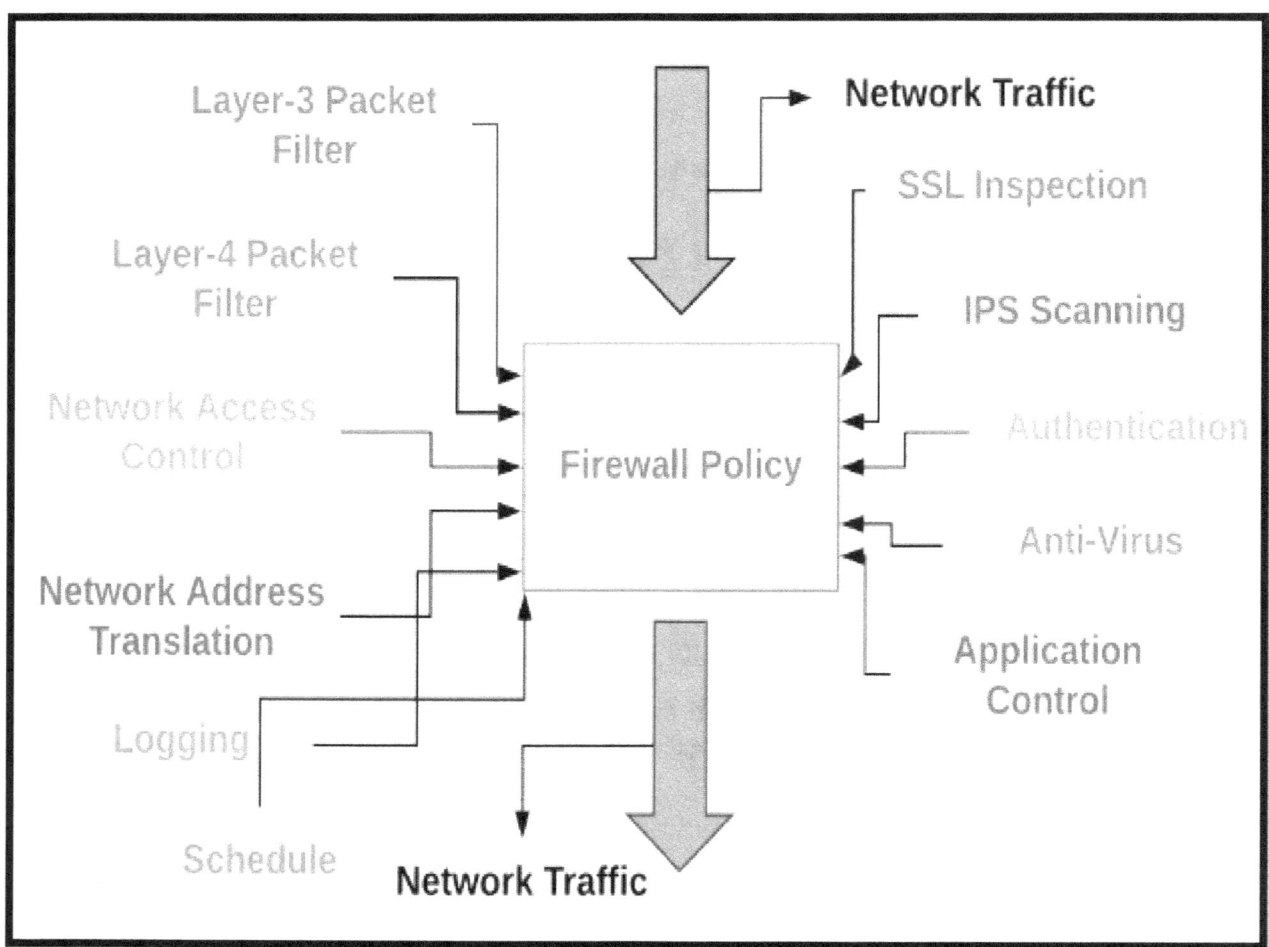

Chapter 4 | Firewall Policy and NAT

Firewall Policy Table

All Firewall Policy Entries are found in the Firewall Policy Table. There are two different tables we are going to be discussing in this chapter, IPv4 and IPv6. Each is autonomous from each other, but both use the same method of matching traffic and then applying features to that traffic. The IPv4 and IPv6 Firewall Policy Tables are found in the GUI via:

Image 4. 2 – GUI Firewall Policy Location

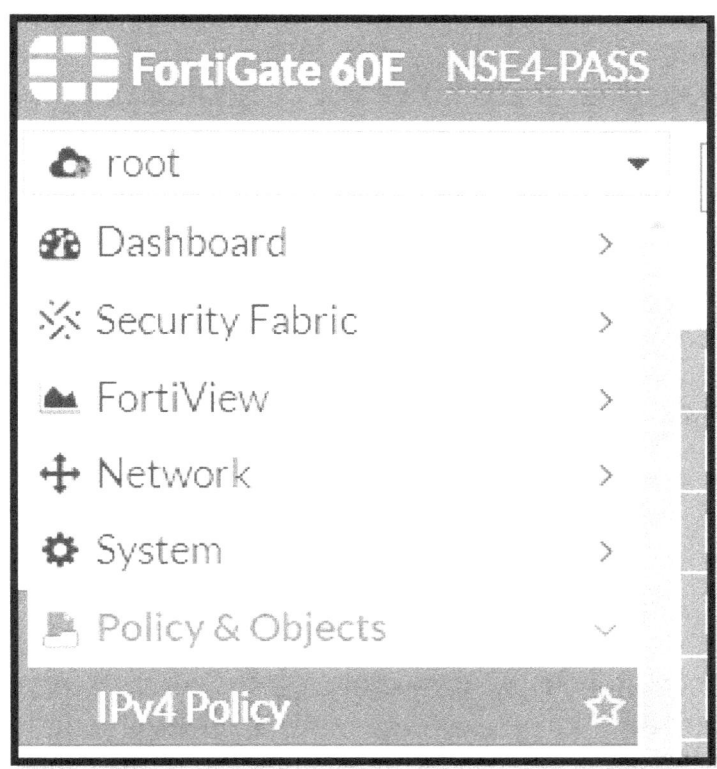

Next, you can also find the Firewall Policy Tables in the CLI as well via:

```
NSE4-PASS (root) # config firewall policy
NSE4-PASS (policy) # end
NSE4-PASS (root) # config firewall policy6
NSE4-PASS (policy6) #
```

Firewall Policy Matching

When a new packet hits the FortiGate (a packet with no active session), the packet will be evaluated by the Firewall Policy Table. The evaluation process starts at the very top of the list, and FortiOS works all the way down through the list, trying to

Chapter 4 | Firewall Policy and NAT

match the packet against a Firewall Policy Entry, and if no match is found, then the packet will take the Implicit Deny Policy Entry.

Note that there are some exceptions regarding rule matching and authentication scenarios, and NAT matching, but to keep things simple, we are going to stay focused on the basic Firewall Policy Entry and talk about the exceptions when we get to that part of the book.

Local-In Policy Table

The Local-In Policy table manages the traffic destined for the FortiGate itself. It is essential to know the difference between transit firewall policies and Local-In Policies. Below is an example of a CLI Local-In Policy that could be used to govern access to the LAN interface.

```
config firewall local-in-policy
    edit 1
        set intf "lan"
        set srcaddr "all"
        set dstaddr "all"
        set action accept
        set service "ALL"
        set schedule "always"
        set status enable
        set comments ''
    next
end
```

In 6.2 FortiOS, the Local-In policies have conveniently been placed in the GUI. This GUI page also categorized the open ports between high-level functions as well. To find this table go to 'Policy & Objects -> Local-Policy'. For you, Linux users out there, think of this as your iptables. Note, these policies cannot be directly modified on this GUI page, see *Image 4.3*. This section is only for reference to see what ports are open. If you wish to close a port open in this Local-In Policy Table, then you must remove or reconfigure the process that opened the port, sometimes this might not be possible, and you will need to explicitly configure a Local-In policy via CLI to restrict access. For example, if you wish to close TCP port 179, then you must go remove all related BGP configurations or configure a Local-in Policy to filter port 179. See *Image 4.3* for GUI details.

Chapter 4 | Firewall Policy and NAT

Image 4.3 – Local In Firewall Policy GUI

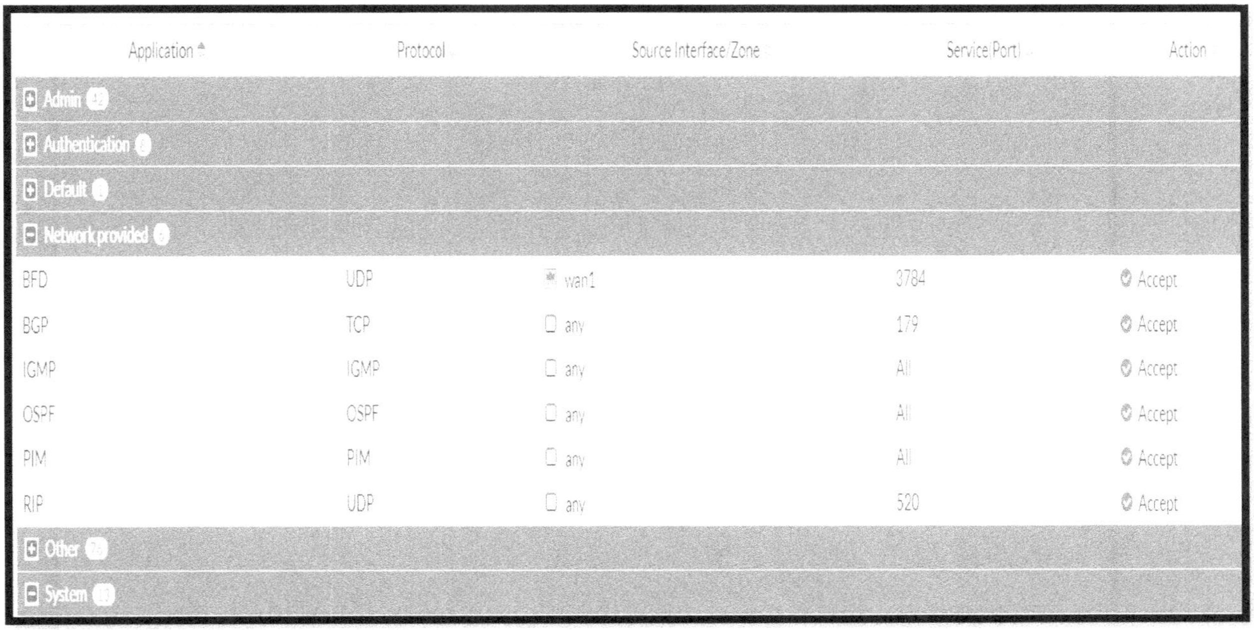

Application	Protocol	Source Interface/Zone	Service/Port	Action
⊞ Admin				
⊞ Authentication				
⊞ Default				
⊟ Network provided				
BFD	UDP	wan1	3784	✓ Accept
BGP	TCP	any	179	✓ Accept
IGMP	IGMP	any	All	✓ Accept
OSPF	OSPF	any	All	✓ Accept
PIM	PIM	any	All	✓ Accept
RIP	UDP	any	520	✓ Accept
⊞ Other				
⊟ System				

Take a moment to review this Image so you can get a feel for the open ports on FortiOS.

Profile Based Policy Components

Before we get started in this section, you should know that there are now two types of Firewall Policies. The first type is Profile Based, which we discuss in this section, and the second is Policy-Based. We discuss Policy Base within the next section. The NSE4 Exam test on both.

Firstly, a row within the Firewall Policy Table is called a Firewall Policy Entry or just a Policy for short. Objects are used to build Firewall Policy Entries. Some of these external objects referenced are found via 'Policy & Objects' Top-Level Menu. Here is the list of objects required to build a Firewall Policy Entry regarding the matching function:

1) Interface and Zone Objects
    a. 'Network > Interface'
2) Address Objects
    a. Found via 'Policy & Objects > Addresses'
3) Service Objects
    a. Found via 'Policy & Objects > Services'
4) Schedule Objects

Chapter 4 | Firewall Policy and NAT

    a. Found via 'Policy & Objects > Schedules'

Image 4.4 – Firewall Policy Required Fields

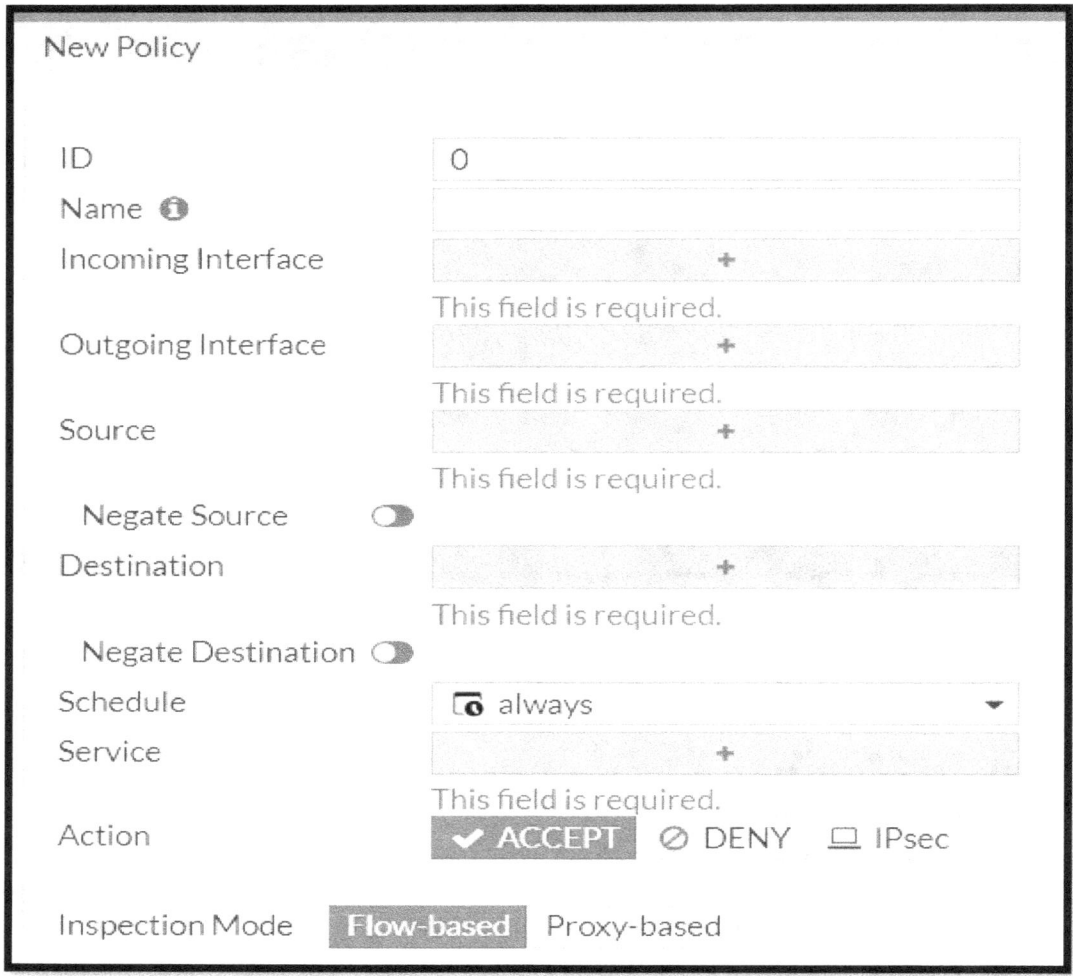

There are six objects a packet must match to be evaluated by a Firewall Policy Entry. That is the Incoming Interface, Outgoing Interface, Source Address, Destination Address, Schedule, and Service. Image 4.4 displays a blank Firewall Policy Entry and its required fields.

Next, to complete this new policy there must be objects to reference. by selecting the plus sign (+) within the icon box next to the descriptor will present the currently objects available on FortiOS for that object type. For example, I am going to fill in this policy with:

Chapter 4 | Firewall Policy and NAT

Source Interface	-> 'internal1'
Destination Interface	-> VLAN_101
Source Address	-> 172.29.101.40/32
Destination Address	-> 10.123.233.0/24
Schedule	-> always
Service	-> HTTP
Action	-> ACCEPT

Check out Image 4.5; this is what the GUI equivalent proposed Firewall Policy Entry would look like.

Image 4.5 – Firewall Policy Complete

The objects seen in this Policy Entry have already been configured before attempting to create this Firewall Policy Entry for convenience. Some objects, by default, are pre-configured on FortiOS. For example, the Service objects show on

Chapter 4 | Firewall Policy and NAT

the right side of Image 4.3 are pre-configured, and as you can see, once you select an object place holder field, the GUI will present all available objects for you to reference on the right-hand side.

If you need to create a custom object to reference in a Firewall Policy Entry, then you must navigate to the appropriate configuration section and create the object or use the short-cut link present in the upper-right hand corner of 4.3 and select '+ Create'.

Custom Service Object in Policy

To create a custom Service Object, we navigate in the GUI via 'Policy & Objects -> Services -> + Create New'. In this example, I want to create a custom HTTP Service Object that allows access to TCP port 8080 named HTTP_8080, see Image 4.6.

Image 4.6 – Custom Service Object

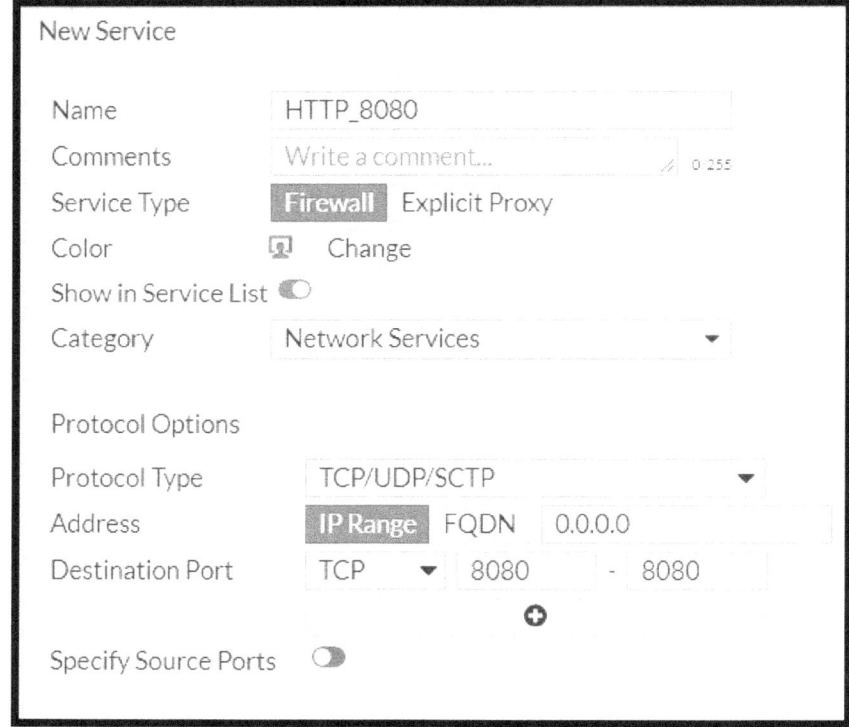

Here we can see our custom Service Object. Note that by creating and referencing this object in a Firewall Policy Entry, FortiOS does not recognize this traffic as HTTP. In HTTP_8080 Service object, FortiOS only recognizes the protocol TCP with a destination port value of 8080. To recognize and enforce protocols at the application level, you must use Application Control. Here is what the CLI configuration would look like for this object:

Chapter 4 | Firewall Policy and NAT

```
0: config firewall service custom
0:   edit "HTTP_8080"
0:     set category "Network Services"
0:     set color 6
0:     unset tcp-portrange
0:     set tcp-portrange 8080
0:     unset udp-portrange
0:     unset sctp-portrange
0:   end
0: end
```

Next, to reference this newly created Service Object "HTTP_8080" into our Firewall Policy Entry, we navigate to the Firewall Policy Entry, and "HTTP_8080" will now be populated when the Service Object place holder is select on the right side of the GUI page. See Image 4.7 for details.

Image 4.7 – Add Custom Service Object to Policy

You repeat this process for the creation and reference of any custom Address Object, Interface, Zone, and Schedule Object that needs to be a part of any Firewall Policy Entry.

Chapter 4 | Firewall Policy and NAT

Configure Service Groups in Policy

FortiOS also allows the group of many Service Objects into one single object. To configure this, navigate within the GUI via 'Policy & Objects -> Services > Create'. See *Image 4.8*.

Image 4. 8 – Service Group Configuration

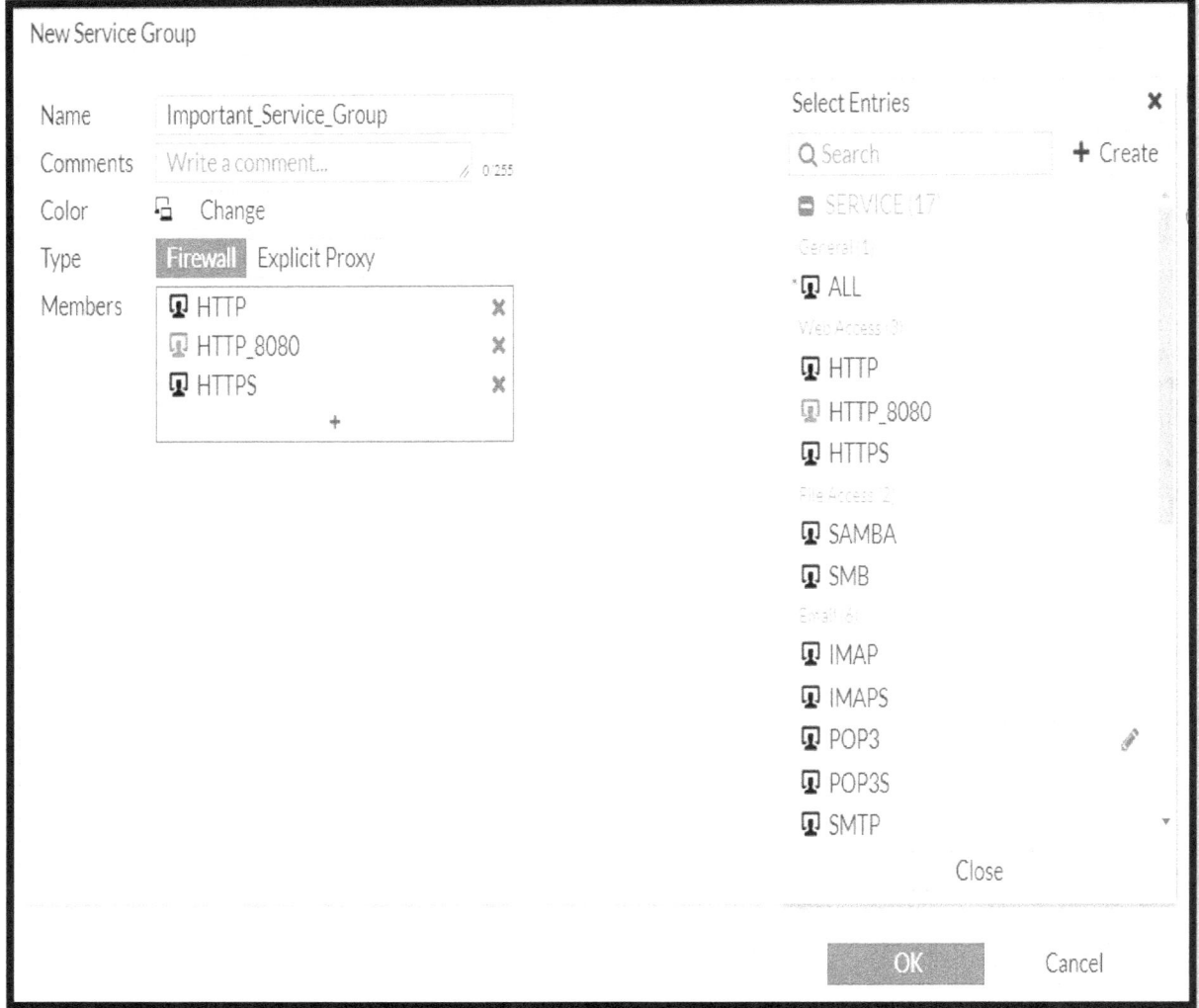

Once created, the Service Group Object 'Important_Service_Group' can be referenced within firewall policies under the Service field.

Chapter 4 | Firewall Policy and NAT

Custom Schedule Object Reference

The Schedule object controls when a Firewall Policy Entry is active. To configure a custom Schedule Object navigate in the GUI via 'Policy & Objects -> Schedules'

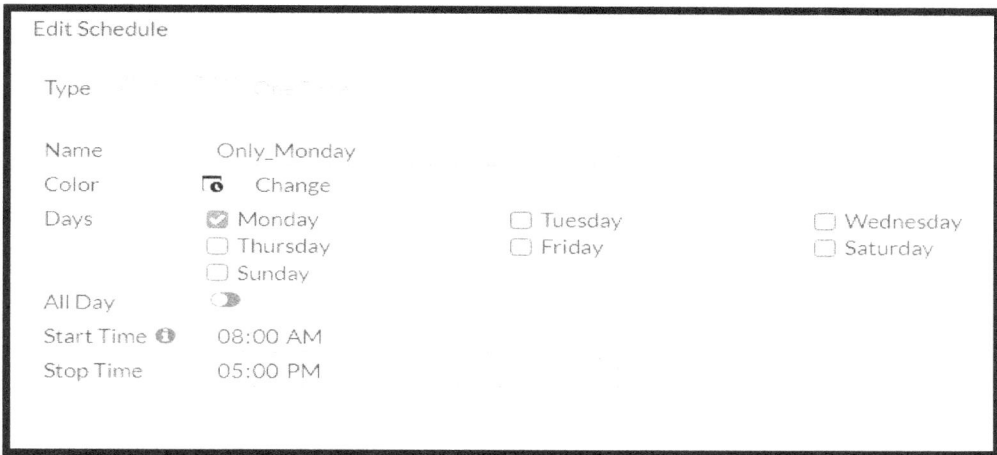

In this example, the custom Schedule object once applied to a Firewall Policy Entry, will only activate the policy on Mondays. A good use case for this, if you only want your employees to access social media on Mondays, you could place the 'Only_Monday' Schedule object as part of the policy configuration. If you navigate back to the Firewall Policy Entry, the 'Only_Monday' Schedule Object is will available. *See Image 4.10.*

Image 4. 10 – Policy Schedule Dropdown Selection

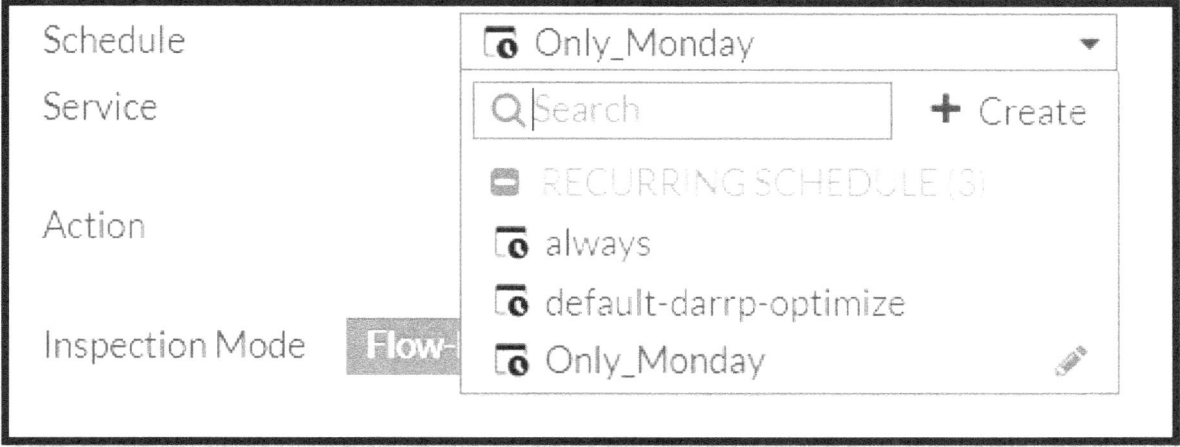

Chapter 4 | Firewall Policy and NAT

Custom Address Object Reference

The next object to discuss is the Address Object which is used to match the source or/and destination IP address within a policy. The same method is used to define an

Image 4. 11 – Custom Address Object

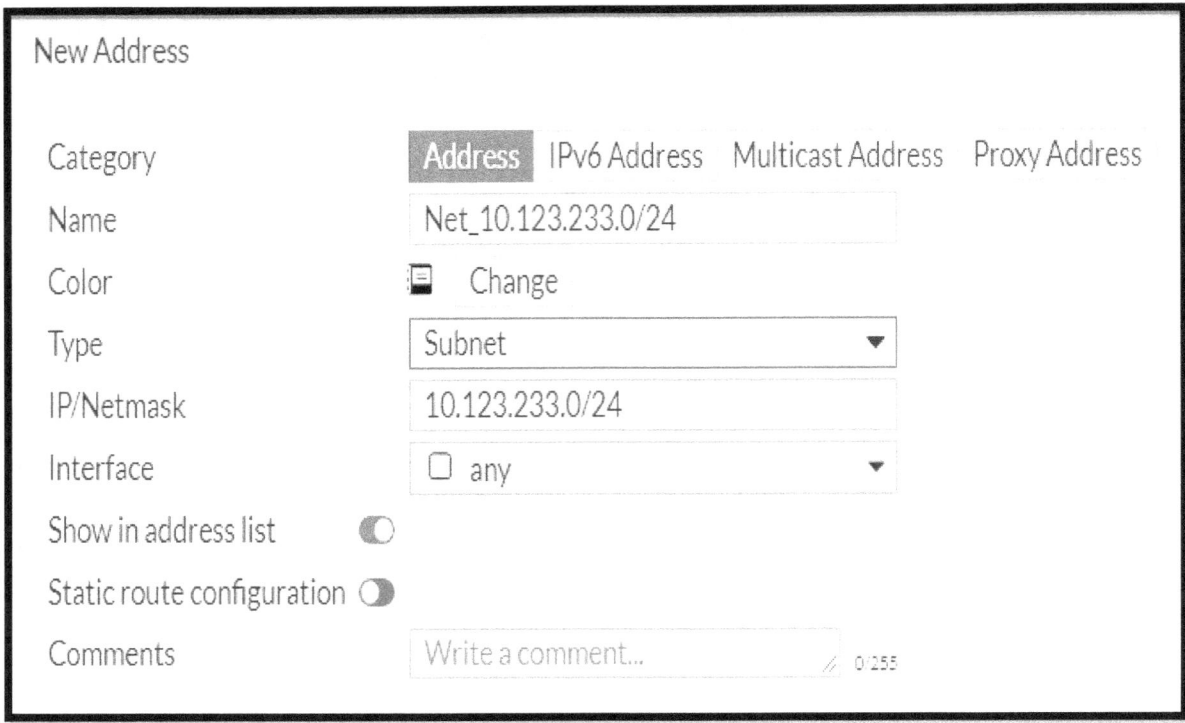

Address Object and reference it within a Firewall Policy Entry. To define a new custom object, navigate in the GUI via 'Policy & Object -> Addresses -> +Create New' as seen in *image 4.11*.

Chapter 4 | Firewall Policy and NAT

Just like Service Objects, you can create Address Object Groups. To accomplish this, navigate to the same location, but choose 'Address Group' in the dropdown. The next step is to create a new Address Group; we call this group 'Important_subnets', and we reference the Address Object that was just created 'Net_10.123.233.0/24'. See *image 4.12*.

Image 4. 12 – New Address Group Configuration

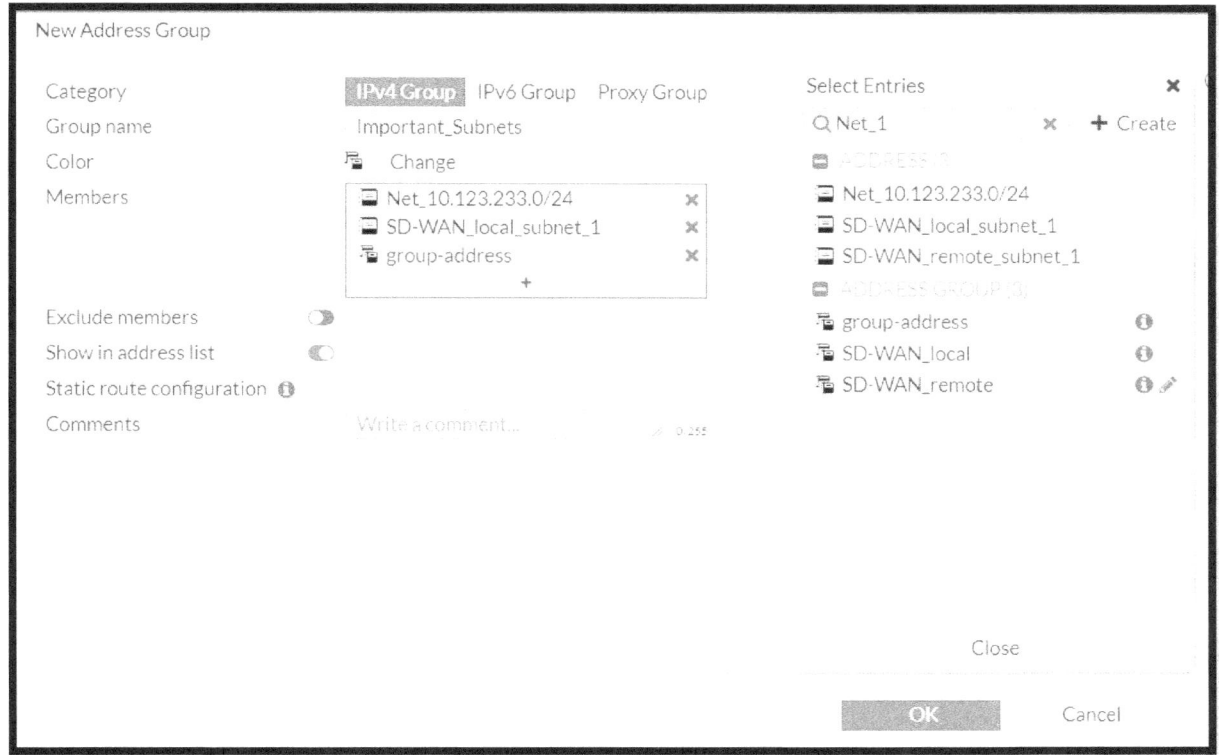

We can see the Address Object we just created within the list on the right-hand side. I have referenced it along with other Address Objects. I also reference another group to show that nested groups are supported as well. To reference this newly created Address Object Navigate back to the policy, we have been working on and select the Source or Destination field and the Address Group 'Important Subnets' and the Address Object 'Net_10.123.233.0/24' are both shown within the list on the right-hand side of the page as seen in *Image 4.13*.

I searched for 'Net_10.123.233.0/24' to filter the available objects. As you can see, this also picked up that 'Net_10.123.233.0/24' is also apart of the Address Group 'Important_Subnets', which I could have just easily referenced here instead of 'Net_10.123.233.0/24'.

Chapter 4 | Firewall Policy and NAT

Image 4. 13 – Policy Address and Group Object Reference

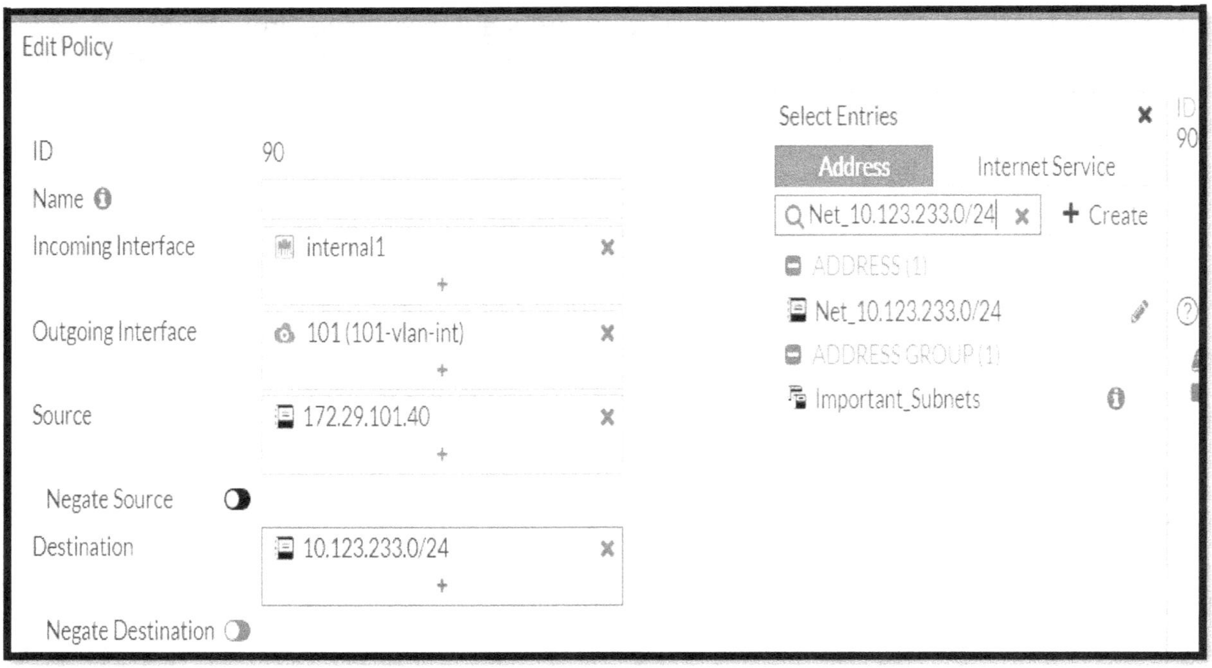

```
Edit Policy

ID                    90                                    Select Entries                    ×
Name                                                        Address       Internet Service
Incoming Interface    internal1              ×              Q Net_10.123.233.0/24  ×    + Create
                      +                                     ADDRESS (1)
Outgoing Interface    101 (101-vlan-int)    ×               Net_10.123.233.0/24
                      +                                     ADDRESS GROUP (1)
Source                172.29.101.40         ×               Important_Subnets
                      +
Negate Source
Destination           10.123.233.0/24       ×
                      +
Negate Destination
```

Firewall Policy Referenced Object

There are methods to lookup an object referenced in FortiOS. In this example, we use the interface internal1. In the GUI, navigate to 'Network > Interfaces' and select the number under the 'Ref.' column, and you should see something like *Image 4.14*.

Here you can see that internal1 is referenced in many places. The interface is referenced in different Policies, routing statements and referenced by a virtual interface which is vlan 101. Note, an object cannot be deleted if it is referenced

> *When creating address objects be sure to configure the value of the IP/Netmask field correctly because this is what matters and not the name of the object when matching traffic.*

somewhere within the configuration. So if you attempt to delete a referenced object, FortiOS displays an error stating it is currently used. So if you wish to delete an object, you must first navigate to the object and find the 'Ref.' column (which

Chapter 4 | Firewall Policy and NAT

stands for reference), and go remove any points of reference. Only then will you be allowed to delete an object. This works the same for most objects on FortiOS.

Image 4. 14 – Internal1 Object References

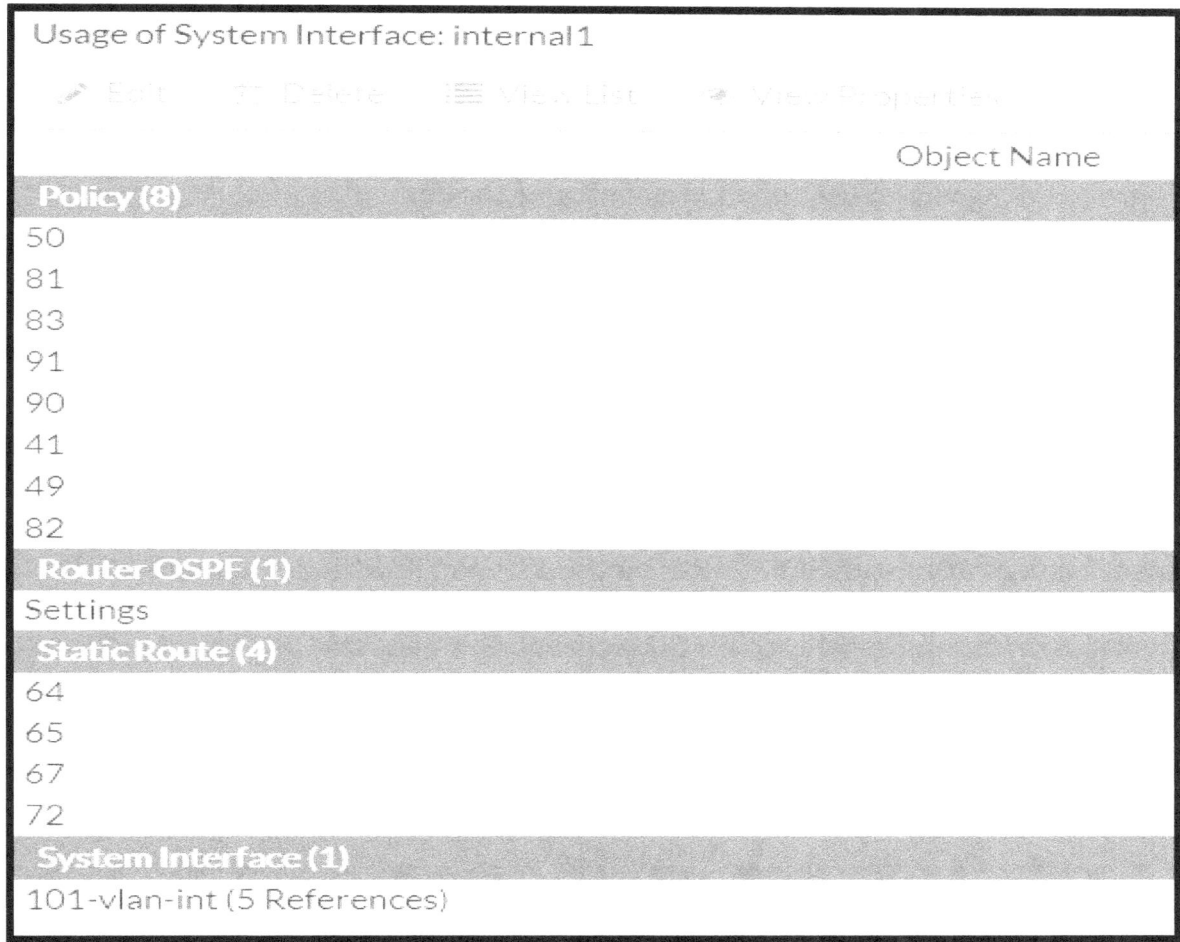

Zone and Interface Policy Reference

The last values to configure within a Firewall Policy Entry are the source and destination interfaces. Within these fields, we can reference zones, logical interfaces, or physical interfaces. I've already discussed how to create VLAN interfaces, which could be referenced along with physical interfaces. The next item to discuss is the Zone.

The purpose of a Zone is to simplify policy management. The way a zones works is, we create a logical object that represents the Zone configuration. In this example, we use ZONE-OUTSIDE. Within this object, we reference physical or logical interfaces; by doing this FortiOS views the interfaces within the zone as one logical interface and no longer separate entities.

Chapter 4 | Firewall Policy and NAT

So, for example, instead of managing policies from LAN->WAN1 and LAN->WAN2, we could just create a zone and place wan1 and wan2 physical interface within it, so we have fewer firewall policies to manage. This, of course, is assuming that traffic going leaving wan1 to have the same requirements as traffic leaving wan2. This might seem like it wouldn't save you a lot of time here, but if you had hundreds or thousands of policies to manage, it would save a lot of configuration and limit the complexity, which is also good.

A Zone can be configured in the GUI or CLI. In the GUI you can navigate to 'Network -> Interfaces -> Create New -> Zone' and select the zone members. But in this example, I am going to use the CLI to configure the zone.

```
config system zone
    edit "ZONE-OUTSIDE"
        set intrazone allow
        set interface "wan2" "wan1"
    next
end
```

In this CLI example, we have referenced wan1 and wan2 interfaces within the Zone Object named 'ZONE-OUTSIDE'. Also, 'set intrazone allow' is configured, which allows traffic to pass freely without policy inspection between wan1 and wan2 interfaces. We could set this to block to change this behavior.

Next, we reference our newly created Zone without our test Firewall Policy Entry. *See Image 4.15.*

Image 4. 15 – Zone Referenced in Firewall Policy Entry

Chapter 4 | Firewall Policy and NAT

Now this policy matches any ingress traffic on internal1 that is destined for wan1 or wan2 because these interfaces are referenced within the ZONE-OUTSIDE object.

Firewall Policy ID and Sequence Numbers

When a new Firewall Policy Entry is created, it will have an ID number. This the

Image 4. 16 – Policy ID Numbers

number used to distinguish the policy within the Firewall Policy Table. It is essential to know this number is not the order the Firewall Policy Table is evaluated. For example, look at *Image 4.16*. The first policy to be evaluated would be policy with ID 91 since it is above policies 90 and 89.

Firewall Policy Context Menu

The next item to discuss is the Firewall Policy context menu found when your right-clicks a Policy within the Policy Table. Navigate to 'Policy & Objects > IPv4 > Right-

Image 4.17 – Policy Context Menu

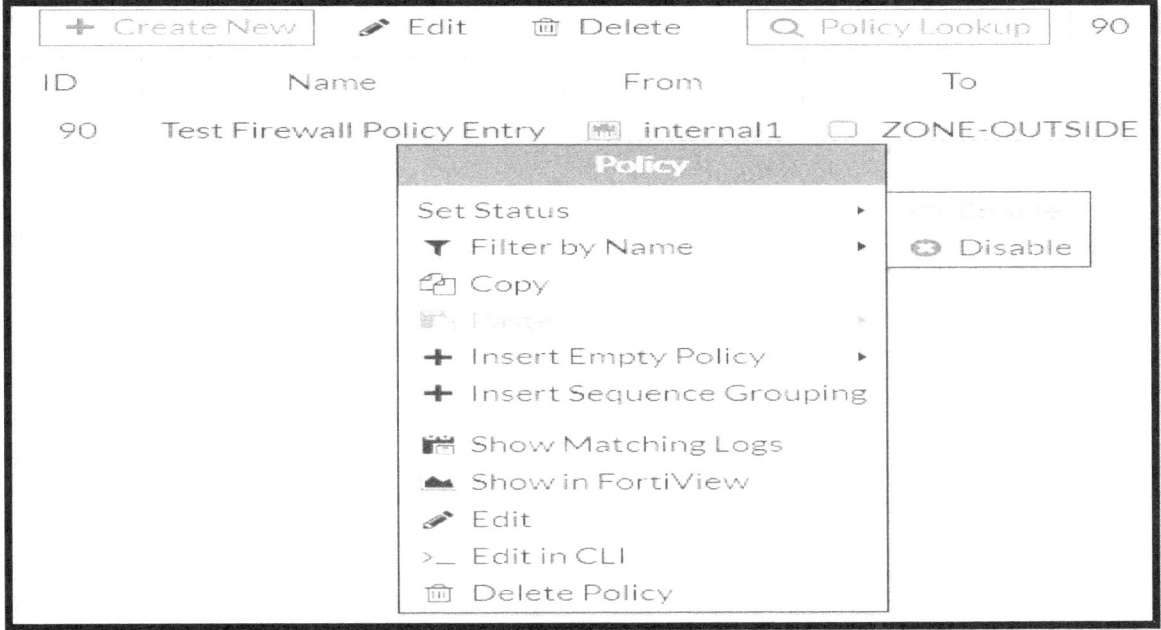

Click a Policy'. You will reference the context menu, as shown in *Image 4.17* here.

Chapter 4 | Firewall Policy and NAT

The context menu allows you to edit or delete policy in the GUI or the CLI directly, which is an excellent feature for quick changes. Also, it provides links to show related logs for traffic using the policy as well. This menu also provides a method to search for policies that have specific attributes. Lastly, the copy feature is useful to create another policy above or below this one and can be used as a template for the new policy, which is a time saver.

Profile Based Policy Entry Components

Remember, there are six components that traffic must match to be evaluated by a Profile Based Firewall Policy, and those are:

1) Source Interface
2) Destination Interface
3) Source IP Address
4) Destination IP Address
5) Service
6) Schedule

This section stepped through each one of these, so you should know now how to navigate to create objects and reference them when building a Firewall Policy Entry.

Policy-Based Next-Generation Firewall

A Policy-Based NGFW is a method used within a Firewall Policy Entry to extend the matching capabilities. This mode also allows admins to apply Application and Web Filtering settings directly to a Firewall Policy without the need to create a profile

Image 4.18 – Enable Policy Based NGFW

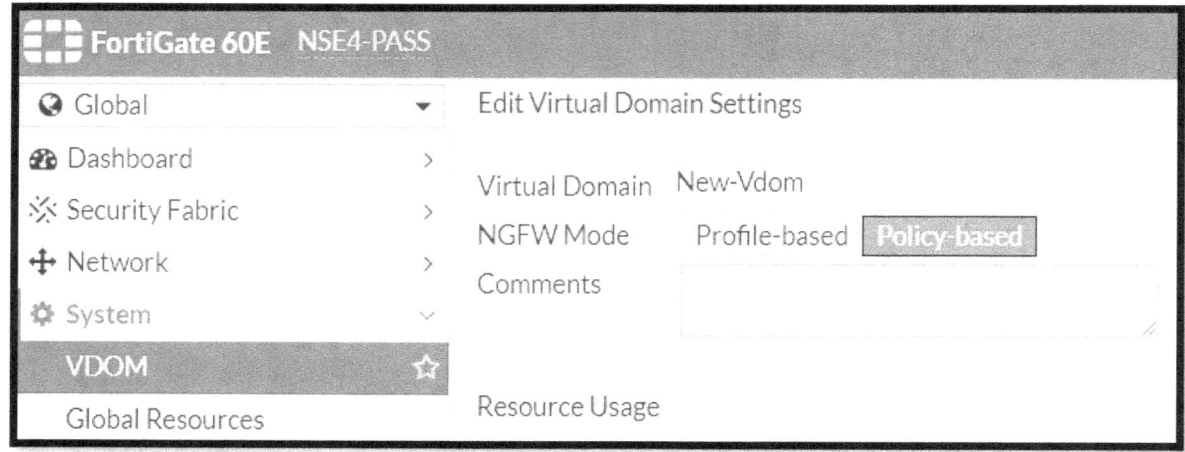

Chapter 4 | Firewall Policy and NAT

first. To enable Policy-Based NGFW on FortiOS with no VDOMs in the GUI goto 'Systems -> Settings -> NGFW Mode'. With VDOMs enabled in the GUI goto 'Global -> System -> VDOM -> Edit VDOM ->NGFW Mode', see Image 4.18 :

In Policy-Based NGFW Mode, note that policy matching changes a little. The ingress/egress and layer-3 and layer-4 matching functions stay the same, but once a packet matches these requirements, it is then sent directly to the IPS engine for further matching requirements depending on Firewall Policy configuration. The IPS engine will try and match the application, URL category, user, and user group as well. If the IPS engine obtains a match for these parameters, then the traffic is sent to the UTM models for security inspection.

Regarding policy matching, if the URL Category is set, then application signatures that are added must be within the browser-based technology category. Once traffic is accepted by Policy Base NGFW Firewall Entry, then you can apply Antivirus Profile, DNS Filter Profile, and IPS Security Profiles to it.

Note, FortiOS Policy-Based Entries traffic is always redirected to the IPS engine for further evaluation. Users and Groups used for authentication must also be configured in the Firewall Policy. Antivirus security configuration is always Profile Based regardless of NGFW mode. Also, Policy-Based NGFW requires the Central NAT table to be used, which we cover in a later section in this chapter.

<u>NGFW Policy-Based Filtering</u>

Here is a more in-depth look at how NGFW Policy-Based Filtering works:

1. Allow all application until they can be defined
    a. Use only IPv4 header information to match the NGFW Policy
    b. Policy accept IPv4 traffic
    c. FortiOS creates a session entry
    d. FortiOS forwards all traffic internally to the IPS module.
2. Once IPS define the application using the session, it will add the Application ID to the Session Entry
    a. The 'dirty' flag is set, which instructs FortiOS to re-evaluation the next packet that matches this Session Entry
    b. The 'valid_app' flag is set in the Session entry, which indicates that the IPS engine has validated the traffic and has set the Application ID.
3. Since Session Entry has a 'dirty' flag set, FortiOS will reevaluate the packet against the Session Entry.
    a. This time, FortiOS uses Layer-4 and Layer 7 information to match the packet against the Session Table Entry.
    b. Lastly, the action configured in the Firewall Policy Entry using Policy-Based mode is applied against the identified application traffic

Chapter 4 | Firewall Policy and NAT

In Summary, for the NSE4 exam, remember that URL Categories and Application Control is configured directly at the policy level. Also, you must use Central NAT in

Image 4.19 – Policy Base NGFW Entry

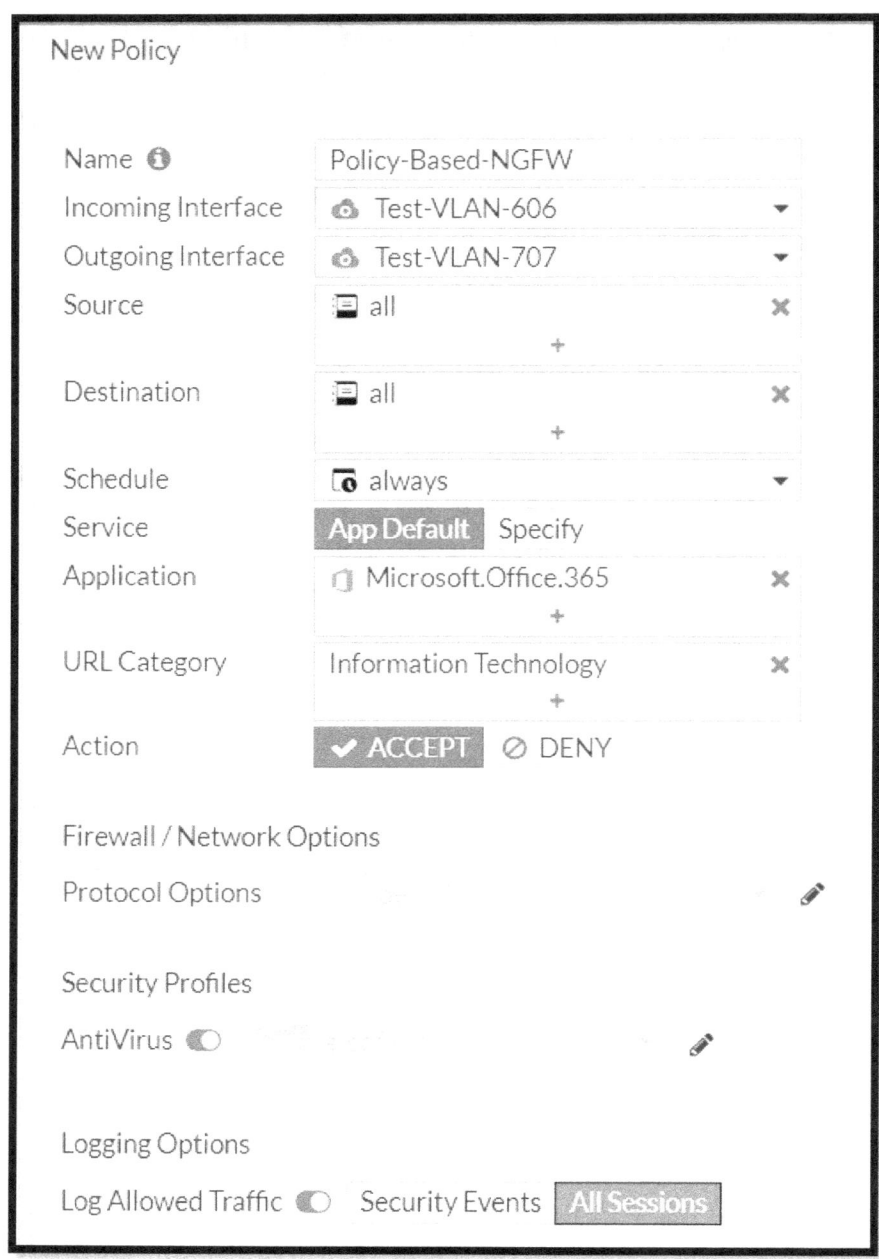

Policy-Based mode. Also, SSH/SSL is configured at the VDOM level. Next, Antivirus security is always Profile Based. Lastly, know that NGFW Policy Base filtering is a relatively new feature on FortiOS, and it has changed many times through each MR, so I recommend to look up the latest information on this feature after you read this section since there have been many changes on it. Next, to configure a Policy-Based

Chapter 4 | Firewall Policy and NAT

NGFW Firewall Policy, navigate to 'Policy & Objects -> Security Policy -> Create New', see image 4.19:

This Firewall Policy Entry reads any IPv4 source or destination that matches Microsoft Office 365 application, which is under the URL Category Information Technology then ACCEPT and then sends traffic to the Antivirus module for further scanning.

Profile Based Policy Entry Features

Now that we know how to build a Firewall Policy Entry to match network traffic. The next thing to configure is what to do with the traffic once we match it or isolate the stream? The obvious one is to ACCEPT or DENY the traffic which we have already discussed. In this section, I discuss some other features we can use within the Firewall Policy Entry.

Real-time Firewall Policy Statistics

In FortiOS 6.2, there are beneficial statistics available to us when viewing the Firewall Policy Entry details in the GUI on the right-hand side. Check out *Image 4.20*.

Image 4.20 – Policy Stats

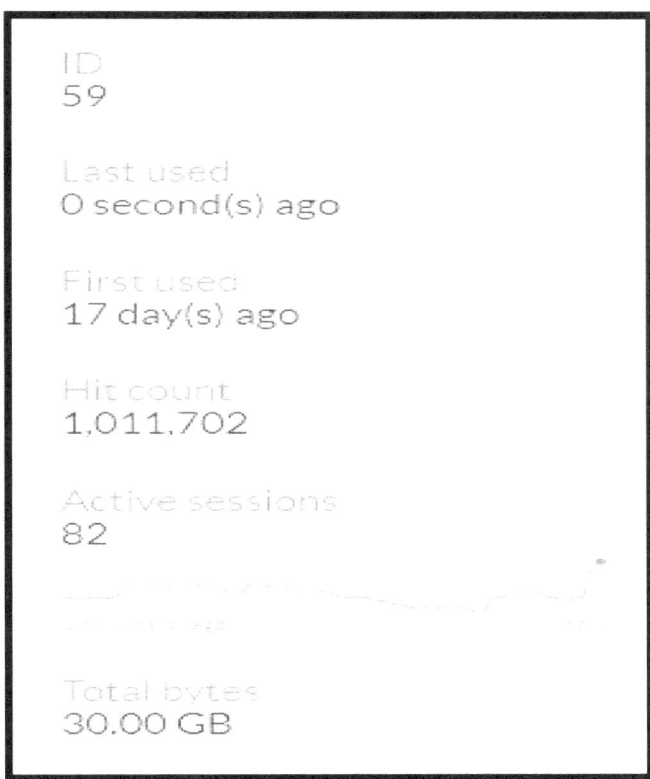

Chapter 4 | Firewall Policy and NAT

As you can see, there is an abundant amount of information that could be gathered from the policy stats. We can tell how much traffic has transverse policy ID 59. Also, we can quickly see how many Session Entries this policy has allowed on FortiOS, which is currently 82. There is even a nice little graph that provides trends. Above Active Session, we see Hit Count, which how many packets have transversed this policy. Lastly, we can see the last time this policy was used, and the first time it was used. This is a great place to go when troubleshooting network issues or trying to get a feel for your network traffic baseline.

Firewall Policy Entry Naming

Another requirement for the NSE4 is to know the naming limitation for Firewall Policies. The reason for naming could be to help understand the purpose of the policy, so another security engineer doesn't delete it. Or the name of a policy could be required if the network is required to meet specific PCI standards. In 6.0, you were required to specify a name, but in 6.2, you are not. No matter the case, you need to know what charters are allowed to be used and which are not within the naming scheme. The allowed characters are:

1) Numbers, 0 to 9
2) Letters, A to Z uppercase and lower case
3) Special characters, hyphen - and underscore _
4) Spaces

Characters like (){} are not allowed to be a Firewall Policy name. Note that some special characters are support in passwords, comments, and replacement messages like *<>()#""'' . My advice here is you are going to find out fairly quickly if FortiOS doesn't like your input because you will receive an error. IF this happens, just check to see if you are using any unusual characters and remove them, and life goes on!

Chapter 4 | Firewall Policy and NAT

Configure Policy Logging

The next NSE4 requirement here is to know about Firewall Policy logging. For FortiOS to generate logs from a Firewall Policy, then the setting must be enabled. See Image 4.21.

Image 4. 21 – Firewall Policy Logging

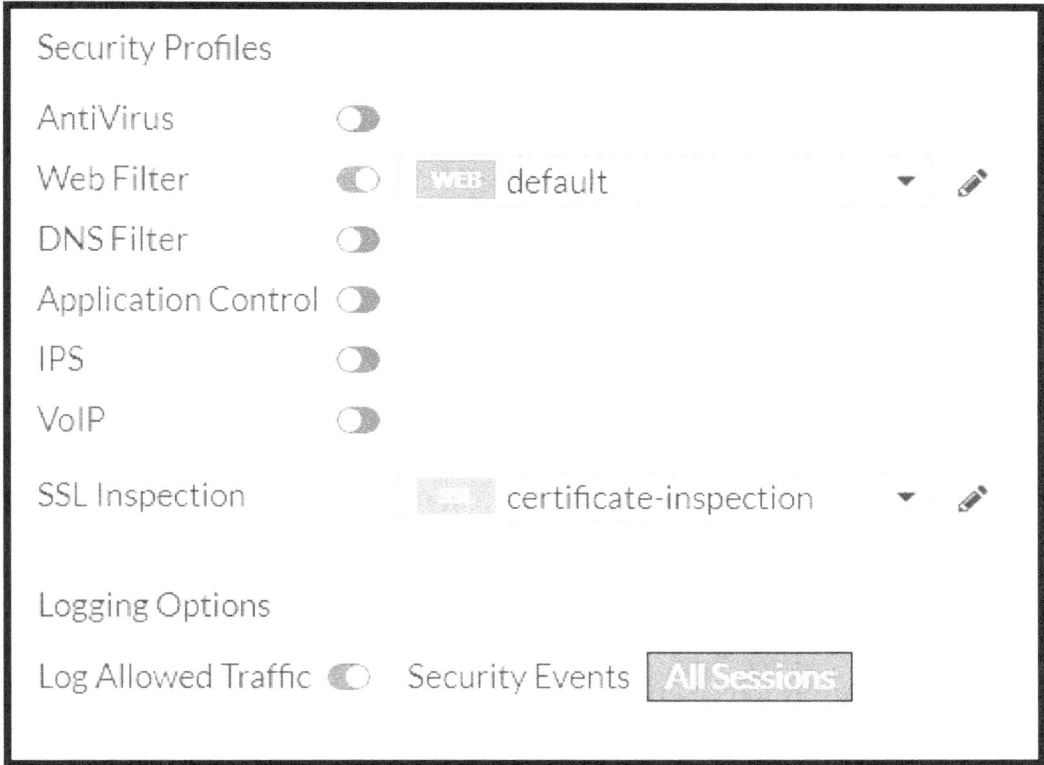

To enable the setting, you must toggle on 'Log Allowed Traffic'. If this setting is disabled, then no logs are generated even if there are Security Profiles attached to the policy. Once on, there are two options presented Security Events or All Sessions. Let me explain the difference:

1) Security Events
   a. If enabled, security event types will be received within the 'forward traffic log' and 'security log'. A 'forward traffic log' is only generated if the packet causes a security-related event. Note, you must have a Security Profile referenced within the policy as well for FortiOS to generate these logging events.
2) All Sessions
   a. If this option is used instead, FortiOS will generate a 'forward traffic log' for every single Session Entry the Firewall Policy generates. Also, if

Chapter 4 | Firewall Policy and NAT

Security Profile(s) is being used, a security log type will be generated for the 'forward traffic log' and also the 'security log'.

In summary, here, the difference between Security Events and All Sessions settings is that All Sessions setting will generate a log for every single Session Entry the Firewall Policy generates, and the Security Events setting will not. Both settings require a Security Profile to be referenced within the policy to generate security log types.

Logging is performed by the **miglogd** *daemon.*

Geographic Policy

The next feature to discuss is a Geographic Firewall Policy. This provides the ability to restructure access on per-country bases. This is accomplished from the GEO-IP database stored on FortiOS. This database is downloaded and updated monthly from FDN. This is useful because this provides tools to make it so that only US-Based IP's can access your web server or only allow your uses to access US-Based IP's for example. Essentially, whatever country your company is doing business in, you can restrict communication to only that country if needed. It is also easy to create a

Image 4.22 – Geography Address Object

Chapter 4 | Firewall Policy and NAT

blacklist of the country not allowed to hit your web server at the IP level. This by itself filters out a lot of potentially malicious traffic way before FortiOS starts performing its layer-7 application inspection Security Profiles.

To configure this feature first, we must create a GEO-IP Address Object. In the GUI navigate to 'Policy & Objects -> Address -> Create New Address', I have configured a GEO-IP Address Object in Image 4.23, In this Address object, we must specify the Type to be 'Geography', and then Country/Region options will be provided in the dropdown menu where I have selected the United States. We are going to use this object in the Firewall Policy so the user can only access US-Based IP space. To

Image 4.23 – Geo IP Firewall Policy

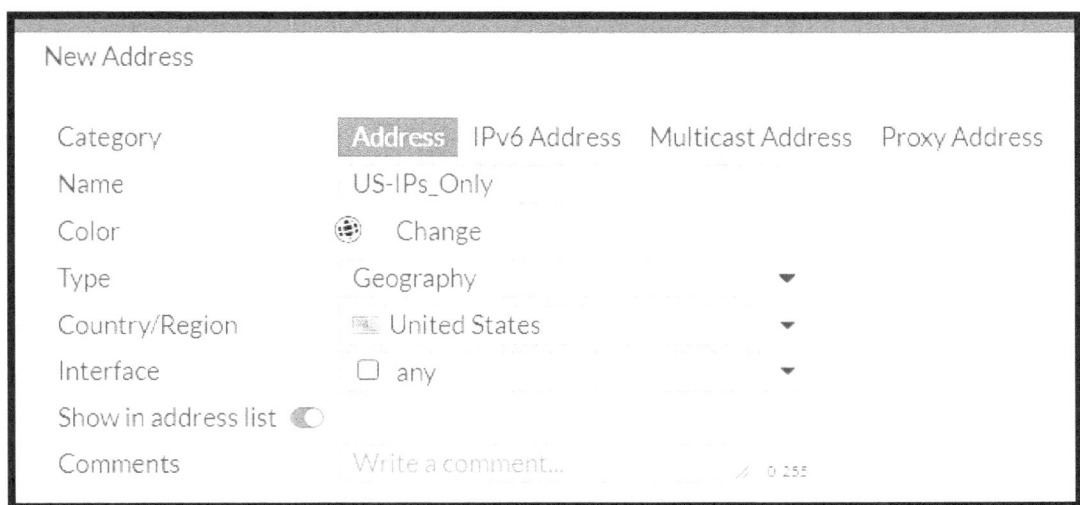

complete this configuration, navigate to our test Firewall Policy Entry in the GUI via 'Policy & Objects -> IPv4 Policy -> Edit 90'. See image 4.22: As you can see, we have referenced the GEO-IP Address Object within the Destination Field of the Firewall Policy Entry. This policy reads, all traffic coming from internal1 going to ZONE-OUTSIDE and is within the IP Space of the United States then allow. I'm sure you might be wondering how GEO-IP works on the backend. We can see the details of the GEO-IP database and IP space of certain counties within the CLI:

```
NSE4-PASS (global) # diagnose autoupdate versions
..
IP Geography DB
---------
Version: 3.00048
Contract Expiry Date: n/a
Last Updated using scheduled update on Tue Feb 18 15:22:50 2020
Last Update Attempt: Tue Feb 25 15:21:57 2020
Result: No Updates
..
```

Chapter 4 | Firewall Policy and NAT

The command 'diagnose autoupdate versions' provides the version of the GEO-IP database currently being used. This may be useful for troubleshooting issues with TAC. Here are some CLI commands we have available when working with the GEO-IP database:

```
NSE4-PASS (root) # diagnose firewall ipgeo
country-list        List all countries.
ip-list             List IP info of country.
ip2country          Get country info for the IP.
override            Print out all user defined IP geolocation data.
copyright-notice    Copyright note.
```

Next, to inspect the IP Space within a particular country us the below CLI commands:

```
NSE4-PASS (root) # diagnose firewall ipgeo ip-list US
..
        223.130.8.0 - 223.130.11.255
        223.201.0.0 - 223.201.3.255
Country name:US Total IP Range:42291
```

So if you ever run into a situation where traffic is not being allowed or is indeed being allowed, and it is not supposed to, then check your IP against the country listed IP space.

Image 4.24 FQDN Address Object

Chapter 4 | Firewall Policy and NAT

FQDN Policy

The next Firewall Policy feature is the Fully Qualified Domain Name policy. FortiOS allows the creations of policies using an FQDN. To accomplish this configuration, then we must first create an FQDN Address Object and then reference this object within the Firewall Policy Entry destination field. In the GUI navigate to 'Policy & Objects -> Addresses -> Create New', see *Image 25*.

Next, we must reference this address object in the destination field of the Firewall Policy Entry ID 90.

This policy reads, any traffic from interan1 going to ZONE-OUTSIDE to the FQDN of www.fortinet.com will be allowed. The way this happens is that FortiOS performs a DNS lookup on the FQDN referenced in Firewall Policy ID 90 and maps the resolved IP as the allowed destination. FortiOS will periodically query its assigned DNS server to resolve FQDN address objects up to 32 entries per FQDN. The commands to view the FQDN resolved IPs are:

```
#diagnose firewall fqdn list
#diagnose test application dnsproxy 6
```

Image 4.25 – FQDN Firewall Policy

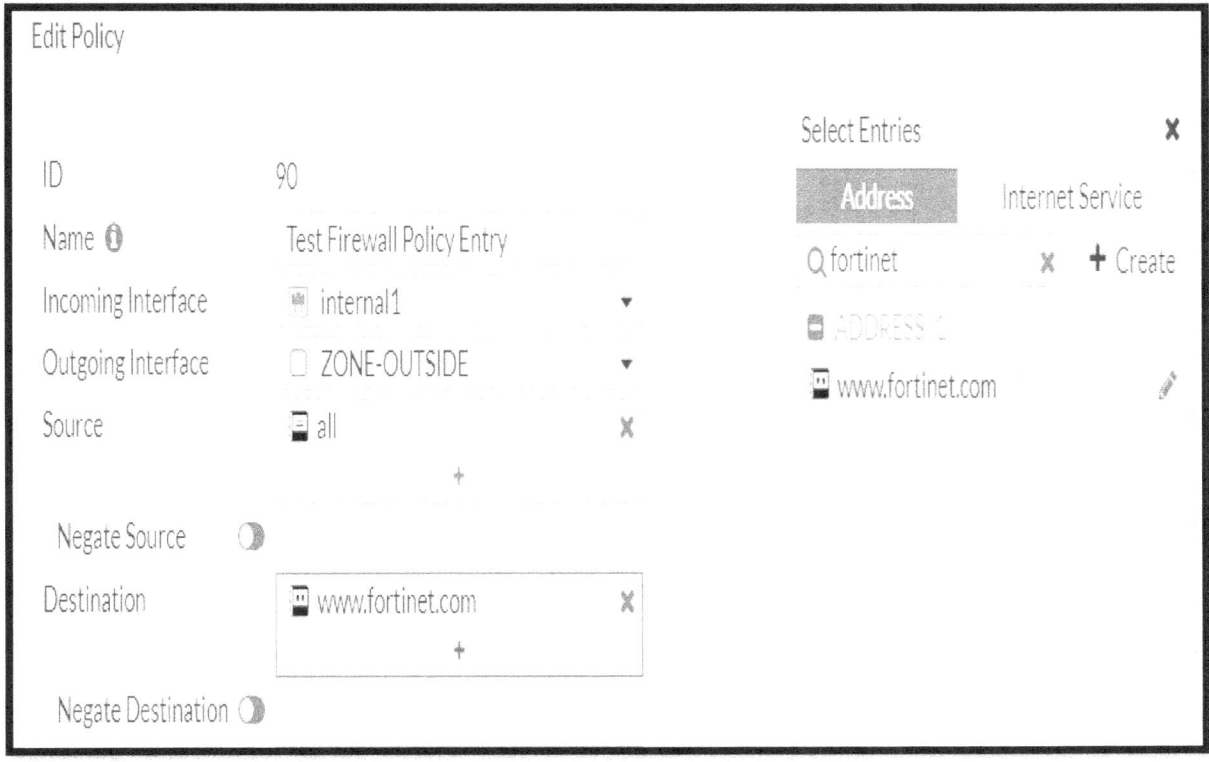

Chapter 4 | Firewall Policy and NAT

The command to increase the cached IPs TTL for an FQDN is the cache-ttl settings found in the CLI via:

```
config firewall address
edit "www.fortinet.com"
set type fqdn
set cache-ttl 86400<--------
set fqdn "www.fortinet.com"
next
end
```

MAC Address Range Policy

The next Firewall Policy feature to cover is MAC Address based policies. This essentially allows FortiOS to permit or deny traffic based on MAC addresses. We could specify a single MAC address or a MAC range. We do both through the Address

Image 4.26 – MAC Based Address Object

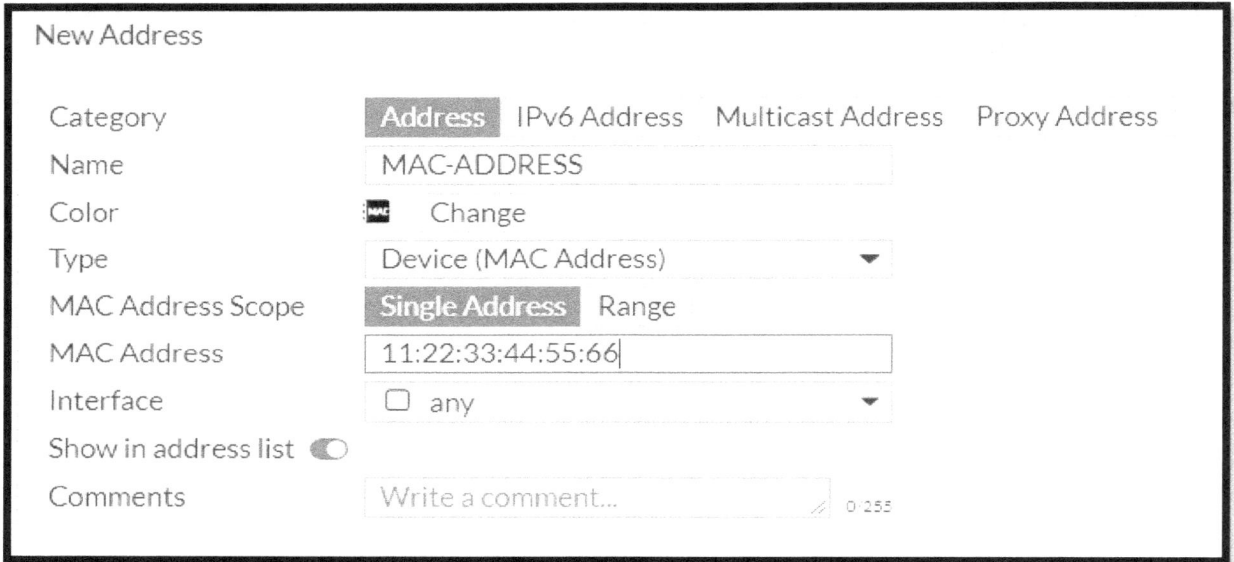

Object. To configure this, firstly navigate to the Address Object configuration page GUI at 'Policy & Objects -> Addresses -> Create New', see *Image 4.26* :

Next, we need to reference this object within the Firewall Policy Entry Source field. See *image 4.27*:

Chapter 4 | Firewall Policy and NAT

Image 4.27 – Mac Based Policy

This policy reads if MAC address of 11:22:33:44:55:66 comes from internal1 and wants to go to ZONE-OUTSIDE, then allow. We could easily specify a range MAC or make this a deny policy to fit the network requirements.

Internet-Service Policy

The next feature to talk about is the Internet-Service Firewall Policy. This is where the ISDB can be referenced within a policy to allow well-known applications. See Image 4.28.

Image 4.28 – Internet Service Firewall Policy

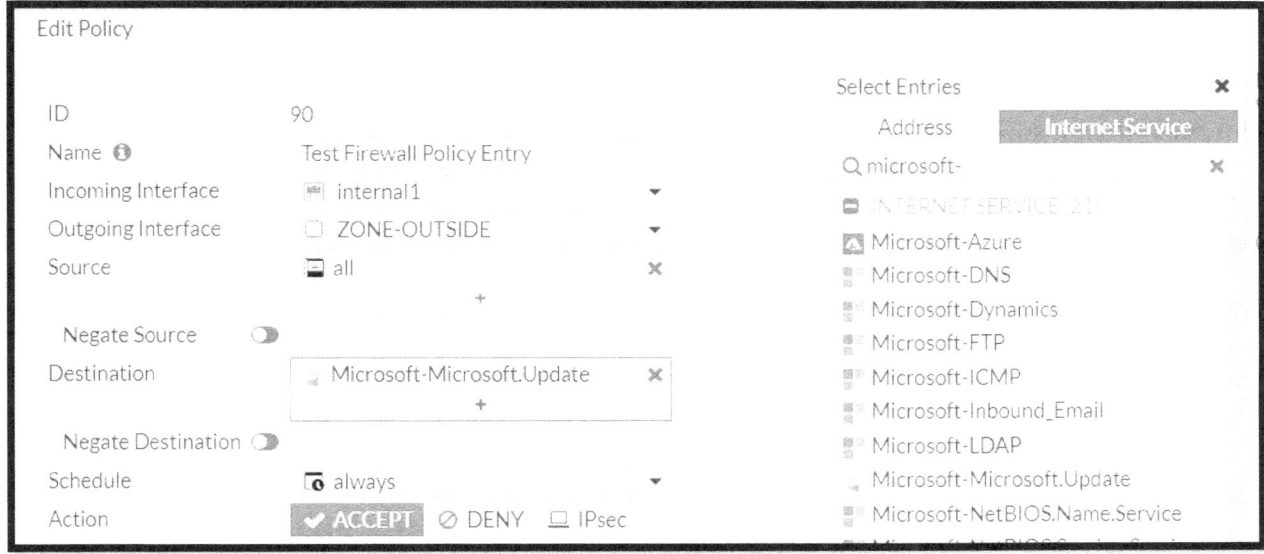

We can reference an Internet Service entries straight from the Firewall Policy configuration GUI on the right-hand side. This policy reads any traffic coming from internal1 going to ZONE-OUTSIDE and wants Microsoft Updates then allow. On the backend, FortiOS maintains an Internet Service Database that maps well-known applications to their related IP, Port, and Protocol. To find details on this database:

Chapter 4 | *Firewall Policy and NAT*

```
NSE4-PASS (global) # diagnose autoupdate versions
..
Internet-service Database Apps
---------
Version: 7.00483
Contract Expiry Date: n/a
Last Updated using scheduled update on Tue Feb 25 15:21:57 2020
Last Update Attempt: Tue Feb 25 15:21:57 2020
Result: Updates Installed
..
```

Next, to obtain details on the ISDB entry, use the below commands:

```
diagnose internet-service id-summary
..
id: 327793 name: "Microsoft-Microsoft.Update"
..
NSE4-PASS (global) # diagnose internet-service id 327793
```

> *Note that wildcard FQDNs can be used in address objects as well:*
> *set fqdn "*.fortinet.com"*

Security Profiles

One of the most essential Firewall Policy features on FortiOS is the ability to quickly reference Security Profiles within a policy. Policies are built under the Top-Level menu Security Profiles. You have a choice to use the default profiles in place or create custom profiles. Suppose you wish to create multiple custom security profiles. In that case, you must enable the feature via 'System -> Feature Visibility -> Additional Features -> Toggle On Multiple Security Profiles'. Now when configuring various UTM Security Profiles, the option is given to create new ones. *Image 4.30* shows the available 6.2 UTM profiles available.

Chapter 4 | Firewall Policy and NAT

Note that the NSE4 Study Guide Part-2 Security book will have entire chapters dedicated to explaining most of these features.

Image 4.29 – Profile Mode Policy UTM Options

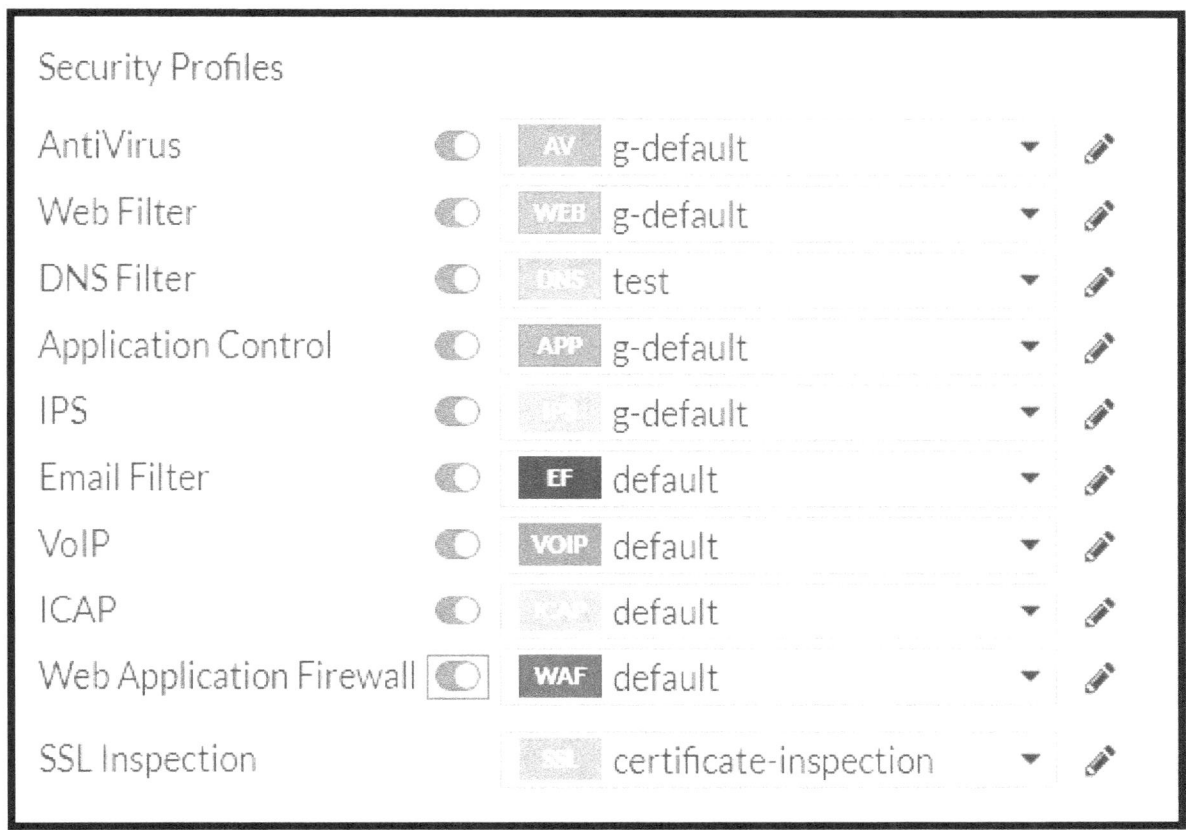

Proxy vs. Flow Based Security Scanning Overview

FortiOS provides us two methods to apply security inspect of network traffic, Proxy Based security inspection, or Flow-Based security inspection. Different security features are supported for each inspection type. Security Profiles have different features available between each of these methods. Some UTM Security Profiles can only operate in Flow-Based, and some only in Proxy Based, and some can operate in both.

Chapter 4 | Firewall Policy and NAT

Before 6.2 FortiOS, inspection mode was a per VDOM configuration settings. Now Proxy and Flow-based security scanning can be configured on a per policy setting. Note that the default inspection mode is Flow-Based. *See image 4.31* :

Image 4.30 – Inspection Mode Default

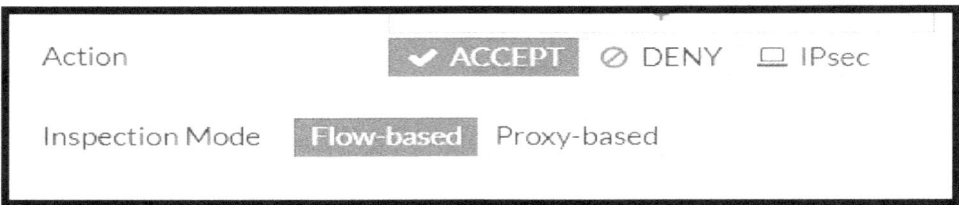

The first question you may be asking yourself is, what is the difference between the two methods? Well, in short, there are a few differences. Let's first look at the high-level advantages and disadvantages of each method, starting with Flow-Based.

1) Flow-Based Security Inspection advantages
    a. Faster Security Scanning
    b. less resource-intensive
    c. It does not require a proxy connection but creates a mirror copy of traffic.
    d. It does not alter or buffer packets.
    e. Less of a chance to time out connection due to server slow response time
2) Flow-Based Security Inspection disadvantages
    a. Less accurate then Proxy Based
    b. Fewer security features available in general

Image 4.31 – **Flow Based Scanning**

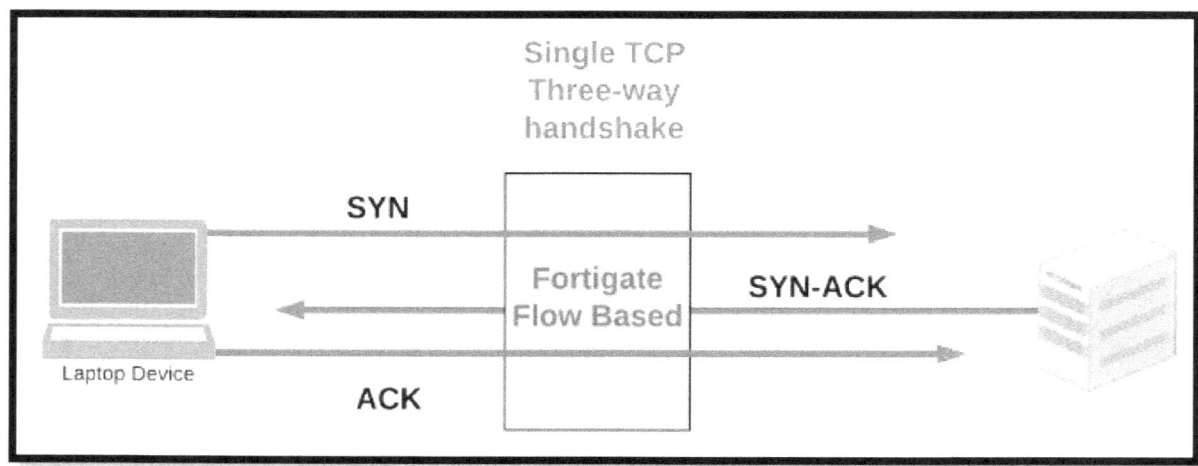

Chapter 4 | Firewall Policy and NAT

Flow-Based inspection operates on a packet to packet basis. The last packet in the communication is held on FortiOS until the Security Scanning returns a verdict on if the traffic is clean or not. If a violation is found in the communicate stream, a TCP reset packet is sent to the receiver, which terminates the connection. The objective of Flow-Based scanning is performance optimization and increased throughput. Flow base is considered a very reliable scanning method.

Next, let us take a look at the advantages and disadvantages of Proxy Based scanning:

1) Proxy Based Security Inspection advantages
    a. More accurate scanning and a higher level of threat protection overall
    b. Fewer false positives
    c. Proxy mode may change HTTP headers like the host of URL for web filter
    d. Proxy mode may send a replacement message to an HTTP client
    e. More security features available
    f. Configure file scanning size limits
2) Proxy Based Security Inspection disadvantages
    a. Higher latency
    b. TCP timeouts more probable
    c. More resource-intensive

Proxy Based scanning is also referred to as a transparent proxy. This is because FortiOS intercepts transit network traffic and buffers all the communication locally, and determines a security verdict on the traffic before dropping it or forwarding it onward. By buffering, the entire communication provides FortiOS the means to capture more datapoint but also creates latency.

Image 4.32 – Proxy Based Scanning

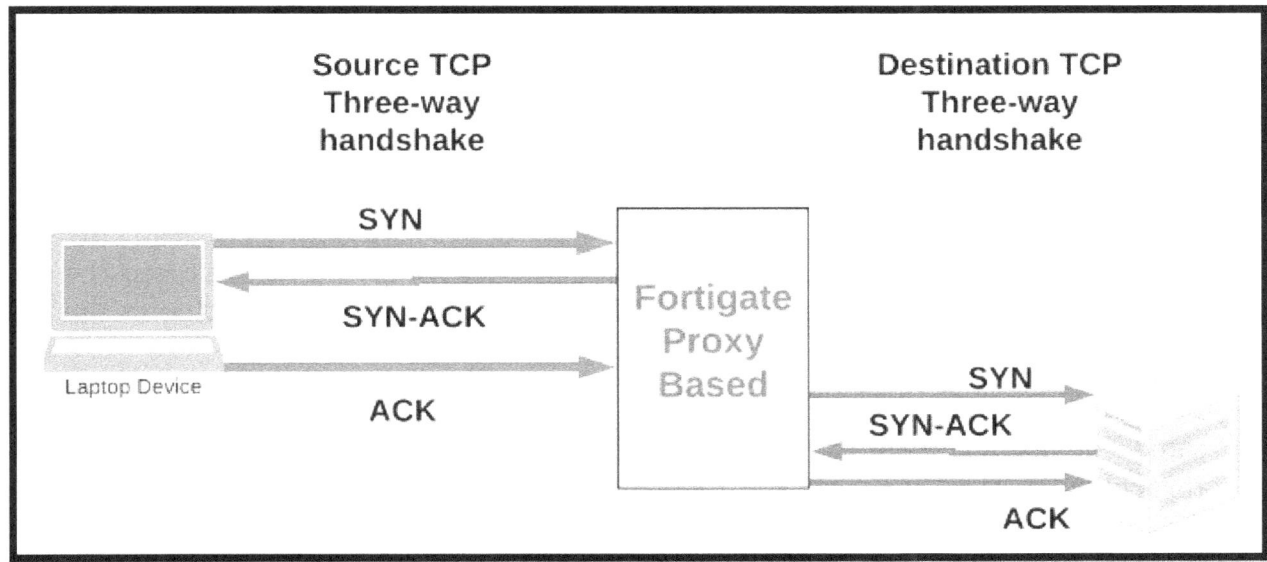

Chapter 4 | Firewall Policy and NAT

When FortiOS receives a new TCP connection request, it will automatically respond to the client with an SYN-ACK and completes the three-way handshake regardless if the intended destination responds. From a server perspective, FortiOS generates another TCP three-way between the egress interface and the destination IP. Necessarily when using Proxy Based scanning, FortiOS generates and manage two autonomous TCP connections between the source and destination of the communication implicitly. The two devices communicating with each other do not know FortiOS has indeed hijacked the TCP session.

In summary, as we work through the NSE4 Part-2 Security book, I will be discussing each scanning method related to the security module at hand. For now, just know there are two different scanning methods and know the high-level difference between them.

Consolidated Policy Mode

The last feature to discuss in this section is Consolidated Policy Mode. This essential provides another method of managing IPv4 and IPv6 policy within the same policy table. Because as you know, by default on FortiOS IPv4 and IPv6 Firewall Policies are kept in separate tables. To consolidate IPv4 and IPv6 policy into the table, you must issue the below CLI command:

```
60F-NSE4-PASS # config system settings
60F-NSE4-PASS (settings) # set consolidated-firewall-mode enable
Enabling   consolidated-firewall-mode   will   delete   all   firewall
policy/policy6.
Do you want to continue? (y/n)
```

As you can see from the warning message, that consolidated firewall command will indeed delete all IPv6 and IPv4 policies, and you should also note that there are many features not available in Consolidated Policy Mode.

Policy Anti Replay Protection

Anti-Replay is a method used by FortiOS to check TCP sequence numbers to make sure the segment is part of a TCP session, essentially. By default, if a segment received falls out of the expected sequence number range, FortiGate drops the packet. This behavior is referred to as strict. This helps prevent SYN flooding in general.

Details on the TCP checking. Note that SYN, FIN, and RST flags cannot be within the same TCP header. Also, FortiOS does not allow more than one ICMP error packet through a Session Entry before it receives an expected TCP or UDP packet. If a TCP RST packet is received and the 'check-reset-range' is set to strict, FortiOS checks the sequence number of the RST to be sure it falls within the unacknowledged

Chapter 4 | Firewall Policy and NAT

segments and will drop the packet if the sequence number is incorrect. This is everything loose checking is accomplished. Strict perform everything as the loose setting in addition to checking the make sure the TCP sequence number has been calculated correctly for each new session. This now a per policy setting found in the CLI via:

```
NSE4-PASS (29) # show ful | grep anti
        set anti-replay enable
```

If you suspect packet loss due to anti-replay, then our diagnose flow debug will show this explicitly:

```
id=20081  trace_id=89  msg="Find  an  existing  session,  id-00061456, original direction"
id=20081 trace_id=179 msg="replay packet, drop"
```

Firewall Policy Table Management

Firewall Policies can get complicated. In this section, I am going to step through and show you what tools we must help navigate through the Firewall Policy Table, how going to discuss how packets are evaluated by the Firewall Policy Table and how to troubleshoot it.

Firewall Policy Views

The items to discuss are Firewall Policy Views. There are two different GUI views on the Firewall Policy GUI page. These are:

1) Interface Pair View
2) By Sequence

I'll discuss Interface Pair View first. Firstly, let us see what this actually looks like in the GUI, see *image 4.33*.

Image 4. 33 – Interface Pair View

Chapter 4 | Firewall Policy and NAT

For this view to be available as an option, you must specify the source and destination interface. You cannot use the value 'any' within source or destination interface fields. Also, you cannot reference more than one interface within the source/destination interface field. I personally prefer this view because it makes firewall policies easier to understand and read. Essentially, this sorts the firewall policies into sections where the source and destination interfaces are the same. As you can see from *Image 4.33*, there is a plus (+) and minus (-) icon right next to the interface pairings. This is used to expand or minimize the list of firewall policies related to the interface pairing.

The next view available is the By Sequence view. This view is forced to be used if you select 'any' within the Source or Destination field within a Firewall Policy Entry. Using 'any' could lower the total amount of Firewall Policies needed but makes the Firewall Policy Table much hardware to read, understand, and ultimately manage. I recommend putting a little more work in the beginning when creating policies and be specific with the Source and Destination fields. See *Image 4.34* as an example of the By Sequence view.

Image 4. 34 – Policies by Sequence view

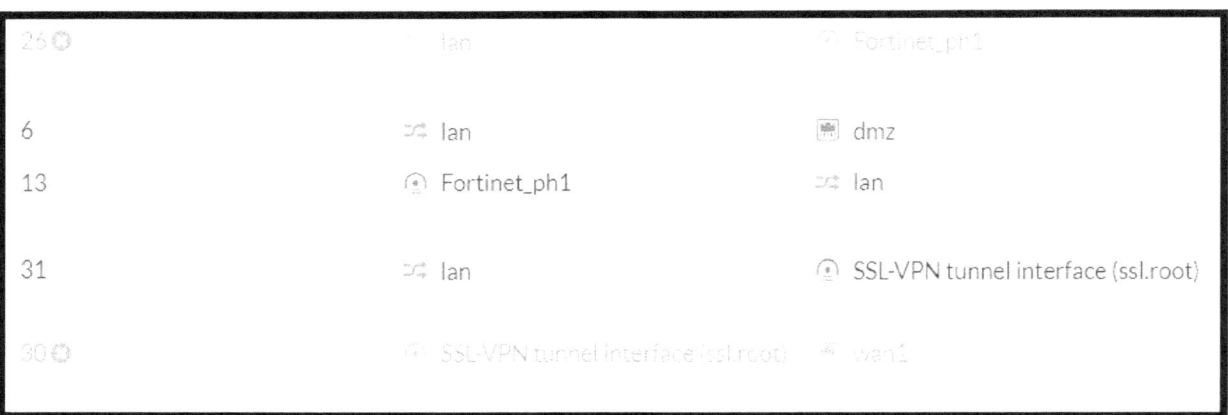

Notice, the Firewall Policy Entries will be presented literally in the order they are configured in the Firewall Policy Table regardless of ID number. Also, remember that Firewall Policies are evaluated from the top down. Lastly, to switch views, navigate to the Firewall Policy Table GUI page, and in the upper right-hand corner, there will be a toggle switch between views, see *Image 4.35*.

Chapter 4 | Firewall Policy and NAT

Image 4. 35 – Change Policy View

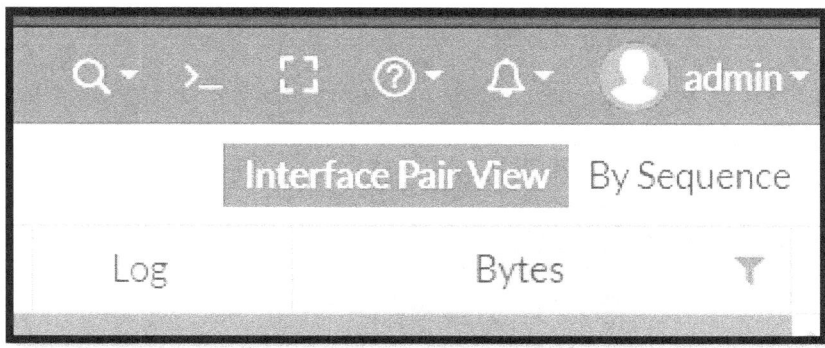

Policy Lookup and Filter Feature

When attempting to find individual policies in the Firewall Policy Table, a search function can be used at the top of the page. See *image 4.36*.

Image 4. 36 – Policy Lookup

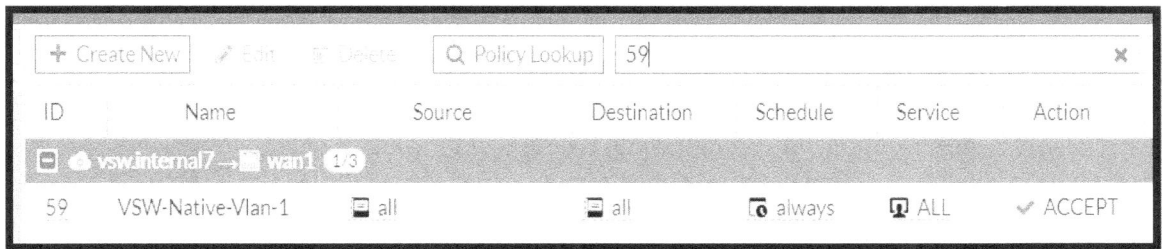

Within the Policy Lookup search filter, you can enter strings to match policy IDs or any object name used to build the Policy Entry. This field is useful when searching for specific attributes within the Firewall Policy Table. The Firewall Policy Table also provides a feature to filter on specific columns using string matching and more advanced regex parsing. Check out Image 4.37 on the next page for details:

Image 4.37 – Policy Table Column Configuration

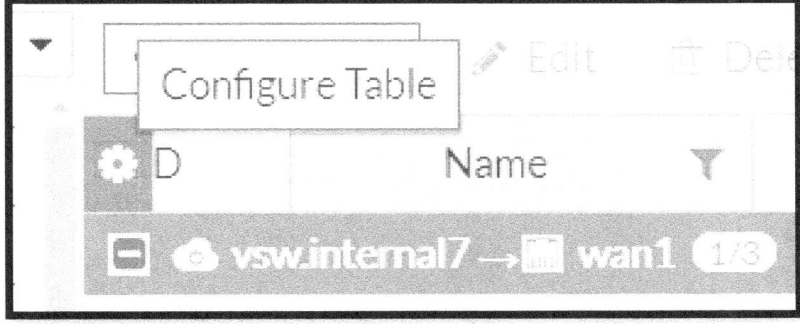

Chapter 4 | Firewall Policy and NAT

Image 4. 38 – Column Filter Feature

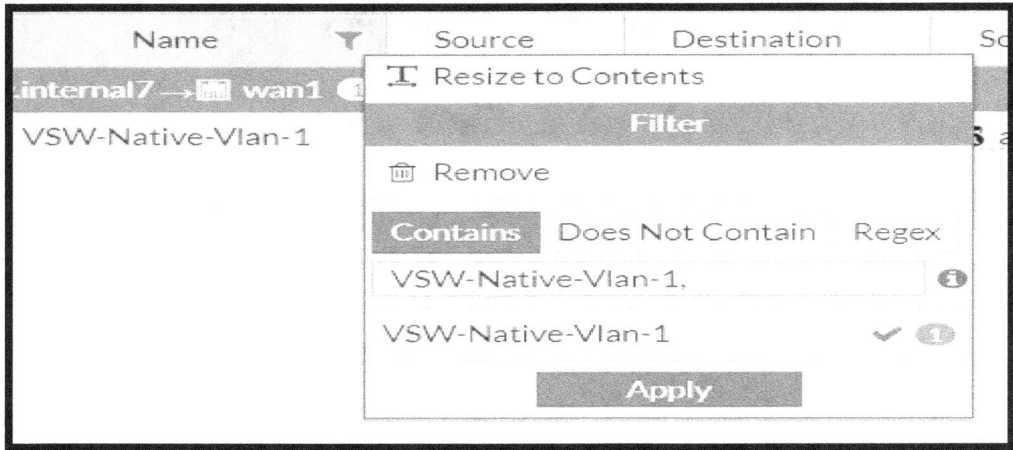

The last feature here to touch on is the column display settings. This setting presents different policy attributes when viewing the Firewall Policy Table within the GUI. See *Image 4.39* on the next page. Once you select 'Configure Table' via the

Image 4.39 – Policy Table Column Filter

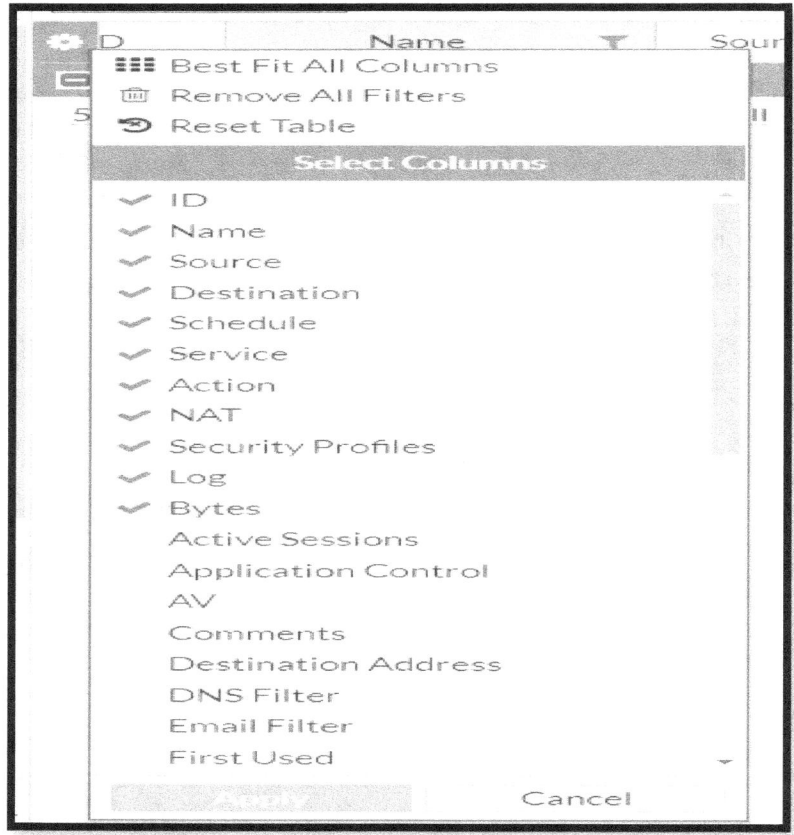

Chapter 4 | Firewall Policy and NAT

gear icon on the Firewall Policy Table page, then you will be presented a context menu where you could select different columns to display. It could be useful when troubleshooting or baselining your network.

Adjusting Policy Sequence

The network table Firewall Policy Management feature to discuss is policy re-ordering. Sometimes it is necessary to re-order policies so traffic matches a particular policy over another. Generally speaking, the more specific policies would need to be configured first and then configure less specific policies configured at the bottom of the table. There are two methods to re-order policies. The first method is to drag and drop from the GUI. The second method is to us the 'move' in the CLI within the Firewall Policy Table context. I will provide an example of both in this section. See image 4.40, The CLI equivalent would be:

```
0: edit root
0: config firewall policy
0: move 96 before 59
0: end
0: end
```

Image 4.40 – Reordering Firewall Policies

As you can see in the CLI output, FortiOS issued the command to move policy ID 96 before policy 59. This causes policy 96 to be evaluated first.

Implicit Deny Policy Zero

The last topic in Firewall Policy Table management to be aware of is Policy 0. This is a special policy that represents the very last policy or the 'catch-all' on the table, which is an implicit deny. This cannot be removed or modified and is the default behavior on FortiOS. Essentially, if there is not an explicit match for certain traffic, then FortiOS drops it. On the NSE4 exam, it is important to know what the diagnose

Chapter 4 | Firewall Policy and NAT

flow debug looks like when traffic hits the implicit deny Policy Entry. Below is an example of this output:

`msg="iprope_in_check() check failed on policy 0, drop"`

This output means there is no firewall policy match. Here is an example of a diagnose flow debug output of an explicit match:

`msg="Allowed by Policy-59:"` or `msg="Denied by Policy-59:"`

The implicit deny policy is listed in the Firewall Policy Table GUI, see *Image 4.41*.

Image 4.41 – Firewall Policy Table Implicit Deny

Firewall Policy Section Summary

This brings us to the end of the FortiOS Firewall Policy section. At this point, you should understand the different policy tables available, the packet to policy matching process, the components of a policy, the available policy features, the difference between Profile Based and Policy-Based, and table management features available. In the next section, we are going to start talking about all the different types of NAT and how they fit into the Firewall Policy Entry.

Chapter 4 | Firewall Policy and NAT

It is crucial that you have a good grasp of the topics we have covered so far in this chapter because we build off this knowledge when we step into NAT and Session Helpers.

Network Address Translation (NAT)

One of the most critical functions on the Internet is NAT (Network Address Translation). So what is NAT? and why do we need it? Fundamentally, NAT is the process of turning a source or destination IP address into a different one… hence the translation. The purpose of doing this most of the time is to turn a private RFC 1918 IPv4 address into an Internet publicly routable IP address. Another reason to use NAT is to hide LAN resources, which inherently increases security.

In this section, we are going to look at the different options FortiOS has for NAT. We are going to talk about DNAT (Destination NAT) and SNAT (Source NAT) and how to implement these functions on FortiOS. Lastly, we are going to touch on NAT troubleshooting and policy matching. Let's get started!

FortiOS Configuration Methods for NAT

FortiOS has two methods to implement NAT, which are Firewall Policy NAT and Central NAT Tables. The first method we will discuss will be Firewall Policy NAT. Here is a quick overview of the two different methods.

Firewall Policy NAT Overview

Firewall Policy NAT method performs the NAT function within the Firewall Policy Entry itself. Just like other objects created to be referenced within a policy, we must create NAT objects as well. There are two base objects to configure for this function, which are:

1) VIP Object or Virtual IP
    a. A VIP is an object that will perform a DNAT on an IP packet.
2) IP Pool Object
    a. An IP Pool is an object that will perform a SNAT on an IP packet

You can locate VIP objects in the GUI via 'Policy & Objects > Virtual IPs'. In the CLI, you can find VIP objects via:

```
NSE4-PASS (root) # config firewall vip
NSE4-PASS (vip) #
```

Chapter 4 | Firewall Policy and NAT

Next, to find the IP Pool object in the GUI navigate via 'Policy & Objects > IP pools'. IP Pool objects can be found in CLI via:

```
NSE4-PASS (ippool) # show
config firewall ippool
```

Central NAT Overview

When using the Central NAT method, there are two different tables to manage on FortiOS, the' Central SNAT' table and the 'DNAT & Virtual IPs' Table. These tables are independent tables from the Firewall Policy Table, and each operates autonomously. This method is not enabled by default. The Central NAT Tables are read from the top down and are evaluated after the Firewall Policy. These tables can be found in the GUI via 'Policy & Objects > Central SNAT' and 'Policy & Objects > DNAT & Virtual IPs'. The CLI location for these table configurations is:

SNAT:

```
60F-NSE4-PASS # config firewall central-snat-map
```
DNAT:
```
60F-NSE4-PASS # config firewall vip
```
   To enable this method, use the following CLI configuration:

```
60F-NSE4-PASS # config system settings
60F-NSE4-PASS (settings) # set central-nat enable
```

Chapter 4 | Firewall Policy and NAT

Image 4. 42 – Central SNAT Entry

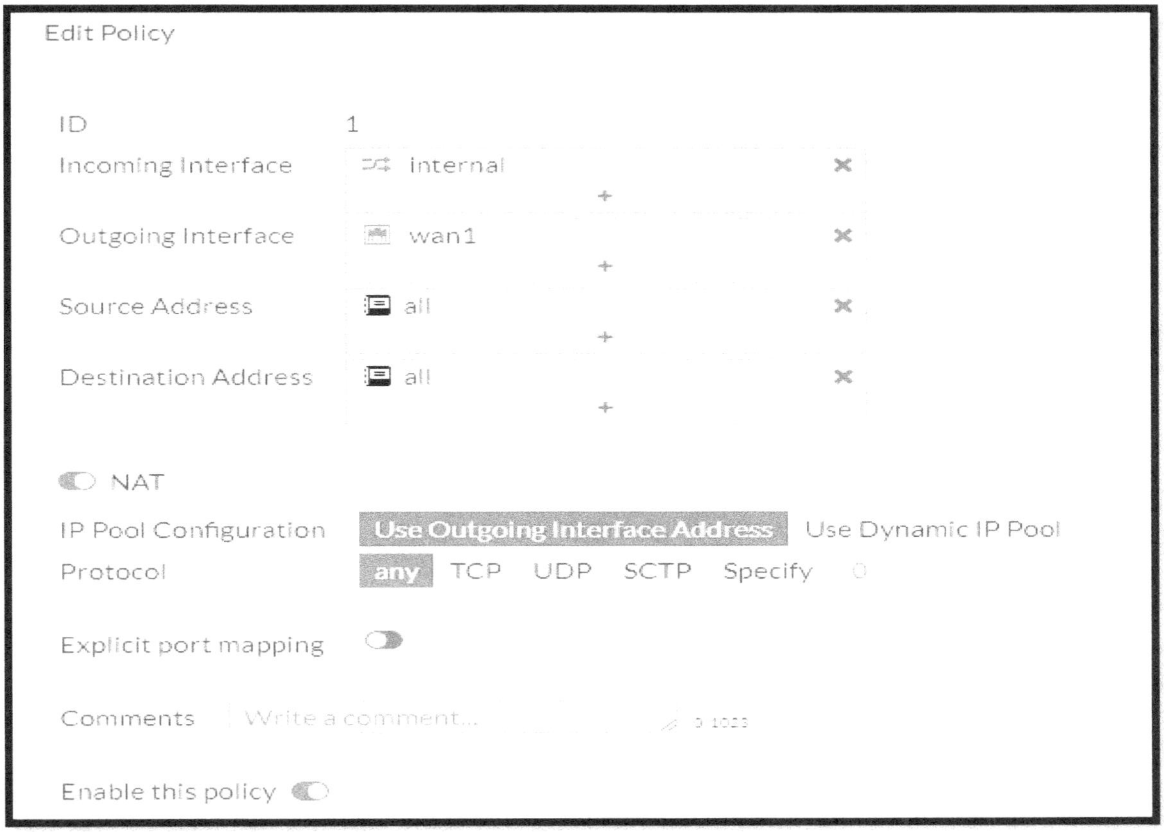

```
Edit Policy

ID                          1
Incoming Interface          ⇄  internal                    ×
                               +
Outgoing Interface          🖥  wan1                       ×
                               +
Source Address              📄  all                        ×
                               +
Destination Address         📄  all                        ×
                               +

  NAT
IP Pool Configuration       Use Outgoing Interface Address   Use Dynamic IP Pool
Protocol                    any  TCP   UDP   SCTP   Specify

Explicit port mapping       ○

Comments       Write a comment...              0 1023

Enable this policy  ○
```

Image 4.42 displays a GUI Central SNAT table entry.

Policy NAT Virtual IP (VIP)

This section goes over the details of VIPs used in the Policy NAT method. In my opinion, this is the more straightforward method and is more commonly used in the community from what I've seen. I'm first going to review all the different types of VIPs we have to work with. Then I will provide a widespread use case example after I will step into more of the fine-grain details of VIP objects and finally finishing on the VIP policy match.

Before we get started, we should go over some terminology. Firstly, when I just say VIP, I mean and IPv4-to-IPv4 VIP DNAT implicitly. There are other VIP object types like IPv6, which is a DNAT for IPv6 addresses. There are also VIP object types to translate IPv4 to IPv6 addresses called VIP NAT46 and IPv6 to IPv4 address, which are called VIP NAT64 Type. We cover all these VIP types in this section. We start with the most common type of VIP.

Chapter 4 | Firewall Policy and NAT

Next, the 'extip' setting is the external facing IP FortiOS expects to receive before any NAT takes place. The 'mappedip' setting is the new destination IP FortiOS will specify. The same logic goes for extport and mappedport settings. These are the expected layer-4 port expected to be received by the VIP object, and the mappedport is the new translated destination port specified by FortiOS. The Setting 'extinft' is the interface FortiOS expects to receive the traffic to be NAT'ed and will respond to ARP on this port for the 'extip' IP address by default. As we go through configuration examples, refer back to this section as needed if you need a refresher of how these settings are related to the DNAT process.

VIP Type Overview

There are many different sub-types of VIPs that can be used for a different reason. Below is the CLI output of the available options. Let's discuss them.

```
NSE4-PASS (FMG_VIP) # set type
static-nat              Static NAT.
load-balance            Load balance.
server-load-balance     Server load balance.
dns-translation         DNS translation.
fqdn                    Fully qualified domain name.
```

VIP sub-types:

1) Static NAT
    a. This type is the most common usage of a VIP. This VIP type is used for your primary port forwarding mechanism and one to one translation.
2) Server Load Balance
    a. As you might suspect, this VIP is used to load balance traffic across multiple internal hosts. We will talk about the load balancing methods and more details on this type later
3) FQDN
    a. the external or mapped IP for a VIP is obtained by resolving an FQDN.
4) DNS Translation
    a. Dynamic VIP used with DNS translation. I recommend to us the DNS Filter profile and not VIP for this functionality.

In this section, we are going to focus on Static NAT and Server Load Balance types.

Chapter 4 | Firewall Policy and NAT

Static VIP Port Forward Example

The first configuration I want to show you is the most basic, which is a port forward, which is commonly used in day to day FortiGate operations. In this exercise, we are

Image 4.43 – VIP Object

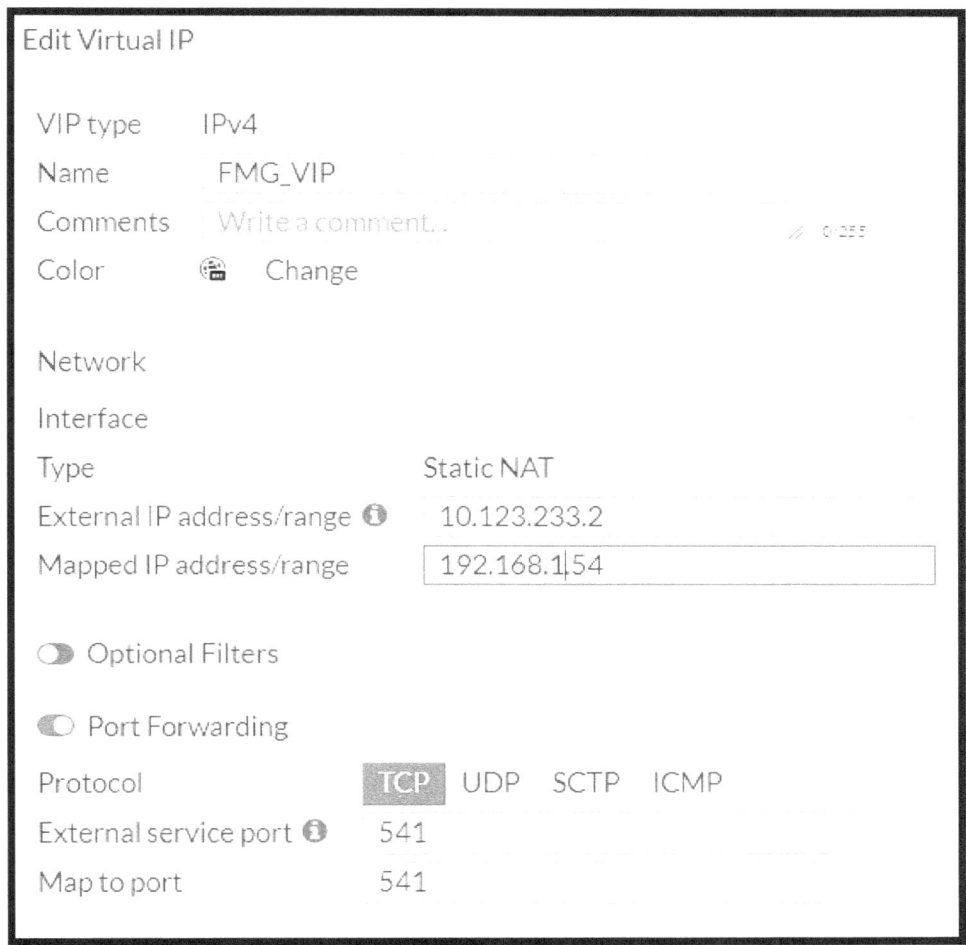

going to create a VIP object and reference it in a Firewall Policy Entry. Remember, a VIP performs DNAT on a packet. Let's create our VIP object first, see *Image 4.43* .

Here is the CLI equivalent:

```
NSE4-PASS (FMG_VIP) # show
config firewall vip
    edit "FMG_VIP"
        set uuid c52417cc-4b7d-51ea-a18f-12d7b371968b
        set extip 10.123.233.2
        set extintf "wan1"
        set portforward enable
        set mappedip "192.168.1.54"
```

Chapter 4 | Firewall Policy and NAT

```
            set extport 541
            set mappedport 541
    next
end
```

Image 4. 44 – VIP DNAT Diagram Flow

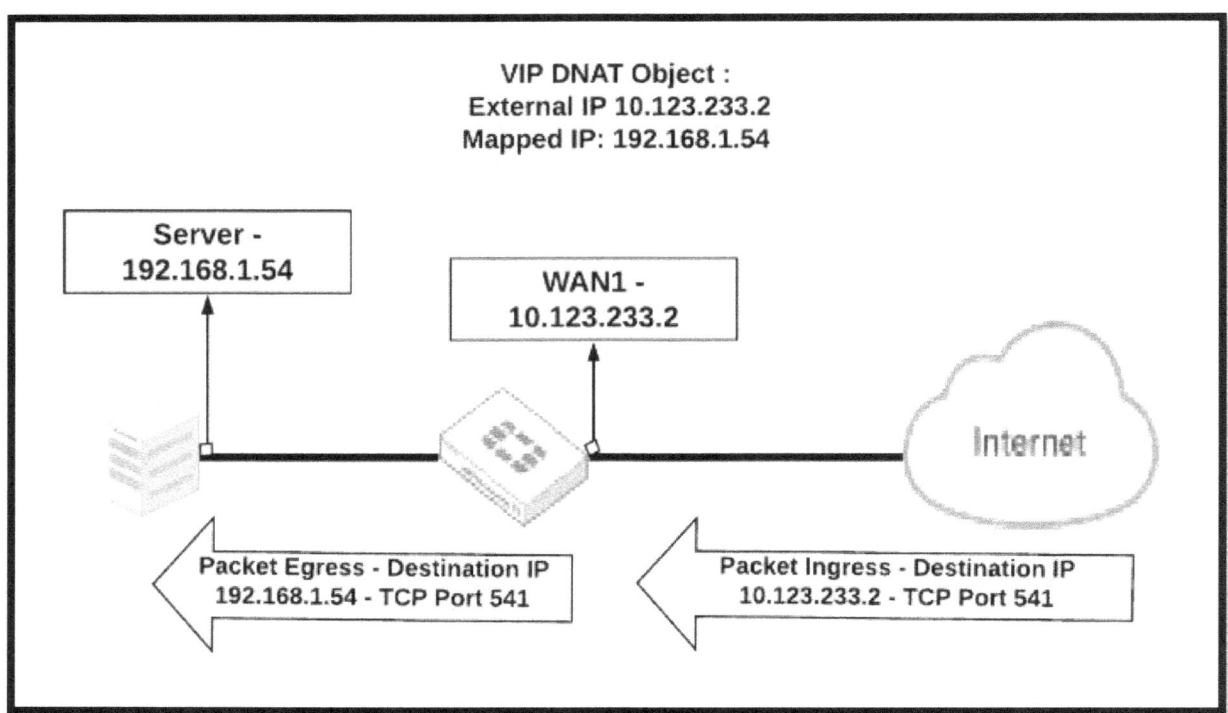

In this example, the external IP used in the VIP object is the same IP assigned to the WAN1 interface 10.123.233.2, and the translated IP is 192.168.1.54. Note that this is not required; any IP can be used as the External IP. The layer-4 port number that is forwarded through FortiGate is 541, which is the FortiManager FGFM protocol port to manage FortiGate. To specify a 1-to-1 NAT, then the 'Port Forwarding' toggle would not be enabled; this would essentially enable the DNAT translation function for all 65535 ports. Also, when the internal server initiates a session outbound, a SNAT is performed by the 1-to-1 VIP. The conditions for a VIP match here are the packet must ingress WAN1 and have a destination IPv4 address of 10.123.233.2, and must be using TCP protocol that has a destination port of 541. Lastly, the packet must be accepted by the policy the VIP object is referenced in.

If all these conditions match, then FortiGate accepts the packet into this VIP object, and the VIP then translates the destination IP within the packet from 10.123.233.2 to 192.168.1.54. Next, FortiOS performs a route lookup for the newly translated IP address and sends the packet onward. This creates a new Session Entry in the Session Table. The reply traffic from 192.168.1.54 matches the newly created

Chapter 4 | *Firewall Policy and NAT*

session, and FortiOS performs an SNAT back to the original IPv4 address of 10.123.233.2 without any additional configuration.

To make this VIP object 'active' when using the Firewall Policy NAT method, it must be referenced in the Destination field within a Firewall Policy Entry. See Image 4.45 as an example of this. This rule reads, if traffic coming from WAN1 going to vsw.internal7, a destination IP is 10.123.233.2 with TCP 541, then perform DNAT to 192.168.1.54 and forward traffic.

Image 4.45 – Firewall Policy NAT VIP

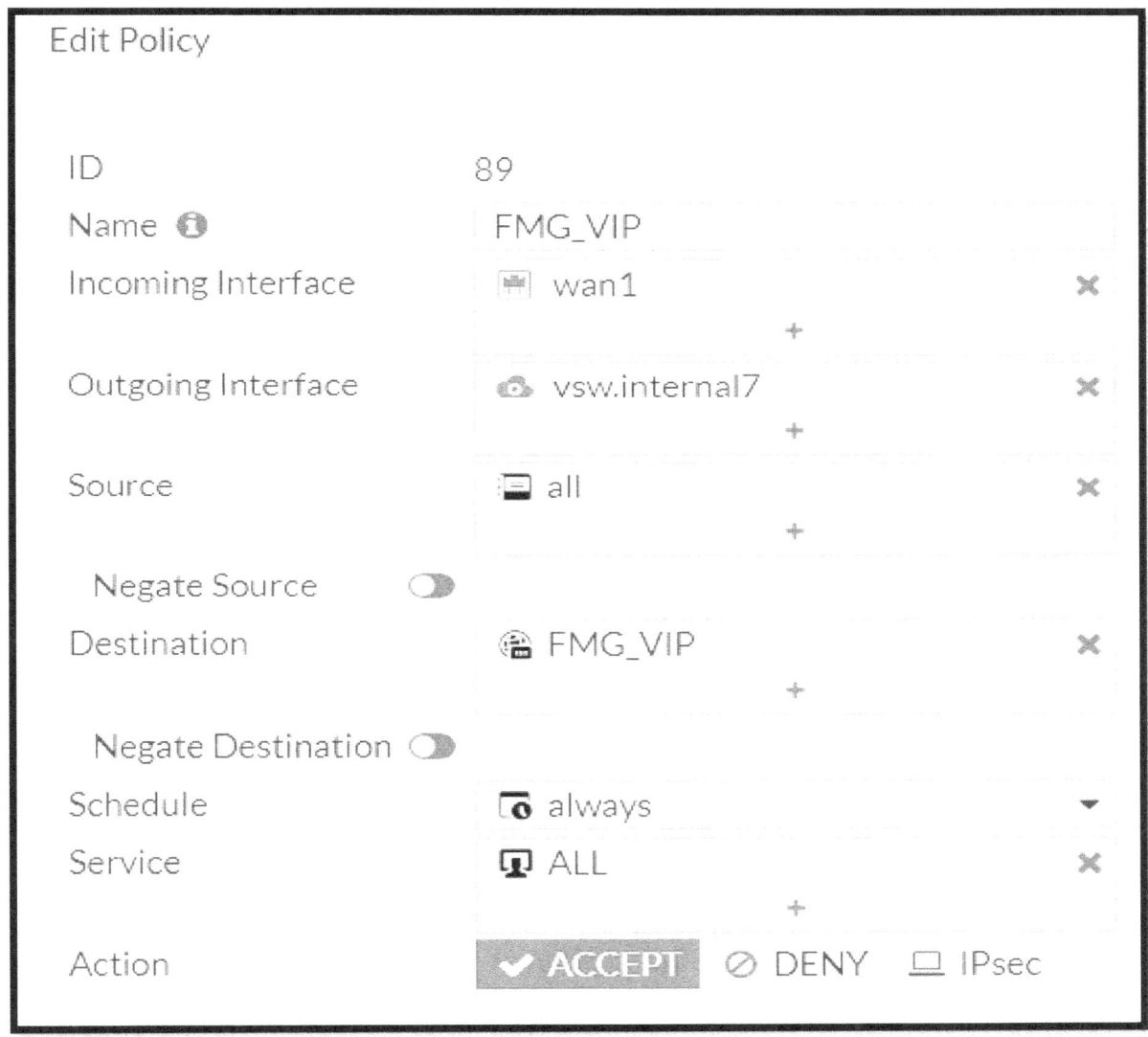

This part might be a little confusing, but we do not need to specify the Service field to allow port 541 explicitly. The VIP object FMG_VIP will only allow port 541 to pass per the configuration. We could specify port 541 in the Service field, but it would

Chapter 4 | Firewall Policy and NAT

not make a difference in this case. The only purpose of doing this here would be to make reading the policy more intuitive.

However, there are situations when using VIP objects; it is required to specify explicitly the ports that are being allowed in the Service field of Firewall Policy Entry. For example, if a one-to-one NAT was used, then by default, the VIP will allow all 65535 ports to pass through the FortiGate. If only a subset of ports is to be allowed, then we must be specified the ports within the Service field within the policy that holds the VIP object.

> *Be careful when using a one-to-one NAT on your WAN1 interface IP because if this interface is used for management you will lose access to your device.*

Remember when using the port forward feature that a single external or public IP can be mapped to many different hosts internally by using different ports. However, if you use a one-to-one VIP, all ports are dedicated to a single internal host.

VIP ARP

VIPs respond to ARP! This is, of course, can be disabled if needed. When using VIPs, know they behave as if they are assigned on the physical/virtual interface itself. They can cause IP conflicts. VIPs can be assigned to specific interfaces, meaning they will only perform DNAT on packets that ingress on that interface and also only respond to ARP request ingress on the interface they are bound to. To disable ARP on a VIP, use the CLI:

```
NSE4-PASS (FMG_VIP) # show
config firewall vip
    edit "FMG_VIP"
        set uuid c52417cc-4b7d-51ea-a18f-12d7b371968b
        set extip 10.123.233.2
        set extintf "wan1"
        set arp-reply disable   ←
        set portforward enable
        set mappedip "192.168.209.54"
        set extport 541
        set mappedport 541
    next
end
```
This could be used when troubleshooting if needed.

Chapter 4 | Firewall Policy and NAT

VIP One to One

The create the VIP object FMG_VIP to be a one-to-one NAT, then all we need to do is disable the port forward feature. This can be done in the GUI by toggled 'Port Forwarding' to off. The CLI configuration is like so:

```
0: config vdom
0: edit root
0: config firewall vip
0: edit "FMG_VIP"
0: set portforward disable
```

Remember, this opens all ports for your internal host allowing access to all ports and services listening on those ports. If you use a one-to-one NAT, then I highly recommend restricting access to the internal host via the Firewall Policy Entry Service field. In the use case where we only want to allow the FortiManager FGFM protocol through FortiGate, then we would specify TCP port 541 in the Service field.

Image 4.46 – Create Custom Service

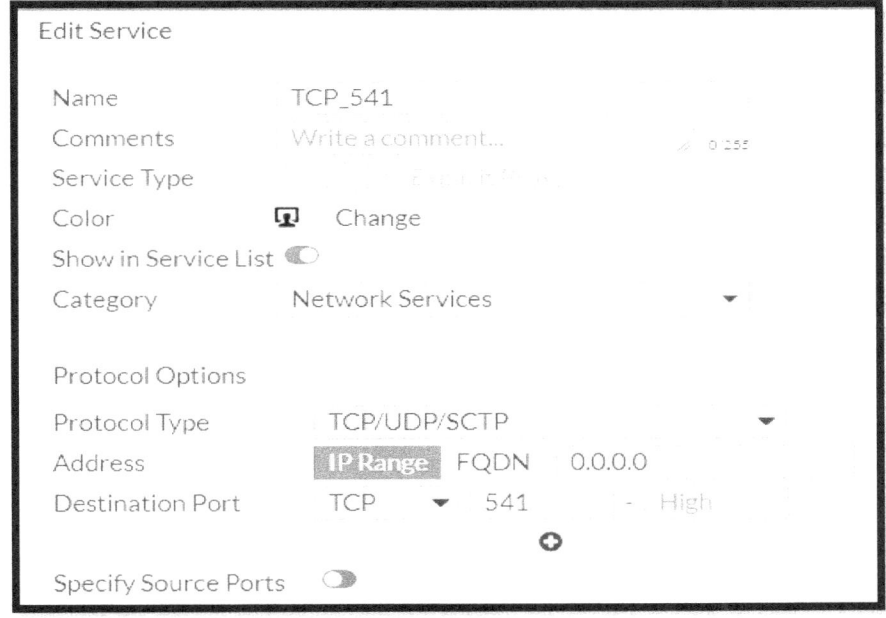

To do this, first, a Service object needs to be created with the required parameters. Navigate to 'Policy & Objects -> Services -> Create New' see image 4.46.

Here is the CLI output:

```
config firewall service custom
    edit "TCP_541"
        set category "Network Services"
```

Chapter 4 | Firewall Policy and NAT

```
            set tcp-portrange 541
    next
end
```

Next, take the object TCP_541 and reference it within the Firewall Policy Entry that holds the VIP FMG_VIP. This will effectively only allow port 541 to pass through.

<u>VIP Range</u>

When using one-to-one VIPs, there is an option to specify a range. Be sure not to create an IP conflict when using this method because FortiOS responds to ARP for the entire range. The purpose of this is if there are many hosts that need one-to-one public IP mapping. For example, if we had four hosts, we could use the configuration:

```
config firewall vip
    edit "VIP"
        set uuid 94cacdb8-6492-51ea-9fad-4c82e8aa6e6d
        set extip 10.10.10.1-10.10.10.4          // external facing IPs
        set extintf "wan1"
        set mappedip "192.168.1.1-192.168.1.4"   // internal host IPs
    next
end
```

The external IP 10.10.10.3 would be mapped to 192.168.1.3 internal IP in this case, and 10.10.10.2 would be mapped to 192.168.1.2 and so on. You can make the range as large as you need. For example, you could map an entire routed block of public IP's to an internal IP subnet, like 100.100.100.0/24 to 172.16.1.0/24. This could be a time saver.

<u>VIP Filtering</u>

This is an option to restrict what source IP address can access the VIP object. You can think of this as a trust host setting. I have not used this setting in a production environment because if I want to restrict what source, I would just use the Source field within the Firewall Policy Entry itself. But there might be specific use cases for this, but just know the feature exists. Here is a CLI example of this configuration:

```
config firewall vip
    edit "FMG_VIP"
        set uuid c52417cc-4b7d-51ea-a18f-12d7b371968b
        set src-filter "192.168.202.0/24"   ←
        set extip 10.123.233.2
```

Chapter 4 | Firewall Policy and NAT

```
        set extintf "wan1"
        set portforward enable
        set mappedip "192.168.209.54"
        set extport 541
        set mappedport 541
    next
```

VIP Load Balancing

VIP Load Balancing is a useful feature with robust functionality that allows you to turn your FortiGate into a full server load balancer, which is when essentially a group of servers share the same application-level configuration and take turns serving new inbound clients. FortiGate is the one that distributes the load and keeps track of each session. There are various load balancing algorithms available. We are going to walk through a basic VIP type Server Load Balancing deployment. See image 4.48.

Image 4. 48 – VIP Server Load Balance Diagram

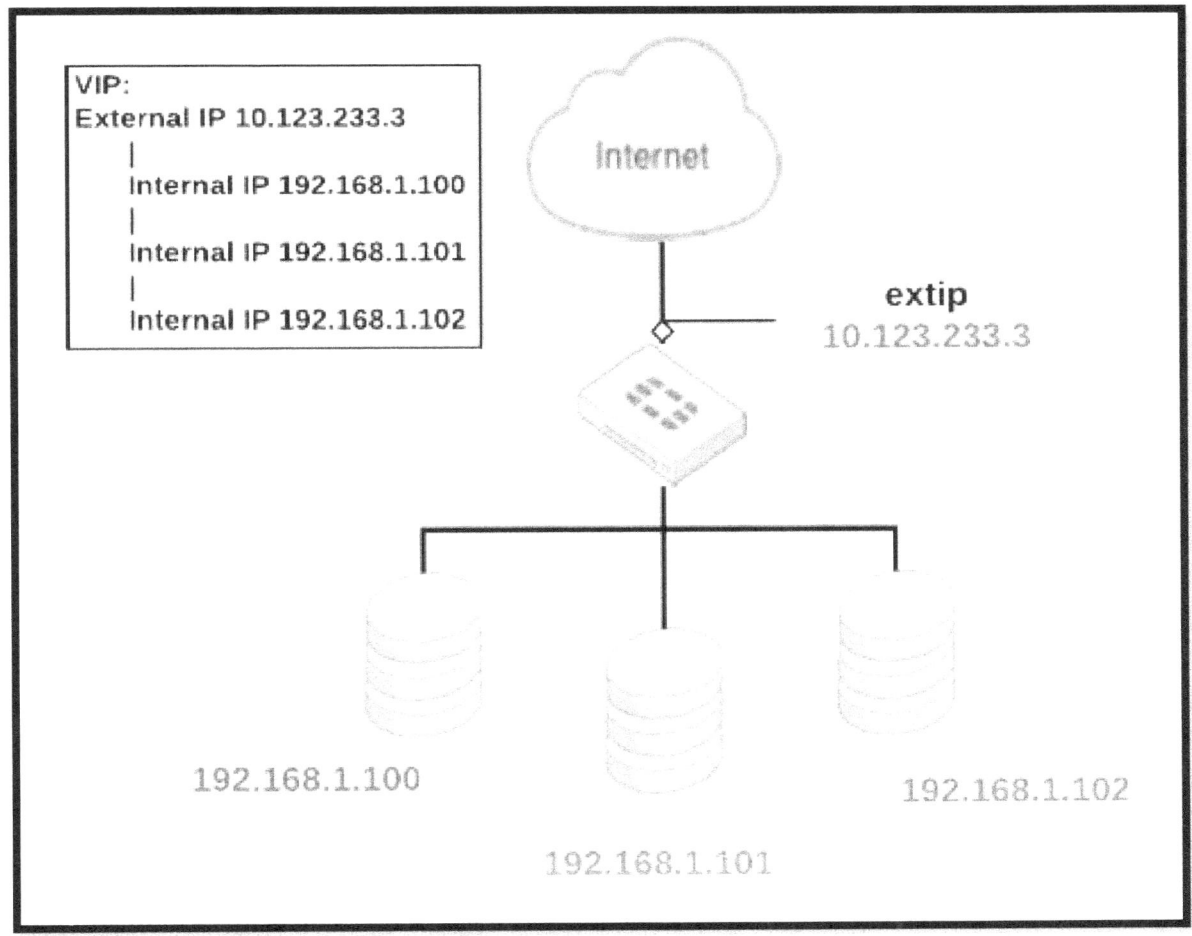

Chapter 4 | Firewall Policy and NAT

In this example, the external (extip) IP address is 10.123.233.2, and the three internal servers that FortiOS load balance to 192.168.1.100, 192.168.1.101, an 192.168.1.102. In the GUI, navigate to 'Policy & Objects -> Virtual Servers -> Create New'

Image 4. 47 – Virtual Server VIP Load Balancer

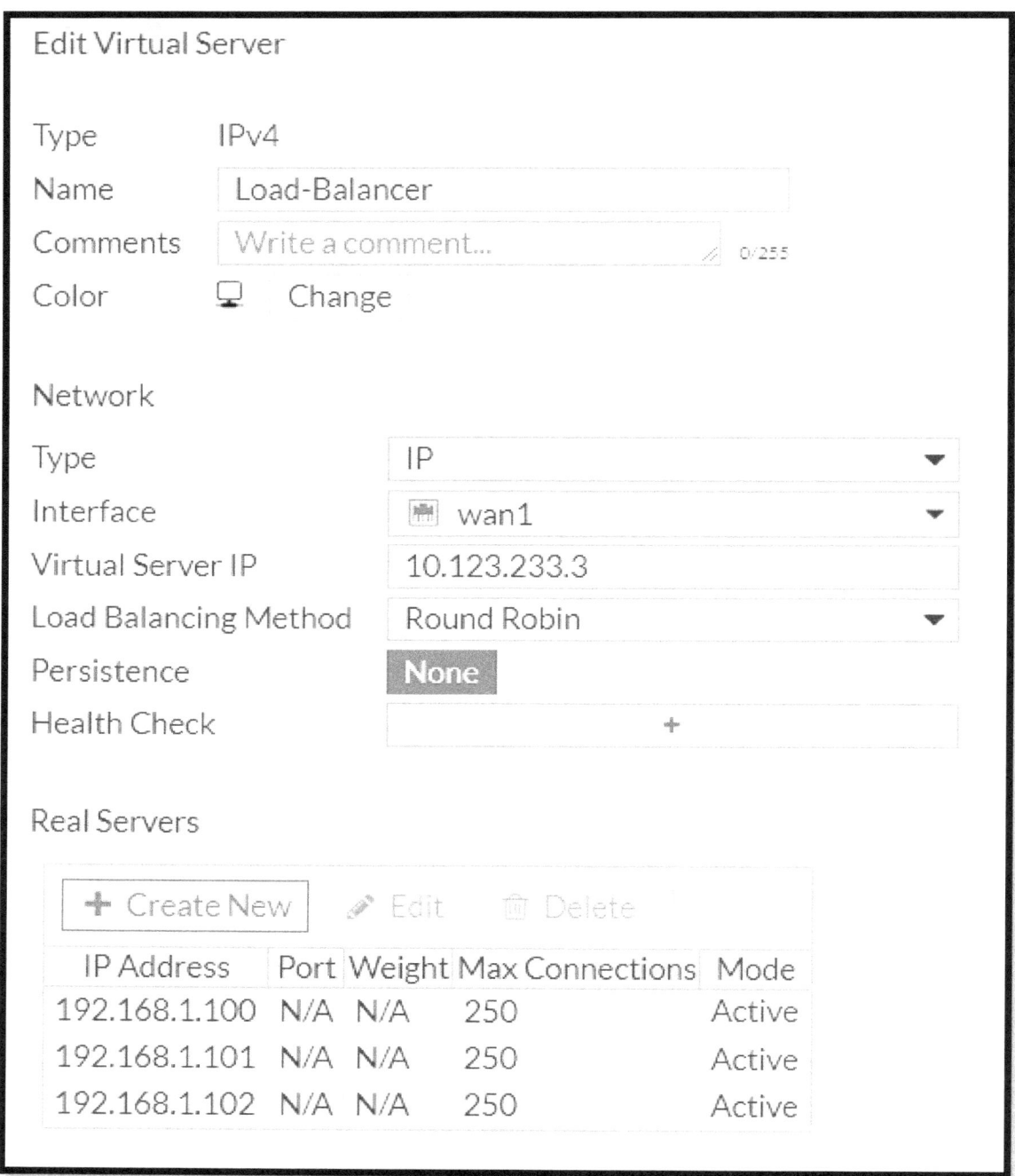

Chapter 4 | Firewall Policy and NAT

See Image 4.48, and this is the most basic example of a load balancing VIP. Even though the GUI locates states 'Virtual Servers' on the backend, this configuration is still held with the other VIPs. See CLI output:

```
NSE4-PASS (vip) # show
path=firewall, objname=vip, tablename=(null), size=724
config firewall vip
    edit "Load-Balancer"
        set uuid 32db404c-654b-51ea-bfd1-06d529d11f6c
        set type server-load-balance
        set extip 10.123.233.3
        set extintf "wan1"
        set server-type ip
        set ldb-method round-robin
        config realservers
            edit 1
                set ip 192.168.1.100
                set max-connections 250
            next
            edit 2
                set ip 192.168.1.101
                set max-connections 250
            next
            edit 3
                set ip 192.168.1.102
                set max-connections 250
            next
        end
    next
end
```

The Virtual Server GUI is just a convince feature. If you wish to make this configuration via CLI, you most certainly can! I really could spend an entire chapter writing on Server Load Balancing. There are many features and useful things we can accomplish with this. However, I am just going to graze the top of these features since we have so much more to cover in this chapter.

You should know that setting *'type load-balance'* is only layer-3 packet distribution and *'type server-load-balance'* by allowing options for server health monitor and application level options.

Firstly, take a look at the different load balancing methods; the CLI gives us a pretty good overview:

Chapter 4 | Firewall Policy and NAT

```
NSE4-PASS (Load-Balancer) # set ldb-method
static              Distribute to server based on source IP.
round-robin         Distribute to server based round robin order.
weighted            Distribute to server based on weight.
least-session       Distribute to server with lowest session count.
least-rtt           Distribute to server with lowest Round-Trip-Time.
first-alive         Distribute to the first server that is alive.
```
Here are the different load balancing algorithms FortiOS provides us to work with. These options allow you to fine-tune your traffic distribution.

Another important thing to know is the VIP Server Load Balance `server-type` setting. This provides options to focus on only certain protocols that provides additional configuration options for each that is specific to that protocol. This can be configured in the CLI as well, and here are the options:

```
NSE4-PASS (Load-Balancer) # set server-type
http      HTTP
https     HTTPS
imaps     IMAPS
pop3s     POP3S
smtps     SMTPS
ssl       SSL
tcp       TCP
udp       UDP
ip        IP
```
For example, if we select HTTP, then more options for the protocol will be provided:

```
NSE4-PASS (Load-Balancer) # set server-type http
NSE4-PASS (Load-Balancer) # show ful | grep http
    set server-type http
    set http-ip-header disable
    set http-redirect disable
    set http-multiplex disable
```

There are many options, and can be very useful to offload the encrypt and decrypt function to the FortiGate CP ASIC's and save resources on your servers. If we set type HTTPS, we have many SSL options.

```
NSE4-PASS (Load-Balancer) # set server-type https
NSE4-PASS (Load-Balancer) # show ful | grep ssl
    set ssl-client-rekey-count 0
    set ssl-hpkp disable
    set ssl-hsts disable
    set ssl-mode half
    set ssl-certificate ''
```

Chapter 4 | Firewall Policy and NAT

```
        set ssl-dh-bits 2048
        set ssl-algorithm high
        set ssl-pfs require
        set ssl-min-version tls-1.1
        set ssl-max-version tls-1.3
        set ssl-send-empty-frags enable
        set ssl-client-fallback enable
        set ssl-client-renegotiation secure
        set ssl-client-session-state-type both
        set ssl-client-session-state-timeout 30
        set ssl-client-session-state-max 1000
        set ssl-http-location-conversion disable
```

This would be a lot of fun to discuss and lab up, but unfortunately, we must move on to the other NSE4 topics you are required to know in this chapter. For now, just tuck this away and know more is coming on this topic. If anything, this can give you a starting point for independent research!

VIP Groups

A VIP Group is a reasonably intuitive feature. This allows you to bundle many VIP Objects into a single group, and this VIP Group object can be referenced within the policy. The purpose of this is to make the Firewall Policy Table easier to manage because it is easier to move a VIP in and out of a VIP Group then it is to create a new Firewall Policy Entry to reference a single VIP object. Also, if there are hundreds of VIP objects, then this would be difficult to manage within a single policy, and the possibility for a mistake to happen increases.

In this example, we create a VIP Group named *MY_WebServers*. We create a few VIP Objects and reference them within *MY_WebServers*. Next, we reference the *MY_WebServers* VIP Group object within a Firewall Policy Entry. The first thing to do is to create the three VIP Objects for the web servers. See *Image 4.49*.

Image 4.48 – Web Server VIP Objects

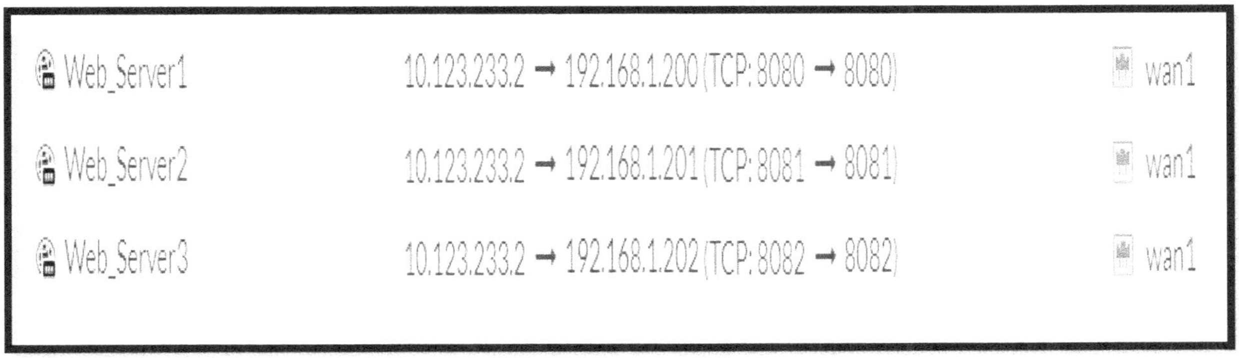

Web_Server1	10.123.233.2 → 192.168.1.200 (TCP: 8080 → 8080)	wan1
Web_Server2	10.123.233.2 → 192.168.1.201 (TCP: 8081 → 8081)	wan1
Web_Server3	10.123.233.2 → 192.168.1.202 (TCP: 8082 → 8082)	wan1

Chapter 4 | Firewall Policy and NAT

Now that the Web Server VIP Objects have been created, next is to create the Group VIP object and reference the VIPs. See *Image 4.50*:

Image 4.49 – VIP Group Object

Now that the VIP Group MY_WebServers have been created, lastly, is to reference this object into the Firewall Policy Entry Destination field. This essentially activated the three VIPs that were created. As you can see, VIP objects can easily be added or removed from a VIP Group, which is very easy to reference in a Firewall Policy Entry.

> *Note that all VIP Objects that share a VIP Group together must be bound to the same interface.*

Chapter 4 | Firewall Policy and NAT

Image 4.50 – VIP Group in Policy

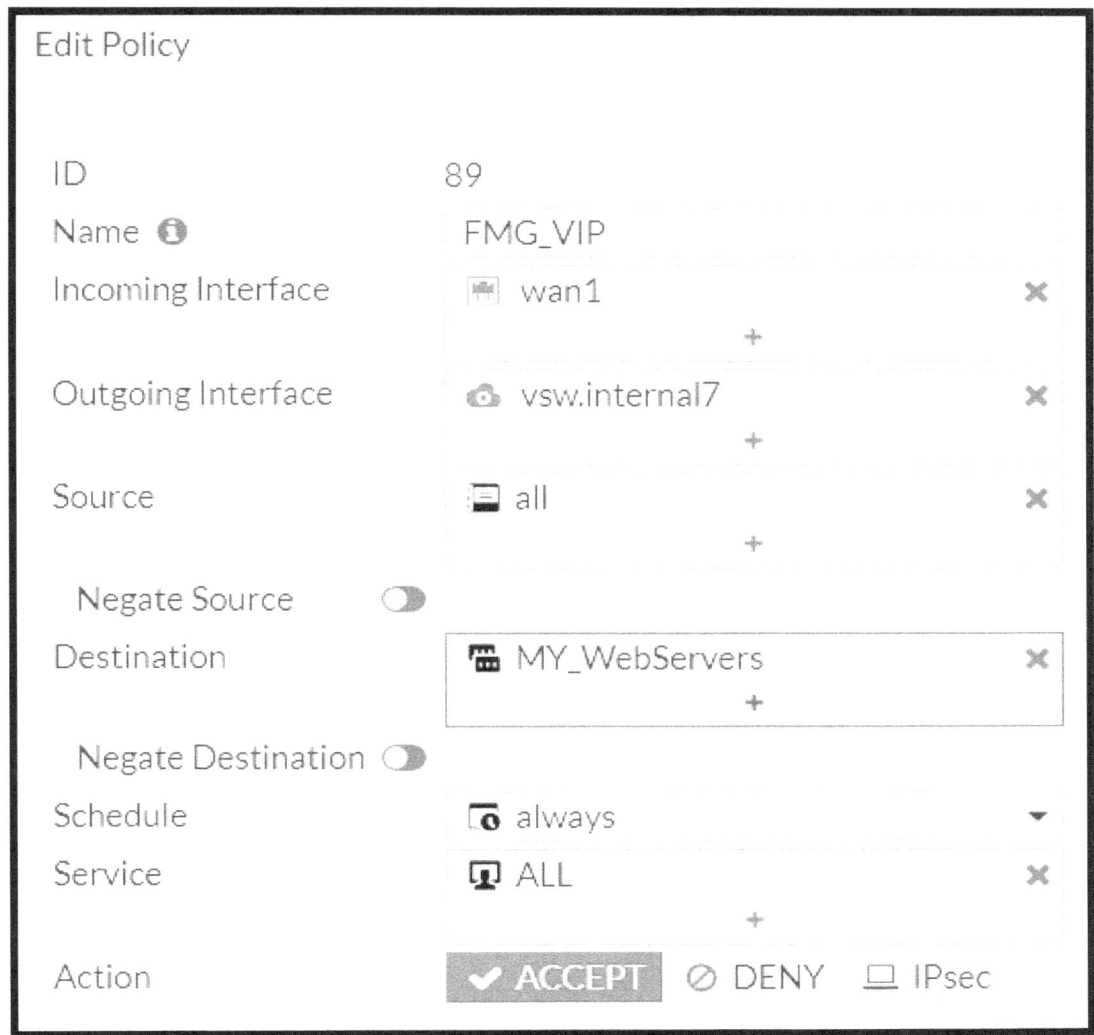

That wraps things up for VIP Groups. Now moving on to our last VIP in this section, policy matching with VIPs!!

VIP Policy Matching

When using VIPs in Firewall Policy NAT, the order of packet evaluation against Firewall Policy Table changes. Essentially, by default, Firewall Policy Entries that contain a VIP are evaluated first regardless of order. Meaning, an inbound WAN-to-LAN connection with a VIP could be at the very bottom of the Firewall Policy Table with many other WAN-to-LAN policies in sequence before it; and however, if those policies do not contain VIP, then they are evaluated after the VIP policy. There is a

Chapter 4 | Firewall Policy and NAT

command that changes this behavior, but I'm going to show you a method of Firewall Policy creation/management before I provide the super-secret command.

Image 4.51 – VIP Policy Matching Example

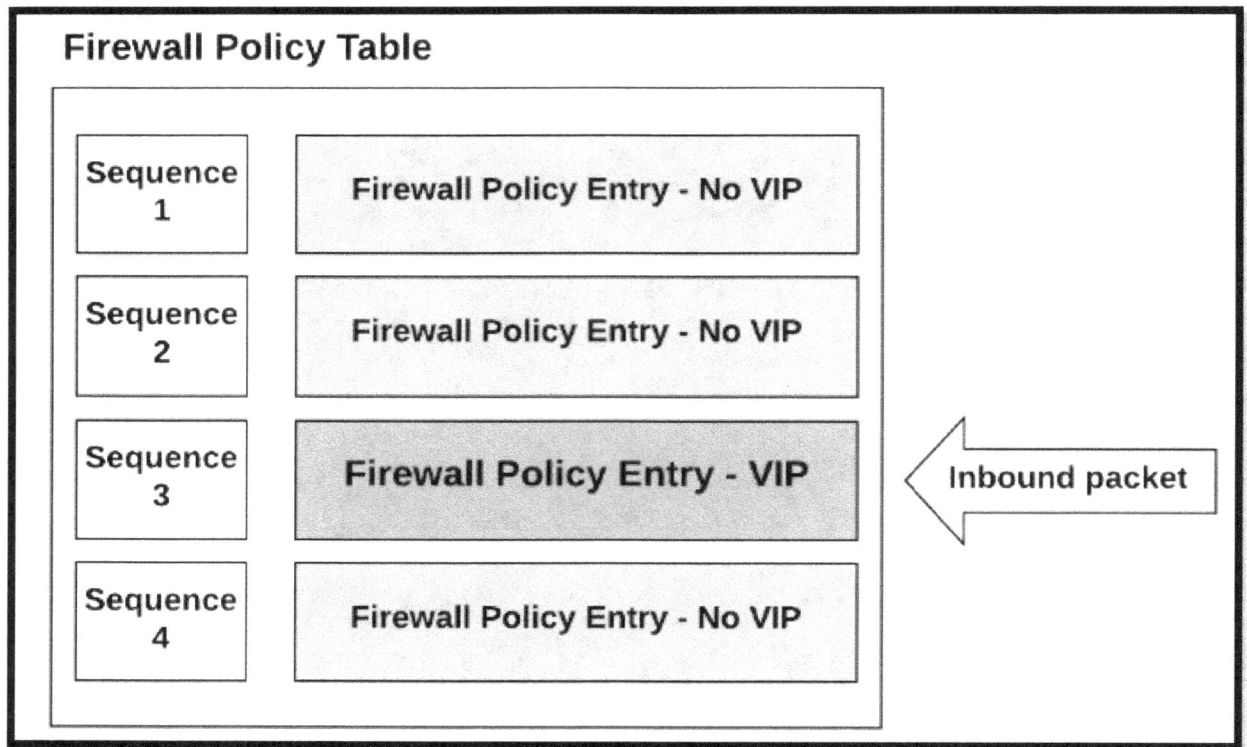

Firstly, I'm going to walk you through a scenario, so we are on the same page. See Image 4.53.

In this example, the Firewall Policy Table only contains four policies. The 3rd one from the top contains a VIP in the destination field. This means policy sequence number three is evaluated first, and if the packet matches the conditions of the VIP and anything else specified in this policy, then it is accepted and processed by FortiGate. Meaning, Firewall Policy Entries sequence one and two are skipped entirely, and this is what usually confuses people. It is honestly not intuitive from a user perspective, but it's how it works, and you need to account for this behavior when management FortiGates. If you configure the first policy here with a source IP list of known 'bad' IPs, then this logic is skipped.

Chapter 4 | Firewall Policy and NAT

There are a couple of methods to handle this situation. Firstly, the easiest method is to configure all your VIP policies first in the sequence since they are evaluated first anyway. If this is done, then all is right with the world; you can still read the Firewall Policy Table from the top down. This would be the method I would recommend if your environment allows it. See *Image 4.54*.

Image 4.52 – VIP Reordered Policy Matching

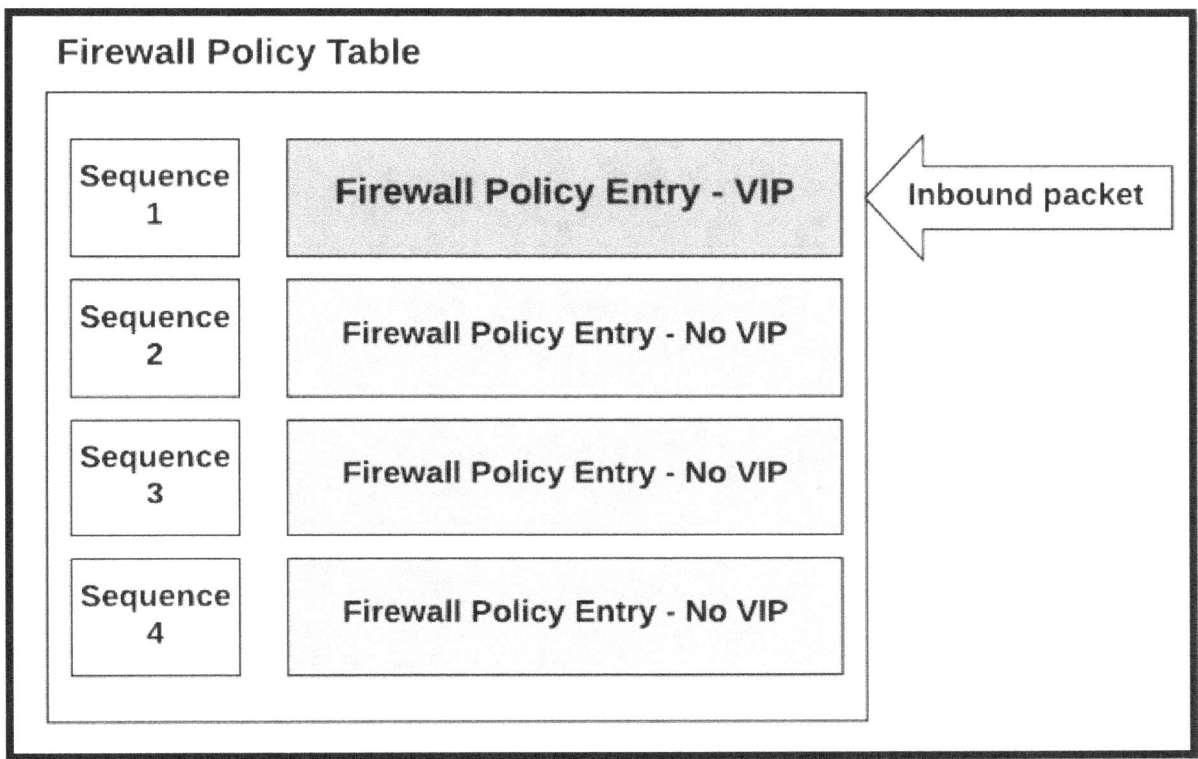

This is how your Firewall Policy Table would look if you place the VIP at the top, and since FortiOS reads all policies from the top down, the logic makes sense. Next, now the super-secret command.

```
config firewall policy
    edit 1
        set match-vip enable    ←
    next
end
```

Chapter 4 | Firewall Policy and NAT

This command is configured on a per policy bases only. Essentially, this command can be configured on a policy that does not contain a VIP and will cause FortiOS to evaluate the policy as if there was a VIP configured in it. So now, if you wish to deny certain source IPs in a policy without a VIP, you can do so. See *Image 4.55*.

Image 4.53 – Match VIP Enable Policy Match

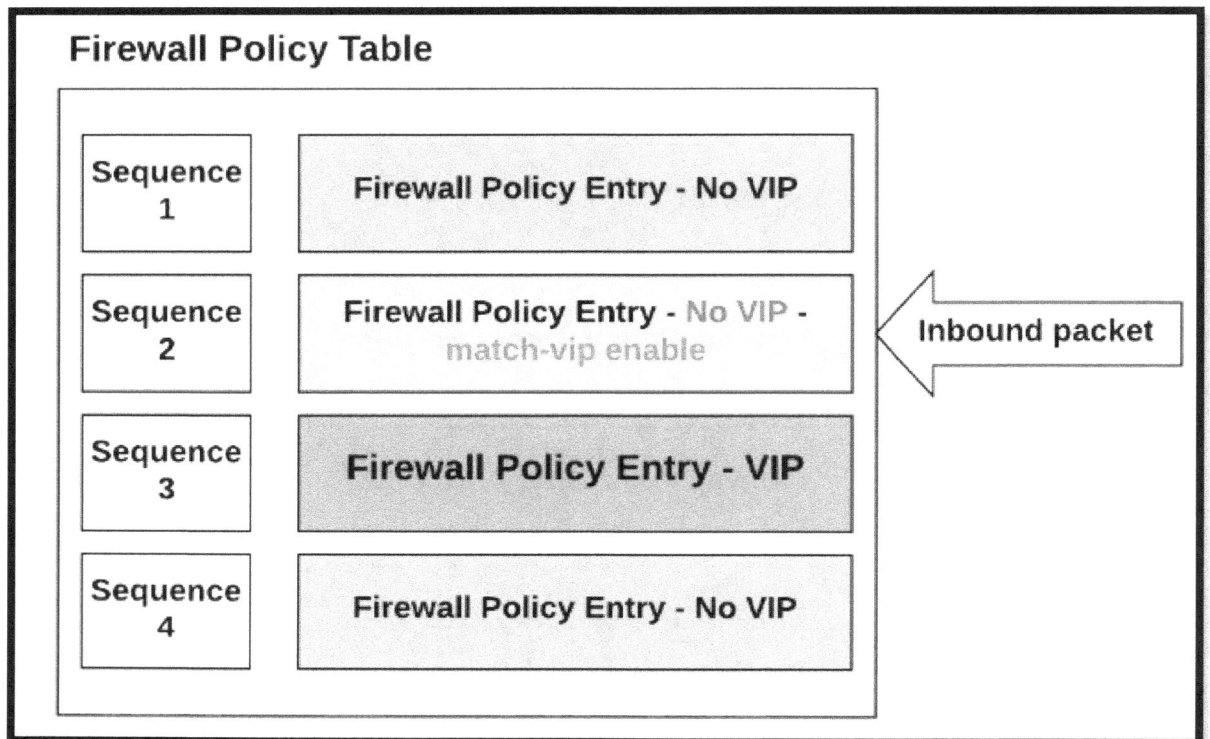

As you can see, an inbound packet is now evaluated by policy at sequence 2 first and then be evaluated by the policy that holds the actual VIP object. Lastly, if the packet does not match policy at sequence 2 or 3 then it will continue to be evaluated by policy at sequence 1 and then sequence 4.

In summary, try to configure your policies that contain VIP objects before policies that do no hold VIP objects so the Firewall Policy Table can be read from the top down intuitively. You should also note there are other use cases for match-vip enable the setting, and essentially, this will make a non-VIP policy be evaluated as a VIP policy.

Chapter 4 | Firewall Policy and NAT

Restricting Traffic to VIP

The last topic on VIPs in this section is how to block traffic from hitting your VIP. There is a whitelist method and a blacklist method. A whitelist is specifying in one Firewall Policy Entry the source IP address that is allowed to access the VIP, which would be the most secure but might be unfeasible for public services like a company web server. The blacklist is where you can create an Address Group that contains known malicious IP addresses and references that object in the Source field. The blacklist method requires at least two policies, and the whitelist method could only require one.

Let's configure this. In the GUI, navigate to your IPv4 Firewall Policy Table via 'Policy & Objects -> IPv4 Policy'. Next, let's say we do not want devices from the 172.20.0.0/16 subnet connecting to our FortiManager VIP Object, so this is the

Image 4.54 – Restricting Traffic to VIP

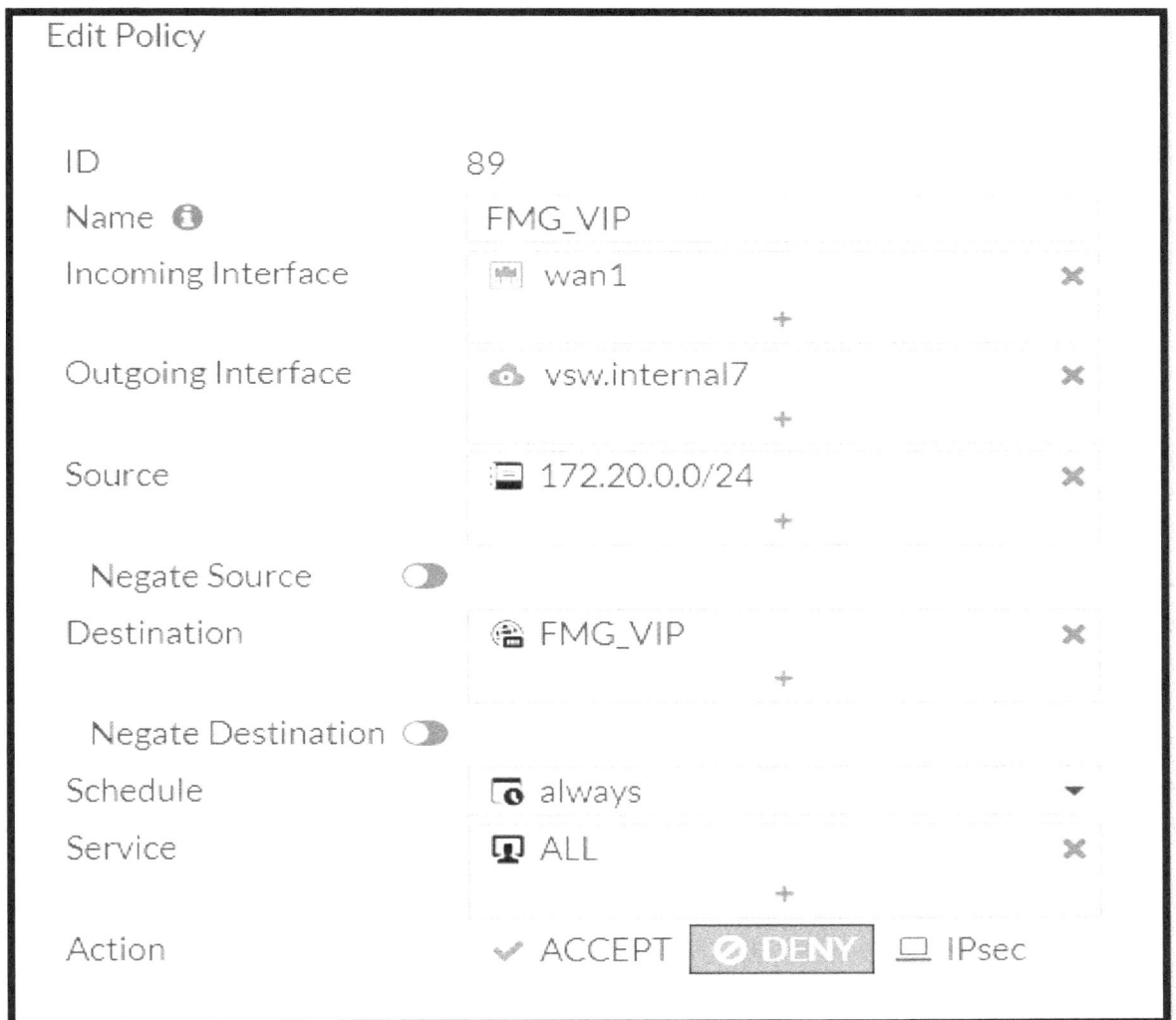

Chapter 4 | Firewall Policy and NAT

blacklist method, so two policies will be used to accomplish this requirement. See Image 4.56.

Image 4.55 – VIP Restricting

After we create this new policy to block access from traffic sourcing 172.20.0.0/24 from accessing the FMG_VIP object, the next thing to do is to place this Deny policy above the allow policy so it is evaluated first. See Image 4.57. As you can see, policy ID 89 is evaluated; first, and if the source comes from 172.20.0.0/24 trying to access the FMG_VIP, then it will be denied, and all other traffic is allowed. For the white list, we could delete policy ID 77 in Image 4.57, and in policy ID 88 set action to allow. This logic would read-only traffic with the source of 172.20.0.0/24 would be allowed to access the FMG_VIP.

VIP Summary

That is for VIPs. At this point, you should know what a VIP is and how to create one and reference it in a Firewall Policy Entry when using the Firewall Policy NAT method. Remember, a VIP is how the FortiGate performs Destination NAT (DNAT) on IP packets. You should know now that VIP policies will be evaluated before the policy that does not have VIPs, and you should know to account for this when managing the Firewall Policy Table. We discussed some VIP filtering options, load balancing, and groups. Note a VIP acts as a real IP and can create an IP conflict on your network if ARP is left enabled.

IP Pool and SNAT

The Egress interface or an IP Pool object is how FortiOS performs Source NAT (SNAT) on packets. When using the Firewall Policy NAT Method IP Pool object can be referenced directly in firewall policies. An IP Pool can be a single IP address or a range. In this section, we are going to discuss SNAT and the different types of IP Pools offer and when to use each one. There are four types of IP Pools that can be configured:

1) Overload or Port Address Translation (PAT)
2) Port Block Allocation (PBA)
3) Fixed Port Range
4) One-to-one

Chapter 4 | Firewall Policy and NAT

Egress Interface SNAT

The most basic method to apply SNAT to egress transit packets is using the IP address assigned to the egress interface. Most of the time, this is wan1, and also, most of the time, there is a public IP assigned to wan1 in production environments. There is a toggle on the firewall policy GUI page that can easily be enabled or disabled for SNAT. Take a look at *Image 4.57*.

Image 4.56 – Firewall Policy Interface NAT Toggle

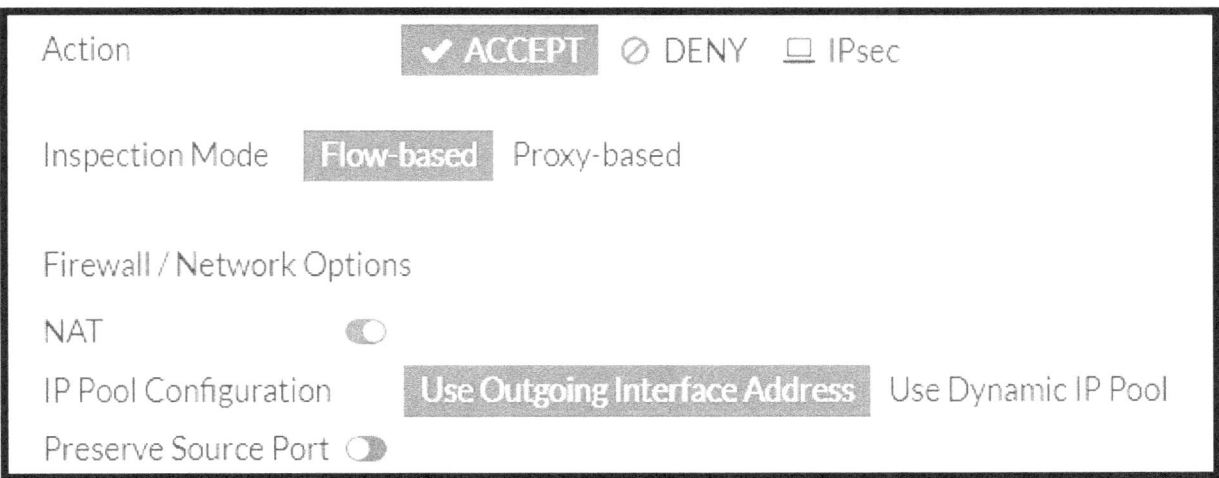

Once the NAT option is toggled on, then two SNAT options are provided. The first is to perform SNAT via egress interface IP "Use Outgoing Interface Address" and the second option is to use an IP Pool via "Use Dynamic IP Pool". Here we use the egress interface IP address. For most branch offices or small networks, this is all that is required to be operational. All traffic that matches the Firewall Policy Entry in Image 4.5.8 has a source IP of the actual IP assigned to the egress Interface.

When this option is used, FortiGate actually uses the Port Address Translation (PAT) SNAT method, which we must explicitly configure for an IP Pool object. At this point, you may be wondering what PAT is, well you're in luck because that is the topic of the next section!

Chapter 4 | Firewall Policy and NAT

IP Pool Overload or PAT

The most common IP Pool SNAT is Overload, and this is also the default. An IP Pool using Overload type is using the PAT SNAT method. PAT is used to map many sources' IP addresses to one a single IP address or many-to-one. Most of the time, a LAN network assigned with private IP space uses a single public IP assigned to the WAN interface when accessing the internet using the PAT method.

Before we get into the IP Pool configuration, let us talk more about PAT and how it works. In FortiOS, when a packet is allowed by a policy using PAT, then a Session

Image 4.57 – Port Address Translation Example

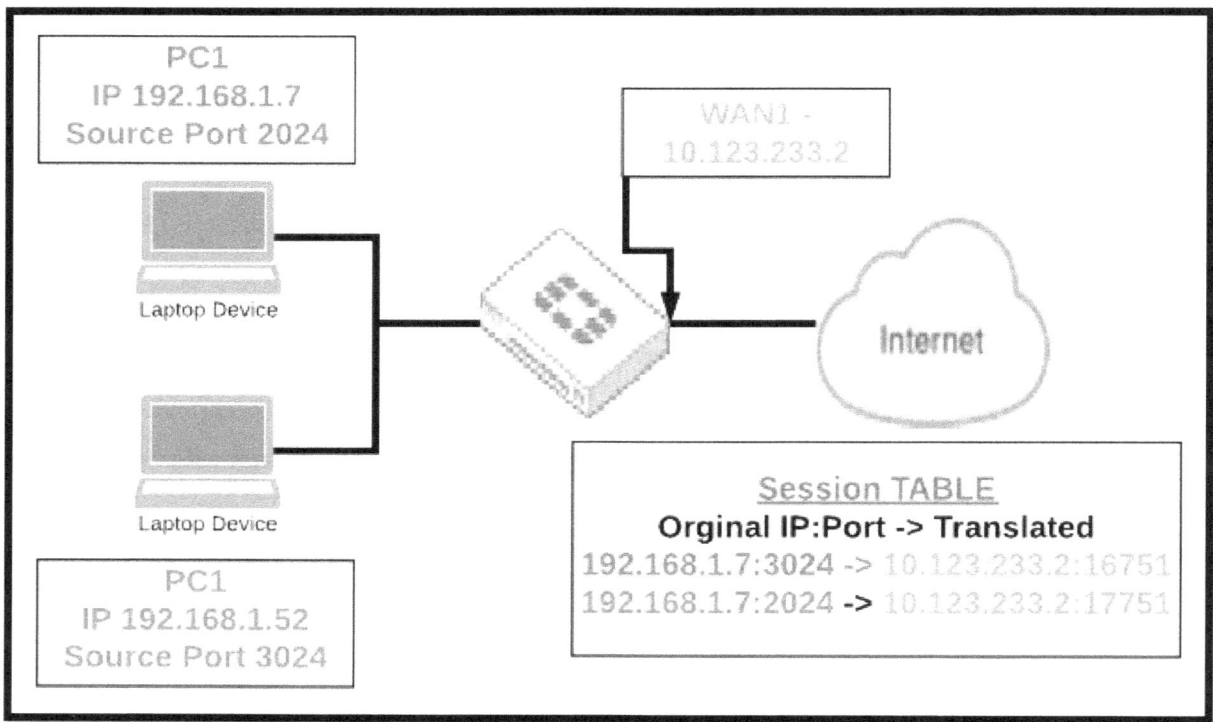

Entry is generated, and within that entry, FortiOS will try to assign a unique NAT session matching values to the egress traffic flow and most the time is done through source port value. That being said, the layer-4 source port is not the only value that makes a SNAT session unique on FortiOS. We talk more about NAT session matching later in the chapter. For clarification, take a look at an example of PAT. See *Image 4.58*.

In the example, there are two machines using 10.123.233.2, which is acting as a public IP in this example. Multiple machines sharing one IP is possible because FortiOS can differentiate between multiple Session Entries by source port alone and map traffic to the correct session using source port.

Chapter 4 | Firewall Policy and NAT

Note one IP address has a port range of 0 to 65,535, and 0 to 1023 is reserved and is normally not used as a client-side source port. Application clients will randomly choose a TCP/UDP port layer-4 between 1024 and 65535. In our example, PC1 has a source port of 2024, and when outbound traffic for this session flows through a policy with SNAT using PAT, this will most likely change by default. FortiOS will generate its own source port for the session, which is 16751 In our example. So when traffic is forwarded to the next hop, the source port will be 16751 in all associated packets, and return traffic will use 16751 as a destination port. Once FortiGate receives this, it will translate the return traffic IP address and port to the original before translation 192.168.1.7:2024. Since FortiOS uses source port to keep track of sessions, where the same source IP is the same, this is where the term Port Address Translation comes from.

As you can see, there is a potential for one IP address to be used to translate hundreds or thousands of internal IP addresses by using ports (PAT). There are sometimes issues with this method like port exhaustion, which we discuss in the NAT troubleshooting section.

Lastly, a quick way to view PAT sessions in FortiOS without having to look at the entire Session Entry is with the below command:

```
NSE4-PASS (root) # get sys session list | grep 192.168.1.7
tcp      3571    192.168.1.7:40933 10.123.233.2:50937 52.226.111.32:443  -
udp      88      192.168.1.7:50583 10.123.233.2:60483 8.8.8.8:53         -
….
```

Here you can see a nice summary of active NAT/PAT sessions. This is a good command to use when looking for malicious activity on your network. If you see 50k outbound connections from a single client machine, then I would recommend running AV on the device because, most likely, it is part of a botnet (a zombie PC ☺) . To count sessions, use 'grep -c' for example:

```
NSE4-PASS (root) # get sys session list | grep 192.168.209.7 -c
73
```

Chapter 4 | Firewall Policy and NAT

IP Pool Overload Configuration

IP Pool is a virtual object like a VIP. It responds to ARP just like an IP address physically assigned to an interface. When using the NAT Policy method, we can reference IP Pools directly into a Firewall Policy Entry to SNAT packets. First, an IP Pool object needs to be created with the IP we want. To do this in the GUI, navigate via *'Policy & Objects -> IP Pools -> Create New'* see *Image 4.59*.

Image 4.58 – IP Pool Configuration

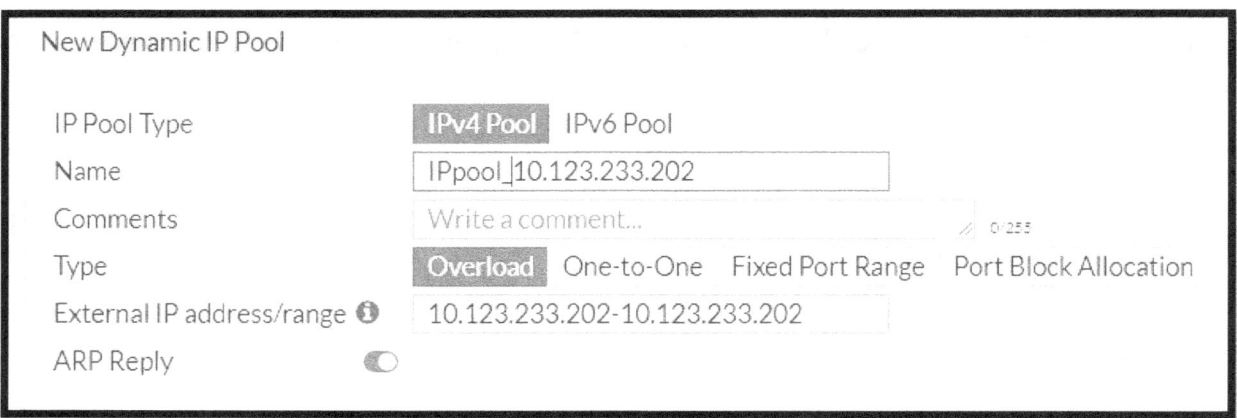

In this example, for the first IP Pool Type, there are options for both IPv4 and IPv6. The Name is 'IPpool_10.123.233.202'. The second Type is where what type of SNAT will be applied to transit traffic, and here Overload is selected. Next, External IP Address/range we configured 10.123.233.202-10.123.233.202. You must select an unused IP address on the LAN, especially if ARP Reply is toggled on. You can see here that it is extremely easy to increase the number of IPs in the range, but I only select one here.

Chapter 4 | Firewall Policy and NAT

Once the object is created, next is to reference 'IPpool_10.123.233.202' into a transit IPv4 Firewall Policy Entry. See *Image 4.60*.

Image 4.59 – IP Pool Policy Example

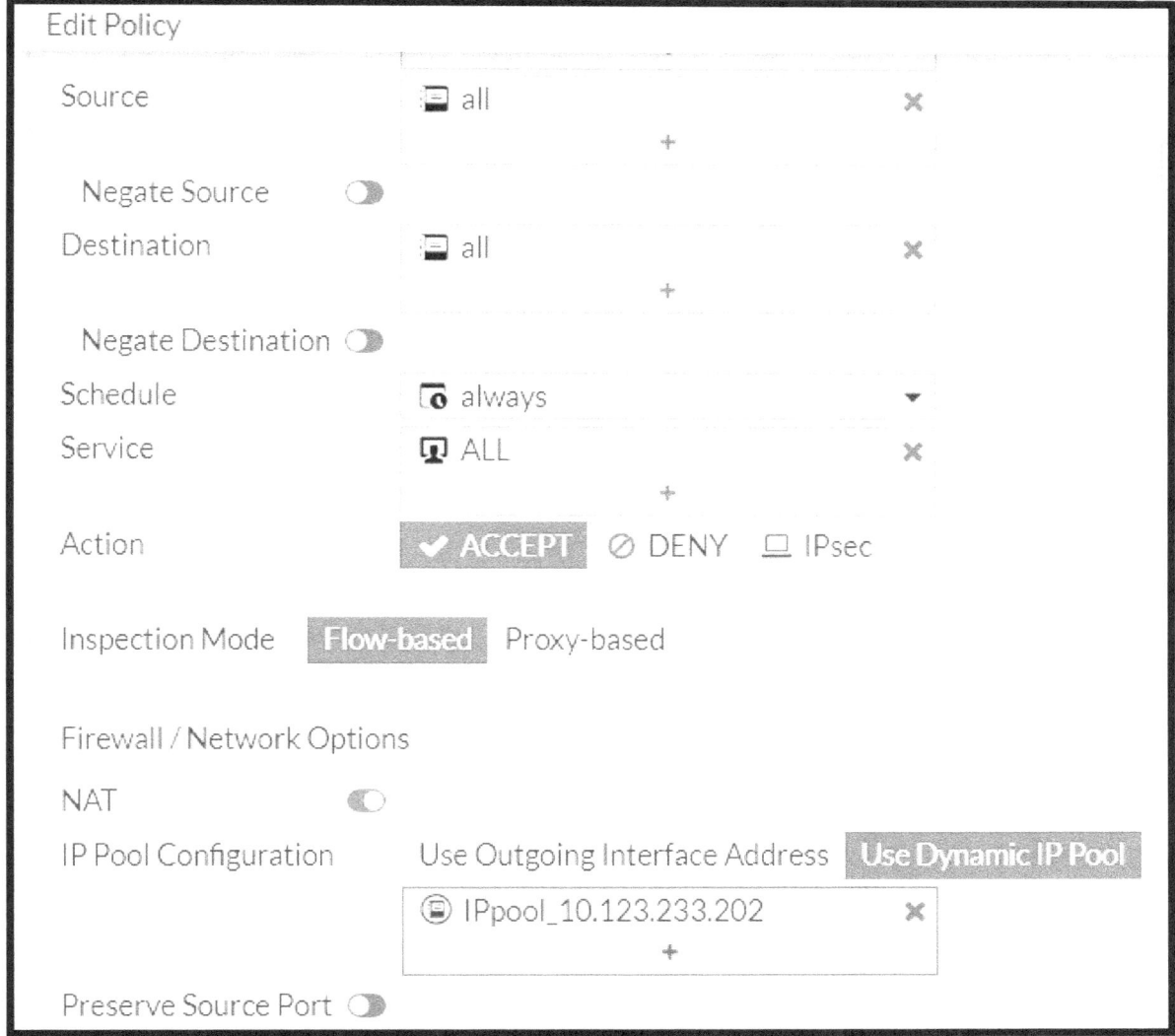

Now every packet that is accepted by this policy SNAT will be applied, and the new source IP would be 10.123.233.202 for the egress packets, which is specified in the IP Pool. As you should know now, not only does the source IP address change, but it also does the source port. Remember, the Overload IP Pool Type uses the PAT method of keeping traffic of sessions, which is a many-to-one method just like when we use the egress interface as the source IP. FortiOS makes it easy to isolate traffic flows within a Firewall Policy Entry and apply NAT features, all within one window configuration pane. Lastly, here, I recommend when making these configuration

Chapter 4 | Firewall Policy and NAT

changes to run `#diag debug cli 7` command so you can see the CLI configuration as well.

<u>IP Pool PBA</u>

Now that we understand the purpose of IP Pools and how PAT works, next, we are going to talk about Port Block Allocation (PBA). This is another IP Pool type and works very similar to Overload Type, but there is a difference. Overload does not care which source IP address receives what source port number; it is random, but PBA does.

Remember, there is a total of 65535 source ports available and are chosen at random to represent a specific traffic flow. What PBA does is provides source IPs certain source port blocks to use when transverse a Firewall Policy Entry; that's where the term Port Block Allocation comes from. FortiOS allocates certain blocks of ports and maps them to certain source IP addresses. The reason for this is control. Some service providers use this method so they can keep track and separate different SNAT entries on a per-customer basis. If your logging to a log aggregator or SIEM, then this could be very useful information when correlating source ports to separate customers.

PBA requires two major additional settings, firstly PBA Block Size, which is how many source ports can be allocated to host(s), and secondly, PBA Blocks Per User, which is blocks of source ports per source IP address. Here are the PBA CLI options:

```
config firewall ippool
    edit "IPpool_10.123.233.202"
        set type port-block-allocation
        set startip 10.123.233.202
        set endip 10.123.233.202
        set block-size 128
        set num-blocks-per-user 8
        set pba-timeout 30
        set permit-any-host disable
        set arp-reply enable
        set arp-intf ''
        set comments ''
    next
end
```

The default PBA Block Size is 128, and the PBA Blocks Per User by default is 8. This means each host or source IP can have up to 8 PBA blocks with a size of 128 each. That means each host, or a single IP can have up to 1,024 source ports allocated. This inherently increases the integrity of a FortiGate and the network as a whole

Chapter 4 | Firewall Policy and NAT

because now a single host cannot overrun the Session Table single-handedly by generating many outbound connections maliciously. They are capped with this configuration.

By changing the '*set num-blocks-per-user 8*' setting the value to 1, this can make things even more restrictive by only allowing a host 1 PBA Block at 128 each. Lastly, here are some PBA IP Pool debugs that could be useful when troubleshooting:

```
#diagnose firewall ippool stats          -(statistics)
#diagnose firewall ippool list pba       -(List PBA in ippool.)
#diagnose firewall ippool list nat-ip    -(List allocated IP in ippool.)
#diagnose firewall ippool list user      -(List users of ippool.)
```

IP Pool Fixed Port Range

IP Pool Type Fixed Port Range is a PAT type, and there is no one-to-one relationship. It is required to define the internal IP range (source-startip - source-endip) as well as the external (startip - endip) range. This method acts a lot like PBA but instead of breaking up source ports with blocks and assigning how many blocks each host can access. Instead, with this method, since the internal or source IP range is explicitly defined, then the max available external IP source ports space is divided by an internal IP range. For example, take a look at below CLI configuration:

```
config firewall ippool
    edit "IPpool_10.123.233.202"
        set type fixed-port-range
        set startip 10.123.233.1
        set endip 10.123.233.1
        set source-startip 172.16.1.1
        set source-endip 172.16.1.10
    next
end
```

In this configuration, there is only one external IP address 10.123.233.1, which contains a total of 65,535 source ports. However, per Fortinet documentation, the start source port is 5117, and the last useable port is 65533, which provides a total of 60,416 usable source ports. Next, since there is 10 source, IP address defines (172.16.1.1 – 172.16.1.10) then each IP address will be provided around 6,041 source ports because 60,416 divided by 10 is 6,041. The same method is used if the

> The equation to map a private IP address to a public IP using IP Pool Fixed Port Range method can be found here:
> https://docs.fortinet.com/document/fortigate/5.4.0/cookbook/414467

Chapter 4 | Firewall Policy and NAT

internal or external IP range changes. Since the number of allocated ports is predetermined hence why this method is called 'Fixed Port Range'.

IP Pool One-to-One

IP Pool Type One-to-One means that all internal and external IPs are one to one mapping. So if a One-to-One IP Pool Type only has 10 external IPs allocated, then only 10 internal IP addresses can you this IP Pool for SNAT. This method is considered to be 'Full Cone' NAT meaning all available source ports for a single external IP are reserved for one IP internal and cannot be shared with multiple internal IP addresses. Remember, with this SNAT method, and one internal IP is mapped to one external IP.

NAT Fixed Port

As you should know now, when using PAT, FortiOS can assign a random source port that doesn't match the original source port pre-translation. This causes a problem for some applications, and sometimes it is necessary to keep the original application source port. FortiOS has a feature called 'Fixed Port' that does just this. This is a Firewall Policy Entry-level configuration. This setting is available via CLI:

```
NSE4-PASS (root) # conf firewall policy
NSE4-PASS (policy) # edit 81
NSE4-PASS (81) # show ful | grep fix
        set fixedport enable
```

Use caution with this command because if FortiOS is handling many sessions within the same policy, then the likelihood of a *clash* increases, meaning no available source port to allocate for a new session in which causes a drop. For example, if source port 12345 is already being utilized and another machine has an application that generates a source port of 12345, then it is more likely to be dropped since FortiOS cannot just assign the new device another port number like 23456. There is more to NAT session matching then what we have discussed so far in this section, and I will clarify in the NAT Session Matching section. So be patience, young grasshopper 😊

Firewall Policy NAT Summary

This wraps up NAT using the Firewall Policy NAT method. We discussed VIPs and how to use them to perform DNAT on packets and reference them in policies. We also discussed the different types of VIPs and some of the available options. Next, we discussed IP Pool and how they are used to perform SNAT on packets and how to reference them in policies. We also touched on the different types of IP Pools. At this point, you should know how to use VIPs and IP Pools on FortiGate.

Chapter 4 | Firewall Policy and NAT

Central NAT

FortiOS Central NAT method is the second method of performing NAT functions. When using this method, VIPs and IP Pools are not referenced in the Firewall Policy Table. This feature is disabled by default and must be explicitly enabled, and once enabled, a Central SNAT Table is created, and the 'nat' setting under Firewall Policy Entries are not referenced. NGFW Mode is required to use the Central NAT method. One major feature only available in Central NAT is the ability to control explicit port translation. So if required to have a specific port translation, Central NAT must be used. To enable Central NAT to run the following CLI commands:

```
config system settings
set central-nat enable
end
```

FortiOS reads Central NAT rules from the top-down, looking for a match and can be found 'Policy & Objects -> Central SNAT' . Here is an example of a Central SNAT Table Entry.

Image 4.60 – Central NAT Table Entry

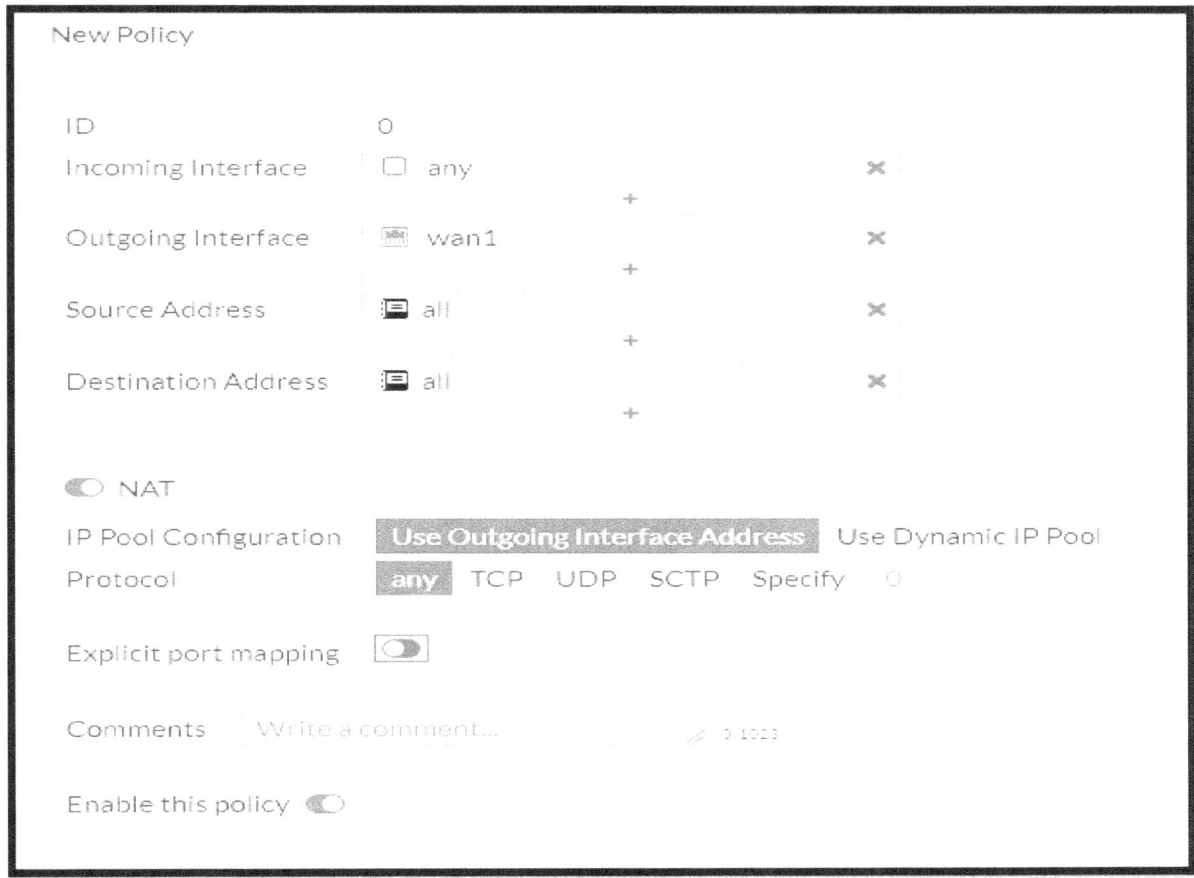

Chapter 4 | Firewall Policy and NAT

This is a very basic example, the rule states traffic coming from any interface going to wan1 with any Source Address and any Destination Address and any layer-4 Protocol then NAT to the egress interface IP *"Use Outgoing Interface Address"*. To use an IP Pool object, then select the option 'Use Dynamic IP Pool' and reference object as we did in the Firewall Policy Entry. This part is fairly straight forward.

Note that when using the Central NAT for SNAT, the Firewall Policy Table and/or Security Policy is evaluated before Central SNAT Table. We go over the full life of a packet in the Diagnose and Troubleshooting chapter in this book. Also note, DNAT cannot be configured on the Central SNAT table but has its own table.

Central DNAT

When using the Central NAT method, there is a separate table created for DNAT or VIPs. The DNAT Table is located in the GUI via 'Policy & Objects -> DNAT & Virtual IPs'. This is the same location as where you would create a VIP and then reference it within a policy. However, when using Central NAT, when a VIP is created here, it is active, and this configuration is now a production altering change.

Once a VIP is creating when Central NAT is being used, they are evaluated first because the destination interface must be found before a Firewall Policy Table look can occur. This is important because when configuring Firewall Policy Entries, you must use the translated IP address or post DNAT function. To elaborate, see *Image 4.63*.

Image 4.63 – Central NAT Packet Flow

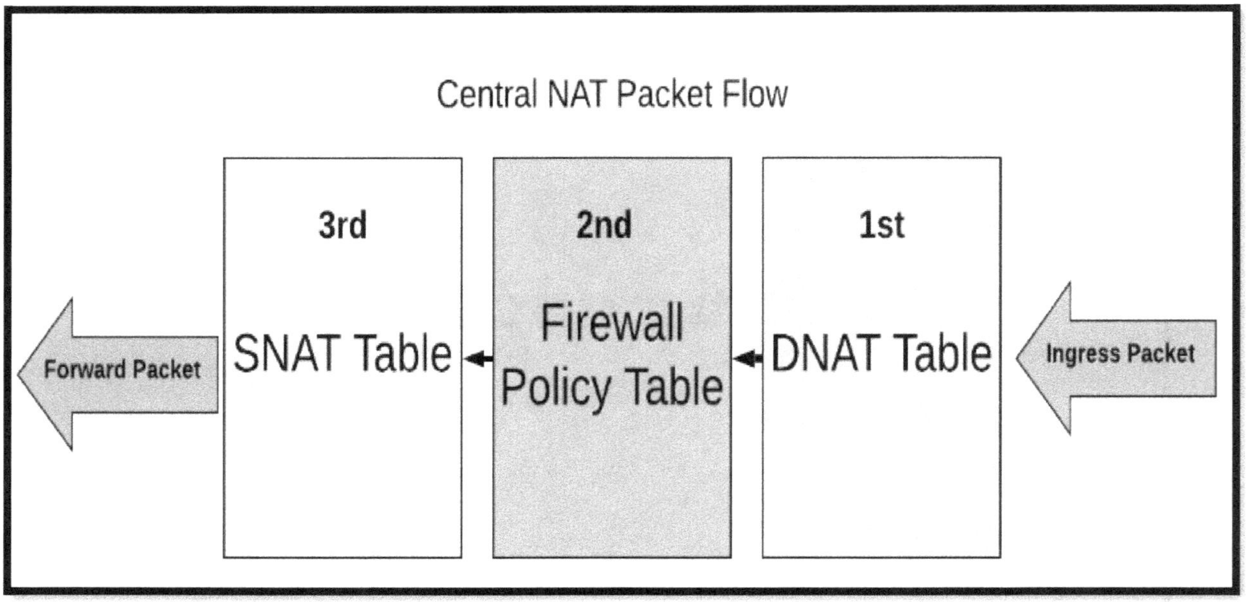

Chapter 4 | Firewall Policy and NAT

As you can see, a new packet will be evaluated against DNAT Table first and then Firewall Policy Table, and lastly, if all security checks out, then FortiOS will try to match a Central SNAT Entry before forwarding the packet.

Central DNAT Firewall Policy Example

In this example, I'm going to create a Firewall Policy Entry to allow a VIP DNAT to flow through FortiGate. The first thing to do is to create the VIP. See CLI output:

```
config firewall vip
    edit "Web_Server1"
        set uuid 6c56f408-6639-51ea-ef0b-43ec70b0c0d7
        set extip 10.123.233.2
        set extintf "wan1"
        set portforward enable
        set mappedip "192.168.1.200"
        set extport 8080
        set mappedport 8080
    next
end
```

We are going to use the VIP object *"Web_Server1"*, which has a translated or 'mappedip' of 192.168.1.200, which is the post DNAT IP address, which is the key

Image 4.61 – Central NAT Firewall Policy

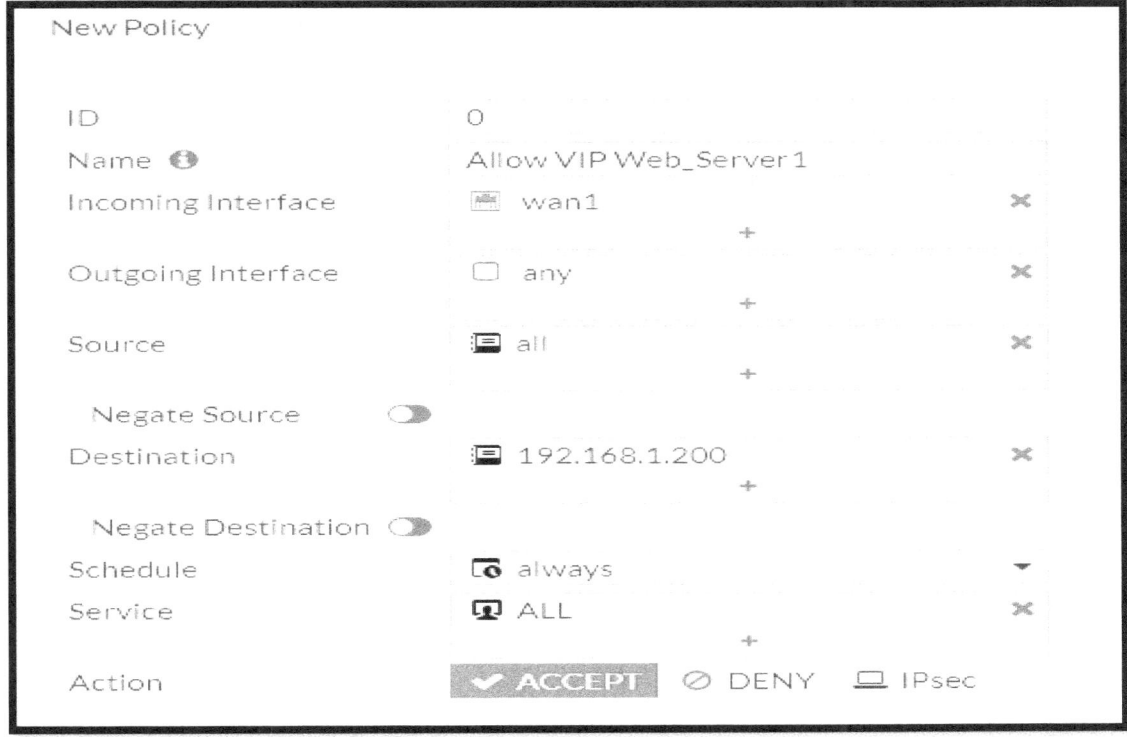

Chapter 4 | Firewall Policy and NAT

here. Also note, this VIP object only allows port 8080. Next, we must create the Firewall Policy Entry to accommodate this traffic flow. I will use the GUI for this, see Image 4.63. The key thing to take away from this example is the translated IP address must be used in the Destination field within a Firewall Policy Entry when using the Central NAT method. At this point, you should know how to configure a VIP with the Central NAT method and create a policy to allow the traffic.

Central NAT Summary

Central NAT is a method of performing NAT on FortiOS by using separate SNAT and DNAT table aside from the Firewall Policy Table. In general, Fortinet suggests using Central NAT only for complex scenarios or while using NGFW policy mode.

IPv4 and IPv6 NAT

FortiGate has the ability to translate IPv4 address to IPv6 address and vice versa. This is important when FortiGate must run both IPv6 networks and IPv4 networks simultaneously, and each must be able to communicate with each other. To allow this, there are special VIPs and Firewall Policy Tables. There is a table to translate IPv4 to IPv6 and IPv6 to IPv4. These tables can be found in the CLI via:

```
NSE4-PASS (root) # config firewall ?
policy      Configure IPv4 policies.
policy46    Configure IPv4 to IPv6 policies.
policy6     Configure IPv6 policies.
policy64    Configure IPv6 to IPv4 policies.
```

The policy46 and policy64 tables are where the vip46 and vip64 objects must be referenced respectfully. To find VIP46 and VIP64 configuration navigates in the CLI via:

```
NSE4-PASS (root) # config firewall vip
vip         Configure virtual IP for IPv4.
vip46       Configure IPv4 to IPv6 virtual IPs.
vip6        Configure virtual IP for IPv6.
vip64       Configure IPv6 to IPv4 virtual IPs.
vipgrp      Configure IPv4 virtual IP groups.
```

And here, we use the same method; first, we must create the VIP object to perform the translation from 4-to-6 or from 6-to-4 and then reference that object within the appropriate table. The last thing to note here to enable NAT64 or NAT46 globally, you must run below cli commands:

Chapter 4 | Firewall Policy and NAT

```
NSE4-PASS (nat64) # show
config system nat64
    set status enable
```

In this last section, I'm going to go into more detail on how FortiOS NAT works in the background and also touch on some common NAT issues.

NAT Session Matching

At this point, you should know what PAT is. Early in the chapter, I said that the source port is what differentiates sessions using the same egress NAT IP. Well.. this is mostly true. The source port with PAT *can* be the attribute to differentiate sessions but doesn't have to be.

FortiOS uses five attributes in a packet to uniquely to a Session Entry. Many vendors strictly use the source port when performing PAT, which maxes out at 65,535 theoretical sessions for one IP address. This is not the case with FortiOS. The five attributes that uniquely identifies a NAT Session Entry are:

Image 4.62 – PAT Session Matching

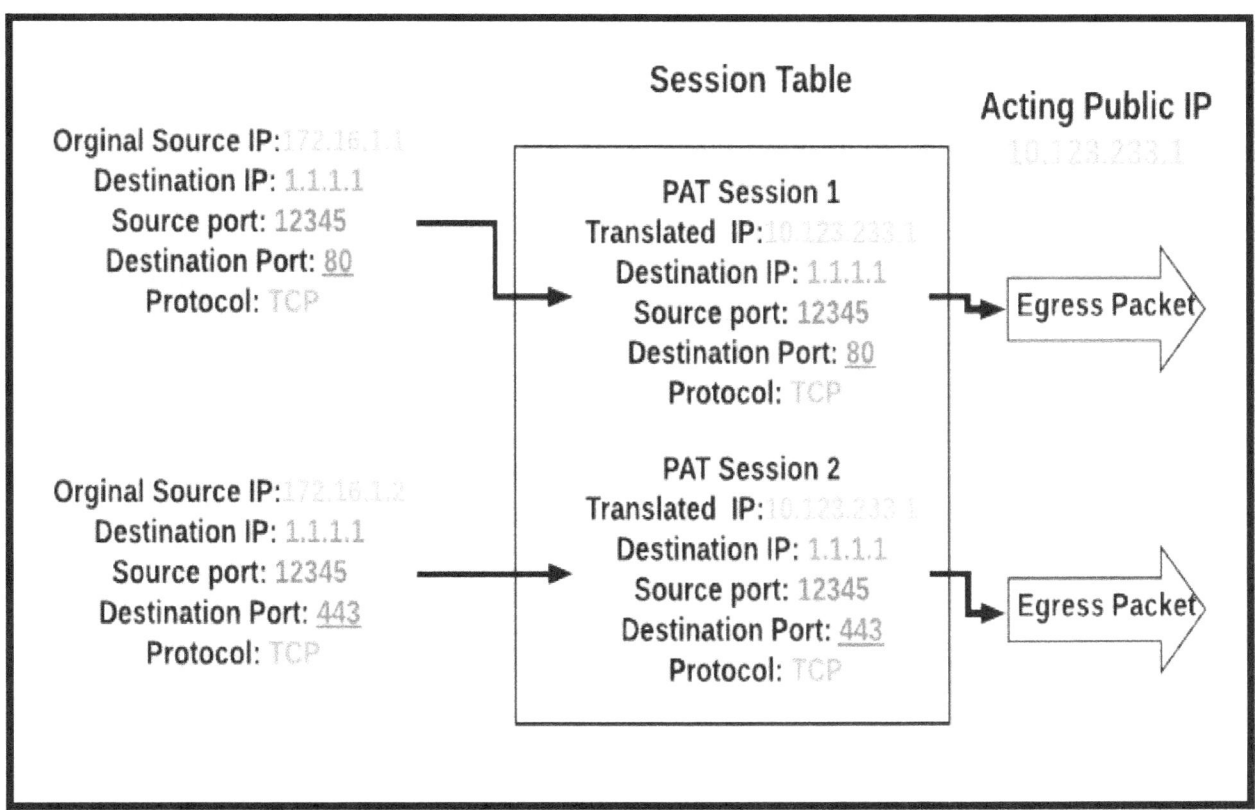

1) Source IP Address

Chapter 4 | Firewall Policy and NAT

          a. This is the post-translation source IP and not the original source IP. Most of the time, this would be the public IP of a WAN interface.
2) Destination IP Address
3) Protocol (TCP, UDP, ESP, GRE..etc)
4) Source Port
5) Destination Port

So, in theory, two machines can share the same source port value post PAT essentially. Only one of the five values here must be different so as to uniquely identify Session Entries. Everything that has been discussed in this chapter, like PBA and Fixed Ports, still holds true. This is only the logic to allocate source port ranges, but the source port is not the sole attribute that makes NAT/PAT sessions unique from one another.

Let's run through an example. Let's take three PC's on a private LAN that uses FortiGate public IP with PAT to access the Internet. See Image 4.65. Here the public NAT IP is shared by the internal LAN. Source IP 172.16.1.1 & 172.16.1.2 share the same source port, and FortiOS also used this source port. The destination IP address is the same, and the protocol, which is TCP. The only difference that can be used is that source ip 172.16.1.1 is using HTTP, which is port 80 by default, and 172.16.1.2 is using HTTPS, which is port 443 by default. Since the destination port value is unique between the two machines, then FortiOS can allocate the same source port post PAT which is 12345.

NAT Port Exhaustion

One of the major issues when using NAT/PAT is port exhaustion. Remember that there are 60,416 source ports available on one IP address used for NAT. Sometimes FortiOS runs out of space to allocate new sessions. Meaning, all 60,416 available ports are in use for a single IP, and the new packet is not unique enough to share a source port with another Session Entry. For example, if there are 60,416 outbound connections using TCP to the same destination IP and same destination port using the same egress NAT IP, then FortiOS cannot add any new Session Entries using these same values and therefore is maxed out. The condition here is called port Exhaustion. When the next packet arrives with these same conditions will cause a clash, and the oldest session will be deleted and replaced by this one, the newest one.

At this point, if more outbound connects using TCP and the same destination IP and destination, then FortiGate would need another fresh IP to be added to the IP Pool to double the available connections. If this did not happen, the likelihood of network degradation because of TCP retransmits would increase.

Chapter 4 | Firewall Policy and NAT

This happens from time to time on a network with a high volume of applications that create many short-lived sessions. Sometimes it is necessary to adjust TCP or UDP session timeout values to counter this situation.

 # diagnose sys session stat
Good command to troubleshoot NAT issues

Session Troubleshoot

To see if FortiOS is having clash Session Entries run the following CLI command:

```
NSE4-PASS (global) # diagnose sys session stat
misc info:        session_count=196 setup_rate=5 exp_count=0 clash=0
        memory_tension_drop=0 ephemeral=0/120832 removeable=0
        npu_session_count=101
        nturbo_session_count=100
delete=48, flush=2, dev_down=26/9616 ses_walkers=0
TCP sessions:
        85 in ESTABLISHED state
        5 in SYN_SENT state
        1 in FIN_WAIT state
        1 in TIME_WAIT state
        2 in CLOSE_WAIT state
firewall error stat:
error1=00000000
error2=00000000
error3=00000000
error4=00000000
tt=00000000
cont=00000000
ids_recv=001dd343
url_recv=00000000
av_recv=00005e99
fqdn_count=0000001b
fqdn6_count=00000000
global: ses_limit=0 ses6_limit=0 rt_limit=0 rt6_limit=0
```

This command, in general, is one of the best commands to investigate NAT issues because it holds critical information on how NAT is performing on FortiGate as a whole. Remember, this commend is a global command that is not per VDOM. This is a lot of output, so let us break some of the more important fields down and

Chapter 4 | Firewall Policy and NAT

understand how they can help us troubleshoot NAT related issues on FortiOS. The first field to recognize is:

`session_count=196`

This is the total number of active sessions on FortiGate counting every VDOM. This could help give a baseline for the network so anomalies can be detected. The next field is:

`setup_rate=5`

This is an important field when troubleshooting network outages. Here you can see if FortiGate is even trying to set up new sessions. This is new sessions per second.

`exp_count=0`

This is the number of currently expected sessions. These expected sessions are created by session helpers and are used for applications that expected return traffic but never sends an initial request for it on at a layer-3/layer-4 level but in the application data. This is sometimes used in SIP or FTP. We cover helpers in the next chapter.

`clash=0`

The clash field is one of the most important fields to know about. This tells you if FortiGate is experiencing NAT/PAT conflicts, which could cause network degradation. Also, if you see odd retransmissions on your network, then check this field counters and see how fast it is incrementing. You may need to allocate more IP space to the IP Pool.

`memory_tension_drop=0`

The memory tension drop field is also a good go-to field for network troubleshooting. If this counter is incrementing, this means FortiGate is low on memory and is deleting session to account for this. The oldest session will be deleted first. Local out TCP sessions will not be deleted.

`ephemeral=0/120832`

ephemeral means lasting for a short time or something in a transitional period. This field means TCP or UDP sessions that are halfway established or closed. For example, TCP has a three-way handshake with certain flags set which are:

```
-> SYN
<-SYN/ACK
 -> ACK
```

Chapter 4 | Firewall Policy and NAT

to be considered established. An ephemeral TCP session, for example, would be a SYN_SENT state. Meaning, an SYN TCP packet has been seen, but no replay was received through FortiGate. The reason FortiOS tracks sessions in this state is because this is a known attack method to perform a DoS on servers by utilizing all open ports by keeping all TCP port space in an ephemeral state. If many ephemeral sessions are seen here, then FortiOS by being witnessing a DoS, or there may be asymmetric routing on the network.

NAT Monitoring

There are some CLI commands on FortiOS that allow us to debug basic information on IP Pools. To list all IP Pools within a VDOM, run the following command:

```
NSE4-PASS (root) # diagnose firewall ippool-all list
vdom:root owns 3 ippool(s)
..
name:IPpool_10.123.233.202
type:overload
nat-ip-range:10.123.233.202-10.123.233.202
```

Next, to obtain the total session per IP Pool that is broken down between UDP, TCP and others, run the following command

```
# diagnose firewall ippool-all stats IPpool_10.123.233.202
name: IPpool_10.123.233.202
type: overload
startip: 10.123.233.202
endip: 10.123.233.202
total ses: 100
tcp ses: 70
udp ses: 25
other ses: 5
```

Another method to monitor NAT issues on FortiGate is via Syslog. Here Is an example of a NAT critical Syslog message:

log_id=0100020007 type=event subtype=system pri=critical vd=root service=kernel status=failure msg="NAT port is exhausted."

For companies that have SIEM solutions, a rule could be written for this message to generate an email to investigate this event.

Chapter 4 | Firewall Policy and NAT

Session Timers

Adjusting session timeout settings could be used to troubleshoot memory and NAT issues caused by session clash or port exhaustion. Timers can be adjusted a few different places on FortiOS, the first place to adjust the timers is the global config level:

```
60F-NSE4-PASS (global) # show ful | grep timer
    set block-session-timer 30
    set tcp-halfclose-timer 120
    set tcp-halfopen-timer 10
    set tcp-timewait-timer 1
    set udp-idle-timer 180
```

The next place to adjust session timers is at the policy level:

```
NSE4-PASS (root) # conf firewall policy
NSE4-PASS (policy) # edit 29
NSE4-PASS (29) # show ful | grep session
        set session-ttl 0
```

CLI info: "session-ttl TTL in seconds for sessions accepted by this policy (0 means use the system default session TTL)." By default, the policy restricts idle 'established' sessions to a 3600 second timeout value, which is one hour. This value could be increased up to 604800, which is 168 hours if needed. The default session TTL value can be found in the CLI via:

```
NSE4-PASS (session-ttl) # show ful
config system session-ttl
    set default 3600
end
```

This is where we could change the default session TTL value. Also, here we could customize session idle timeout for certain ports. For example, we could have port 443 timeouts in 7200 seconds via:

```
config system session-ttl
    config port
        edit 443
            set protocol 6
            set timeout 7200
        next
    end
end
```

Chapter 4 | Firewall Policy and NAT

Next, there are also configuration options to adjust established TCP session with a custom service object in CLI via:

```
config firewall service custom
    edit "HTTPS_10443"
        set tcp-portrange 10443
        set session-ttl 300
    next
end
```

Lastly, the idle session value could be adjusted with application control as well, which we cover in our application control chapter.

In summary, if all methods are used, the more specific configuration overrides the global configuration. Here is the list of precedence when adjusting the session TTL timeout values:

1) Application Control – Most preferred
2) Custom Service Object
3) Firewall Policy Entry
4) VDOM or Global level configuration - least preferred

This wraps things up for NAT matching and troubleshooting. It is important to know how FortOS performs NAT/PAT and how to identify problems when using these methods. Take note of the commands referenced in this section and put them in your tool bag because you never know when you will need to troubleshoot some FortiGate NAT issues. Lastly, be sure to understand session timers and how they could be used to triage certain memory or NAT issues that occur from time to time.

Chapter 4 | Firewall Policy and NAT

Summary

Wow, what a chapter to write, so much great material to cover with policies and NAT/PAT on FortiGate! Let's recap and make sure you touch on all the topics where covered in this chapter.

We touched on the Firewall Policy Tables, and I explained that these tables hold the Firewall Policy Entries that provide security to transit traffic. There are different tables for IPv4, IPv6, and multicast traffic in regards to transit traffic. There is another table for local in traffic called the Local-in Policy Table. I explained how policy matching works on FortiOS and how to create objects like Address objects, Schedule objects, and Service objects to be referenced in the Firewall Policy Entry, and how to group these objects together.

I discussed six components that traffic must match to be evaluated by a Profile Based Firewall Policy, and those are Source Interface, Destination Interface, Source IP Address, Destination IP Address, Service, and Schedule. I explained how interfaces are referenced in various places within FortiOS, including the Firewall Policy Entry. Also, we covered how to use zone to logically bundle individual interfaces so as to simplify the management of the Firewall Policy Table. We discussed how the Policy ID related to the Sequencing number considering the Firewall Policy Table. I reviewed how to change policy order and how to use the Firewall Policy Table context menu.

Next, we discussed the NGFW Policy and how traffic is matched against this type of policy. This mode also allows admins to apply Application and Web Filtering settings directly to a Firewall Policy without the need to create a profile first. With this method, the application must match what is configured in the policy to be accepted by the Firewall Policy Entry.

Next, we discussed Profile Based Policy Entry features; these include Real-time Firewall Policy Statistics, policy naming, policy logging, geographic type policy, FQDN type policy, MAC address policy, ISDB policy, Security Profiles, Proxy vs. Flow scanning, Consolidation Policy Mode, and anti-replay protection.

Next, we took a look at the Firewall Policy Table management as a whole and what tools are available to assist us. We review the different policy views and how to change policy sequence numbers. We also discussed the implicit deny policy that will drop traffic by default if not matched to a prior ACCEPT policy.

In the second half of the chapter, we review FortiOS NAT methods. We learned about VIPs and IP Pools on how to use them. We learned about Policy NAT and Central NAT methods and how to use them. I touched on the different types of NAT/PAT and how to use these methods in VIPs and IP Pools. Lastly, we discussed

Chapter 4 | Firewall Policy and NAT

NAT session troubleshooting and some tools to help investigate and correct common issues.

There is a lot of keystone information in this chapter. I feel like I say that about every chapter, but if you do not understand how FortiOS policies and NAT works by now, then I highly recommend going back and re-read the chapter because we build on this knowledge, and these features are honestly the basics. Know this chapter true before moving to the next chapter. You can test yourself by going through the end of chapter questions next! Outstanding job go ahead and give yourself a 'pat' on the back (do you get it… PAT, come on, it's a little funny) and keep at it!

Chapter 4 | Firewall Policy and NAT

Chapter Four Review Questions

1) With Profile Based Policy, for traffic to match a Firewall Policy Entry, it is required to match the Source Interface, Destination Interface, Source Address, Destination Address, Service, and Schedule.
    a. True
    b. False

2) With NGFW Policy-Based Filtering This time, FortiOS uses Layer-4 and Layer 7 information to match the packet against the Session Table Entry.
    a. True
    b. False

3) What is Anti Replay?
    a. A method to detected spoofed source IPs
    b. Keeps track of UDP packets by tagging them
    c. A method to keep track of TCP sequence numbers
    d. used solely to detect asymmetric routing

4) New packets are evaluated against the Firewall Policy Table from the top down by using Policy ID's.
    a. True
    b. False

5) What does the diagnose flow message Denied by Policy 0 mean?
    a. It means the packet was matched denied by a configured Firewall Policy Entry.
    b. It means that the packet did not match any policy on the Firewall Policy Table.
    c. It means that the source IP was spoofed and, therefore, dropped by policy 0
    d. It means the packet was dropped due to the Anti Replay mechanism.

Chapter 4 | Firewall Policy and NAT

6) Describe the Policy Proxy Scanning method.
   a. Buffers the entire packets and performs security scanning before forwarding packets.
   b. Does not buffer packets but forwards and sends RST packet if a security issue is found
   c. Is the fastest security scanning method
   d. Can be offloaded to the NP6 chip

7) How many source ports are available when using a single IP within a IP Pool type Overload?
   a. 65535
   b. 64512
   c. 61416
   d. 60416

8) What tools could be used to troubleshoot memory issues caused by NAT.
   a. Anti Replay
   b. Session Timers
   c. Fixed Port Range
   d. Use VIPs instead of IP Pools

9) What is a NAT clash?
   a. When there is no IP Pool configured on egress policy
   b. When there is a one-to-one NAT used by multiple source IPs
   c. When a VIP and an IP Pool is configured within the same Policy, will cause this condition
   d. When all unique values to allocate a new PAT session are used.

10) What happens after a clash occurs. Pick two.
   a. The oldest session will be removed from the Session Table.
   b. The newest Session will be removed from the Session Table.
   c. The new packet will create a new Session Entry.
   d. The new packet will be dropped because of port exhaustion

11) When using Central NAT, what is the order of tables evaluation?
   a. SNAT -> DNAT -Security Policy

Chapter 4 | Firewall Policy and NAT

      b. DNAT-> Security Policy -> SNAT
      c. Security Policy -> DNAT -> SNAT
      d. SNAT -> Security Policy -> DNAT

12) What does PBA stand for in regards to IP Pool?
      a. Protocol Based authentication
      b. Port-Based authentication
      c. Port Block Allocation
      d. Protocol Block Allocation

13) Policies with a VIP are always evaluated before Policies without a VIP configured.
      a. True
      b. False

14) What command will show NAT clash counter?
      a. *diagnose sys session stat*
      b. diagnose sys nat list
      c. diagnose sys session list
      d. diagnose sys clash ippool

15) If you saw many ephemeral sessions, what would this signify? Choose two.
      a. This could point to a layer one issue
      b. This could point to a layer two issue
      c. This could point to a potential DoS attack
      d. This could point to asymmetric routing
      e. This is caused by many idle TCP sessions in the established state

16) A FQDN Firewall Policy Entry matches the host header information in HTTP(S) type of packet to allow access to the policy.
      a. True
      b. False

17) The NGFW Policy-Based method is required to use Central NAT.
      a. True
      b. False

Chapter 4 | Firewall Policy and NAT

18) When you delete an object that is referenced in FortiOS this will cause all other objects where the object is being used to be deleted as well.
    a. True
    b. False

19) The Firewall Policy Table can be used to govern transit, and local-in traffic flows.
    a. True
    b. False

20) What command will show the details about an IP Pool utilization?
    a. diagnose firewall ippool-all stats
    b. diagnose sys session list
    c. diagnose sys session stats
    d. diagnose firewall ippool-all list

Book Summary - Intro to FortiGate Part-1

I hope you have enjoyed the book and found the information here useful! Please feel free to email me directly if you have any comments, recommendations, or suggestions at howardsinc@gmail.com. I hope to have Part-II publish by the end of 2020.

Stay updated on the progress of the other books I'm working on by following my Facebook page, Amazon author page, or the Fortinet Press website.

https://www.facebook.com/fortinetpress/

https://www.amazon.com/Daniel-Howard/e/B08BS3B4NY

https://fortinetpress.com/

Until next time, keep studying and see you soon!

Best Regards,

Daniel Howard

Chapter 4 | Firewall Policy and NAT

Appendix A: End of Chapter Answers

Chapter One – End of Chapter Question Answers

1. C
    a. Content Processor helps with SSL Encryption and Decryption
2. A
    a. For 6.2+ FortiOS the live query FQDN is securewf.fortiguard.net
3. C
    a. For 6.0 and below, the live query FQDN is service.fortiguard.net
4. B
    a. AV and IPS are some UTM modules that store a local database on FortiOS
5. False
    a. by default FortiGate will look for updates daily for UTM features with local databases on FortiOS.
6. False
    a. In Transparent mode IP address cannot be configured on physical interfaces and only has management IP configured only that is not bound to any particular interface.
7. True
    a. sessions that requires flow-based security scanning can be offloaded to NP if FortiGate supports the NTurbo feature.
8. C
    a. System Information widget holds information on things like serial number and firmware version
9. D
    a. maintainer is the backdoor account for FortiOS and the password for this account is bcpb + 'Serial Number'
10. D
    a. Trust host restricts the source IP of where admin users can login to FortiGate from.
11. D
    a. The default IP and subnet for LAN interface for lower end models is 192.168.1.99/24
12. D
    a. The default user and password login for FortiOS is admin and no password (Blank)
13. B
    a. This is a deny policy because if it was an accept policy then it would explicitly show configuration for 'action accept'
14. C

Chapter 4 | Firewall Policy and NAT

   a. Fortinet supports new Version and Major Release code base for a total of 54 months. Note, engineering support ends in 36 months in this timeline.
15. C
   a. FortiCare is an entitlement that is purchased for a single platform that allows for vendor support and hardware replacement.
16. B
   a. RMA team requires HQIP test to be perform if bad NIC is reported
17. B
   a. Fortinet TAC will not support firmware passed EoS date.
18. False
   a. FortiGate processes Firewall Policies in sequence from top to bottom and Policy ID is just an identifier of a particular policy. Policy ID 25 would be hit before any other policy if match occurs.
19. D
   a. maintainer account password is bcpd + 'Serial Number'
20. D
   a. FortiGate clean install requires console access, TFTP server and firmware.
21. C
   a. Show sys interface , will display FortiGate interfaces

Chapter Two – End of Chapter Question Answers

1. B
   a. virtual interfaces inherit MAC address and MTU from parent interface
2. C
   a. diagnose hardware deviceinfo nic wan1 – this is one command that will show interface MAC address
3. False
   a. Software Switch cannot offload traffic
4. C
   a. Current_HWaddr is the field that points to the active MAC for an interface.
5. B
   a. The virtual-switch object hold will reference the hardware switch interface which is under physical-switch
6. A
   a. switch-interface CLI object holds configuration for the software switch
7. C

Chapter 4 | Firewall Policy and NAT

       a. 5 minutes is the default time FortiOS will retain ARP cache entries
8. False
       a. hardware switch does not run STP by default
9. C
       a. get sys stp list – will show current STP status on FortiGate
10. D
       a. main benefits of LACP is redundancy and throughput
11. D
       a. A good operational state flags for LACP is ASAIEE
12. C
       a. Forwarding Domains
13. A
       a. The local MAC has the attribute Local Static
14. C
       a. ARP resolves IP addresses to MAC addresses for IPv4
15. D
       a. LLDP-MED can dynamically assign a voice VLAN to VOIP devices.
16. True
       a. Virtual Wire Pairing are bound to each other and communication is exclusive
17. True
       a. vlanfoward enabled will forward VLAN traffic to all other VLANs on sharing parent interface
18. True
       a. FortiOS TP will forward ARP packets by default
19. D
       a. Forwarding Database FDB is used to forward Ethernet frames at layer-2
20. False
       a. VLANs in TP FortiOS does not separate broadcast domains

Chapter Three – End of Chapter Question Answers

1. B
       a. get router info routing-table database – will show ALL route entries.
2. C
       a. RFC 1918 is IPv4 private IP space
3. D
       a. Default Distance for static route is 10
4. A
       a. The default Priority for static routes is 0

Chapter 4 | Firewall Policy and NAT

5. D
    a. The Distance shown in the route entry is 10
6. C
    a. The Priority shown in the route entry is 5
7. B
    a. The Session Table is responsible for keeping try of what traffic has passed through the firewall and tracks the current state of the connection
8. C
    a. RPF is the anti-spoofing mechanism on FortiOS
9. C
    a. Sniffer verbosity level 4 will show IP headers and interface name
10. False
    a. Policy Based Routes are defined separately from the routes in the Routing Table.
11. C
    a. ISDB stands for Internet Service Database
12. D
    a. The default Distance for OSPF is 110.
13. False
    a. RPF Strict requires the best route must match the egress interface for the source IP of a packet.
14. C
    a. The line shown in the Session Table Entry show that this is a UDP (protocol 17) packet and a replay has been seen per the 01
15. C
    a. This line in the Session Table Entry shows traffic ingresses port with index 34 and egress port with index 5.
16. A
    a. get router info routing-table all – displays only active routes
17. A
    a. Destination Subnet, Distance, Metric and Priority
18. D
    a. FIB stands for Forwarding Information Base, which is the kernel routing table.
19. A
    a. >* indicate a route is active
20. B
    a. diagnose firewall proute list – will list all PBR

Chapter 4 | Firewall Policy and NAT

Chapter Four – End of Chapter Question Answers

1. True
    a. Profile Based Policy, traffic must match Source Interface, Destination Interface, Source Address, Destination Address, Service and Schedule
2. True
    a. NGFW Policy Based Filtering uses layer-4 and Layer 7 information to match packet against Session Table Entry
3. C
    a. Anti-Replay is a method to keep track of TCP sequence numbers
4. False
    a. Policy ID's are only a label for a Firewall Policy Entry and does not indicate the order of precedent regards to policy matching.
5. B
    a. Policy 0 in flow debug means packet did not many any rules in the Firewall Policy Table.
6. A
    a. Proxy scanning method, FortiOS will buffer the entire packet(s) and perform security scanning before forwarding.
7. D
    a. the start source port is 5117, and the last useable port is 65533, which provides a total of 60,416 usable source ports
8. B
    a. Session timers could be used to reduce memory usage by aging out sessions faster
9. D
    a. A clash is where all unique values to allocate a new PAT session are used
10. A, C
    a. The oldest session will be deleted and replaced by this one, the newest one.
11. B
    a. Table evaluation for central NAT are DNAT -> Security Policy -> SNAT
12. C
    a. Port Block Allocation
13. A
    a. policy with VIPs as a destination will be evaluated before policies without VIP configurations or do not have match-vip setting.
14. A
    a. diagnose sys session stat – will show clash counter
15. C , E
    a. High ephemeral session count could point to a possible DoS attack

Chapter 4 | Firewall Policy and NAT

16. False
    a. FQDN Firewall Policy Entry matches based on resolved IP of FQDN
17. True
    a. NGFW Policy-Based method is required to use Central NAT
18. False
    a. You cannot delete objects with dependencies
19. False
    a. Firewall Policy Table cannot be used to govern local-in traffic
20. A
    a. diagnose firewall ippool-all stats – shows details on IPpool utilization

www.ingramcontent.com/pod-product-compliance
Lightning Source LLC
Chambersburg PA
CBHW080450220526
45465CB00006B/2225